The Economics of Public Education

Third Edition

The Economics of
Public Education

Charles S. Benson
University of California, Berkeley

Houghton Mifflin Company   Boston
Dallas   Geneva, Illinois
Hopewell, New Jersey   Palo Alto   London

The chapter opening illustrations are reproduced from 1800 Woodcuts by
Thomas Bewick and His School, *edited by Blanche Cirker and the*
Editorial Staff of Dover Publications *(New York: Dover Publications,*
Inc., 1962).

Contents

Preface

In the decade since the second edition of this book was published, much work has been done in two closely related fields: economics of education, and productivity and finance of educational systems. Findings and analyses from these fields bear directly on the further development of our elementary and secondary schools; hence, knowledge of these elements is an essential part of the intellectual toolkit, may I suggest, of school administrators, students of school administration, teachers, and other professional workers in education. It is to these persons primarily that this book is addressed.

No previous knowledge of economics is assumed, though readers who have taken an economics course are likely to proceed through the arguments faster than those who have not. Every effort has been made to develop major points step by step and to explain terms clearly. Should a reader find a particular passage difficult, I suggest that the reader continue through the chapter, possibly find clarification on subsequent pages, and then return to the troublesome material.

The basic plan of the book follows. Chapters One and Two provide essentials of the viewpoint and terminology of the economics discipline. Illustrations show applications of economic thinking to educational decision-making. Chapter Three addresses the important question of how much of our gains in material welfare can be attributed to the provision of educational services. Chapter Four takes up a closely intertwined topic: What is the economic value to individuals and to society of investment in the educational system? Thus, Chapters Three and Four help to establish a rational procedure for analyzing the willingness of households to support schools.

Chapters Five and Six consider household choice with respect to the provision of public education, that is, how the different types of school services that may be offered can be better adjusted to the preferences of families. The alternative of distributing educational funds directly to families, rather than to school districts (vouchers), is examined on its merits. Chapter Seven reviews the work done to date in discovering means to affect the outcomes of public educational activities—how best we can decide, for example, whether to spend budget increments on teachers' salaries across the board or to use the money on alteration of students' access to different types of teachers. Chapter Eight presents a set of common-sense approaches to raising the productivity of educational systems.

The remaining chapters of the book deal with educational finance. Chapter Nine considers the equity aspects of alternative sources of revenue. Chapter Ten traces the history of the grant-in-aid systems that link state and local revenue sources in the support of schools. Chapter Eleven portrays the roots and the consequences of the educational finance reform movement, with special reference to the higher courts' role in demanding an adjustment in equity vis-à-vis distribution of school services to different groups in the population. Chapter Twelve explores the federal role in finance of schools and suggests that the federal government should accept responsibility for halting deterioration and near collapse of school services in our central cities.

I hope the reader will join me in a continuing exploration of these topics. Most research findings to date are either tentative or partial in nature. More can be learned to guide the development of educational policy. *Much* more can be done to use knowledge that we already have to make educational policy. Seeking to raise the quality of life in our country and to gain a higher degree of social equity is a grand adventure.

In the first two editions of this book, Herold C. Hunt, late Charles William Eliot Professor of Education at Harvard, kindly offered a foreword. It is my sorrow that he cannot offer one for this edition. I am deeply indebted to the following individuals who kindly read all or part of this manuscript and gave me the benefit of their wise and scholarly advice: Henry M. Levin, Center for Advanced

Study in the Behavioral Sciences, Stanford University; Gary P. Johnson, The Pennsylvania State University; J. Alan Thomas, The University of Chicago; Richard K. Miller, Washington and Jefferson College, Washington, Pa.; Richard A. Rossmiller, The University of Wisconsin, Madison. Also, I thank Gareth E. Hoachlander and Elliott Medrich for many new insights and much stimulation of thought. Both are members of The Childhood and Government Project, Boalt Hall School of Law, University of California, Berkeley, a project sponsored by the Ford Foundation and the Carnegie Corporation. I am happy to say I continue to learn a lot from my co-principal investigator of that same project, John E. Coons. The manuscript was prepared with great care by Viviane Dutoit. As always in my writing, my chief support is Dorothy Merrick. But not even she can claim responsibility for my errors or omissions! They rest with me alone.

C.S.B.

List of Tables

The Economics of Public Education

Chapter One

Relationships in Our Society

Economics deals with the choices that people make. Many of these choices relate to production, or work activity. The entrepreneur, say a manufacturer, makes choices about which new lines of product, if any, should be developed, about whether or not to buy high-output machinery and substitute it for human workers in production processes, about whether to expand or contract the company's advertising expenditures, and about many other things. An educational administrator, on the other hand, makes choices when deciding to recommend that the school board hire certificated teachers in place of paraprofessionals—or vice versa—or when deciding to advocate expanding early elementary education in place of programs for handicapped children—or vice versa. (Of course, when the educational administrator has received a budget increase, the choices do not necessarily have to be approached as a set of all-or-nothing decisions; rather, it becomes a matter of *how much* of the increased budget shall be spent on certificated teachers, how much on paraprofessionals, etc.) At the present time of declining enrollments, many choices in education center on selecting for reduction those expenditures whose loss will do least damage to the main activities of the school district.

Decision making in the work world is not confined to owners, managers, and administrators. Workers are free to decide where they will work and which employment opportunity, among the possible job openings, they will accept. Workers, including teachers, make choices about how much of their time and income they will devote to their occupational and professional growth.

Another whole class of economic choices is to be found in the decisions that families make in spending and saving their incomes. The questions commonly take the following forms: Shall we buy a book or a sweater? Shall we go out to dinner or to a movie (or shall we do both)? Shall we replace the car, furnish the extra room, or put the money into a savings account for Henry's or Jane's college educations? The economic decisions of the family do not deal with monetary allocations only; decisions also establish priorities for the uses made of leisure time (outside the work place). Families seek a distribution of their money budget *and* their available time that will make them as happy as possible—this is what the completely rational and all-knowing family would do anyway. Different types of consumer goods require different amounts of time for their use and enjoyment, and allocations of money budgets and time budgets are therefore *joint processes*, that is, they are decision-making processes that are interdependent and simultaneous. Education helps shape the tastes and preferences of families in the use they make of their monetary and time budgets. Thus, it should be clear that schooling has its own influence on economic choices.

Economists believe that the kinds of choices we have been discussing, that is, about what goods and services to produce, about how to produce them, about savings and investments, about what to spend income on, are made in a systematic manner. To predict how the management of a given company will react to a change in the price of a certain type of raw material, economists do not need to know the personal characteristics of that management nor the history of the business. To predict how a family will respond to, say, a change in food prices, it is not necessary to have information on the dietary patterns of members of that family. Economic choices are seen as grounded in assumptions about what it is that businesses seek to maximize (profits) and that households seek to maximize (satisfactions or utility). From these assumptions, an elaborate structure of response relationships has been developed to analyze the nature of economic choice. This structure is called an *economic system*. As we shall shortly see, it can be described simply. First, however, let us draw some distinctions between *public* and *private* economic activity.

The Mixed Economy

Both private and public activities consume economic resources in order to provide the households of the country with goods and services. Both private and public activities seek to obtain an efficient use of the resources at their command. What distinguishes private enterprises from their counterparts in the public sector, that is, from those activities in which government functions in its service role, is this: A private firm obtains money receipts from market sales, while public activities obtain money receipts, ultimately and essentially, from compulsory levies on the population, that is, through taxation. Both kinds of activities must obtain money receipts to continue to purchase the service of resources that are necessary in their productive operations, or they will cease to exist. Now, what is the ultimate controlling agent over the use of those resources?

In the theory of a democratic, capitalistic society, the *ultimate* controlling agent over the use of resources is the individual household. Consumers direct the use of resources in the private sector by their actions in the market place, that is, by their willingness to buy various kinds of goods and services at prices that yield (or do not yield) profits to the firms that produce them. Likewise, individuals determine the allocation of resources between the private and public sectors (and also *within* the public sector) by their actions at the polls. In the first instance, it can be said that householders "vote" with the dollars of income at their command; in the second, that they vote, of course, with ballots.

Though it is generally agreed that we continue to live in a democratic, capitalistic society, it has become common to refer to the U.S. economy as a *mixed* economy. Since 1929 there has been a large expansion of the government's role in financing goods and services. In that year, approximately 8.9 percent of all employees worked for the government; by 1975 the figure had increased to 19.2 percent. Likewise, in 1929 approximately 8.1 percent of gross national product (GNP) was represented by "government purchase of goods and services"; this proportion had risen to 22.3 percent in 1975. (We discuss GNP in detail in Chapter 2.) Although it is still true that private financing produces the largest part of goods and services and that most incomes originate in the private sector, the expansion of publicly financed services has led some observers to apply the designation *mixed* to our economic system. It is no longer so largely private (capitalistic) that the share of resources devoted to satisfying public wants can be ignored; but, of course, by no means is it so largely independent of private production for profit that it can be called socialistic. Some of the privately financed production yields finished goods for household consumption; some of it yields producers' goods, that is, capital goods of various sorts. This same description can be applied to publicly financed output. Also, let us note that much government output provides goods, such as highways and police protection, that are "consumed" by private firms in their own productive operations.

With respect to public education itself, we note in Chapter 2, that it is our largest civilian governmental function. This is true whether we measure the size of public education in terms of dollar expenditures or in terms of personnel employed. It is interesting to observe that public spending on schools, colleges, and universities in the United States in 1975–76 ($98 billion) exceeds the total incomes of all the people who live in such relatively large nations as Pakistan or Indonesia.

In fact, it is clear that the private and public sectors are mutually related. No modern industrial system could function without such public services as universal education, streets and highways, fire and police protection. Similarly, public activities are strongly affected by changes in the private economy. How does it affect education?

First, taxes to support schools are levied for the most part on incomes earned in the private sector. As we will see in the next chapter, there is a strong relationship between level of national income and public education expenditures. Accordingly, it is probable that the rate of growth in the private economy will be a major determinant of future changes in the size of those expenditures. Second, changes in the private economy affect the character of the specific demands for educational services. Since an ever larger number of parents can afford to send their children to college, the demand for first-rate college preparatory programs has increased. Similarly, changes in industrial techniques alter the nature of the vocational programs. Third, and very important, the private economy sets the prices that school systems must pay for the goods and services they buy. Teachers' salaries, for example, are regulated significantly by what a newly trained candidate for a school post could obtain in alternative (private) employment. Costs of school construction, textbooks, and laboratory equipment are largely determined in the private sector. Fourth, improvements in goods that school systems purchase may reflect the increasing effectiveness with which resources are used in the private economy. For example, school buses are safer today than they were twenty years ago; this is a contribution that research in private firms has made in school systems. Fifth, if the private economy is disturbed by inflation, the orderly management of school finances is adversely affected in many ways.

Because of those (and possibly other) relationships between public education and the private enterprise system, it is appropriate for us to take a summary view of the workings of that system. This actually takes us to the heart of the discipline of economics.

Operation of the Economy

The central topic of economics is the *allocation of resources*. The central concept is *scarcity*. It is assumed that a society does not have—and cannot be expected to attain—a superfluity in all kinds of goods and services. Why is it assumed that a condition of scarcity exists, and why does the making of this assumption lead to concern with the allocation of resources? To answer these questions requires us to explore briefly a few definitions.

First, let us distinguish between free goods and economic goods. A *free good* is anything that yields satisfaction (or possesses the quality of "desiredness") and is available in superfluous quantities. Examples are air for breathing and ocean water for swimming. *Economic goods* possess the quality of desiredness, but they exist in something less than superfluous supply. For any one of them, the people in a society have less of it to use than they would prefer to have. Examples are strawberries, diamonds, travel, and education.

When we think of goods and services, it is only the class of economic goods that comes to mind; free goods are taken for granted. When economists speak of the "production of goods and services," they are referring only to the class of economic goods. But why are not all goods free, so that we would read nothing in the "dismal science of economics"?[1] The answer is that the supply of resources is limited. Resources, as stated, are those things that have the capacity to contribute to productive processes (productive in the sense of creating economic goods). From the beginnings of modern economics, it has been the practice to classify resources as *labor, land,* and *capital.* Labor includes all the many kinds of human services that enter into production, including management and enterprise. Land represents not just agricultural land but, more broadly, natural resources as the term is commonly used. Capital is not money but stands for produced means of production or goods that have been made, not to satisfy the desire for consumption immediately, but to be used in further acts of production. Examples are factory buildings, machines, highways, bridges, and blackboards.

The amount of each of the three resources is limited in supply—the amounts of resources available are not indefinitely large. We should also note that under a modern system of private property, it is the claim to the productive powers of resources that constitutes the household's claim to income. For example, a person may undertake a contract, formally or informally drawn, to supply the powers of

---

[1] The phrase is Thomas Carlyle's. *Thomas Carlyle's Works: Miscellanies* (London: Chapman & Hall, 1874), XII, 84.

his or her mind and body in the performance of certain tasks in exchange for a money wage (a person "takes a job"). Or, to use an example of another type of resource, a person may yield the productive powers of a certain amount of land that she or he owns to another individual in exchange for a rent payment.

The class of economic goods by definition, then, is scarce. Scarcity is related to the existence of only a limited supply of productive resources. Now, what does this have to do with the central topic of economics—the allocation of resources? First, scarcity alone requires that the end products (the finished goods) be allocated among competing uses, assuming that behavior is rational. Suppose that packages of resources of certain kinds (pasture, herds, and farmers) can be employed only in the production of cow's milk. Suppose further that the quality and proportion of each separate factor of production in the package are fixed. There is still an allocation problem. No milk should be put to an inferior use. Let us assume initially that the supply of milk is relatively abundant. Now, imagine that the human birth rate increases, and that there are more babies per household than formerly. But nothing has happened, say, to increase the milk supply. It would then be an easy decision to no longer lavish milk on cats when there is a danger of malnutrition of children. This is a case of the allocation of the end product of resources. It is a kind of decision normally made within the households of the economy.

This order of decision making is not in itself very interesting. But limitation in supply, *together with certain other attributes of economic resources,* establishes the necessity for some very complex (and interesting) types of decisions. First, it is possible to use the same kinds of resources to make different kinds of goods. Resources have *alternative uses.* Steelmaking capacity can be used in producing automobiles as well as in building schoolhouses. Mathematicians can work in the research laboratory of an automobile company or they can teach school, but they cannot undertake both of those tasks full time or at the same time. Given (a) the condition of scarcity and (b) alternative uses of resources, competition in the employment of resources exists. Somehow, decisions must be made about what kinds of goods are to be produced and in what quantities each is to be provided. These are complex decisions.

Second, resources can be combined in different proportions to turn out a particular commodity. (Our earlier assumption that resources are combined in fixed packages is pedagogically useful but plainly unrealistic.) A certain amount of wheat can be grown by using much land and little labor or by using less land and more labor. Given (a) the condition of scarcity and (b) the possibility of producing commodities with varying proportions of *inputs,* decisions ideally should be made that employ the minimum-cost combination of resources for making various commodities. This is simply to say that, since we all have unsatisfied demands, it is foolish to engage in wasteful schemes of production.

Third, it is a matter of common observation that the yield of economic resources is greater if they are subject to specialization in product or function. Among a group of people, it will normally be found that there are differences, inborn or acquired, in their abilities to do various things. Certain of these abilities are more scarce than others at any one time. It makes sense that those of rare abilities concentrate as nearly full time as possible in their area of special competence. Given (a) the condition of scarcity and (b) the likelihood of increasing output through specialization, it becomes clear, ceteris paribus, that a society should encourage the extension of the division of labor. But as a society becomes more specialized it becomes less self-sufficient. It moves to an *exchange economy,* where people use the resources at their command to produce goods, not for their own consumption, but for the market. An exchange economy functions smoothly only if there is a satisfactory medium of exchange (money). It also calls for the existence of economic power to assemble highly specialized resources for the production of commodities—hence, in our society, the corporation. But the highly specialized economy must face the problem of how to divide the economic product among the owners of resources. How much is this grade of labor, or that type of skill, or the use of that piece of land "worth"? As these questions are answered, the income of the various households is determined. This, too, is a complex decision.

Fourth, resources may be used for improvement in the economy. This process of improvement takes one of three forms: an increase in quantity and quality of resources, the development of a higher level of technology, or a refinement of tastes so that a given level of output yields a greater amount of satisfactions in the households. The means for obtaining improvement—such as investment in plant and equipment (manufacturing), the fertility of the soil (agriculture), transportation facilities (distribution), training of workers, research and education—generally require the use of scarce resources. Total output of consumption goods could be increased in the short run if society lost all its bent toward improvement, since resources would be released from investment in all types of capital (broadly defined) to supply more fully peoples' immediate desires. But output in the long run will be greater than it is now because society does have a bent for improvement, that is, because people are willing to sacrifice some of the goods they could have today in order to live in a better world tomorrow.[2] The choice exists of how much the bent for improvement is to be satisfied. This is the last major question that we mention under the topic of allocation of resources.

Five Questions on Allocation of Resources

To recapitulate, allocation of resources involves five major questions:

1.   What kinds of goods are to be produced?
2.   What amounts of various goods are to be produced?
3.   How are resources to be combined in efficient schemes of production?
4.   How is the total economic production to be shared among the households (that is, owners of resources)?
5.   At what level are various kinds of improvements in the economy to be sought?

Unless a society answers these questions reasonably well, most people will live in poverty and chaos. The mechanism for getting answers, as we stated earlier, is called an *economic system*. Ancient Egypt had a different kind of economic system from that of ancient Greece. Clearly, the system under which we live in the United Stated is different from that of feudal England; it is also different in important respects from that of the Soviet Union. Economic systems take various forms.

The Price System

As is well known, the U.S. economy is called a *price system*. Another term is *self-regulating market economy*. Let us explore briefly how the price system works to give answers to the five major resource allocation questions.

The price system is a mechanism that operates under a high degree of decentralization. Millions of units of hundred of thousands of different goods and services are produced. The products are distributed throughout the country so that households are able to obtain them at convenient places in conveniently sized lots and with dispatch. The system operates smoothly: Except under the strain of war,

[2] Improvement may be financed by savings of households (subsequently to be made available to firms through financial intermediaries), taxes, or simply paying high enough prices for goods to finance research, development, and training activities in the firms that supply them.

our economy is largely free of the phenomenon of queuing, which is a demonstration of the existence of at least temporary shortages of some goods. The workings of a smoothly operating system are often taken for granted; but it is startling to see that the goods we need for our very existence—goods without which we could not survive more than a few days—are produced under absolutely no plan at all. There is no central economic bureau to oversee production and to assure that we are supplied with enough food to eat and enough fuel oil to keep us from freezing to death in the winter. To a good mercantilist we could hardly be more foolhardy. Not only are we unconcerned at the absence of a central production plan, but we also tend to support the sporadic efforts to destroy large concentrations of economic power (for example, monopolies), the very things that would make broad, systematic, and long-range planning effective.[3]

How, then, can this decentralized system work? It is necessary that economic units—households, business firms, and owners of resources—be able to communicate with one another. The means of communication are afforded by prices—prices of products and prices of factors of production (that is, human labor; natural assets, such as land; and instruments produced by human labor, such as machines).

In any economic system it is desirable for everyone to more or less agree on who holds the ultimate authority. In our system it is generally agreed that the consumer is the ultimate authority. When consumers desire a particular kind of commodity, they indicate this to the producers by their willingness to pay a price of it. When consumers come to desire *more* of a particular kind of commodity, they so indicate by offering to pay a *higher* price for it. As the demand for a product increases and its price goes up, the affected firms see an opportunity to make an extra amount of profit by producing more units.[4] To do so, they must hire additional amounts of economic resources, but the higher selling price of the finished product allows them to bid resources away from other businesses whose lines are not expanding. What consumers demand, they get; and their wishes are communicated to the business community through prices. When

[3] In the words of James Gould Cozzens, "In the present, every day is a miracle. The world gets up in the morning and is fed and goes to work, and in the evening it goes home and is fed again and perhaps has a little amusement and goes to sleep. To make that possible, so much has to be done by so many people that, on the face of it, it is impossible." *The Just and the Unjust* (New York: Harcourt, Brace, 1942), p. 434.

[4] During the period of temporary short supply, the price system also serves to ration the goods so that those families who have the strongest desire for certain items get the most of them, considerations of income distribution aside.

consumers desire *less* of a particular commodity, its price will fall, inventories will pile up, production will be cut, and—the final result—economic resources will be released for use in making more of those things that the consumers do want. In this simple way, the price system affords a means of communication between consumers and business firms to deal with the first two major questions in resource allocation: What goods are to be produced and in what quantities they are to be supplied?

In viewing the various alternative combinations of resources that may be employed to turn out a given amount of product, firms will seek that form of production that is available at lowest cost. That is, competitive pressure will lead them to discover the ideal combination of factors of production, given the level of output they seek to maintain and the relative prices of the various factors. Some firms may seek to solve the problem by refined methods of analysis, such as linear programming; others may follow a procedure of trial and error. All firms, however, have the strong incentive of the market economy to obtain a reasonably accurate approximation to the best combination of resources. It stands to reason that their survival as business firms depends on finding a good approximation; otherwise, they will be underbid in product markets and overbid in factor markets. In this manner our third major question of how goods may be produced efficiently is solved by the price system.

To consider how the price system operates to solve the fourth question—how the total product is to be shared among the households of the economy—we must recognize that households meet business firms not only in the markets of consumers' goods but also in factor markets, that is, in places where households exchange the economic resources at their command for money wages, rent, and interest. Competition among business firms will insure that the prices of the various factors of production will be bid up to the point at which owners each receive a money payment equal to the full value of the contribution of their resources to the productive process. Competition will also insure that no business firm will overpay the owner of a factor of production, because the competition will then be able to undercut it in its selling markets. The income of a household, then, depends on the kind and amount of economic resources it is able to place on the market. Each unit of resources will be evaluated in terms of its contribution to the production of certain goods.

The existence of a system of communication is a necessary condition for the operation of the price system, but it alone does not explain the response of business firms to a change in consumer demand. Our system is characterized by private ownership of resources. Any extra return that accrues to the owner of a particular amount of resources is his or hers to claim. Further, there is a considerable degree of freedom in the disposition of these privately owned resources. Except in wartime, price and production controls of a compulsory nature are largely absent. Finally, there is general acceptance of the goal of private material gain. It is accepted that the men who control the affairs of private firms will seek to maximize the profits earned by these companies. These conditions lead to the fact that firms exist in a state of competition—or rivalry—with one another. The firm that supplies consumers with what they most want is able to bid strongly for resources and to make a profit. The firm that is unresponsive to consumer needs will be able to make only a weak bid for resources and will soon vanish from the scene.

Long-run Improvement in the Private Economy

The price system, as we have said, provides answers to four of the major economic questions. But what about the fifth question—at what level are improvements in the economy to be sought? Actually, present-day economics does not have a great deal to say about improvement, broadly considered. Motivations for improvement are complex. Economists have preferred to build their theoretical superstructure on simple kinds of motivations—the desire of the businesses to maximize profit, for instance. Improvement takes time to accomplish, and since uncertainty is always attached to future events, economists have concentrated their efforts on examining the short-run operation of the price system. Improvements are often of an intangible character, and economists, until lately, have chosen examples of improvements in terms of tangible things (investment in new factories and new equipment in factories). With respect to these tangible improvements, the classical approach has been to point to the capital markets as the institutions that provided the mechanism to balance the society's desire for present consumption against its desire for greater amounts of consumption in the future. Prices in these markets are interest rates.

Much is said about society itself failing to place a sufficiently strong emphasis on those activities, such as basic research and education, that are centrally important in long-run developments. Our task in this book is to examine the economic aspects of one main agent of improvement, public education. It is evident that the quality of the public schools affects (1) the ability over the long run to undertake both basic and applied research from which the improvements in technology will occur, (2) the skill of the labor force (professional worker as well as manual worker), and (3) the level of performance of tasks of the households.

Allocation of Resources in the Public Sector

Aside from the problems of, perhaps, giving sufficient attention to long-range needs and to income distribution, it seems to be generally agreed in the United States that the price system operates effectively. Consumers' desires for the various kinds of products are taken account of (sooner or later), resources are brought together in economically efficient ways, and the firms are responsive to such changes in technology as do appear. It might seem that this privately managed, decentralized system will best promote the welfare with only the smallest amount of interference from government. But such apparently has not been the judgment of the people. Under our democratic form of government we have seen an enormous expansion in the range and level of governmental activity.

To see why, let us note that the beneficent operation of the price system rests on certain assumptions of *economic rationality*. It is assumed that households know their own needs and will make a wise selection of purchases. It is assumed that businesses will seek to maximize profits. It is assumed that owners of factors of production have both the information and the motivation to obtain the highest price they can get. Unless people behave the way they are expected to under these assumptions, the price system cannot be expected to operate in the manner we have outlined above.

To a limited degree, government enters the picture because some people do not behave in an economically rational way. Households may be ignorant of their needs and susceptible to false or misleading claims of advertising; hence, the Federal Trade Commission acts as a policeman to promote truth in advertising. Some businesses may be apathetic in their search for profits, and so the U.S. Department of Commerce provides substantial help to business people, showing them how to cut costs and open new markets. Some households may not know how best to dispose of the economic resources at their command, and governmental units offer help to them also.

But the main roles of government—insofar as they can be justified in economic conditions—exist because society has been unwilling to accept completely the results, the unfettered pursuit, let us say, of economic rationality. In terms of economic rationality, a household may desire that its children enter the work force at a very young age to supplement the family income. The society has decided, however, that children should stay in school, though not necessarily in public school, beyond the time when they are physically and mentally capable of undertaking work for pay. Thus, laws exist in all states that establish a minimum school-leaving age (sixteen years, in most instances). By such mandates government seeks to establish a milieu in which the self-regulating market economy can operate effectively. It would not be economically rational for a household voluntarily to pay taxes, since it would be able to consume approximately the same amount of government services whether or not it paid its share (a very small part, of course, of government receipts); hence, sanctions exist against those who seek to evade taxes. These are examples of the government's role in exercising control.[5]

Government also finances a range of services used by the households of the country. For government to undertake to supply a service, it is necessary, presumably, that two conditions be met: (1) The service must be important to the households of the economy, and (2) the service will not be supplied in sufficient quantity or quality wholly through private financing. The government then uses its powers to tax, charge fees, and borrow so that the service may be supplied at a more adequate level.

As soon as it is recognized that government consumes resources to supply services, it is possible to draw up a list of major questions on resource allocation for the public sector, corresponding to those for the private economy we have been discussing. We can use this list as a frame of reference for much of the discussion in the succeeding chapters:

1. What kinds of services shall be provided by the government?
2. At what level shall the various services be provided?
3. Shall the distribution of a given public service be equal among members of the population or client groups, for example, schoolchildren, or shall it be intended to favor some certain class?
4. What unit of government shall provide what share of financing of the services?
5. How shall the several units of government finance their shares of the services?
6. How shall the operational responsibility of specific tasks be assigned among the different units of government, and between the government and private firms?

---

[5] Other examples are minimum wage and antitrust legislation. Often different government policies, each of which can be separately defended, turn out to be inconsistent with each other. Patent legislation strengthens monopoly power; antitrust legislation seeks to tear it down.

7.   How shall the existing qualities of resources be combined efficiently under existing technology to provide the services?

8.   How shall long-term improvements in the productive processes (quality of resources and technology) be obtained in the publicly financed activities?

Government often stands as a monopolist supplier in relation to the consuming households. For publicly financed services, there is less competitive pressure to see that resources are combined under efficient schemes of production. It can be taken for granted that firms in the private economy will make reasonably efficient use of resources in production, but it cannot be taken for granted that, say, public school teachers work in an environment that allows them to concentrate their energies on those tasks that they can do best at different stages in their careers. Under the private economy we mentioned only one category of improvement: *long-term* betterment of tasks, resources, and technology. It is assumed that the private economy in the *short run* is operating at maximum efficiency. For tax-supported activities, one goal of public policy must be to strive for improvement in *both* the short run and the long run.

Now, let us recognize that the degree of government involvement in providing services shows a great diversity. Conceivably, the contribution of government might be limited to finance only. For example, a town may grant a contract to a private firm to collect trash. At the other extreme, it is conceivable that the government would initiate, plan for, and itself completely provide certain services, as well as taking the responsibility for financing them. Generally speaking, the degree of involvement of the government can be considered as lying somewhere between these two extremes. In the case of highways, government finances the program, undertakes planning activities, and initiates specific projects; but the highways are built by private construction companies. In the case of defense, installations are manned by members of the armed forces; but the equipment (for example, missiles, nuclear-powered submarines), which has become so important in national protection, is often manufactured by private aircraft and electronics firms. Research on new weapons and on defense systems is also often done by private firms under government contract; and, then, planning for the initiation of specific projects is also strongly influenced by private, as distinct from public, agencies. Again, the postal service is largely operated by the government, but even here, long-distance hauling of mail is done by private carriers. A measure of the degree of public involvement (beyond the financing aspect) is the ratio of salaries of public employees in an activity to the total cost of the particular service: the higher the ratio, the greater the degree of public involvement. The degree of public involvement is very high in elementary and secondary education. For example, approximately 60 percent of school budgets in the United States are spent for instructional salaries. Frequently, the share of all salaries in districts, instructional and noninstructional together, exceeds 80 percent.

Even so, school systems do turn to private firms to build and equip the schools and, in some instances, to provide such services as pupil transportation. Standardized tests are obtained from private firms, as are texts and library books. Increasingly, the following types, at least, of consultative services are obtained under contract: architectural, legal, medical, and personnel development.

Where there is a fairly large degree of private participation in providing the public service, the responsibility for attaining a reasonable degree of efficiency in the short run and improvement in the long run can be shared between the government and the private firms.[6] In such instances, a substantial part of the basis for gains in the quality of public services rests on the same incentives that exist in the private economy. Since it is commonly held that private business firms, on the average, are more flexible and dynamic than government agencies, this is a comforting thought. In those instances, on the other hand, where governmental units themselves are almost wholly responsible for providing a public service, for example, public education, almost the entire burden for efficiency and improvement rests on these agencies. How well they fulfill their responsibility is a matter of major concern. Just as we want higher quality goods to be produced over time in the private sector of the economy, so also we want improvement in the quality of public services, especially in so important an activity as elementary and secondary education.

The Special Issue of Distribution

Education is valuable not only as it promotes national development but it is also valuable to the individual. The simplest way to see this is to observe the relationship between number of years of schooling completed by persons and their incomes. In 1972, taking all males aged 18 and older, average income of high school dropouts was

---

[6] In a sense, the government is acting as agent for the households of the country in buying various articles from private industry for collective consumption. Government efficiency is, in effect, its astuteness as a purchasing agent.

$7,500; average income of males who completed high school but did not go beyond was $9,200; and average income of male college graduates was $15,200.[7]

No one would seriously propose that families be urged to be indifferent about the present and future welfare of their children. Parents act, generally speaking, in the belief that quality of education is important in determining both present and future well-being. In spite of the changes we see taking place in family structure, as a child-rearing institution, the nuclear family holds a place of supremacy. The family possesses moral and legal rights to raise its children as it sees fit, unless, of course, its practices depart so far from social norms as to entail chances of serious injury to the child. Included in these rights is the family's right to seek preferential educational services for its children. Our system of schools is locally administered, and this gives parents the means to choose a school for their children by choosing a particular residential location. Thus, school services at present are distributed under a policy of *geographical entitlement.* How tightly this power is held is shown by the political resistance to proposals to extend the boundaries of central-city school districts to embrace suburban districts of a metropolitan area or, as it happens even more dramatically, by resistance to consolidation of contiguous suburban districts. Parental choice of educational opportunities for children is reinforced by the existence of a large private sector in higher education and, in the public sector of higher education, by the existence of hierarchically arranged structures of educational quality— universities at the top and community colleges at the bottom. We might even say that the exercise of parental choice in education is itself a powerful stimulus toward maintaining a set of superior educational institutions, which provide criteria on standards for mediocre ones.

A major problem arises, however, because of the probability that some parents are much more adept than others in gaining preferential educational treatment for their children. Rich families tend to cluster in districts where the schools meet high standards of excellence. The richer families then encourage their children to use their superior preparation to enter superior universities and to attend high-grade professional schools and, finally, to enter the ranks of the elite professional occupations. At the same time, poorer families, especially if they are minority families, find themselves effectively restricted to schools of low academic performance. This, together with other inhibiting conditions, reduces the probability that children

[7] U.S. Department of Commerce, *Statistical Abstract of the United States* (Washington, D.C.: U.S. Government Printing Office, 1976), p. 128.

of poorer families will accumulate as many years of education as do children of richer households; it also reduces the probability that children of poorer families will attend colleges and universities of great prestige. From the child's point of view, there is an element of injustice in the present distribution of educational opportunities.[8]

Injustice, it might be said, is a condition of life, so why be concerned? The point here is that injustice in the distribution of education strikes at the heart of the ideals upon which this country was founded. As Abraham Lincoln said, speaking once in Independence Hall,

> I have often pondered over the dangers which were incurred by the men who assembled here and framed and adopted that Declaration. I have pondered over the toils that were endured by the officers and soldiers of the army who achieved that independence. I have often inquired of myself what great principle or idea it was that kept this Confederacy so long together. It was not the mere matter of separation of the Colonies from the motherland, but that sentiment in the Declaration of Independence which gave liberty not alone to the people of this country, but hope to all the world, for all future time. It was that which gave promise that in due time the weights would be lifted from the shoulders of all men, and *that all should have an equal chance.*[9]

The same principle was elaborated by R. H. Tawney in 1931:

> It is the fact that, in spite of their varying characters and capacities, men possess in their common humanity a quality which is worth cultivating, and that a community is more likely to make the most of that quality if it takes it into account in planning its economic organization and its social institutions—if it stresses lightly differences of wealth and birth and social position, and establishes on firm foundations institutions which meet common needs and are a source of common

---

[8] In the public sector, institutions that are, in essence, bankrupt are not required to turn their affairs over to trustees, not in the short run, at least. For example, a given elementary school in a large city may have a very bad record in teaching reading, writing, and numbers skills. And still it will remain "in business" year after year because parents who live in its attendance zone and who presumably cannot afford to live elsewhere are required by law to send their children to it, unless, as is often unlikely, they can find a private school alternative. See Annie Stein,"Strategies for Failure," *Harvard Educational Review*, 41, no. 2 (May 1971): esp. 195–198.

[9] Philadelphia, February 22, 1861. (Italics added.)

enlightenment and common enjoyment. The individual differences of which so much is made . . . will always survive, and they are to be welcomed, not regretted. But their existence is no reason for not seeking to establish the largest possible measure of equality of environment, and circumstance, and opportunity. On the contrary, it is a reason for redoubling our efforts to establish it, in order to ensure that these diversities of gifts may come to fruition.[10]

We must face the conflict, likely to continue into the distant future, between principles of social justice, as embodied, for example in Lincoln's remarks about equality of opportunity, and the principle of granting just rewards to individual families that try to give their children a good start in life. It is a truism that the future well-being of our society rests in the hands of the rising generations. As long as our society places its primary trust in the family to mold the character and guide the educational development of the individual members of the rising generations, it cannot logically also take action to frustrate the human developmental efforts of the conscientious family. That is to say that society cannot arrange an equal distribution of rewards of child-rearing between the conscientious family and the careless. Indeed, we then might expect conscientious families to band together, as they do now to some degree, to take defensive action against government in order to protect their children's advantages; and not all such actions would be socially desirable.[11]

Society acts to compound the effect on talent development by seeing that children of "good homes," living in "good neighborhoods," are placed in "good schools." The only certain means of accomplishing a real redistribution of life chances is to place barriers in the way of those children who appear to be favored by circumstances, for example, to deny the bright children of conscientious parents the opportunity to attend secondary school. This is clearly impossible.

Nevertheless, there is little in the practice of granting just rewards for child-rearing that requires maintaining *class differences* in the distribution of educational services. To remove the influence of hereditary class on educational opportunity and attainment is a proper long-run objective of our society. And the main point of this

---

[10] R. H. Tawney. *Equality*, 4th ed. (London: Allen & Unwin, 1952), p. 47.
[11] One such action would be to try to protect the child's interest by financial inheritance; another would be to rely upon nepotistic practices in job appointments and promotions. Not all families would be able to use these means or to use them more intensively, but the pressure would exist to do so.

book is to consider certain of the means available to accomplish that task.

Presently, we may assert that educational services are distributed more strictly in accordance with social class than in accordance with the effectiveness of a given family's parenting. That is, the upper-middle-class family typically sends its children to a school with well-trained and experienced teachers and in which time devoted to disciplinary problems is rather small. The poor family is likely to find that the schools to which it is entitled have teachers who are beginning their careers; moreover, these inexperienced teachers are forced to spend a lot of time on disciplinary control at the expense of instruction. Consequently, an earlier drive to reward effective parents by allowing them the right to seek preferential educational treatment for their children has been transmitted into a general incentive for households to acquire wealth. As long as a family is upper middle class, it can be effective or ineffective and still see its children provided with superior educational opportunities. No matter how hard parents in a poor household strive to give their children a good start in life, they are generally unlikely to be able to enroll them in schools that successfully encourage academic excellence. This seems wrong.

We might hold that the problem arises because society has chosen basically the wrong criterion—economic status—to measure effective parenting. Unfortunately, it is hard to imagine a measurable criterion that would be given general acceptance. Early measures of student aptitude, given the nature of the instruments used, almost certainly will favor the upper and middle classes as long as we have as much inequality in early childhood environments as we do.[12] Beyond this, we enter the field of attempting to measure moral worth or character.

On the other hand, there is sufficient diversity in human nature, and sufficient opportunity to enjoy each other's variety of performance. And this suggests that qualitative differences in education should be enhanced, under the immediate objective of releasing the child's curiosity and developing the child's understanding in as many different fields of human accomplishment as educational budgets will allow, as long as the effect is not to increase social

---

[12] In England there has been, until recently, a government policy under which all students at (or near) age 11 were given an examination to test their academic prowess. Those who got high marks on their "11+" exams were admitted into state-financed grammar schools, in which they received intensive instruction in scholarly fields. Their period of secondary school education might last until age 18 or 19. Students who received lower marks on the 11+ went to secondary modern or technical schools, in which standards of instruction were less intellectually demanding and more oriented to clerical and blue-collar trades. Such secondary education concluded at age 15. This

isolation. The proviso is important and so also, in this author's opinion, is the objective. The objective would seem to be, not so much to reinforce incentives for effective parenting, but to allow human intelligence to bloom wherever it can.

So the basic policy objective becomes equal education for all children in standard areas of learning, together with plentiful opportunities for children to specialize in topics of special interest, so long as the provision of such opportunities does not serve to produce a socially stratified distribution of educational services. Having got this far, we must recognize that a number of operational problems attend the implementation of such a policy. What is equal basic education? As long as we rely on school districts to administer educational services and as long as the amount of money we must pay to hire teachers of a certain level of proficiency is different from place to place (and it certainly appears to be different), then equal dollars spent per student cannot represent equal education. Should we not also be concerned about what the dollar buys in terms of student learning? Yes, but experience so far with compensatory education gives us no clear guide about what resources are required to achieve equal average attainment by social class of student. Rather than rely on financial distribution to equalize educational outputs by social class, we might seek to establish schools in which enrollments are balanced by social class over a whole metropolitan area and, at the same time, try to distribute teachers so that each school had equal proportions of highly experienced, highly trained, and professionally motivated staff. To so equalize the distribution of students and teachers would require, however, considerably centralizing the administration of education. Such centralization might carry with it the possibility of

---

whole arrangement was an attempt to establish a meritocratic distribution of educational services. But it does not appear to have been free of class bias. The preponderant groups of children in grammar schools were sons and daughters of professional workers and the predominant groups in secondary moderns were children of manual workers. This was so clear that a respected English sociologist, Jean Floud, was led to say in 1961 "that there is a substantial reserve of uneducated ability in the offspring of working-class fathers cannot be doubted." (Quoted in David Rubenstein and Brian Simon, *The Evolution of the Comprehensive School, 1926–1972*, 2nd ed. [London: Routledge, 1973], p. 63.) Beginning in 1965, the British government began to back away from its policy of early selection and urged local authorities to establish comprehensive secondary schools. The 11+ screening is now a thing of the past, and selection for the higher tracks in the comprehensive schools is based on broader evidence (not just on a series of exams given over a period of two or three days) and occurs a few years later in the life of the student than it did under previous policy. In summary, then, the English experience with early screening of children is not encouraging for the use of tests to regulate the just distribution of education.

undue control of the curriculum by political organizations and might also entail bureaucratic oppression in unwarranted degree. There are other measures to take to improve distributive justice in education, and we shall discuss certain of these in the chapters to follow. Here we wish simply to indicate that the policy issues are complex.

Summary

Production in the private sector of an economy is subject to the discipline of the market. Businesses discover what consumers will buy or can be persuaded to buy and then seek to provide them with these products and services at prices they can afford. Consumers, on their part, make allocations of their income and, correspondingly, of their nonwork time, to maximize their satisfactions in accordance with their tastes and preferences. A system of prices is the link that joins decisions on production and consumption; the price system is intended to provide a necessary degree of stability in our complicated, specialized economic life. To improve the functioning of the private economy, government regulates activities, for example, seeks to prevent fraud, and also provides services that for various reasons are inappropriate for private firms to supply. Education is by far the largest of civilian governmental functions in the United States, and its importance is by no means established by size alone. Education is an engine of economic growth. It is also important in the formation of consumers' tastes and preferences. Education, finally, is our chief means to provide social mobility. It is thus important that educational activities be conducted in an efficient manner.

Selected Bibliography

Blechman, Barry M., Edward M. Gramlich, and Robert W. Hartman. *Setting National Priorities: The 1976 Budget.* Washington, D.C.: Brookings, 1975.

Conant, James Bryant. *Slums and Suburbs.* New York: McGraw-Hill, 1961.

Fusfeld, Daniel R. *Economics.* 2nd ed. Lexington, Mass.: D. C. Heath, 1976.

McWilliams, Wilson Carey. *The Idea of Fraternity in America.* Berkeley: University of California Press, 1973.

Rawls, John. *A Theory of Justice.* Cambridge: Harvard, 1971.

Chapter Two

Education and the National Economy

Education is a very large economic activity. Consider the following summary magnitudes:

▶ Total expenditures in the United States of formal public and private educational institutions, including elementary, secondary, and higher institutions, was $120 billion in 1976. This was 7.5 percent of GNP. (GNP is a measure of total economic activity in a given country in a given year; we shall explore its meaning thoroughly in this chapter.)

▶ Expenditures in publicly administered educational institutions in 1976 were $98 billion, which represents approximately 20 percent of the dollar value of all federal, state, and local government services in that year.

▶ For each man, woman, and child in the United States, outlays on public education in 1976 were $458. This established public education as the second largest functional activity of all levels of government, being exceeded only by national defense and international relations at $461 per capita. Education is by a considerable margin the largest civilian function of government.

▶ In 1976 there were 59.9 million students enrolled in educational institutions. One of every 3.6 persons in the country in that year was a student.

In 1976 there were 2,824,000 persons employed full time as teachers in public and private educational institutions. This number exceeded by over 300,000 the total of full-time paid civilian employment in the whole of the federal government. It also exceeds employment in the automotive, aircraft, and printing and publishing industries, taken all together.[1]

The maintenance level of an educational system is functionally related to an economic base. Consider an economically poor country such as Pakistan, where the financing of education is substantially under the control of the central government. The economy of the country at large is thus available to support its educational system. For the sake of argument, ignore differences in real costs of education. Imagine that Pakistan wanted to provide its children of elementary and secondary school age with the same level of educational services as we do in the United States. This would be impossible, as we noted in Chapter 1, because the cost would exceed Pakistan's entire annual economic output.[2]

The United States relies in large degree on state governments, and the local educational agencies they have created, to maintain elementary and secondary schools. Thus the relevant economic base is that of the state. And the capacity of different states to finance schools—a capacity determined by the level of economic activity within each state—varies markedly. Figure 2.1 shows the statistical relationship in 1972–73 between personal income per capita (the state measure that corresponds to national income per capita in describing the wealth of nations) and current expenditures per student in the public elementary and secondary schools. Differences in personal income per capita appear to account for 65 percent in the variance in expenditure per student. (We say "appear to," because for simplicity we ignore other variables, such as urbanization, that may affect school expenditures.) On the average, a $24 rise in expenditure per student is associated with a $100 increase in state personal income per capita.

---

[1] These figures were obtained from Bureau of the Census, U.S. Department of Commerce, *Statistical Abstract of the United States* (Washington, D.C.: U.S. Government Printing Office, 1976), pp. 5, 115, 248, 256, 259, 368–369; and U.S. Department of Health, Education, and Welfare, National Center for Education Statistics, *Projections of Education Statistics to 1984–85* (Washington, D.C.: U.S. Government Printing Office, 1976), pp. 61, 67.

[2] See Charles S. Benson, *Finance of Education: Training and Related Service in the Public Sector* (Islamabad, Pakistan: Planning Commission, Government of Pakistan, 1970), pp. 59–63.

Figure 2.1
Relationship between personal income per capita and current expenditures per student in public schools, by state, 1975–76[a]

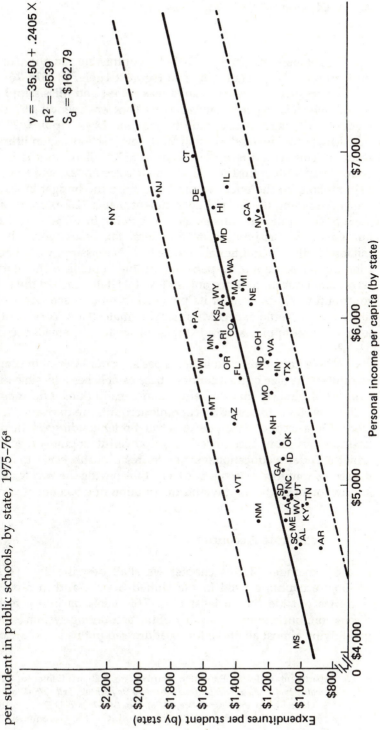

$$y = -35.50 + .2405 \, X$$
$$R^2 = .6539$$
$$S_d = \$162.79$$

[a] Alaska with personal income per capita of $9,448 and school expenditures of $2,096 per student is not shown.

Source: Data from U.S. Department of Health, Education, and Welfare, National Center for Education Statistics, *Statistics of Public Elementary and Secondary Day Schools, Fall, 1975* (Washington, D.C.: U.S. Government Printing Office, 1976), pp. 36–37; U.S. Department of Commerce, *Survey of Current Business* (Washington, D.C.: U.S. Government Printing Office, vol. 56, no. 8, August 1976), p. 17.

Let us consider in detail the contrasting situation of New York and Mississippi (all figures in Figure 2.1 refer to 1975–76). New York's personal income per capita was $6,564 and Mississippi's was $4,052, which is 38 percent lower. New York was spending $2,179 per student in its current operating budget and Mississippi, $997. Suppose Mississippi wanted to equal New York's school expenditures per student. This would represent a *rise* of $577 million in Mississippi's educational budget (in 1975–76, the state's current expenditures were $478 million, so the effect would be to raise the budget by 121 percent). Assuming the federal government meets 21.2 percent of Mississippi's educational outlays, as it was doing in 1975–76, the added burden on Mississippi's state and local tax bases would be $455 million. With this additional expenditure, Mississippi would be contributing 8.7 percent of its personal income to public elementary and secondary education. Since only one state, Utah, reached the point of contributing 7.1 percent of its personal income to schools, it is unlikely that we could expect Mississippi to match New York's outlay as long as Mississippi has the advantage of a markedly smaller economic base.[3]

We have thus established a basis for our interest in economic accounts—the size of the economic base establishes a feasible level of support of publicly financed educational institutions. Our main task in this chapter is to see how economic accounts are derived. There is, moreover, a second reason why such an understanding will be useful: Education is now recognized as a powerful engine of economic growth. Today's educational expenditures probably serve to increase the size of tomorrow's economic base, thus paving the way for further improvement in the supply and distribution of educational services.

Economic Accounts

In the remainder of this chapter we shall describe the system of national accounting used in the United States—and in most other countries outside the socialist bloc. This takes us into a technical discussion, but an understanding of the accounting system is helpful in studying almost all of the topics addressed in this book. Success in

---

[3] U.S. Department of Health, Education, and Welfare, National Center for Education Statistics, *Statistics of Public Elementary and Secondary Day Schools, Fall 1975* (Washington, D.C.: U.S. Government Printing Office, 1976), pp. 36–37; and U.S. Department of Commerce, *Survey of Current Business* (Washington, D.C.: U.S. Government Printing Office, 1976), 56, no. 8: 17.

Figure 2.2
The circular flow of the economy

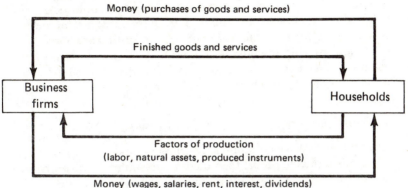

Money (purchases of goods and services)

Finished goods and services

Business firms

Households

Factors of production
(labor, natural assets, produced instruments)

Money (wages, salaries, rent, interest, dividends)

measuring national income was not achieved until the 1930s. Fortunately, we have today a whole set of conscientiously derived estimates of various totals of national income and product. The data are prepared by the U.S. Department of Commerce and are the most comprehensive tools for measuring the performance of the economy.[4]

The fundamental organization of an economy, excluding foreign trade, can be presented in the form of a diagram. The rectangles of Figure 2.2 represent the business and household sectors of the economy. The upper loop, representing the product market, shows the process of households sending money to the firms in exchange for finished goods and services. The lower loop, representing the market for factors of production, indicates that firms exchange money—in the form of wages, salaries, and so on—for the use of factors of production owned by the households. Factors of production, as we noted in Chapter 1, are human labor; natural assets, such as land and minerals; and instruments produced by labor, such as machines and factory buildings. Households claim ownership to land and mineral assets and other instruments of production, either as single households (owning one's own farm, say) or as shareholders in corporations. Such assets are classified as *capital goods*. In all modern societies, households are entitled to the fruits of their labor (that is, slavery is outlawed), and they receive these returns in the form of wages, salaries, and fringe benefits. The sale of goods and services by the business firms provides them with the money to buy the services

---

[4] The reader who has a particular interest in the national income measure might want to consult J. W. Kendrick, *Economic Accounts and Their Uses* (New York: McGraw-Hill, 1972), esp. chaps. 2–4 and 6.

of factors of production in order to keep turning out finished goods. As the households provide factors of production to the firms, the households receive money, which enables them to continue to buy the finished products. On the upper loop, money leaving the households represents to them the *cost of living,* or consumption expenditures. Money entering the business firms is their *sales receipts.* On the lower loop, money leaving the business firms is their *cost of production,* while money entering the households is their *consumer income.*

National Output as Value of Final Product

It might appear that we could measure national income by asking (1) heads of households to report their incomes to some central office and (2) the central office to cast up a sum for the whole country. This procedure, of course, would be inefficient: A statistician could design a sample to draw the same information and it would be unnecessary to tabulate the returns from millions of forms. But the difficulty in using any household reporting scheme is basically the difficulty in obtaining consistent treatment of different items of income and nonincome. For instance, we would need to state whether the respondent should include both *earned* and *unearned* income—earned income refers to salaries, wages, and fees; unearned income represents returns from property, for example, dividends, interest, and rental payments. We would have to specify whether income should be reported before or after taxes; and the treatment of taxes would be complicated because there are many different kinds of levies and some are more easily measured than others. Unless we laid down a rule, the treatment of increases or decreases in the value of assets would be different in different households. A household that receives periodic gifts from a rich uncle, absent any service provided to that uncle, might properly regard these as a part of its income. But, since both the recipient and the uncle cannot spend the same sum of money, there could well be an overstatement of income reported by the two parties. We would even need to specify whether such things as employer contributions to retirement plans and insurance dividends applied to reduce premiums should be counted. These may appear insignificant in the single household, but they become substantial when added up for all households in the country. The problems are manifold, and their existence shows the need for a workable concept of national income.

The conceptual framework of national income measurement that has been developed over a period of years stresses the identity of income and product. Income and product are two ways of describing the end result of some economic activity. Let us note that the concept makes a certain amount of sense. A business firm makes and sells a flow of product values over a period of time. During the same time, *and in order to turn out the product,* the firm makes income payments to factors of production: labor, land, and capital. Once the basic identity of income and product is accepted, it is possible to devise a scheme for measuring national income that yields consistent results over time and allows special measurements, for example, disposable income, to be developed for particular uses.

How could we estimate *national output?* It would be improper to cast up the sales receipts of all firms. We do not want to count the market value of the flour, for example, that was used by a bakery in making bread. Since we cannot eat the bread and then, as a separate act, eat the flour, the inclusion of the value of both the flour and the bread, each counted separately, would overstate the amount of product that was made available to the consumer. It would be a case of *double counting.* So we include only the market value of all *final* goods and services produced in the country over a given period. The test is this: Is an article or service *at the point of final sale?*

Income as Factor Income

The discussion so far enables us to understand such a standard definition as this: GNP is the market value of all final goods and services produced in a given period. Now, let us turn to the measurement of income. As we noted, we could obtain an estimate of income by casting up the money receipts of all households in the economy, but there is a conceptual difficulty akin to the one we considered in product measurement. Such a summation of money receipts would involve a double counting of income. One example of double counting we have already given (the rich uncle who gives money to his impecunious nieces and nephews). Double counting may also occur when a household sells a capital asset. Let us say that a member of household A negotiates a private sale of securities with a member of household B. The securities are transferred from A to B, and cash is transferred from B to A.[5] Each household has undergone a change in the composition of its stock of assets, but this transaction per se does not affect the income of either, in spite of A's receiving a sum of money in the transaction.

What we have described is called a *transfer payment.* The two households swapped assets (securities for cash). Transfers, as in our example of the rich uncle, can also be unilateral—gifts or inheritance.

---

[5] We assume that the transaction is private. If there is a brokerage fee involved, it is counted as part of national income.

If the payments are made from capital, the increase in assets of one party is matched by a decrease in holdings of the other.

When we exclude transfer payments from our income measure, we arrive essentially at a statement of returns to households for their contributions to current production, that is, *factor income*. It has seemed desirable that the estimate of national income be restricted to factor returns. Thus, money receipts of households must be adjusted to exclude the effects of capital gains and losses also.

We consider income, then, as a payment to factors of production in return for the current contribution of the factors in some productive process. In what specific forms are the payments made? One form is the compensation of employees. Under this heading are included wages, salaries, and supplements to wages and salaries (employer contributions for social insurance, pension funds, health and welfare funds, and related items). A second form is rent, which is defined as "the return to persons from the rental of real property." A third form is interest. A fourth is corporate profits. A fifth is income of unincorporated enterprises. These kinds of payments are the major types of factor income. A single household may receive income under several of those classifications. All that is required is that the household include one or more employed members or some members who own some rental property, stocks, or bonds.[6]

Value of Final Products and Factor Income: The Concept of Value Added

How is it that the sum of factor payments is actually the same magnitude as the market value of final products? Let us recall our statement about a business firm. The firm is engaged in producing and selling certain goods. Over any period there is a flow of output, or product values. During the same period there is payment of income to the factors of production. Production does not take place without the use (and, hence, remuneration) of productive factors; likewise, factor payments are made as—and only as—the factors are contributing to the process of production.

---

[6] Naturally, we think of these payments as being received in (or during) a given length of time. Thus, one might say, "My income in (during) 1973 was approximately $15,000." One would not say, however, "My income on December 31, 1973, was $12,000." So we are brought to the distinction between income (a *flow* of receipts of or claims to a supply of goods and services) and wealth (a *stock* of assets). It would also be perfectly proper to say that "My net worth, or the value of my assets less liabilities, on December 31, 1973, was $40,000. Here the statement of a money magnitude refers properly to a point, not a span of time.

Table 2.1
Arithmetic example of computing value added

Contributor	Sales receipts	Purchases from other firms	Value added
Farmer	$1,000,000	—	$1,000,000
Flour mill	3,000,000	$1,000,000	2,000,000
Bakery	6,000,000	3,000,000	3,000,000
Retailer	8,000,000	6,000,000	2,000,000
Total	18,000,000	10,000,000	8,000,000

To see this more clearly, let us look, not at a single business firm, but at a series of operations that carry a product from raw material to consumer. Suppose we start with a group of self-sufficient farmers who market $1 million worth of wheat during a given period. This wheat is transformed by a flour mill into $3 million worth of flour. The flour goes to a bakery, where bread worth $6 million is produced. Finally, the bread is sold in grocery stores for $8 million. The market value of final goods is thus $8 million.

But consider the sums of the contributions of the retailer down to the farmer. First, what is the magnitude of the *separate contributions* of the retailer, the baker, and so on? The retailer bought something (bread) worth $6 million and sold it for $8 million; his contribution to final value is $2 million. By the fact of his performing the service of retailing, the value of the product was increased by $2 million. Likewise, the baker bought flour at $3 million and produced bread worth $6 million. By the act of manufacturing flour into bread, $3 million was added to the worth of the product. The rationale is plain: At each step of ownership, we subtract from *sales receipts* the amount of *purchases from other firms* to obtain a measure of output that is *value added*. The results are shown in Table 2.1.

From the figures we see that the sum of value added at the several stages of production is equal to the market value of the final product ($8 million). Now, what does value added represent? If we examine an income statement of a firm, what will we see remaining after cost of materials is subtracted from sales receipts? Mainly wages and salaries, rent interest, and profits.[7] Two major items other than factor income would be included: (1) depreciation of capital goods

[7] Considerable interest was shown during the early 1970s in substituting value added taxes to allow governments in our country to phase out the use of property taxes for schools (see Chapter 9).

and (2) indirect business taxes. But the point is that value added in a firm can be taken, with certain adjustments, to represent factor income created by that firm. Because the value of *intermediate goods*—that is, goods bought by a *firm* to be manipulated or processed before sale—is subtracted at each stage of production, the sum of value added in a given line of activity is also equal to the market value of final goods. Hence, the sum of factor incomes in a line of production is equal to the value of final goods. Income and product are simply two ways of looking at the same magnitude.

That point aside, the concept of value added is useful in thinking about such activities as education. The teacher at the start of a school year receives students, each of which stands at a certain point of capacity to learn and receive knowledge. At the close of the school year, each of those same students has presumably advanced to some higher point of knowledge and capacity to learn. The difference in these two points of progress for each student is "value added in education," associated with the work of the given teacher during the year. Ideally, teachers would be evaluated in terms of the progress their students make—or in terms of value added—rather than in terms of the absolute standing of their students at the close of a school year.

Private Investment

We have been discussing national income and product under the assumption that all economic activity is directed toward supplying goods and services for household consumption. In a fundamental sense this is true, but such a simple approach does not satisfy the national income statisticians. The use of durable capital goods in our economy causes the statisticians to divide the output of the private economy into two sectors: the household and the business enterprise. Expenditures in the first sector are called *personal consumption;* in the second, production of durable goods is described as *private domestic investment,* measurable in *gross* or *net* terms. Gross investment reflects the entire output of *capital goods* (plant and equipment) in a current period of production. We know, however, that a certain amount of capital goods will wear out in any given period. Hence, a part of the total output serves simply to replace the worn-out plants and machines, that is, to keep the existing stock of capital equipment up to its previous level. By subtracting the amount of capital goods that serves as replacement from the total, we arrive at a net figure that reveals how much in any given period has been added to the stock of capital goods in our economy. The estimate of net private investment is one measure of economic growth, since it shows the change in quantity of physical resources produced by labor at our command. (If the net private investment figure is negative, the economy is "eating up its capital.")

In passing, we note that private domestic investment does not include estimates of the increase in the stock of *human capital*. Expenditures on elementary and secondary schools, higher education, industrial training, and research all serve to increase human capital. At the same time, the stock of human capital is subject to depreciation when trained workers retire or die. The size of this stock is crucial in determining the productivity of a country or region. Such an omission by national income statisticians serves to undervalue the role of school expenditures in promoting or preserving economic welfare.

Capital goods are not fully used up in any current period of production, whether this is defined as a month, quarter, or year. Hence, the full cost of any piece of capital equipment is not charged to current expenses of production but only a certain part of that full cost as determined under a depreciation formula. Accordingly, capital goods are not intermediate but final goods. Once this is accepted, our earlier statements about exclusion of intermediate goods in computing value of output applies. The market value of a newly produced piece of machinery would be counted in national product but not *both* the machine and the steel that went into making it.

Government Activity in National Economic Accounts

We have not yet considered the contribution of the government to national product. Governments do not have output measured in monetary terms, and governments do not make profits.[8] A large part of government debt is incurred for reasons unrelated to productive activity in any direct sense. The existence of government poses substantially different problems for the national income statistician from those raised in measuring private activity.

The position of government in the national economy can best be seen by expanding the circular flow diagram in Figure 2.2 to include a public sector, as shown in Figure 2.3. The loops joining business firms and households are by now familiar in meaning: Business firms deliver goods and services to households in exchange for

[8] There are exceptions to that statement. Public power plants are examples. The activities represented by such government enterprises are not quantitatively important in the measurement of national income.

Figure 2.3
The circular flow of the economy, including the
public sector

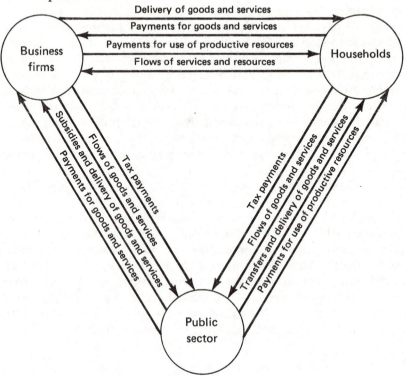

payments in money; at the same time households, as owners of
productive resources, supply services of labor and capital to business
firms in exchange for monetary returns. The public sector stands
apart both from business firms and households, but it has characteristics of each. It also has characteristics peculiar to itself, such as the
legal power to levy taxes, that is, compulsory claims, on business
firms and households alike.

From business firms and households, government *purchases*
goods and services. Government makes purchases from business
firms of such things as fire hoses, school buildings, and the advice of
professional consultants. From households, government obtains
labor and, inter alia, the services of rental properties. A corresponding reverse flow of money is represented in the diagram as "payments

for goods and services," directed to both businesses and to households.

Government *supplies* services to households, services such as schooling. These services as provided to households represent final goods. But government also supplies services to industry: police, fire protection, highways, for example. And when government serves industry, it is providing not final but intermediate goods. Lastly, we observe that government provides one more major item: money to businesses and households in amounts unrelated to any reverse flow of goods or services. In the case of business, these payments are called *subsidies*—agricultural subsidies are a prime example. For households, the payments are called *transfers*. Unemployment insurance, veterans' benefits, and social security benefits are examples of governmental transfers to households. All these relationships are displayed in Figure 2.3.

In early days of national economic accounting, the problems posed by the existence of a public sector were solved by ignoring government, which was equivalent to saying, as some business people still maintain, that public activity is nonproductive or sterile. One could move to the opposite extreme and equate total tax levy with sales of output by the government to the consumer, in which case, a great many transfer payments would necessarily be included. The actual practice in computing the government contribution to GNP is to define that contribution as "government purchases of goods and services." This sum is intended to represent what the government, acting as an agent for the households, buys of goods and the services of individuals, including, for instance, the services of public school teachers. Effectively, this procedure excludes public transfers and subsidies from national product measurement in the first instance. However, this procedure may result in an overstatement of the governmental contribution, since much of what the government offers is actually provided to business, that is, it falls in the class of intermediate goods and, hence, has already been counted in the market value of privately produced outputs. For example, government defends and protects the property of corporations as well as that of households. At the local level, this can be seen in the provision of police and fire services; these services are made available to business establishments in at least as full measure as they are available to individual households. The highway system carries the trucks and buses of private corporations as well as the cars of private households. On the other hand, interest on public debt is (rather arbitrarily) defined as a transfer item; since some government debt, particularly that of state and local governments, results in the creation of durable assets (as distinct from government debt incurred to fight wars), the treatment of total government interest in this manner excludes the current yield of services to the community that flow from these publicly financed assets. Whether there is a net over- or under-statement of government contribution, it is impossible to say.

The increases in amounts of public expenditures during recent years are notable. This statement applies to government purchases of goods and services and to that category of public expenditures called transfers and subsidies as well (see Table 2.2). For example, between the years 1970 and 1974, government purchases of goods and services rose by $89.3 billion (up by 40.7 percent in the four years) and transfers and subsidies rose by $55.3 billion (up by 70.0 percent).

National Income Accounts

There are, then, three major sectors in national income accounting: household, business enterprise, and government.[9] We have examined the major concepts that lie behind this scheme of accounting. Let us list the definitions of the specific measures of income and product that are available. There is not just one measure of national product or income but a set of measures. We will describe the major ones briefly.

Gross national product (GNP) is the final market value of the output of goods and services of the economy over a given period. All nondurable business products used up in that period are excluded, but no deduction is made for depreciation of durable capital goods. GNP thus represents essentially the purchases of goods and services by consumers, the purchase of goods and services by government, and gross private investment (including changes in business inventories).

Net national product (NNP) is GNP minus depreciation of durable capital goods. Since GNP includes double counting in capital consumption, NNP is the more precise estimate of the actual output of the economy. That is, NNP is the closest measure we have of the sum of market values of the output of final goods.

[9] The purist would state that there are actually four sectors. The additional one is called the *foreign*, or *rest-of-the-world* sector. If we export more goods and services than we import, the net difference is added to GNP. And, conversely, a net import balance would be subtracted from GNP. The dollar magnitude is small, relative to the other major sectors.

Table 2.2

Federal, state, and local government in the national income accounts, selected years (in billions of dollars)

Calendar year	Purchases of goods & services	Transfers and subsidies	Net interest
1950	$ 37.9	$ 18.2	$ 4.8
1960	99.6	28.8	7.8
1970	219.5	79.0	14.2
1971	234.2	92.7	13.4
1972	255.7	103.6	13.2
1973	276.4	116.2	15.5
1974	308.8	134.3	17.2

Source: Council of Economic Advisers, *Annual Report* (Washington, D.C.: U.S. Government Printing Office, 1975), pp. 329–330.

National income is NNP minus transfer payments made by business firms and indirect business taxes. Indirect business taxes include excise taxes, custom duties, capital stock taxes, state and local sales taxes, and property taxes levied on business enterprise. These sums are included in the market price of products but cannot be claimed by any factor of production. By excluding them from NNP, we arrive at an estimate, called national income, or what we described earlier as factor income.

There are two more significant measures, *personal income* and *disposable income*. Both include receipts and deductions unrelated to factor income. Hence, with respect to these two measures, the identity between income and product that we have in national income is lost. However, both give a better picture of current receipts in the household than does national income.

Personal income is national income minus such items as corporate profits and contributions for social insurance and plus dividends, interest paid by government and by consumers, and government transfers. In computing personal income, those portions of factor income earned, but not received, by households are subtracted. On the other hand, government transfer payments are added. Personal transfers are still excluded.

Disposable personal income is personal income minus personal taxes (federal, state, and local). It represents the amount of receipts available for personal consumption expenditures and for personal savings. Table 2.3 shows the relationships among the accounts in 1975.

Table 2.3
National income accounts, 1975 (in billions of dollars)

Gross national product (GNP)	$1,516.3
Less: Capital consumption allowance	
Equals: Net national product (NNP)	1,355.0
Less: Business transfers	
Indirect business tax	
Statistical discrepancy	
Plus: Subsidies	
Equals: National income	1,207.6
Less: Corporation profits and inventory valuation adjustment	
Contributions for social insurance	
Wage accruals *less* disbursements	
Less: Government transfer payments to persons	
Interest payments by governments and by consumers	
Dividends	
Business transfer payments	
Equals: Personal income	1,249.7
Less: Personal tax payments	
Equals: Disposable income	1,080.9

Source: U.S. Department of Commerce, *Survey of Current Business* (Washington, D.C.: U.S. Government Printing Office, 1976), 56, no. 11: 4, 6.

Problems Associated with National Income Accounts

There are several measurement and interpretation problems associated with national income accounts. The first of these that we will discuss has to do with inflation.

Changes in the Price Level

Between 1958 and 1974 the price of a family-size Chevrolet increased from $2,081 to $4,119, a rise of 97.9 percent. The price of the daily *New York Times* went up from a nickel to 20 cents, a rise of 300 percent.[10] Changes in price level make interpretations of national income accounts difficult. Comparisons over time are strongly affected by change in the price level. National product and income figures reported through the normal channels of public communication are

---

[10] *New York Times,* August 25, 1974, sec. 4, p. 2.

generally in *current dollars*—dollars uncorrected for the effect of price-level change. Hence, the GNP estimates announced quarterly in the newspapers represent an overstatement, generally, of the gain in the output of the economy. (This is so as a matter of post–World War II experience, for the price level has gone up rather consistently. If the price level went down, GNP in current dollars would underestimate the change in national output.)

National income statisticians prepare estimates corrected for the effect of change in the price level. These are referred to as estimates of, say, GNP in *real dollars* or, more commonly, as estimates of GNP in *constant (1972) dollars.* The latter phrase indicates that GNP is measured for each year at the level of prices that prevailed in the base year 1972. (The choice of the base year is arbitrary.) The procedure is to deflate GNP in current dollars by dividing the estimates for particular quarters by a *price index,* that is, by a measure of the average level of prices in the given quarters as compared with the average level of the base year. For example, the price index applicable to GNP stood at 134.34 in the third quarter of 1976 (1972 = 100). This means that the prices of goods and services included in GNP were 34.34 percent higher, on the average, than they were in 1972. To obtain an estimate of third quarter GNP in constant (1972) dollars, we divide $1,708.4 billion—the estimate in current dollars—by 1.3434. The required estimate is $1,271.7 billion.[11] Figure 2.4 shows changes from 1955 to 1975 in constant (1972) dollars of GNP and of its major components: personal consumption, private investment, and government purchases of goods and services.

There are serious problems, however, in the construction of price indexes. The 1974 Chevrolet mentioned earlier may be a higher quality vehicle than the 1958 model. Part of the $2,038 price increase between 1958 and 1974 thus would represent not inflation but a higher price for a "better" car. Judgments about change in quality are highly subjective; they are not generally recognized in price indexes.

A second main problem has to do with the process of averaging many different prices. If all prices went up by the same percentage, the problem would not exist. Unfortunately, for price statisticians, this is not the case. To complicate the matter further, certain articles are very important in the budget of given types of families, while other articles may bulk large in the purchases of other sorts of households. In the ordinary American family it is of greater interest that the price of round steak went up by 74 percent between 1958 and

[11] U.S. Department of Commerce, *Survey of Current Business* (Washington, D.C.: U.S. Government Printing Office, 1976), 56, no. 11: 3, 9.

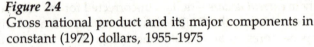

Figure 2.4
Gross national product and its major components in
constant (1972) dollars, 1955–1975

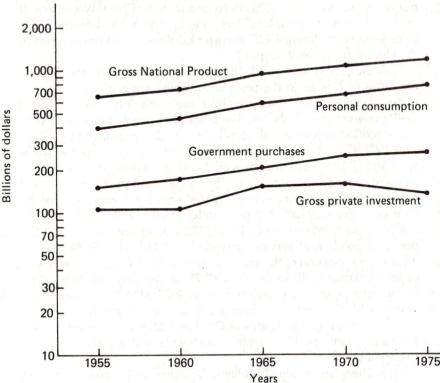

Source: Data from U.S. Department of Commerce, *Statistical Abstract of the United States*
(Washington, D.C.: U.S. Government Printing Office, 1976), p. 394.

1974 than that the price of a ranch mink coat rose by only 13 percent.[12]
So a simple average of the changes in prices of a set of commodities
and services is seldom appropriate. Various schemes have been devised to recognize, that is, give weight to, the relative significance of
price changes of different items of production or consumption.[13]

[12] *New York Times*, August 25, 1974, sec. 4, p. 2.
[13] In the case of preparing a *consumers' price index* (CPI), the procedure is empirically to
determine the budget allocations made by representative families of middle income.
The *market basket* of goods and services is priced at different points of time and the
changing (generally rising) amount of dollars needed to purchase the stated goods and

Sex Roles

There is a major omission in computing national product and income. All nonmarket transactions are excluded. Thus, no account is taken of the contribution to production of unpaid workers in the home. Vast amounts of work in cooking, cleaning, washing, driving, and child care are ignored because they are done in the home without pay. Arthur O. Dahlberg has put the matter succinctly: "If a rich bachelor hires a cook and pays her wages, then her services are counted as part of the national output. But, if he marries the cook, her same service contribution is not counted, and the national output figure goes down.[14]

Aside from this blatant omission, it is also true that as more and more women enter the labor force, they still fail to receive adequate recognition for their real contribution to GNP. This is because (1) national income accounting records their contribution in money salaries and wages and (2) such wages and salaries are paid to women at depressed levels that reflect sex discrimination in the labor market. *The Manpower Report of the President* recently noted:

> Even among continuously employed women . . . earnings are generally lower than those of men workers of comparable age, occupation, education, and experience. According to a recent analysis, a sample of professional and technical women who had been working most of their adult lives ". . . earned only 66 percent of the male average in these occupations. A similar comparison made for clerical workers showed that career women earned 79 percent as much as men, and among operatives and services workers . . . only half as much as men." In other words, a significant proportion of the wage differential between continuously employed women and similarly qualified men must be attributed to discrimination.[15]

---

services is taken to represent price-level change. The difficulty is that consumption patterns of families change gradually, and it is thus hard to separate price changes from the consumer's response to changes in his or her tastes and real income.

[14] Arthur O. Dahlberg, *How U.S. Output is Measured* (New York: Columbia, 1956), p. 5.

[15] Office of the President, *Manpower Report of the President Including Reports by the U.S. Department of Labor and the U.S. Department of Health, Education, and Welfare* (Washington, D.C.: U.S. Government Printing Office, 1974), p. 120.

In the next chapter we shall see that income differences attributed to education are commonly taken to represent the economic *return to investment in schooling*. On account of sex discrimination in the market, such assessments of the economic value of schooling will record lower returns to the education of women than of men.

Income Distribution

National output and income measures are commonly assumed to reflect the economic well-being of a country. Yet the process of preparing the counts is peculiarly value free. Guns and butter, cigarettes and vitamins, high-style sunglasses and seeing-eye dogs are all rated strictly in terms of the monetary values of their final products or in terms of factor costs. That some of these items might be of greater intrinsic importance in determining the state of happiness of the people is not judged independently of values assigned in the market. Moreover, an expensive bauble that might amuse a rich person for a few moments stands as being of the same economic significance as resources of equal total market value that are used to supply school lunches to needy children; that is to say, inter alia, national income accounts accept the prevailing, or existing, pattern of income distribution among households.

If the pattern of income distribution were basically even, this peculiarity in measuring the national accounts would pose no special problem. But it is not. Neither passage of time nor greater equality in educational attainments seem to be effective in reducing income disparities. In 1947 the average income received by the highest fifth of families, ranked by income, was $13,955. The lowest fifth received an average income of $1,616. Thus, the average income of the highest fifth was 8.64 times that of the lowest fifth. A quarter century later, in 1971, the highest fifth received, on the average, $24,559 and the lowest fifth, $3,247. The ratio of the highest fifth to the lowest was still of a high magnitude at 7.56.[16] The share of aggregate income in the nation received by the lowest fifth of families was 5.1 percent in 1947 and 5.4 percent in 1974, while the share going to the top fifth of families was, respectively, 43.8 and 41.0. With regard to wealth, that is, to assets of real estate, stocks, bonds, mortgages, insurance equities, and the like, the top 1 percent of adults, ranked by personal

---

[16] U.S. Department of Commerce, Social and Economic Statistics Administration, *Social Indicators* (Washington, D.C.: U.S. Government Printing Office, 1973), p. 178.

wealth, held 20.8 percent of the total of wealth in the country in 1949 and 20.7 percent in 1972.[17]

Externalities

Productive activities conducted in private markets or in the government sector may generate either costs or benefits that are *external* to the main productive activity. Such externalities are seldom captured in national income accounts (or when they are captured, they may carry an unusual meaning). Consider the following examples. Suppose that a group of wood pulp manufacturers establish themselves on a clean river. Under normal procedure, the mills would dump waste chemicals into the river, killing the fish and rendering the land area near the banks unsuitable for human habitation. The nonavailability of the river banks for summer cottages and for recreation, such as picnicking and fishing, is the external cost levied by the mills on the society; it is in addition to the private costs paid by the mills to manufacture their product. The value added reported by the mills would take no account of these external costs, only the private ones. At some later date a decision, perhaps enforced by government edict, may be made to clean up the river. The value of the final product of the firms would at that time show a rise, reflecting the additional cost of running nonpolluting mills or, alternatively, reflecting the absorption of social costs into private costs. As value added goes up, so does GNP. This particular addition to GNP would not indicate a gain in social welfare over the original position of unspoiled rivers but, rather, a delayed recognition of the more complete counting of costs of manufacturing a particular product.

On the other hand, a firm may produce external benefits, which, though they are initially measured in money cost, may be grossly undervalued in the current period. A given research program in a private company, financed, say, by a modest budget, may produce findings that are of immense value to the society for many years. The firm hopes to make its private return (profit) from its investment in research, but there are limits to the extent any company can exploit new knowledge through the market mechanism, even that share of new knowledge provided by its own research program.

Education is generally presumed to be characterized by externalities to an unusually large degree. Assume, as is reasonable, that not all people are equally talented in all lines of human endeavor. (This is not to deny that all people may have, in some sense, equal

---

[17] Bureau of the Census, *Statistical Abstract*, pp. 392, 408.

talents all around.) There is then likely to be a generalized social benefit produced when the education system identifies particular kinds of talent, nurtures its development, and guides persons possessing those talents into those lines of work that are most appropriate for them. For example, our country is presumably better off when the school system succeeds in encouraging people who have a natural bent toward physical science to study and prepare themselves well for that demanding line of work. The same observation about the role of an educational system in helping to discover talent would hold true for the selection of future violinists, ballet dancers, and opera singers.[18] We might say the same thing about the beneficial effects of screening candidates for such professions as medicine and law. However, when the line of work involves face-to-face contact of practitioner and client and when the practitioner holds power to regulate the quality of service offered to different types of clients, then the humanitarianism of the practitioner is important to the goal of social justice. There is little evidence, alas, that preference is given to those of equal technical aptitude who are relatively altruistic.

Education may produce social costs as well as benefits. Two examples will suffice. First, education may raise expectations in the individual about what kinds of work she or he is qualified to do. If at the same time the economy is not offering a sufficiently large number of superior work opportunities to meet the expectations of recent graduates, they may be driven—or succumb—to antisocial action.[19] As James O'Toole notes:

> The rub is that no industrialized nation has been able to produce an adequate number of jobs that provide the status and require the skills and educational levels that their work forces are achieving. . . . There is thus a disjuncture between the expectations raised by educational policy and the inability of the economic order to make good on society's promises. There simply are not enough good jobs to go around to everyone who thinks he or she deserves one. If it were not for the Marxist overtones, this disjuncture could be called a contradiction, one that stems from the very success of nations in their efforts to become more egalitarian! To the extent that developed countries are solving the centuries-old problems of

[18] We do not, of course, contend that the educational system performs its sorting function as effectively as it should. On this point, see David Kirp. "Schools As Sorters: The Constitutional and Policy Implications of Student Classification," *Pennsylvania Law Review*, 121, no. 4 (April 1973): 705–797.

[19] This is a problem that the developing nations have faced for nearly 20 years.

providing freer access to education, they are paradoxically creating a situation that in the future threatens to countervail their efforts to achieve greater equality and political stability.[20]

This argument applies to persons who are educational successes, but the educational system produces persons who are school failures as well as successes. The failures (like some who are school successes but nevertheless unlucky in work) are largely channeled into dead-end jobs. Since to be a school failure and to obtain at best a dull job is, in most instances, a worse fate than to be a school success and lack the job one would like to have, the creation by the educational system of school failures that are preventable is an unconscionable social act.

The second example of a social cost produced by the educational system was alluded to in Chapter 1. Insofar as an effort is made to minimize parental frustrations about choice of school by emphasizing local control in the distribution of educational resources, pressure is at the same time created to maintain a pattern of social isolation, that is, segregation by race, income, and age in residential location. If the question of where a family lived in a given metropolitan area had less to do with the kinds of schools its children might attend, then residential choice would obviously become freer. Hence, the functioning of the educational system is a contributing factor to social-class isolation of neighborhoods.

Quality of Life

As we have seen, national income figures tell us little about whether the society is providing people with the kinds of jobs they would like to have. And surely the economic well-being of the households of a nation is not determined solely by their levels of consumption, for satisfaction in work is itself an important source of economic well-being. To achieve a high level of GNP, and a high level of GNP is generally assumed to represent an advanced state of human welfare, society may have sacrificed too much in accepting conditions of work that lack enjoyment, that have turned work into chores that people perform only for pay. And one of the worst cases may be that society has accepted means of satisfaction that are terribly expensive. Consider the automobile, one of the main *consumer durables*. Automobiles

[20] James O'Toole, "The Reserve Army of the Underemployed," *Change*, May 1975, p. 28.

are assumed to provide a flow of services, that is, personal transport, over a given period. But, as Tibor Scitovsky has stated,

> they also provide something else. Thanks to constant model changes and style changes, the latest models also provide the pleasant stimulation of novelty. They are new gadgets to play with, to show off, and to enjoy. This aspect of durable goods is definitely nondurable, because the attraction and stimulation of novelty wears off rather quickly. . . . This is very costly entertainment. . . .[21]

Scitovsky goes on to suggest that we as a nation run the danger of placing too much emphasis on "defensive consumption" at the expense of "creative consumption." Defensive consumption serves to protect the body from hunger, thirst, and pain of all kinds, including the pains of bother and boredom. Creative consumption, on the other hand,

> consists in the delectation of the senses, the exercise of one's faculties, and in the sophistication added to the simple satisfactions of life to enhance their enjoyment. The enjoyment of extending or deepening one's experiences and knowledge of the world in any of its aspects, from taste sensations to literature and intellectual concerns, is creative consumption. Much of this is a process of learning: learning to know or to know better for the sake of enjoyment.[22]

A rise in GNP does not necessarily connote growth of creative consumption. Above a minimum level, we might say that GNP has little to do with creative consumption, although provision of educational services has a lot to do with it.

[21] Tibor Scitovsky. "The Place of Economic Welfare in Human Welfare," *The Quarterly Review of Economics and Business*, 3, no. 3 (Autumn 1975); reprinted as Reprint no. 117 (Palo Alto, Calif.: Center for Research in Economic Growth, Stanford University), p. 12.

[22] Tibor Scitovsky. "Notes on the Producer Society," *The Economist*, 121, no. 3 (1973): 241.

Economic Resources and Economic Growth

Nevertheless, if education is an instrumental variable in improving the quality of life, education must be financed. And its level of financing is functionally related to the size of national income. Educational expenditures grow most easily when material income itself is rising. How, then, does material income become larger? To comprehend basic ideas about economic growth, we require familiarity with the concept of *economic resources*. From the beginnings of modern economics, it has been the practice to classify resources as *labor, land,* and *capital.* Labor includes all the many kinds of human services that enter into production, including management. Land represents not just agricultural land but, more broadly, natural resources as the term is commonly used. Capital is not money but produced means of production, or goods that have been made, not to satisfy the desire for consumption immediately, but to be used in further acts of production. Examples are factory buildings, machines, highways, bridges, and blackboards.

Resources are used to make goods and services. Economic resources possess the special attribute of scarcity. A chemical plant, for example, uses ordinary air in its productive processes, but air is available in sufficiently plentiful quantities that no one is able to send the chemical company a bill for the ordinary air it is using, not a bill that the company would take seriously, anyway. But the company may also use the services from time to time of consultants in chemical technology. Obviously, consultants are in limited supply; she or he is able to send the company a bill that it would see fit to honor.

At any given time, the national output of a country is limited by the amount of economic resources available to its firms; its independent entrepreneurs, including farmers; and to its government.[23] Fortunately, the amount of economic resources available to the productive agencies of a country can be increased from one period to the next, and that is what the process of economic growth is all about.

For instance, suppose the population of a country increases. As the rising numbers of children grow up, a certain proportion, ordinarily something over half, will enter the labor force. These extra workers act to increase the national product, in total. But, if the new workers are given less than the traditional amount of capital goods to work with or if they have been poorly educated, *output per worker* may

[23] Of course, there may be unemployed resources in the country; when such exist, output can expand without new resources being created.

fall. A country in which GNP is growing, but growing more slowly than the size of the work force, is commonly regarded as getting poorer, not richer.

The key variable in measuring the results of economic growth is, thus, national (or regional) output per worker.[24] Assuming that the supply of land is fixed (land meaning natural resources), the modern view of growth holds that output per worker goes up primarily as (1) the quality of labor is increased, (2) the quantity or quality (or both) of capital goods is increased, and (3) advances are made in technical knowledge.[25] Improvements in the quality of labor, increases in the effective stock of capital goods, and advances in knowledge all are the result of the process of investment, which is the deliberate application of a share of today's resources to enlarge the supply of resources for tomorrow's use. This is the main topic of the next chapter.

Summary

The national income accounts described in this chapter are our chief means of measuring economic progress. As national income advances, so does the capacity to support schools. The accounts are derived in the first instance from the simple idea that income and product are identical concepts of economic progress. Special difficulties are attached to incorporating government activities into the national income accounts, but this does not contradict the basic point that rising national income is associated with an expansion of the absolute, if not the relative, size of the public sector. Finally, though the accounts represent the best statement of economic progress, they remain a less than complete description of changes in the quality of life. In various ways, the remainder of this book is concerned with the role of education in contributing to the quality of our lives.

---

[24] Unless average family size is changing immoderately, output per worker and output per capita will move in step. Either can be used to measure change in a nation's economic well-being.

[25] For a more detailed statement on factors affecting economic growth, see F. C. Mills, *Productivity and Economic Progress*, National Bureau of Economic Research, Occasional Paper 38 (New York, 1952).

Selected Bibliography

Eckaus, Richard S. *Basic Economics*. Boston: Little, Brown, 1972.

Johnson, Harry G. *The Theory of Income Distribution*. London: Gray-Mills Publishing, Ltd., 1973.

Kendrick, John W. *Economic Accounts and Their Uses*. New York: McGraw-Hill, 1972.

Lerner, Abba P. *Everybody's Business*. New York: Harper & Row, 1964.

Musgrave, Richard A., and Peggy B. Musgrave. *Public Finance in Theory and Practice*. New York: McGraw-Hill, 1973.

Rainwater, Lee. *What Money Buys: Inequality and the Social Meanings of Income*. New York: Basic Books, 1974.

Willis, James F., and Martin L. Primack. *Explorations in Economics*. Boston: Houghton Mifflin, 1977.

Chapter Three

Relationship of Economic Growth to Educational Investments

Our task in this chapter is to gain an understanding about the process of economic growth and to see how investment in education contributes to that process. The basic ideas concerning economic growth, applicable in any society regardless of its political structure, can best be presented by a simple "fable."

A Simple Fable of Economic Progress

Imagine that Robinson Crusoe is cast up on a rather barren island, all alone. Suppose that the only food available to Robinson is fish. Let him be able, by working diligently, to catch six fish a day in the lagoon of his island and suppose that he can live satisfactorily on the daily output of six fish. So far, all production is consumed, day by day.

Imagine next that Robinson discovers how to store fish, possibly by salting it, using some dry salt he found on the island. Let Robinson put aside a half fish a day for eleven days and on the twelfth day, let him fish not at all but spend his working time building a net. Imagine that Robinson, using the same energy as before, can catch with the net, not six fish a day, but eight.

The act of building a net is an act of *investment*, resulting in an increase in economic resources available to Robinson. He has his own labor, and he has acquired capital goods as well. When resources are increased, output per worker goes up—by two fish a day. However, the process of investment required sacrifice, which we call *saving*. For twelve days, Robinson lived less well than he might if he had not planned to invest in the net, putting aside half a fish until he had enough to support himself during the time he devoted his attention to building the net. In this case it is obvious that the value of resources saved—5.5 fish—is equal to the value of resources invested, for they are the one and same magnitude. In the real world, acts of saving and acts of investment may be done by different people who never expect to see each other. Yet, it still holds true that savings and investments, in total and including inventories, are of equal magnitude.[1]

Once his investment begins to yield returns, Robinson has a number of interesting choices to make. He may simply catch more fish, that is, live better. (But unless he takes time off from fishing once in a while to keep his net in repair, his standard of living eventually will fall back to the old level: *capital depreciates*.) Or he can work fewer hours while still consuming, say, six fish per day; he could use his greater productive capacity to "purchase" leisure. Or he could use some of his added productive capacity to finance additional investments. And, because he is now richer, the required sacrifice should seem less painful. Quite possibly Robinson would use his new output to accomplish all of these things in some measure at the same time— that is what most societies do.

Next, let Robinson be joined by Friday. Assume for sake of argument that Friday is a fisherman of equal skill with Robinson. Various situations are possible. Perhaps the net was too big for Crusoe to gain full advantage from its use, so that output per man actually increases when two men join forces on the one net, and maybe output goes up to a total of 20 fish a day. This would be a situation of *increasing return to scale*. Or perhaps the one net, shared between the two men, gives a total yield of only 14 fish a day, so that output per man drops to 7 fish. This is the ordinary and expected result when we observe an increase in supply of one factor of production—in this case, labor—while supplies of other factors are held constant: Output per unit of the factor of production in increased supply falls. (This makes sense. If there are 10 farmers working 100 acres of land, we could hardly expect to get a 10-fold increase of yield from that same [fixed] amount of land if the number of farmers

---

[1] If we save and put our money in the bank, the bank does not actually put it away in a vault. Rather, the bank, as a financial intermediary, lends the money to some person or to some company who will most probably use it for investment purposes.

increased to 100. After a point the extra farmers would just get in each other's way.) This is called the *principle of diminishing returns.*

At this point, perhaps Robinson and Friday would decide to invest more and build a second net. Or they could invest by taking time off to improve their skills, either as net builders, net repairers, or fishermen. The latter exercise would be an *investment in human capital.* To judge whether to invest in a net or in training requires an estimate of the extra (marginal) yield of varying amounts of investment in the two alternative forms, physical or human capital. At some point, however, increments of investment would begin to yield smaller and smaller additions to output. This is because the size of the lagoon in which Robinson and Friday do their fishing is itself fixed. (In real life, there is almost always some element of production that is not readily expandable.) The only hope for higher output then becomes creation of new technical knowledge: for example, discovering of a new lagoon or discovering how to attract fish from other islands to theirs, etc. Ordinarily, new technical knowledge is created by acts of investment.

The Concept of Opportunity Cost

The observations we have so far made about the nature of economic resources lead inevitably to this conclusion: When resources are fully employed—and full employment is a recognized objective of all enlightened governments—additional goods or services of one type can only be produced when output of some other economic product is curtailed. The idea applies whether or not we live in a money economy. If Robinson Crusoe broadens his diet to include coconuts as well as fish, and if he is fully employed in the pursuit of food, he can increase his consumption of coconuts only if he is willing to *forego* a certain amount of fish. The *opportunity cost* of one type of consumption is the opportunity we forego to enjoy some other type of consumption. Economics and magic do not mix well: Economics tells us that goods and services do not, like a rabbit, pop out of a hat but require hard work and capital to make. And hard work and capital through all of human history have been in short supply, relative to peoples' wants.

A difference, moreover, should be noted between the business person's measure of costs and the economist's definition of opportunity costs. The businessperson measures costs to reveal the profit or loss situation by comparing outlays with revenues. Imagine that a person is operating a proprietary vocational school. The main

items of cost that would be recognized would be salaries of professional staff, salaries and wages of nonprofessional staff, depreciation
of plant and equipment, purchase of consumable supplies, and interest. The economist, in assessing opportunity cost, would modify these
accounts in two ways:

1.   Instead of measuring salaries and wages by the amount the
      employer pays to his staff, the economist would wish to
      know what are the possible earnings of staff in their best
      alternative employment.
2.   The economist would include a cost not recognized by the
      employer, namely, the amount of earnings, or extra earnings,
      the students could make if they were working instead of
      going to school. (If the students were working and going to
      school, then the appropriate figure is the additional earnings
      they could have if they lengthened their workweek by the
      time they spend in school and in studying.)

The concept of opportunity cost is shown graphically in Figure 3.1. Consider two economic goods, bread and schooling. (Bread
may refer to all types of goods and services that yield immediate
satisfaction and schooling to all types that yield delayed satisfaction,
or satisfaction extending over a longer period. Or bread may refer to
private market goods and schooling to output of the public sector.)
Along the vertical axis of Figure 3.1 we measure the output of bread
with each small distance, $l'm'$, say, equal to 1,000 loaves. The horizontal axis indicates the output of schooling, with each small segment,
$q''r'$, being set equal, say, to successfully completing 100 hours of
instruction. (All such measurements are illustrative only.) The line *AB*
indicates the maximum amount of the two commodities a society can
turn out when all its resources suitable for the production of the two
goods are fully employed. It is called the *production possibility curve*. If
all resources are devoted to the production of bread, we can have *0B*
units of bread; and if all resources are directed toward schooling, we
can have *0A* units of schooling. Or we can have any combination on
the line extending between *A* and *B*.

Note the position of the point *U*. Here we have production of
0C bread and *0D* schooling. By moving to the point *E*, we can have
more of both outputs, *0F* bread and *0G* schooling. The reason is that
U represents a point of unemployment of some resources; when
resources are unemployed, we can increase output of both products
simultaneously. What we cannot do is obtain the output associated
with a point such as *E'* because the line *AB* reveals the maximum
combinations of the two goods that can be produced. On the line *AB*,

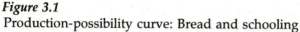

Figure 3.1
Production-possibility curve: Bread and schooling

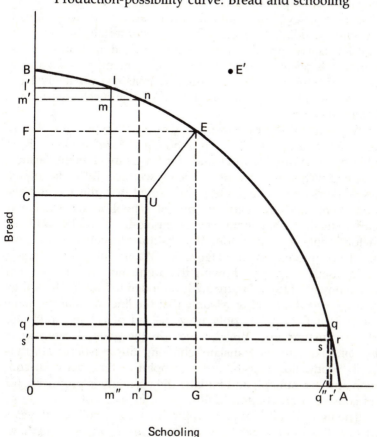

Schooling

it is possible to have more schooling only if we are willing to accept less bread—in the short run, at least.

The other feature of Figure 3.1 to note is that the line *AB* bows out to the northeast. Why? Consider the two small triangles *lmn* and *qrs*. Let the vertical distances *lm* and *qs* be the same, equal to 1,000 loaves of bread. When we move along the production possibility curve (line *AB*) from *l* to *n*, we sacrifice a small, fixed amount of bread to obtain a rather large additional amount of schooling, *mn*. Now, let us make the same kind of trade off, starting at point *q*. Here we give up the small amount of bread (*lm* = *qs* = 1,000 loaves); but as we go from *q* to *r*, we acquire in exchange a very small extra amount of schooling, *sr*. The bowed shape of the curve produces this kind of difference and it is intended to portray the general principle of *diminishing returns*. At point *l*, we have much bread and little schooling. Those resources devoted to making bread are much overstrained. Persons who are skilled teachers but rather poor farmers are working the field, let us say. So, when we give up a fixed amount of bread production, we release resources that are eminently suited to the production of education. As a result, we obtain a relatively large increase in the amount of educational services in exchange for the given amount of bread.

At point *q*, just the opposite kind of situation prevails. We are producing little bread and much schooling. Farmers have been drafted into the classroom, and some of them are much better farmers than teachers. When we give up *qr* bread, we push into educational services workers who are even less well suited than those who have preceded them, and the extra output of schooling we receive is necessarily small. A shorthand way of expressing this idea is to say that factor inputs are not perfectly substitutable between the two outputs. To continue, consider Figure 3.2. Whereas Figure 3.1 was a kind of economic snapshot, showing the production possibilities that exist at a moment of time, Figure 3.2 is intended to indicate how they may change over time. Let us assume that the line *AB* is of the same order as *AB* in Figure 3.1, only now instead of calling goods for immediate consumption "bread," we use the general category of *consumption*. Likewise, we translate schooling into *investment*. *AB* thus represents production possibilities at a point of time between consumption and investment; and initially the economy is producing O*H* units of consumption goods and O*I* units of investment.

The line *TV* might represent productive possibilities 10 years later, when the prior allocations of resources to investment have heightened the productive capacity of the country. One possible response to the new level of productive capacity could be to take all the extra yield in favor of consumption, to choose, that is, O*J* units of consumption and O*I* units of investment. A more likely response is for the country to increase its production of both consumption and investment goods, a combination, say, of O*K* consumption and O*L* investment.

Figure 3.2 also illustrates the plight of underdeveloped countries. If the population is below adequate standards of nutrition, and this is substantially true in a country like Bangladesh, it is very difficult not to take any extra yield of the economy in the form of immediate consumption. And so the underdeveloped countries, lacking means of investment, continue to fall behind the rich nations in

Figure 3.2
Dynamics of production and economic growth:
Consumption versus investment

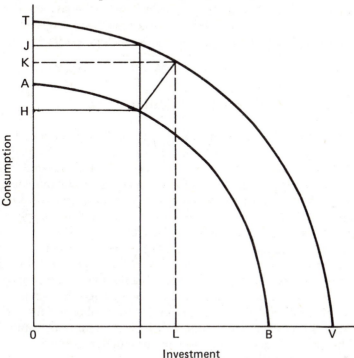

economic progress. Education does not compete well with food if people are continually hungry. Indeed, the problem is compounded because what resources are devoted to education are likely to be ineffectively utilized because the intellectual power of the students has been stunted by lack of protein in their diets.

Thus, Figure 3.2 illustrates the final relationship we mentioned earlier: Today's investments increase tomorrow's productive possibilities.[2] As tomorrow's production possibilities expand, it becomes possible to further increase investment while also expanding consumption. These points are important to educators, for education is very much a form of investment expenditure. To urge educators to

---

[2] To put it another way, choices on the production possibility curve *TV* are not independent of those on *AB*. If the society had chosen point *A* in the first place, *TV* would never come into existence (ruling out international grants and loans).

be concerned about the contribution of schooling to economic growth is not necessarily to adopt a blatantly materialistic view of human progress, for economic growth can serve to release resources for investments in education and other socially beneficial activities. It is unrealistic to think we shall dismantle our complex and interdependent economic system. As long as it exists, material advance and cultural development are natural allies, not enemies.

Accounting for Growth: Education's Share

We have seen that in the economist's view, economic growth occurs when supplies of resources, including the resource of technology, increase.[3] Traditionally, the supply of land, meaning natural resources, is assumed to be fixed.[4] This leaves gains in capital (meaning physical capital), labor, and technology as sources of growth. Our next task in this chapter is to see how education affects the supply of labor inputs by serving to improve their quality.

The most commonly used model of economic growth is one or another variant of the *Cobb-Douglas production function.*[5] In its simplest basic formulation, this model asserts that a percentage change in national output is the sum of the percentage change in the size and quality of the labor force (assuming that labor is fully employed) plus the percentage change in physical volume of capital. Each of the percentages is weighted by production coefficients or elasticities, which are treated as constants.

---

[3] If unemployment of labor or capital goods—or, more likely, both—increases at the same time that supplies of resources increase, then national output does not necessarily rise. Generally speaking, growth theory does not deal with the problem of unemployment.

[4] This is true in the physical sense of conservation of resources, but the supply of economically useful natural resources is actually not rigidly fixed but is subject to some control (and abuse) by man.

[5] The Cobb-Douglas production function is generally written

$$Q = AK^\alpha L^\beta$$

Q = national output; A = a constant, standing as an indication of the general state of technology; K = capital supply; L = labor supply, and α and β are positive fractions. In natural logarithms, this can be written

$$\ln Q = \ln A + \alpha \ln K + \beta \ln L, \qquad \alpha + \beta = 1$$

and the additive nature of the function is seen. For discussions of the development of the Cobb-Douglas function, see C. Cobb and P. Douglas, "A Theory of Production," *American Economic Review,* supplement (1928), pp. 139–165.

Let us consider a numerical example. To make things easy, let's measure everything in money—in billions of dollars, say. And let us adopt a standard set of symbols. Let Q = national output. ΔQ stands for a small (marginal) change in output. $\Delta Q/Q$ represents percentage change in output. Let K equal supplies of capital and L equal supplies of labor. Let S_k equal the weight, or elasticity, used to modify the percentage change in capital, $\Delta K/K$; and let S_1 represent labor's weight. The basic Cobb-Douglas formula then reads

$$\frac{\Delta Q}{Q} = S_k \cdot \frac{\Delta K}{K} + S_1 \cdot \frac{\Delta L}{L} \tag{3.1}$$

Suppose there are 125 units worth of capital in the economy and 375 units worth of labor. Let each type of input be increased by one tenth—or by 10 percent. Let $S_k = 0.25$ and $S_1 = 0.75$. What is the rate of change in national output? We have

$$\frac{\Delta Q}{Q} = (0.25)\frac{12.5}{125} + (0.75)\frac{37.5}{375}$$

$$= (0.25)\,(0.10) + (0.75)\,(0.10)$$

$$= 0.025 + 0.075 = 0.100$$

$$= 10.0\% \tag{3.2}$$

Therefore, output Q rises by 10 percent. When the two inputs of labor and capital each increase by a given percentage amount, the Cobb-Douglas function tells us that national output goes up by precisely that same percentage.

It is a property of the basic formulation of the Cobb-Douglas function that labor and capital change always in equal proportions: That is, the *capital-labor ratio* is constant. A constant capital-labor ratio means that average products of capital and labor (the national output per unit of capital and per unit of labor, respectively) remain constant as the supplies of capital and labor change. Also, marginal products of labor and capital (that is, the extra output (Q) associated with very small changes in either capital (K) or labor (L), the amount of the other factor of production being held constant) remain constant.[6]

Under constant returns to scale (meaning that if we double all inputs, we precisely double all outputs; and if we increase all inputs by any given percentage, call it x, output rises by precisely x), and

[6] For a proof that marginal products are constant in the Cobb-Douglas function, see A. Chiang, *Fundamental Methods of Mathematical Economics* (New York: McGraw-Hill, 1967), pp. 373–375.

when each factor is paid the value of its marginal product, then capital's constant relative share of national product will be S_k in equation (1) and labor's constant share will be S_1. S_k and S_1, moreover, will add up to 1, which is to say that the relative shares exhaust the entire national product.

This is a very important point, and to see why, let us consider the numerical example again. Suppose that the increase in labor inputs of 37.5 billion dollars was the result of improvements in quality of labor as achieved through education. We might conclude that at the given point in time, education was responsible for 75 percent ($\Delta L/\Delta Q = 37.5/50 = 75$ percent) of economic growth. (An illustrative magnitude only; education is apparently responsible for a somewhat smaller share.) S_1 then—and S_k too—represents *weights* to assess the contribution of a particular asset to national growth.

The early attempts to provide theoretical verification for the Cobb-Douglas function were noted for the relative simplicity of the data they employed. Labor was treated as a homogeneous unit, and the number of employed persons was totaled to obtain measures of labor supply. (Adjustments were made, however, to recognize changes in length of work day, work week, etc.)[7] Capital was physical capital, essentially, and the capital estimates were corrected for price changes. Assuming that growth is related to changes in supply of labor and capital only, and recognizing that the early Cobb-Douglas work treated labor as homogeneous, it followed that, abstracting from matters having to do with the length of work year and work week and rates of unemployment, the route to higher output *per worker* was strictly through increasing the amounts of physical capital assets in production. Under that older view, education was not investment, it was consumption. This view has now changed.

In most current measurements of the economic significance of education, however, certain major ideas from Cobb-Douglas production function theory are carried over.

1.   It is assumed that the rate of growth in national product is related in a proportional way to changes in quantities of inputs. A given percentage change in input A, weighted by an appropriate constant, will equal a share of a given percentage change in GNP.

2.   It is assumed that factors of production are paid in accordance with the value of their marginal products.

[7] See Paul H. Douglas, *Real Wages in the United States 1890–1926* (Boston: Houghton Mifflin, 1930), part 3.

These assumptions allow us to translate changes in the quantity of education possessed by members of the work force into changes in quality of labor inputs by weighting years of schooling by average salaries and wages associated with different amounts of education. On the other hand, it justifies using shares of national product paid to different factors of production as weights (in relating growth changes by each factor to growth changes in GNP). These assumptions are rather extreme—determination of sources of growth, including contributions of education, rests on grounds that are not unassailable theoretically.

To continue, in 1957 Robert Solow published an article, based on new data, showing that less than half of the increase in output per man could be accounted for by increases in the physical volume of capital goods.[8] Something else, obviously, was affecting productivity change. One possible explanation for Solow's finding was that the quality, as well as the quantity, of physical capital was rising. Another was that the quality of labor was going up. Additional studies indicated that improvements in the quality of capital fell far short of accounting for the unexplained portion of productivity advance. That left the improvement in the quality of labor, and the stage was set for economists to consider the investment aspects of educational expenditures and of other expenditures—on health, for example—that affect the quality of labor.

To see further how economists now deal with the value of education, let us imagine first of all that we live in a slave society. Imagine that most of human labor, as well as most of physical capital and land, is owned by a small minority. The owners of capital would see that they could maximize their profits by regulating investment in various types of capital in terms of relative profitability. For example, they would purchase additional slaves—or purchase services to improve the health, strength, or quality of mind of their chattels—whenever the anticipated returns from various specific types of investments in human capital exceeded anticipated returns from various specific investments in physical capital. National product would grow at a high rate whenever resources invested by individual entrepreneurs were substantial and were made in accordance with the rule of relative profitability.

The economic value of a slave at auction would be a function of such factors as age, sex, health, and mental characteristics in general. But the slave's specific skills would be a major consideration

[8] R. Solow, "Technical Change and the Aggregate Production Function," *Review of Economics and Statistics*, 39, no. 3 (August 1957): 312–320.

in determining that value. In part, the slave's skills might be natural or hereditary; in part, they might have been obtained by education or training. The education economists would seek to isolate this last component of value—that is, seek to determine the contribution to productivity of training as distinct from other sources of acquired characteristics of the human agent, taking the natural characteristics (age, sex, intelligence, and the like) as given.

The entrepreneurs would likewise attempt to estimate the marginal productivity of increments of training, recognizing that training is lumpy, segmental, and specific to different skills; that the time span over which the yield of training may be garnered is a function of the age and possibly the sex of the trainee; and that skills of imparting training are themselves reproducible assets subject to ordinary principles of cost minimization (education, that is, has its own production function). Once a set of skills possessed by a set of slaves had been identified, the value of those skills would be depreciated over the average working lives of those individuals, just as the value of a piece of machinery would be depreciated in conventional accounting practice.

Of course, we do not live in a slave society, and ownership of value of skills is not permitted to be sold. Aside from that fundamental point, the contribution of education to productivity is dealt with in terms similar to those we have used just above. Consider the following summary statement by Edward F. Denison:

> A sharp upward shift in the educational background of the American labor force has upgraded the skills and versatility of labor and contributed to the rise in national income. It has enhanced the skills of individuals within what is conventionally termed an occupation, often with considerable changes in the work actually performed; it has also permitted a shift in occupational composition from occupations in which workers typically have little education and low earnings toward those in which education and earnings are higher. Education also heightens an individual's awareness of job opportunities, and thereby the chances that he is employed where his marginal product is greatest. A more educated work force—from top management down—also is better able to learn about and use the most efficient production practices.[9]

[9] Edward F. Denison, *Accounting for United States Economic Growth, 1929–1969* (Washington, D.C.: Brookings, 1974), p. 43.

Measuring Education's Contribution to National Economic Growth

The Denison Approach

One of the chief questions that economists seek to answer about education—and about other sources of growth—is what share of the increase in national output can properly be attributed to changes over time in the given factor of production. This aspect of economic inquiry is called *accounting for growth*. A basic procedure in accounting for education's share is shown in Table 3.1. (The figures for this hypothetical case are deliberately made simple to reveal the underlying principle of measurement; actual results of measurement are given below.) Column (1) indicates a distribution of a labor force of 10 million workers by education level in a base period, and column (3) shows a distribution of precisely the same size work force by education level in a comparison period 10 years later. Average school years completed in the work force rises from 11.6 in the base year to 12.8 in the comparison period. (Base magnitudes are identified by the subscript 0; comparison magnitudes by the subscript 1.) How can we relate the increase in education level of the work force to growth in national product? One procedure is to cast up a sum of wages earned in the base period and compare it with a wage estimate in a later period. It is, however, necessary to use only one set of wages in making the comparison. Otherwise we confuse effects of changes in educational level—and its assumed effect on productivity—with changes in wage rates per se, which may have various causes. (Admittedly, the procedure prevents making any adjustments for rising productivity or falling costs of education. We are not comparing benefits with costs: the fact that productivity *within* educational institutions may be rising or falling does not enter into the calculations.) Thus, columns (5) and (6) show earned income in the given and comparison period priced at wages prevailing in the base period, that is, the figures shown as P_0 in column (2). Total labor income rises from $124 billion to $140 billion.

The next step in accounting for education's contribution to economic growth is to convert such a rise in labor income to an average annual rate. This is 1.29 percent (bottom of column 9). Assuming that wages represent 75 percent of national output and, by the argument of the previous section, weighting the average annual growth in labor income by 0.75, we arrive at an average annual increase in factor supply of 0.968. That is, education served to push

Table 3.1
Hypothetical computation of education's contribution to economic growth, case 1

	Base year		Comparison year[a]	
	No. of workers (in millions) N_0 (1)	Average earned income (in thousands) P_0 (2)	No. of workers (in millions) N_1 (3)	Average earned income (in thousands) P_1 (4)
Degree				
Elementary	3	$ 8	1	$ 8.5
High school	5	12	6	12.5
College	2	20	3	18.0
Totals	10		10	
Average school years completed	11.6[b]		12.8[b]	

	Labor income priced at P_0		Labor income priced at P_1		Change in labor income priced at:	
	Base year (in billions) (5)	Comparison year (in billions) (6)	Base year (in billions) (7)	Comparison year (in billions) (8)	P_0 (in billions) (9)	P_1 (in billions) (10)
Degree						
Elementary	$ 24	$ 8	$ 25.5	$ 8.5	$ -16.0	$ -17.0
High school	60	72	62.5	75.0	+12.0	+12.5
College	40	60	36.0	54.0	+20.0	+18.0
Totals	124	140	124.0	137.5	+16.0	13.5
Average annual rate of change					1.29%	1.09%

[a] Comparison year = Base year plus 10.
[b] Assuming eight years of elementary school, four years of high school, and four years of college.

up the annual contribution of labor inputs by approximately 1 percent a year. Assume, finally, that national output is going up during the given period of time by 3 percent. The relative contribution of education to that growth rate is 0.968/3.00 = 32.3 percent. Thus, in this hypothetical instance, education accounts for approximately one-third of economic growth.

What assumptions underlie the model? The chief assumption is that we are able to isolate the effects of education on productivity. In the computation reflected in columns (5) and (6), only education is allowed to vary between the base period—not the size of work force, not the utilization of capital goods, not wage rates—and presumably not hours of work nor noneducational characteristics of workers. But if the comparisons of Table 3.1 are to have real meaning, it is required that the wage rate differences be related to skill differences, which skills, in turn, are acquired through the process of education. Suppose, on the other hand, that the higher wages of college graduates are simply traditional or are determined primarily in relation to socioeconomic status. This would mean, for example, that jobs held by college graduates could be performed just as well by high school graduates, if the latter could gain access to such jobs. In such case, the changes in labor income *by education class* in columns (5) and (6) would display, not real increases in national product, but a redistribution of income against those persons holding less education capital and, indeed, against persons holding physical capital. (We shall return to this point later in discussing the work of Ivar Berg.) The general assumptions, therefore, of economists who relate shares of national economic growth to education is that wage differences are productivity based and that a major determinant of productivity is the amount of formal education possessed by members of the work force.

There is one special difficulty in making the computations of Table 3.1, however. Wage rates may change from one period to the next. As shown, wages in the comparison period, P_1, reflect the relatively greater scarcity of the less educated worker and the relative abundance of the highly trained. Columns (7) and (8) show national income change due to education based on comparison period wage rates. Using these latter wage rates, we would conclude that the average annual change in labor income due to education was 1.09 percent, not 1.29. Unfortunately, there is no real reason to choose base year wages over comparison year wages. Although both estimates are technically acceptable, neither is fully accurate. In economics, measurement of changes over time are frequently subject to such inaccuracy, known as the *index number problem*.

Table 3.2
Hypothetical computation of education's contribution
to economic growth, case 2 (in percent)

Degree	Percentage distribution of work force		Change in percentage points (3)
	Base year (1)	Comparison year (2)	
Elementary	30%	10%	−20%
High school	50	60	+10
College	20	30	+10
Total	100	100	

Degree	Average earned income (4)	Relative to weighted average income[a] (5)	Product of change in distribution of labor force and relative labor prices (6)
Elementary	$ 8,000	0.645	−12.90%
High school	12,000	0.968	+9.68
College	20,000	1.613	+16.13
Total	Mean =	Total change 12.91	
	12,400	Annual change 1.29	

[a] As shown, based on base year wages of Table 3.1.

Table 3.2 presents the same data and results as Table 3.1, but the format of the analysis is the one preferred by economists. Columns (1) and (2) show percentage distributions of workers by education class in the base and comparison years. Column (3) gives changes in the distribution of education in percentage points between the two years. Column (5) shows wage rates expressed relative to the weighted, economywide average wage rate in P_0 of $12,400. Column (6) is the product of columns (3) and (5). The sum of column (6), 12.91 percent divided by 10, the length of the comparison period, gives the same value for annual increase of labor income, 1.29 percent, as Table 3.1 (using base period wage rates). One advantage of the format of Table 3.2 is that we need not separate the effects of education on growth in product from the effects of increase in size of labor force by the artificial device of holding size of labor force constant.

Table 3.3
Sources of growth of total national income, 1929–1969
(contributions to growth rate in percentage points)

National income	3.33%
Total factor input	1.81
Labor	1.31
Employment	1.08
Hours	−0.22
Age-sex composition	−0.05
Education	0.41
Unallocated	0.09
Capital	0.50
Land	0.00
Output per unit of input	1.52
Advances in knowledge and growth not elsewhere classified	0.92
Other[a]	0.60

[a] Includes improved resource allocation, dwelling occupancy ratio, economies of scale, and irregular factors (weather in farming, labor disputes, and intensity of demand).
Source: Edward F. Denison, *Accounting for United States Economic Growth, 1929–1969* (Washington, D.C.: The Brookings Institution, 1974), p. 127. Copyright © 1974 by The Brookings Institution. Reprinted with permission.

Using basically the scheme of measurement described here but taking extraordinary care to isolate the effects of education on productivity from the effects of changes in hours of work per year, sex, age of workers, race, urban versus rural work environment, socioeconomic status of workers, etc., Denison conducted a number of studies to assess the contribution of education to economic growth (the first of his major studies was published in 1962).[10] It should be added immediately that Denison seeks to account for economic growth in terms of shares assigned to a large number of different types of resources and causal factors, not just to education. Table 3.3 gives a summary of his most recent results. Between 1929 and 1969 real national income rose at an average annual rate of 3.33 percent. Education is estimated to have been responsible for 0.41 percentage points of that growth; thus, (formal) education accounted for 12.3 percent of the national growth rate. This is the share of growth

[10] Edward F. Denison, *The Sources of Economic Growth and the Alternatives Before Us* (New York: Committee for Economic Development, 1962), pp. 67–77.

attributable to education for its role in improving skills of the work force.

Growth occurs as well in a related manner through advances in technology and in knowledge in general. Denison estimated that 27.6 percent of national growth was relative to knowledge (in Table 3.3, 0.92 percent/3.33 percent = 27.6 percent). How much credit is due our education system for training scientists and other persons responsible for increase of knowledge, credit over and beyond that attributed to education through the earned income of such persons (and thus included in the education assessment itself), is impossible to say, but some part surely is.

Let us turn back to education's role in improving the quality of the labor force. For the period 1929–1969, this aspect of education accounts for 12.3 percent of the annual rise of national output, as we have just observed. In his first major study of sources of growth, Denison assigned a larger share to education, 23 percent, which covered the period 1929–1957.[11] This brings us to an important point: Accounting for growth in the past does not predict very well future sources of growth.

In his early study, Denison actually predicted that education's relative share would fall. His argument is interesting. Because the United States has succeeded in extending educational opportunities very broadly throughout its population, future rates of advance in educational provision cannot approximate those of the past. There is no way that the increase in average number of school years per member of the work force can grow in the 1970s and 1980s at the rate it grew, for example, during the decade of the 1930s; it was in the 1930s that the United States essentially completed the task of establishing a system of universal secondary education. As Denison says,

> The past great increase in schooling has been stimulated by the geographic expansion of 12-year public school facilities to cover the nation, the prohibition of child labor, and compulsory school attendance laws, as well as the decline in agriculture and such continuing influence as rising income. Though still exerting a strong delayed impact upon the educational level of the labor force, the effect of these great reforms on school attendance is running out. The remaining possibilities for increasing education through the high school years, though important in absolute terms and especially so in the

[11] Ibid.

South, are slight compared with past achievements. The average number of days a year that students spend in elementary and secondary schools is twice that of 1870. But in recent years it has been almost stationary. Indeed, except for some possible further reduction in absenteeism, to double it again would require the schools to remain open for all students 365 days a year. . . . [W]hat is required to maintain the contribution of more education to the growth *rate* is maintenance of the *percentage* increase in the amount of education received, adjusted for the greater importance of the upper grades. For the long pull, this seems simply unattainable.[12]

Denison admits that improvements in the quality of education might be an important future source of growth, and we should be clear that he has assigned to education a share of economic growth strictly on the basis of the *quantitative expansion* of the educational system. Furthermore, he deals almost exclusively with the formal system of education, not taking account of night schools, correspondence courses, and the like, unless they lead to diplomas or degrees.

The Schultz Approach

A different approach to accounting for education's share of economic growth has been taken by Theodore Schultz. Though the conclusions of his classic study might be regarded as having historical interest only, his methods are sufficiently clear and interesting to warrant extensive treatment. Schultz begins his analysis by estimating the cost of education for various years since 1900. The procedure is involved, but essentially the steps are as follows: From gross expenditures of educational establishments, the sums spent on capital outlay and auxiliary enterprises are subtracted, yielding estimates of *net expenditures*. To net expenditures is added a value for interest and depreciation on physical property, and the sum represents *annual resource costs*. (The figures for interest and depreciation represent how much physical capital is used up each year by educational establishments.) To the sum of resource costs is added a value for income foregone of students, that is, the amount of money they could make if they take a job instead of spending their time studying. Resource costs plus foregone income plus *additional expenditures* (the money

[12] Ibid., p. 77.

Table 3.4
Cost of education in labor force in 1957 as measured
by year of school per member

Level	Average years of school completed (1)	Cost per year in 1956 prices (2)	Cost per member of labor force (3)
Elementary	7.52	$ 280	$2,106
Secondary	2.44	1,420	3,458
College	0.64	3,300	2,099
Total	10.6		7,663

Source: Theodore W. Schultz, "Education and Economic Growth," in *Social Forces Influencing American Education* (Chicago: National Society for the Study of Education, 1961), p. 70.

spent on books, supplies, extra clothes, and privately financed travel to and from educational institutions) equals the total cost of education. Total costs are converted to a per-student basis for elementary, secondary, and college levels.[13]

In preparing his estimates of the stock of physical capital, Schultz chose to use cost figures for the base year of 1956. In that year, the cost figures were: elementary, $280; high school, $1,420; college and university, $3,300. The main procedure in estimating the stocks for 1957 is illustrated in Table 3.4.

Column (1) of Table 3.4 indicates the average school years completed per member of the labor force. On the average, workers had 7.52 years of elementary school, 2.44 years of high school, and 0.64 years of college in 1957. The cost figures in column (2) are those to which we referred just above. Column (3) is the product of columns (1) and (2), yielding cost per member at each level of education. The total stock of education per member of the work force in 1957 was $7,663, as measured by dollar cost. The costs per member are then converted to average cost per school year, $7,663/10.6 = $723.

The next step is to compute the number of years of education possessed by members of the work force in 1957: The figure is 740 million. Multiplying this figure by the cost per year, $723, yields a total stock of human capital valued at $535 billion. A similar procedure is employed to compute stocks in other periods, and the results are shown in Table 3.5. For comparison, changes in the stocks of

[13] This presentation is drawn from Theodore W. Schultz, "Education and Economic Growth," in *Social Forces Influencing American Education* (Chicago: National Society for the Study of Education, 1961), pp. 46–88.

Table 3.5

Total value of the stock of human capital and of reproducible nonhuman wealth in the United States, 1900–1957, in 1955–1956 prices (in billions of dollars)

Year	Human capital stock of labor force, 14 years and older	Index of percentage change, 1900 = 100	Stock of reproducible nonhuman wealth	Index of percentage change, 1900 = 100	Total stock of capital	Index of percentage change, 1900 = 100
1900	$ 63	100.0%	$282	100.0%	$ 345	100.0%
1910	94	149.2	403	142.9	497	144.1
1920	127	201.6	526	186.5	653	189.3
1930	180	285.7	735	260.6	915	265.2
1940	348	552.4	756	268.1	1104	320.0
1950	359	569.8	969	343.6	1328	384.9
1957	535	849.2	1270	450.4	1805	523.2

Source: Theodore W. Schultz, "Education and Economic Growth," in *Social Forces Influencing American Education* (Chicago: National Society for the Study of Education, 1961), p. 70.

nonhuman capital also are shown. Clearly, human capital has been increasing at a greater rate than nonhuman capital.

Table 3.5 does not show the change in the total stock of human capital in the whole population since it deals only with members of the labor force. This is the way Schultz chose to allocate the production of education between its investment (work force) and consumption (nonwork force) uses. The procedure removes about 37 percent of the stock of education from the investment category.

What contribution did the rise in the stock of human capital make to national economic growth? Schultz approaches the question in the following manner. Taking the period 1929 to 1957, he notes that real national income in the United States rose from $150 billion to $302 billion, a gain of $152 billion. During this same time, the stock of human capital in the labor force went up from $180 billion to $535 billion, a gain of $355 billion. However, during this time the size of the labor force rose by 38 percent. Hence, to hold the stock of education per member of the work force constant, the 1930 value of that stock, $180 billion, had to be increased by 38 percent, which is $69 billion. Thus, the net value of the increase in human capital was $286 billion ($355 billion minus the $69 billion for "maintenance"). The only further requirement is to apply a *rate of return* to this net increase in educational stock.

Schultz suggested it was appropriate to apply a rate of return of 11 percent, for the reason, inter alia, that the ratio of the additional earnings of college graduates over those of high school graduates to the cost of college education had a value of approximately 11 in 1958. (In the next section we explore how rates of return to education are computed.) Applying a rate of return of 11 percent to the $286 billion net investment in human capital gives a dollar yield of $31.5 billion. Between 1929 and 1957, then, the net increase in human capital accounted for $31.5 billion of the increase in real national income. This figure represents approximately 21 percent of the rise in real national income between 1929 and 1957 (31.5/152 × 100 = 21 percent). Schultz's estimate of 21 percent contribution by education to economic growth is very close to Denison's estimate of 23 percent for the same period, 1929–1957, even though their methods of accounting are different.

Some Limitations of Growth-Accounting Procedures

The contributions of Denison and Schultz to understanding the relation between educational outlays and economic growth have been widely hailed around the world. Their results have been used, especially in the developing countries, to justify major expansions in provision of educational services. In our own country the Denison-Schultz analysis has served to promote the growth of higher education. Yet their analytic procedures have limitations.

One has already been noted—the analysis is grounded in a highly aggregated, abstract model, the Cobb-Douglas production function. This model does not address the question of whether a given rate of physical capital formation poses different requirements for educated manpower from one point of time to the next, depending on the composition of new physical capital. That is, education may be more or less highly valued from one period to the next for reasons related to the mix of goods ultimately to be produced in the society.[14] Such differences in the need for educated persons would be reflected in wage and salary differentials and, finally, in the contribution that education makes to national economic growth.

[14] These points were taken up by this author some years ago. See Charles S. Benson (with P. R. Lohnes), "Skill Requirements and Industrial Training in Durable Goods Manufacturing," *Industrial and Labor Relations Review*, 12, no. 4 (July 1959): 540–553.

For example, in the 1960s the population of the country was growing at a rather high rate. This led to a considerable expansion in the size of the educational system, which is the single largest employer of educated persons. This fueled a demand for college and university graduates, and so also did space exploration and defense industries. In the late 1970s, national income is larger than in the 1960s, but the demand for graduates has shrunk relative to the supply. Educationally related salary differentials are also declining.[15] To a degree, these changes can be seen as a result of the fall-off in the rate of growth of the educational system and in expenditures for governmental research and development. Both changes are reflected in differences in the composition of new physical capital between the 1960s and the 1970s. In sum, the Denison-Schultz analysis is interesting as a description of what has happened in the past. But it should not be used uncritically to predict the future, that is, to estimate what the contribution of education to economic growth will be in the years ahead. As we have noted, however, the Denison-Schultz analysis has been employed in developing countries to justify expansion of their educational systems; in short, the analysis has been used as if it were a predictive device. This might represent no great problem if educational policy decisions were readily reversible, but our own difficulties in trying to deal with excess supply of Ph.D.'s in a number of highly specialized fields indicate that those policy decisions are not readily reversible.

We will note a second shortcoming of the analysis more briefly: The Denison-Schultz procedure deals only with the contribution to economic growth of the formal educational system. Both economists in the works cited here related growth to years of schooling per worker, not to years of schooling plus on-the-job training. Yet, because on-the-job training is often supplied at the expense of the employer, it should be that type of education which is most closely tied in with productivity advance. In comparison, there is much in the formal education curriculum that has little to do directly with the effectiveness of workers in their jobs.

Summary

In this chapter we have examined the basic nature of the process of economic growth. Growth occurs when resources are invested, that is, when resources are converted into capital. Creation of capital

---

[15] Samuel Bowles and Herbert Gintis, *Schooling in Capitalist America* (New York: Basic Books, 1976), pp. 220–223.

enhances the productive power of the people in the work force. Until recently, most economists regarded capital as being physical assets. Land is an example and so are mineral deposits, but chief interest attaches to reproducible forms of capital: machinery, buildings, highways, etc. A major discovery of the present generation of economists is that capital also exists in human form, that is, in the skills of the educated, productive worker. This is a reproducible form of capital created by our educational system. Economists have gone on to estimate, with some precision, the proportion of economic growth attributable to investments in education. The techniques they use were described in this chapter. Basically, the argument derives from the fact that, on the average, persons with more years of schooling earn more in income than persons with less.

Selected Bibliography

Cohn, Elchanan. *The Economics of Education*. Cambridge: Ballinger Publishing Company, 1975.

Denison, Edward F. *Why Growth Rates Differ: Postwar Experience in Nine Western Countries*. Washington, D.C.: Brookings, 1967.

———. *Accounting for United States Economic Growth, 1929–1969*. Washington, D.C.: Brookings, 1974.

Freeman, Richard B. *The Market for College-Trained Manpower*. Cambridge: Harvard, 1971.

Hansen, W. Lee, ed. *Education, Income and Human Capital*. New York: Columbia, 1970.

Schultz, Theodore W. *Investment in Human Capital*. New York: Free Press, 1971.

Chapter Four

The Economic Returns of Education

In considering the relationship between investment in human capital and economic growth, we have been dealing with the question of what share of past economic growth may properly be assigned to education. This is an important matter in economic theory. There is a second major question to be dealt with, which is more attuned to policy issues: How large should investments in human capital be? Though economics cannot provide a precise answer to this question, it can take us part way to an answer.

Analyzing Rates of Return

Determining the appropriate size of education investments is an exercise in computing *rates of return,* and there are two fundamental ideas involved. First, earned income of individuals, on the average, is higher the more schooling they have. As we saw in Chapter 1, there is a clear, positive relationship between years of education of members of the work force and the average level of their incomes. This extra, or *incremental,* earning associated with a given segment of a person's education career can be regarded as a *return to schooling.* The average extra earnings of college over high school graduates stands as a first approximation of returns to college education. But these extra earnings must be related to the *costs* of attending college. With respect to the question, for example, of whether we should establish in this country a system of free universal undergraduate education, the voter might properly ask the following question: Do college graduates, on the average, earn sufficiently more than high school graduates to offset the cost of providing them with a college education, including as a cost the income they give up while they are attending college? If the answer is affirmative, the voter should be willing to explore further the question of whether universal higher education is a good investment.[1] If the answer is negative, the voter could be justified in turning the proposal down without further evidence.[2]

The above example serves to clarify the process of estimating returns to education. We could just as well assess the desirability of making national investments in, say, the *quality* of elementary and secondary education. But, unfortunately, there are not readily available and generally agreed upon definitions of educational quality; and measurement of the relationship between quality of education, as distinct from length of schooling, and the earned income of individuals is still in a primitive stage.[3]

The second fundamental idea in rate of return analysis is *discounting.* Education outlays are made over a period of time; returns to education, measured as income differentials, are received over an even longer period. The time pattern of outlays and receipts vary from one set of individuals to the next. If we were all completely indifferent about the dates on which we made education outlays and

[1] The voter should be interested to try to find out whether differentials between earnings of college and high school graduates that have existed in the past are predictive of future differentials. The voter should also compare the relative profitability of investment in education with investments in other activities that promote economic growth. Even if these answers favor expansion of higher education, the voter might still, of course, be reluctant to vote for expansion if he or she thought that all of the returns would be kept by college graduates; the voter might then believe the persons receiving the education should pay for it themselves.

[2] Of course, the voter might support the stated policy on grounds of social equity, cultural advancement, or whatever. But in doing so she or he would be trading economic growth for these other objectives. The problem is complicated because a policy of universal undergraduate education does not guarantee that all youth attend college. Those who choose not to do so might be penalized if, as a result, private returns to high school education would be reduced. The problem is further complicated because there exist complementary relationships among different types of investments. For example, investment in the training of workers may not be profitable unless there are simultaneous investments in new capital equipment that utilizes the skills of the workers.

[3] What can now be done on this point is shown in G. E. Johnson and F. P. Stafford, "Social Returns to Quantity and Quality of Schooling," *Journal of Human Resources*, 8, no. 2 (Spring 1973): 139–155.

on which we received the related salary adjustments, variations in the time patterns of expenditures and receipts would need no special treatment in analysis. But they do require such treatment.

Take the case of two college graduates, one of whom becomes a successful professional football player and the other a successful academic. Assume that the total lifetime *earned* income of both is the same. Are they equally well off in terms of income? One would think not. The football player is likely to receive his peak earned income between the ages of 30 and 35; the academic will most likely receive her or his peak earned income between the ages of 60 and 65. Now, the football player can set aside a part of his peak income in his early thirties, invest it, and receive a notably higher total lifetime income, earned and unearned together, than can the academic. In economics, money received quickly is considered more valuable than money to be got in the distant future.

We will now examine the following problem, using greater analytical refinement. Suppose Steve asks Lois for a dollar today and pledges to return it in one year. Let Lois be absolutely certain that Steve will pay back whatever he has pledged to pay, so risk considerations do not enter into the agreement. Also, let both agree that they want to make an agreement that is economically sound. Lois should then tell Steve that she cannot give him a dollar today for a dollar one year from now because her dollar could be earning interest in the bank. Assume that the bank, with deposits fully guaranteed, pays interest at 6 percent, compounded annually. Lois would then say, "I will give you $0.94 for $1 a year from now, because $0.94 × 1.06 = $1.00. That is, Lois can have a dollar a year from now by putting away $0.94, so the *present value* of $1 one year in the future is $0.94, assuming an interest rate of 6 percent. Having got this far in their discussion, Steve might say, "Actually, I want to repay you a dollar two years from now, not one year. What is the most that you can lend me?" Lois answers $0.89 because

$$\$0.89 \times 1.06 \times 1.06 = \$1$$

This recognizes that banks pay interest on interest previously earned and left on deposit. Rearranging terms, we have

$$\$0.89 = \frac{\$1}{(1.06)\,(1.06)}$$

for the two-year arrangement. For a three-year arrangement, we would have

$$\$0.84 = \frac{\$1}{(1.06)(1.06)(1.06)}$$

And $0.84 is the present value of $1 three years in the future, again assuming that the interest rate is 6 percent. In the general case, then, we compute the present value of an amount of money at a future date under the following formula:

$$PV = \frac{F_t}{(1 + i)^t} \tag{4.1}$$

where PV = present value; i = a rate of interest (or, more properly, a rate of discount; t = time, and F_t is the amount of a future payment t periods of time in the future. Likewise, when we deal with a series of future payments, not just a single one, the present value of that whole series can be written as

$$PV = \sum_{t=1}^{n} \frac{F_t}{(1 + i)^t} \tag{4.2}$$

The symbol $\Sigma_{t=1}^{n}$ indicates that the calculation we have described for a one-shot future payment be conducted for each separate future payment and the sum of all the future values be cast with a single estimate. The individual values of F_t need not be equal, of course. But ordinarily a single value of i will be used in the computation.

What applies to Lois and Steve in this hypothetical example regarding the valuation of future receipts also applies to government when it seeks to assess the relative worth of programs in which benefits and costs—either or both—extend forward in time: Benefits and costs must be discounted.

In Table 4.1 we see in column (3) the differential earnings between community college graduates and high school graduates. The first two figures are negative and indicate that community college students could expect to earn $8,000 and $8,500 in the two years of their program if they had joined the labor force instead of becoming students; this is foregone income. The positive annual benefits are discounted in column (8), using a discount rate of 5 percent. Over a 16-year period—for computational ease, assume that this is the chosen period for the valuation of alternative investments—the total of discounted benefit is $19,386. Costs are the sum of direct costs in column (4), representing public expenditures per student per year, plus fees charged to the student, etc., and foregone income. The total discounted value, column (6), is $19,977. (Since costs, like benefits, are spread over time, they must be discounted too, and the same arguments just developed apply as well to discounting costs.) Thus, yield to community college graduates in this hypothetical illustration

Table 4.1
Hypothetical calculations of returns to education, community college graduates over high school graduates (5 percent discount rate)

Year (1)	$(1 + 0.05)^t$ (2)	Excess of earnings (3)	Direct costs (4)	Total annual costs (5)	Annual costs discounted (6)	Annual benefits (7)	Annual benefits discounted (8)
1	1.0500	$-8,000	$2,500	$10,500	$10,000	$ —	$ —
2	1.1025	-8,500	2,500	11,000	9,977	—	—
3	1.1580	+ 500	0	0	0	500	432
4	1.2160	+ 500	0	0	0	500	411
5	1.2760	+ 750	0	0	0	750	588
6	1.3400	+1,000	0	0	0	1,000	746
7	1.4070	+1,500	0	0	0	1,500	1,066
8	1.4770	+2,000	0	0	0	2,000	1,354
9	1.5510	+2,500	0	0	0	2,500	1,612
10	1.6290	+3,000	0	0	0	3,000	1,842
11	1.7100	+3,000	0	0	0	3,000	1,754
12	1.7960	+3,500	0	0	0	3,500	1,949
13	1.8860	+3,500	0	0	0	3,500	1,856
14	1.9800	+4,000	0	0	0	4,000	2,020
15	2.0790	+4,000	0	0	0	4,000	1,924
16	2.1830	+4,000	0	0	0	4,000	1,832
Total			5,000	21,500	19,977	33,750	19,386

does not equal costs, and we would have to conclude the investment in community college programs would be unwise.[4]

Table 4.2 repeats the exercise for four-year college graduates, using the same discount rate of 5 percent. Even though discounted costs are doubled, total discounted returns exceed costs; and we might say that four-year college programs qualify as a growth-inducing investment. However, by comparing Tables 4.2 and 4.3, we can see the important effect of choice of discount rate. The absolute magnitudes in Tables 4.2 and 4.3 are the same—the undiscounted amounts of benefits and costs, that is. The only difference is that the discount rate in Table 4.2 is 5 percent and in Table 4.3, 10 percent. In the case of Table 4.3, returns that were positive in Table 4.2 become negative. If the discount rate were 10 percent, neither community college nor four-year college programs would qualify for funding, under our economic criteria.

One rule for the allocation of resources between consumption and investment—and among competing types of investments—is that the society should select and fund all projects for which the present value of benefits exceeds the present value of costs, all projects, that is, where Tables 4.1–4.3 make it plain that the determination

$$\sum_{t=1}^{n} \frac{b_t}{(1 + i)^t} > \sum_{t=1}^{n} \frac{c_t}{(1 + i)^t} \tag{4.3}$$

of what is to be funded under the *net-present-value* rule is a function of the discount rate that is chosen.[5] Low discount rates favor investment in general and especially investments that offer payoffs far into the future. High discount rates favor current consumption and investments offering short-term yields.

At this point, we should pause to note the difference between the *social discount rate* and rates of interests in general. Rates of interest represent a cost of borrowing money; and it is essentially the

[4] Suppose, however, that the direct costs are paid in full by the state so that community college education is free to the individual student. The figures in Table 4.1 indicate that it would then pay the student to attend because the benefits in extra income exceed the private costs of attending. When there is a divergence between social costs (those borne by the society at large, through, say, taxation) and private costs (those costs on the individual's budget, not of taxes), the society and the individual may reach opposite conclusions about the economic worth of a particular type of education.
[5] Because education is intended to serve the objectives of social mobility and improving the distribution of income, it is especially important that educational investments be expanded up to the stated point. Otherwise, the educated obtain what might be regarded as monopolistic returns to investments in their schooling; after all, one person's income is another person's price. See J. W. Walsh, "Capital Concept Applied to Man," *Quarterly Journal of Economics*, 49, no. 2 (February 1935): 255–285.

Table 4.2
Hypothetical calculations of returns to education, four-year college graduates over high school graduates (5 percent discount rate)

Year (1)	$(1 + 0.05)^t$ (2)	Excess of earnings (3)	Direct costs (4)	Total annual costs (5)	Annual costs discounted (6)	Annual benefits (7)	Annual benefits discounted (8)
1	1.0500	$− 8,000	$2,500	$10,500	$10,000	$ —	$ —
2	1.1025	− 8,500	2,500	11,000	9,977	—	—
3	1.1580	− 9,000	4,000	13,000	11,226	—	—
4	1.2160	− 9,500	4,000	13,500	11,102	—	—
5	1.2760	+ 2,000	0	0	0	2,000	1,576
6	1.3400	+ 2,500	0	0	0	2,500	1,866
7	1.4070	+ 3,000	0	0	0	3,000	2,132
8	1.4770	+ 5,000	0	0	0	5,000	3,385
9	1.5510	+ 8,000	0	0	0	8,000	5,158
10	1.6290	+12,000	0	0	0	12,000	7,366
11	1.7100	+12,000	0	0	0	12,000	7,018
12	1.7960	+15,000	0	0	0	15,000	8,352
13	1.8860	+15,000	0	0	0	15,000	7,953
14	1.9800	+15,000	0	0	0	15,000	7,576
15	2.0790	+10,000	0	0	0	10,000	4,810
16	2.1830	+10,000	0	0	0	10,000	4,581
Total		13,000		48,000	42,305	109,500	61,773

Table 4.3
Hypothetical calculations of returns to education, four-year college graduates over high school graduates (10 percent discount rate)

Year (1)	$(1 + 0.10)^t$ (2)	Excess of earnings (3)	Direct costs (4)	Total annual costs (5)	Annual costs discounted (6)	Annual benefits (7)	Annual benefits discounted (8)
1	1.100	$- 8,000	$2,500	$10,500	$ 9,545	$ —	$ —
2	1.210	− 8,500	2,500	11,000	9,091	—	—
3	1.331	− 9,000	4,000	13,000	9,767	—	—
4	1.464	− 9,500	4,000	13,500	9,221	—	—
5	1.610	+ 2,000	0	0	0	2,000	1,242
6	1.771	+ 2,500	0	0	0	2,500	1,412
7	1.948	+ 3,000	0	0	0	3,000	1,540
8	2.143	+ 5,000	0	0	0	5,000	2,333
9	2.357	+ 8,000	0	0	0	8,000	3,394
10	2.593	+12,000	0	0	0	12,000	4,628
11	2.852	+12,000	0	0	0	12,000	4,208
12	3.137	+15,000	0	0	0	15,000	4,782
13	3.451	+15,000	0	0	0	15,000	4,347
14	3.796	+15,000	0	0	0	15,000	3,952
15	4.176	+10,000	0	0	0	10,000	2,395
16	4.594	+10,000	0	0	0	10,000	2,177
Total			13,000	48,000	37,624	109,500	36,410

same cost to the borrower as an individual, as a corporation, or as a government. The social discount rate, on the other hand, does not exist in any money market. It is a fictional rate, used by government for computing purposes to screen public investment projects for acceptability. There is no consensus among economists about the proper level of the social discount rate. (This is why we said above that economics can take us only part way in the process of deciding how much the country should invest in education—and in other types of growth-producing activities.) There are actually a number of different ways to calculate a social discount rate.

Some economists hold that the social discount rate should be set at or near the rates of interest established in private money markets. Such rates may be interpreted—assuming that capital markets are perfectly competitive—as reflecting consumers' preferences between present and future consumption. This position holds that public-sector investments should be guided by the same time preference criterion as prevails in the private economy. A problem with this approach is that private capital markets are not perfectly competitive. This means that the money market displays a complex structure of interest rates, so the question becomes which private market rate to choose.

Other economists argue that, in principle, the social rate of discount should be established at a level below the range of private market interest rates. One reason is that public investments may generate external benefits, resulting in the *social rate of return*—the yield of the investment to the society as a whole—being higher than the private rate of return—the yield that can be claimed by private households on their own exclusionary behalf. Another is that voters may be shortsighted and fail to appreciate the future benefits that investments will yield, and they may also fail to take account of the fact that the taxes required for debt service will become relatively less burdensome in the future as the standard of living rises through investment and technological advance. These arguments suggest that when the social discount rate is to be used for the purpose of project evaluation, it should be set arbitrarily at a level below interest rates in the private market, but the arguments unfortunately do not inform any agency how much below private rates the social rate of discount should be pegged. In the end, economists turn to their values and government turns to a rule of thumb—such as setting the social discount rate equal to the interest rate that government is currently paying on its long-term debt.[6]

[6] For a thorough discussion of alternative views about the level of the social discount rate, see Richard A. Musgrave and Peggy B. Musgrave, *Public Finance in Theory and Practice* (New York: McGraw-Hill, 1973), pp. 146–155.

Individuals may make investments voluntarily in education in accordance with their private discount rates, which correspond in function to social discount rates; that is, private discount rates serve to regulate the distribution of resources between a household's present and future consumption. Private discount rates presumably display a wide variation from one household to the next. Consider two families of similar income and station in life: One may invest heavily in the education of its children, while the other may devote practically all of its resources to near-term pleasures. The first family could be said to have a lower discount rate than the second. Government then steps in to make investments in education on behalf of the whole group of households in the country, and this action obviously reflects dissatisfaction with results obtained when decisions about educational investments are left strictly in private hands.

Government action is not altogether a result of divergence between private and social discount rates. It also reflects concern for distribution of income, in that poor families may be unable to pay for the further schooling of those of their children who are talented or who are simply eager to learn. Here is where disagreement about a proper level of social discount rate becomes a problem; we are left without a clear guide to how far government action should supplement or supersede private action.

In any case, rate of return analysis allows us to rank and compare net yields of alternative investments; it thus improves the allocation process. The procedure is a simple extension of what we have already discussed, and it is described as calculating an *internal rate of return*:

$$\sum_{t=1}^{n} \frac{b_t}{(1 + r)^t} = \sum_{t=1}^{n} \frac{c_t}{(1 + r)^t} \tag{4.4}$$

This is the rate of interest, r, that serves to make equal flows of benefits and costs. More specifically, the internal rate of return is that particular, precise rate of interest that makes the present value of benefits exactly equal to the present value of the costs. Of two alternative investments, the one that displays the higher internal rate of return will be characterized by a larger present value of benefits than the second, or a smaller present value of costs, or both: In short, it is the preferred investment.

To calculate the internal rate of return, we must estimate costs and benefits and attach dates to them. From that point on, the calculation of the internal rate of return used to require a tedious series of arithmetic exercises (trial and error) to approximate true value.[7] Nowadays, computers project a very accurate estimate of internal rates of return in seconds; even the more expensive types of hand calculators give one an internal rate.

Once government has done its homework—that is, has estimated benefits and costs in alternative investment programs, dated them, and computed their internal rates of return—it could base its funding decisions on the following rule: Commence all programs in which the internal rate of return exceeds the social discount rate. The higher the social discount rate, the less likely it is that many programs will qualify for funding; the lower the social discount rate, the more likely it is that the number of programs undertaken will be large. Once again, we see how the social discount rate serves to regulate, in principle at least, the size and direction of the public sector.

The pioneer in computing internal rates of return in education is Gary Becker.[8] His general conclusion regarding the relative profitability of education is as follows:

> A first approximation to the social rate of return on business capital can be found by relating profits to capital, with profits including the corporate income and other direct taxes. The before-tax rate of return on corporate manufacturing capital averaged about twelve percent for both 1938–1947 and 1947–1957, compared to an after-tax rate of seven percent. If the before-tax rate on all corporations were between ten and thirteen percent and that on unincorporated forms between four and eight percent . . . the rate on all business capital would be between eight and twelve percent. The first approximation to the social rate of return to white male college graduates would be between ten to thirteen percent after adjustment for differential ability. Since the rates to dropouts, workers, and nonwhites, would be a few percentage points lower, the rate to all college entrants would be between eight and eleven percent. *The rates on business capital and college education seem, therefore, to fall within the same range.*[9]

[7] To see how straightforward (in principle) the calculation actually is, the reader may wish to examine James C. Van Horne, *Financial Management and Policy*, 3rd ed. (Englewood Cliffs, N. J.: Prentice-Hall, 1974), pp. 15–23.

[8] Pioneering, that is, among economists of the capitalist world. S. G. Strumilin of the Soviet Union had calculated returns to education as early as 1924. His work substantially influenced Stalin's educational policy of the late 1920s. See V. N. Turchenko, "The Revolution in Science and Technology and Problems of Education," *Voprosy Filosofii*, 1973, no. 2, p. 51.

[9] G. S. Becker, *Human Capital: A Theoretical and Empirical Analysis, With Special Reference*

One policy implication to be drawn from that analysis is the importance of assuring that students have as good access to capital markets to finance their educations as businessmen have to finance their purchases of physical capital, since returns to the two forms of investment "fall within the same range." Another possible policy implication is more difficult to deal with, namely, that we should concentrate higher education expenditures on white males because their returns are higher than those of Blacks, females, etc. To some extent, this question has been mooted by later studies that indicate Blacks do gain relatively high returns from education.[10] In any case, discrepancies in returns between white males and other groups in the economy may be assumed to reflect some amount of discrimination in the hiring and promotion policies of employers. And it would be unwise to reinforce discrimination against certain groups in the workplace with discrimination against those same groups in education.

The process of computing rates of return for education investments has spread since the time Becker made his pioneering contribution. In 1973, for example, George Psacharopoulos published a volume in which he analyzed rates of return in both developing and developed countries.[11] Table 4.4 is a summary of his data. In general, rates of return are higher in developing countries than in those that have already attained economic growth.

Such work ordinarily does not draw distinctions among students with respect to their social class. Thus, Henry M. Levin added an important dimension to the analysis of economic returns to education when he estimated the "costs to the nation of inadequate education."[12] Since it is primarily youth of low-income families that receive

---

to Education (New York: National Bureau of Economic Research, 1964), pp. 120–121. Italics added. Computation of internal rates of return does not, however, solve the question of how much to invest in education. As E. Cohn has said, "Note that the utilization of the internal rate of return . . . although simplifying the analysis, still cannot dodge the question of which rate of discount is the 'proper' one, since the resulting rate of return must be compared to the *chosen* rate of discount . . . unless the purpose of the analysis is merely to rank projects. . . ." See his *Economics of Education* (Lexington, Mass.: Lexington Books, 1972), pp. 176–177.

[10] See particularly Finis Welch, "Black-White Differences in Returns to Schooling," *American Economic Review*, 53, no. 5 (December 1973): 893–907.

[11] George Psacharopoulos, *Returns to Education: An International Comparison* (San Francisco: Jossey-Bass, 1973).

[12] Henry M. Levin, *The Costs to the Nation of Inadequate Education,* a report prepared for the U.S. Senate Select Committee on Equal Educational Opportunity, 92nd Cong., 2nd sess. (Washington, D.C.: U.S. Government Printing Office, 1972).

Table 4.4

Overall social rate of return in 29 countries, various years

Country	Rate of return	Country	Rate of return
United States	13.6	Greece	3.9
Canada	12.4	Israel	9.6
Puerto Rico	19.6	India	17.2
Mexico	21.9	Malaysia	10.6
Venezuela	42.0	The Philippines	12.7
Colombia	25.9	Japan	5.1
Chile	19.3	South Korea	9.4
Brazil	13.7	Thailand	25.2
Great Britain	4.6	Nigeria	18.5
Norway	7.2	Ghana	15.1
Sweden	10.3	Kenya	18.9
Denmark	7.8	Uganda	39.0
Netherlands	5.3	N. Rhodesia	12.4
Belgium	9.3	New Zealand	17.6
Germany	4.6		

Source: George Psacharopoulos, *Returns to Education: An International Comparison* (San Francisco: Elsevier North-Holland, 1973), p. 85. Reprinted with permission.

inadequate education, Levin's study can be regarded as a set of estimates of returns to education in a particular economic class, namely, the poor.

Levin concluded that inadequate schooling represented a loss of $237 billion in foregone income for male high school dropouts alone over their working lifetimes; and he put the cost of providing suitable education at $40 billion. Discounting aside, better education for the poor would seem to be a good investment. Levin also estimated that inadequate schooling was itself responsible for about $3 billion annually in avoidable welfare expenditures and $3 billion in avoidable costs of crime. [13]

The main point, however, concerns the greater income that might be earned by high school dropouts if they continued their education for a longer period. This assumes that

1.   either the private economy or the government would be able to create a level of aggregate demand sufficiently high to

[13] Ibid., chaps. 2, 4.

provide employment opportunities for the would-be-educated poor, and

2.   the employment opportunities so created for the formerly uneducated poor would be commensurate with their higher levels of education.

In the light of the performance of the economy in the 1970s, these are formidable assumptions. Hence, the main result might be redistribution of opportunities amongst persons, not a major rise in national income.

Recent Rate of Return Studies

Most rate of return studies investigate the relationship between education and other independent variables, on the one hand, and wage and salary earnings, on the other. Fringe benefits—such as medical insurance, pension rights, paid vacations, stock options, etc.—have generally not been dealt with, nor have such working conditions as safety, overtime hours control, and employment stability. Greg J. Duncan, using data from a survey on the quality of employment conducted by the Survey Research Center for the Employment Standards Administration and the National Institute for Occupational Safety and Health, was able to include nonpecuniary benefits in his analysis of returns to education. The results are favorable toward the significance of education:

> The principal finding is that education's well-documented, pervasive importance for pecuniary benefits carries over to fringe and nonpecuniary benefits as well. Education is a significant determinant of fringe benefits and all but one (income stability) of the six nonpecuniary variables. . . . When pecuniary and nonpecuniary variables are combined into a single composite earnings measure, the estimated coefficient on education is considerably greater than when earnings are measured by wage rates alone. This added importance of education persists even when cognitive ability, achievement motivation, and socioeconomic background are taken into account.[14]

[14] Greg J. Duncan, "Earnings Functions and Nonpecuniary Benefits," *Journal of Human Resources*, 11, no. 4 (Fall 1976): 462–483 (quote on p. 481).

Another possible shortcoming of most rate of return studies is that they are confined to measuring the relationship between years of schooling completed and income; that is, they are seldom constructed to deal explicitly with economic returns to different *quality* levels of education. Thomas Ribich and James Murphy have sought to close this gap. Using data from the Project Talent National Survey of high schools, they constructed a model consisting of these variables: ability, achievement, and aptitude of students, number of school years completed, school costs during the elementary and secondary years of the student (as a measure of educational quality), socioeconomic status of family, and estimated lifetime income (as the dependent variable).[15]

Their results suggest that increase in earnings is not as great as increase in school costs, a finding entirely consistent with the proposition that education provides nonmonetary as well as monetary returns. The primary effect of quality of education on earnings operates through the stimulus leading to a lengthening of school life. The effects of higher quality of schooling on income is roughly equal for high-status and low-status individuals. Hence, the analysis does not support "the argument that underprivileged children are especially resistant to benefiting from increased educational spending."[16] Low-status individuals appeared, moreover, to benefit strongly from the opportunity to attend schools that were integrated by social class.

Finally, we will note a more recent examination of the extent to which parental characteristics affect earnings streams. Mary Corcoran, Christopher Jencks, and Michael Olneck conducted eight separate surveys in which information was included to relate parental characteristics to earnings. Five of the studies included educational data as well. Two main findings were the following: "(1) Employers do not often discriminate directly against employees on the basis of parental characteristics *other than race* . . . [and] (2) Parental characteristics exert considerable influence on children's test scores and educational attainment, which in turn influence their earnings."[17]

Rate of return analysis, in summary, is intended to inform policy decision makers about *how much* is to be spent on different kinds of educational programs. (On the other hand, it is not intended

---

[15] Thomas E. Ribich and James L. Murphy, "The Economic Returns to Increased Educational Spending," *Journal of Human Resources*, 10, no. 1 (Winter 1975): 56–77.

[16] Ibid., p. 75.

[17] Mary Corcoran, Christopher Jencks, and Michael Olneck, "The Effects of Family Background on Earnings," *American Economic Review*, 66, no. 2 (May 1976): 430–435 (quote is on p. 435; italics added).

to provide information to improve resource allocations *within* the educational system, for example, on how much a school district should spend, say, on salaries of regular teachers versus salaries of teacher aides.) Before education came to be regarded as "investment" in the economic sense, educational outlays had to be defended primarily on the grounds of paternalism, altruism, and human-itarianism. Now education, along with other programs for human development, such as health, competes with various uses of *investment funds*, both in the public and the private sector, because it has been shown that developing human capital is of equal importance with developing physical capital. From there on, the argument in the recent past has centered on the adequacy of techniques to measure benefits and costs of alternative human resource investments and on the level of the social discount rate to use to screen worthwhile from less worthwhile projects. In the next section, however, we shall see that basic criticism of human capital theory has mounted and become, in the past few years, quite severe.

Criticisms of Analyses of Economic Returns to Education

The work done since the mid-1950s in analyzing economic yields of investments in education has been subject to heavy criticism. We shall mention several of the major criticisms.

Disaggregation of Returns to Ability Versus Education

The argument about disaggregation of returns to ability takes the following line. Skills of labor force members are not created full-blown by the educational process; instead, they are built on a base of inborn ability or talent. Thus, to relate income differentials to education overstates the contribution of education to economic growth, unless we make a downward adjustment in those returns to recognize the ability component. To put it another way, on the average, college graduates have higher lifetime incomes than high school graduates. Thus the differences result from the fact, in the first instance, that people who manage to get through college are brighter, on the average, than those who stop their formal education short. The argument then proceeds to show that there are no means available to disentangle accurately the separate contributions of ability and income. Hence, the assessment of returns to education either will overstate the amount of those returns by including the ability component in full measure or will give unreliable estimates if we make a downward adjustment for ability essentially on some rule-of-thumb basis.[18]

On the other hand, it is perhaps more appropriate to regard ability and education as complementary, not competitive, sources of productivity. Surely an educational system that did no ability sorting would be regarded as one that was failing to meet its responsibility to support and undergird productivity increase. As Zvi Griliches has said:

> "Ability," "intelligence," and "learning" are all very slippery concepts. . . . We do know, however, the following things: 1. Intelligence is not a fixed datum independent of schooling and other environmental influences. 2. It can be affected by schooling. 3. It, in turn, affects the amount of learning achieved in a given schooling situation. 4. Because the scale on which it is measured is arbitrary, it is not clear whether the relative distribution of "intelligence" or "learning abilities" has remained constant over time. . . . Actually, IQ and achievement tests are so intimately intertwined with education that we may never be able to disentangle all their separate contributions. IQ tests were originally designed to determine which children could learn at "normal" rates. Consequently, children with above average IQ's are expected to learn at above normal rates. The effect of intelligence on learning is presumably twofold (or are these two sides of the same coin?): Higher IQ children know more to start with and this "knowing more" makes it easier to learn a given new subject (since knowing more implies that it is less "new" than it would otherwise be), and higher IQ children are "quicker." They absorb more from a similar length of exposure, and hence know more at the end of a given period. Since schools try, in a sense, to maximize students' "achievement" and since achievement and IQ tests are highly enough correlated for us to treat them interchangeably, one might venture to define the gross output of the schooling system as ability. That is, schools use the time of teachers and students and their respective abilities to increase the abilities of the student. From this point of view, the student's ability is both the

---

[18] Edward F. Denison, *Accounting for United States Economic Growth, 1929–1969* (Washington, D.C.: Brookings, 1974), pp. 228–240.

raw material that he brings to the schooling process, which will determine how much he will get out of it, and the final output that he takes away from it. Hence, at least part of the apparent returns to "ability" should be imparted to the schooling system. How much depends on what is the bottleneck in the production of educated people—the educational system or the limited number of "able" people that can benefit from it. If, as I believe may be the case, ability constraints have not been really binding, very little, if any, of the gross return to education should be imparted to the not very scarce resource of innate ability.[19]

Upgrading Jobs in Terms of Educational Requirements

A more damaging criticism, in our view, is the one that suggests that, outside a few professional fields, there is little association between educational attainment and the ability to perform in a given line of work. The salary and wage differentials reflect, not differences in performance, but the simple regard that employers hold for educational attainments per se. This argument strikes at the heart of the contention discussed earlier in this chapter.

A well-known proponent of this line of argument is Ivar Berg, who has conducted a number of studies to test his ideas. One such was in a Mississippi textile company:

> The data . . . gave no support to the contention that educational requirements are a useful screening device in blue-collar employee selection. The education of high producers did not differ from that of low producers to any statistically significant degree, although the less productive ones were slightly *better* educated.[20]

Speaking of employment of scientists in the electrical industry, Berg notes,

> Men with masters' degrees who were designated by *management* as among the 20 percent of their scientists who were "relatively" most valuable in terms of present performance

[19] Zvi Griliches, "Notes on the Role of Education in Production Functions and Growth Accounting," in *Education, Income, and Human Capital*, W. Lee Hansen, ed. (New York: National Bureau of Economic Research, 1970), pp. 94–95.
[20] Ivar Berg, *Education and Jobs: The Great Training Robbery* (Boston: Beacon Press, 1971), pp. 87–88.

and potential were paid an average salary which was *$1,000 less* than that paid to Ph.D.'s, who were reportedly less valuable. Other data show that Ph.D.'s are paid substantially more even when they are younger and less experienced . . . some less educated men (may, of course) earn through performance salaries that men with Ph.D.'s are given for their degrees.[21]

Let us see what this argument implies. Suppose companies gradually replaced M.A.'s with Ph.D.'s. At best, output per scientist would remain constant, but the costs to the companies of scientific work would go up. Assuming the companies seek to maintain their going rates of profit, how can they adjust successfully to this situation? One way is to raise the prices of their products—gradually over time, of course—and these prices eventually would be passed to consumers. Another way would be to rearrange the wage and salary structure so that less well educated people receive smaller increments over time than they would have in the absence of job upgrading at the Ph.D. level. In either case, the final outcome of employing increasing numbers of highly educated people is, not a gain in output for all to share, but income redistribution. The real income of the highly educated rises over time relative to the real income of the less well educated.

This is not necessarily the kind of income redistribution we would like to see. A major reason is that we may be compounding an inequity. To raise incomes of the less well educated is possibly an appropriate form of compensation for the less interesting and agreeable jobs such persons hold. Berg's analysis would indicate that such compensation is not being provided.[22]

The problem we are discussing here is a serious one in the developing countries. Those governments have used estimates that forecast high returns to educational investments to justify substantial expansion of student places in their schools and colleges. This policy is, at the same time, politically popular because the masses see education as the route to an individual's attainment of a better life, free of

---

[21] Ibid., p. 98.
[22] Putting this in a slightly different context, Harry G. Johnson has written: "If poverty or inequality is considered a problem, one whould recognize that the poorest among us, and the one most deserving of help from his fellowmen, is the one whom nature forgot to endow with brains—and that the way to make it up to him is not to exclude him from school and tax him to pay part of the cost of educating his intellectually well-endowed and no-longer-poor peer group among the children of poor parents, but to give him money in lieu of the brains he lacks." "The Alternatives Before Us," *Journal of Political Economy*, 80, no. 3 (May-June 1972): pt. 2, S 280–S 289 (quote on p. S 289).

the poverty and squalor in which many presently exist. Thus, rate of return studies have been used to justify actions that governments were under strong pressure to take for essentially noneconomic reasons. Unfortunately, expansion of educational systems is not often accompanied by curricular reform. The result is that the countries are forced to find employment for a rising number of classically trained graduates, whose preparation is better suited for routine duties in an already overloaded government bureaucracy. Thus, some educational systems in the developing world have attributes of exploitation devices.

Inappropriateness of Economic Growth as Social Objective

E. J. Mishan has asserted that economic growth is an inappropriate social objective.[23] His argument has three main parts:

1. The effects of economic growth on the character of man's *work*.
2. The effects of growth on *environment*.
3. The effects of growth on standards of *taste*.

Mishan states the following about the effects of growth on work:

> modern technology could hardly be more ingeniously fashioned than it is for depriving men of the exercise of their character as men. From the beginnings of the "industrial revolution" men have become progressively more specialized in a narrow range of tastes whether they work in an office, factory or laboratory. Whatever the particular skill employed, all the other qualities of a man, important enough in earlier times—qualities like courage, loyalty, perseverance, integrity, resourcefulness, attributes that once entered heavily into his future and the esteem in which he was held—have begun to lose their value in this unheroic push-button age.[24]

On environmental conditions of life, Mishan offers this observation:

> The incidence of a single spillover alone—be it foul air, endless traffic bedlam noise, or fear of criminal violence—can be

---

[23] E. J. Mishan, *The Costs of Economic Growth* (London: Staples Press, 1967).
[24] Ibid., p. 142.

enough to counter all of the alleged gains of economic prosperity. Let a family have five television sets, four refrigerators, three cars, two yachts, a private plane, a swimming pool, and half a million dollars' worth of securities. What enjoyment is left if it fears to stroll out on an evening, if it must take elaborate precautions against burglary, if it lives in continuous anxiety lest one or another, parent or child, be kidnapped, mutilated or murdered?[25]

Mishan has said about the effects of growth on standards of taste that:

> never was a younger generation so ill-equipped to withstand the siren songs of the entrepreneurs. Nor poverty, nor filial bonds, nor idealism, nor inhibition of any sort stand between them and the realization of any freak of fancy that enters their TV-heated imaginations. Social workers and journalists who have entered the candy-and-tinsel world that teenagers increasingly seek to inhabit, and have witnessed their mawkish raptures, their cultivated gluttony, their drug sessions, and their stylized reductions, are uncertain whether to be appalled or exhilarated by these near-hysterical attempts of the young to divest themselves of responsibility. . . . It is incomparably more efficient to turn the knob of a panel in order to capture the music of a celebrated symphony orchestra than to depend upon a solo or duet . . . by members of the family . . . [but] some essential sweetness in the lives of men has also passed away.[26]

Plainly, there is much that is sound in Mishan's analysis. And insofar as the existence of great educational systems are justified by the contributions those systems make toward the objective of economic growth, as we have understood that objective in the past, they are justified, in part at least, by the creation and perpetuation of the excesses that Mishan describes.

A more balanced view might suggest that economic growth has brought us "goods" and "bads," and we should try to arrange priorities so that the process of growth itself is better justified in human welfare. It would be a mistake to assume that a no-growth policy will bring us inevitably to a blissful state. And it is a misreading

---

[25] E. J. Mishan, "Growth and Antigrowth: What are the Issues?" *Challenge*, May-June 1973, p. 29.
[26] Mishan, *Costs of Economic Growth*, pp. 151, 162–163.

of history to imagine that conditions of human existence before the industrial revolution, conditions marred by rural poverty, famine and plague, were idyllic.

Reanalysis of Returns to Education

The research on human capital that was begun in the mid-1950s emphasized a relationship between only two variables: length of schooling and annual earned income. In comparing the incomes of any two individuals, obviously many other variables are important—where the persons live, industrial classification, health, natural talent, amount of work experience, the amount of time (and possibly money) invested in on-the-job training, access to labor market information, parental status, motivation to work hard (to find satisfaction in work rather than in leisure-time activities), sex, race, and luck. Several of these variables are hard to measure and some, like luck, impossible. Accordingly, though the average incomes of high school graduates are higher than the average incomes of dropouts (and the average incomes of Harvard Law School graduates are higher than those of persons who obtained law degrees at night school), the variation within any educational category is likely to be large. Looking at incomes of individuals, instead of incomes of groups of individuals averaged over educational categories, is almost certain to show a smaller influence of length of education on incomes than had previously been estimated.

Specifically, Jacob Mincer's examination of the incomes of white, nonfarm males as of 1959 (in a study published in 1974) shows that *years of schooling alone* explains only 7 percent of variation in income. Adding two variables—length of work experience and weeks worked in the year—raises the proportion of income variation that is explained to 55 percent.[27]

These findings alone by no means destroy the validity of human capital theory. It still remains true that, on the average a person improves his or her income prospects by acquiring additional years of schooling. And length of schooling is a variable that most young Americans can place under their own control. On the other hand, individuals cannot control such variables as parental status or their luck. Secondly, early versions of human capital theory were admittedly deficient in terms of emphasizing formal, compared with informal, education in determining incomes. Mincer's inclusion of a variable for "experience" serves to substantially correct that de-

---

[27] Jacob Mincer, *Schooling, Experience, and Earnings* (New York: Columbia, 1974), p. 92ff.

ficiency, since experience is a measure of the length of time a worker has been in a position to receive on-the-job training.

Mincer's findings suggest that if the policy objective is to reduce inequality of income distribution, concentrating on the distribution of years of formal education as the exclusive policy instrument may not be wise. Better to deal as well with access to programs of nonformal (on-the-job) education and with the distribution of involuntary unemployment (for example, through work-sharing schemes.[28]

At the present time there appears to be an overproduction of Ph.D.'s in the United States. The National Board on Graduate Education has stated:

> The two principal sources of employment for Ph.D.'s that have traditionally made direct use of the advanced education and research skills provided by doctoral education—college and university teaching and non-academic R. & D. [research and development] employment—will fall far short of the likely number of new Ph.D.'s entering the labor market. Allan Cartter's analysis suggests that, by the early 1980's, as few as 3,000–5,000 new Ph.D.'s may find academic employment per year, on average, and the National Science Foundation's projections for the period 1972–1985 indicate that, on average, approximately 4,000 new doctorates per year in the sciences (covering the physical sciences, engineering, mathematics, life sciences, and social sciences) will secure non-academic R. & D. employment. Consequently, if these projections are broadly accurate, within five years as few as 7,000–9,000 and probably no more than 15,000–20,000 new Ph.D.'s per year may secure employment that is closely related to the education provided in graduate school. In fiscal year 1974, 33,000 doctorate degrees were awarded, and most projections foresee slow but continuing growth in this number, reaching perhaps 40,000 in the early 1980's. Even if we allow for a substantial margin of error in each computation, those figures point to a massive (and not temporary) shift in the labor market for Ph.D.'s during the next decade.[29]

[28] Similar findings about the limited significance of length of education in accounting for individual differences in earnings are reported in Paul Taubman and Terence Wales, *Higher Education and Earnings: College as an Investment and a Screening Device* (New York: McGraw-Hill, 1974), p. 171ff. However, these authors also report that how the individual perceives the quality of the institution of higher education he or she attends has a significant effect on his or her learnings.

[29] National Board on Graduate Education, *Outlook and Opportunities for Graduate Education* (Washington, D.C. 1975), pp. 34–35.

This problem was not anticipated in the empirical work of the human capital theorists, one reason being that estimates of return to education are based either on current or historical data and have assumed that present conditions will continue to exist in the future. Not only do many Ph.D.'s face prospects of underemployment (working in jobs that do not call upon or make use of the highest skills acquired) but, in the mid-1970s, so also do many persons with baccalaureate degrees. However, the extent to which this latter phenomenon is a short-term cyclical one is not clear.

Because the United States is now facing a problem of *educated unemployment,* or underemployment, similar to that which has plagued developing nations for the last decade, we need to re-examine the structure and functioning of higher education. The change in conditions of employment also serve to cast doubt on the usefulness of internal rates of return to guide public-sector investments, at least in educational fields. Economics remains fallible as a predictive science.

One consequence of present conditions may be inflation of degrees. To get the kind of job today held by M.A.'s, a person tomorrow may need a Ph.D., not because of any change in the nature of the work itself, but because the higher degree allows holders to move ahead in the job-seeking queue. This would be wasteful in the extreme, not only in university expenditures but also in cost of time to students.

Another means to maintain fictionally high rates of return to education—this is done already to a degree—is to relate salary differentials to degrees and not to the content of the job. Putting the matter this way, we see that returns to education from the private point of view are related to income inequality. Generally, the more income inequality we have, the higher will be private rates of return to education.

A short-term solution to the problem of educated unemployment is to shift emphasis in universities from the training of scientists at high levels and from education of undergraduates in liberal arts and social science fields toward professional education (law and medicine, say) and toward applied fields in undergraduate programs, such as business administration and engineering. In the present state of the economy (mid-1970s), these fields could also become overcrowded very quickly.

A more fundamental approach to the problem of educated unemployment is for the country to engage in a political dialogue about its social goals. Once the goals were further clarified, we might see the extent to which educational institutions might make contributions toward meeting those goals. One thing, however, seems fairly plain: Work and preparation for work will gradually become less important activities in the lives of most people. Education could make, this author believes, a major difference to many people in the way they use their nonwork time and in the satisfaction they derive from that time.

Almost all work is repetitive in some degree. Reduction in work requirements could be a liberating force and could pose requirements on the educational system far in excess of those imposed by the need to prepare people for occupations.

In Chapter 9 we shall consider the distribution of opportunities for nonwork education, exploring the idea that its present distribution is "perverse" in the sense that people in highly repetitious jobs and people who have the most free time at their disposal are least well equipped to use their nonwork hours in meaningful and boredom-relieving ways.

The Radical Economists' Critique of Human Capital Theory

Human capital theory rests on two basic assumptions:

1. Education helps develop skills of work, that is, improves the capacity of the worker to be productive.
2. Earned income reflects marginal productivities of different categories of workers.

The view of radical economists is somewhat different. In the first place, they postulate a general oversupply of work skills, such that American industry could function just as well if the skill development function of schools was substantially reduced. But this is not to say that the educational system does not have a significant role in a capitalist society. Under capitalism, owners and managers of enterprises are free to seek private profits, and they do. Profits are created as and when managers and owners pay workers less than the value of their output. For workers to accept being shortchanged in this way, owners and managers could rely on police power or private power. This exercise of brute force would produce social disharmony. Better to rely on a system of thought control under which workers are convinced that they deserve no more in economic rewards (salary and status) than their employers are willing to give them. And so the role of schools is to convince a majority of the population that they are unfitted for anything more than low-paying, low-status work, and to convince a minority of the population that they are prepared to be owners and managers. Samuel Bowles and Herbert Gintis write:

Different levels of education feed workers into different levels within the occupational structure . . . the lowest levels in the hierarchy of enterprise emphasize rule-following, middle levels, dependability, and the capacity to operate without direct and continuous supervision while the higher levels stress the internalization of the norms of the enterprise. Similarly, in education, lower levels (junior and senior high school) tend to severely limit and channel the activities of students. Somewhat higher up the educational ladder, teacher and community colleges allow for more independent activity and less overall supervision. At the top, the elite four-year colleges emphasize social relationship comformable with the higher levels in the production hierarchy. Thus schools continually maintain their hold on students. As they "master" one type of behavioral regulation, they are either allowed to progress to the next or are channeled into the corresponding level in the hierarchy of production. Even within a single school, the social relationships of different tracks tend to conform to different behavioral norms. Thus in high school, vocational and general trades emphasize rule-following and close supervision, while the college track tends toward a more open atmosphere emphasizing the internalization of norms.[30]

The conclusion to draw from this argument is that the educational system is dominated by requirements of economic enterprise. It will be impossible to reform education, in the sense that the system lives up to its ideal of promoting the full development of each individual, as long as the system is dominated by monopolist capitalist enterprise and as long as hierarchical patterns of relationships exist in the workplace.

What may we make of their argument? The answer to that question depends very much on one's world view, that is, whether one is or is not a Marxist. However, we can certainly agree that our society is characterized by hierarchical relationships. (Indeed, so are most socialist societies, as Bowles and Gintis note.) The basic question is whether schools reinforce or moderate the nonegalitarian forces that exist in our society. Do they, that is, preserve privilege from parent to child or interfere with the transmission of privilege? The case is not yet proven on either side.

[30] Samuel Bowles and Herbert Gintis, *Schooling in Capitalist America: Educational Reform and the Contradictions of Economic Life* (New York: Basic Books, 1976), p. 132.

Obviously, the intent of radical economists is to lead us to a more humane society. But what the nature of the society is to be is not at all clear.

Summary

On the average, persons who spend more years in acquiring formal education have higher incomes than those who spend fewer years. Starting from this observation, economists have developed techniques to measure the financial returns to investment in schooling. Both education-related income differentials and costs of education, including foregone income, are discounted (adjusted to reflect that future dollars are worth less than today's dollars because of the opportunity to put today's dollars out to compound interest). How worthwhile a given sum of educational investment is, is sensitive to the choice of a discount rate. And economists are in disagreement about what the appropriate rate to regulate educational investments should be. Moreover, the ability of the educational system to produce more graduates than the economy can absorb in their preferred lines of work casts some doubt on the actual estimates of returns to education. In spite of such criticisms, the concept of human capital is generally regarded as a valuable addition to the body of economic theory.

Selected Bibliography

Becker, Gary S. *Human Capital.* New York: Columbia, 1964.

Bowles, Samuel, and Herbert Gintis. *Schooling in Capitalist America.* New York: Basic Books, 1976.

Mincer, Jacob. *Schooling, Experience and Earnings.* New York: Columbia, 1974.

Noah, Harold J., ed. *The Economics of Education in the U.S.S.R.* New York: Praeger, 1969.

Psacharopoulos, George. *Returns to Education: An International Comparison.* San Francisco: Jossey-Bass, 1973.

Taubman, Paul, and Terence Wales. *Higher Education and Earnings: College as an Investment and a Screening Device.* New York: McGraw-Hill, 1974.

Chapter Five

Economic Decision Making
Examined Further

In the United States, as in virtually all countries, the central government is responsible for economic policy. One of the primary objectives of central government is a rising level of national income. Insofar as educational expenditures contribute to increases in GNP, we would expect the federal government to seize initiative to control those expenditures and so regulate them that marginal returns to education are equal to those in other major public-sector programs, for example, health, scientific research, transport, housing, and the like. On the contrary, the federal government turns over policy decisions about educational expenditures to state and local government. Indeed, it typically is the school district that holds the initiative to regulate educational expenditures, although state governments contribute substantially to such outlays. In 1975–76, there were 16,376 such districts in our country.

When expenditure policies are set in such a disaggregated fashion, it is appropriate to imagine that the processes of decision making conform somewhat to those of a small collection of households. Therefore, we turn now to the *theory of household demand*. The ideas we develop in the following sections are useful in analyzing economic problems generally; and they will be especially helpful in understanding later discussions about responses of local districts to state and federal subsidies and about the nature of tax incidence.

The Theory of Household Demand

The theory of household demand properly begins with consideration of the concept of *utility*, which is defined as an attribute of economic goods. In particular, it is the attribute of *desiredness*. There is no ethical or semiethical connotation in the term as used here. It is not necessary that the commodity be useful, only that it be wanted. Education, as an example, affords utility to the households in the country.

Special interest is attached to the change in utility as a household obtains more units of the same commodity. *Marginal utility* of a commodity may be defined as the "desiredness of one more unit of that commodity." What is the expected behavior of marginal utility; that is, does it increase or decrease as a household acquires more units of the same commodity? The answer given in economic theory is that marginal utility decreases. This property of increments of utility is, in fact, called the principle of *diminishing marginal utility*. [1]

Marginal utility diminishes, it is held, on two accounts. First, since we are dealing with acquisition of commodities at a point of time (not spread over time), we expect that repeated doses of the same commodity in the same use will lead gradually to satiation. This is certainly true of a commodity like milk. After acquiring a fairly small number of units of milk, people ordinarily seek to divert their purchases to other types of goods. Marginal utility of milk approaches the value of zero. The operation of satiation can supposedly be observed in a household spending a relatively small share of its income on any one commodity, even on the one that might be regarded as that household's favorite.

At first glance, education may appear to be unique on this score. There is some reason to believe that those households whose members are highly educated are the ones that place a high value on schooling. This would be a case of supply creating its own demand. But note that the analysis of marginal utility specifies that we consider a short period. Now, it takes time to acquire education. In any short period, we would thus expect eventual satiation of demand, not because of a general lack of interest in education, but because the number of hours in the week that can be devoted to schooling and study is limited.

The second basis of diminishing marginal utility is the observed pattern of behavior under which households put goods to

---

[1] We are speaking of additional units of the *same* commodity that are acquired by a single household over a relatively short period.

successively less important uses as they acquire additional units of the goods. Since the uses become less important, the desiredness of one more unit becomes less and less. Again, we can use the example of milk. If the supply is very short, it will be given only to sickly children. As it becomes more plentiful, it will be given to all children. Next, it will be drunk by adults. Additional units will be fed to animals. Finally, so it is said, people may use it for beauty care.

The principle of diminishing marginal utility allows us to dispose easily of a point that was extremely troublesome to the early economists. Why, they asked, are people willing to pay only a few cents for an additional unit of water, which is necessary for survival, when at the same time they will pay many dollars for trinkets and baubles that catch their fancy at the moment? The answer is that people are already acquiring so many units of water that the marginal utility of water is low even compared with relatively useless novelties.

The principle of diminishing marginal utility also allows us to establish the concept of household *equilibrium* in the consumption of privately produced goods. Let us assume that households seek to maximize the satisfactions they can obtain from their disposable incomes. Given the amount of its income, how can a household arrange its expenditures so that it gets as much satisfaction as possible? Should it buy more of commodity A and less of B or C? Under the assumption that it wants to maximize satisfactions, the household seeks a *position of equilibrium* in which it cannot gain any additional satisfaction by shifting a part of its income from one commodity to any other. Marginal utility diminishes, for all commodities, as additional units are acquired. Hence, the rule for maximizing satisfaction is to carry forward consumption of the various commodities until the ratios of the marginal utilities of all commodities to their prices are equal. That is, the marginal utility of the last dollar spent in every different line of consumption is equal; no transfer of purchases between commodity A and any other commodity can increase total satisfaction. This is the desired position of equilibrium.

Let us assume, once again, that education is a service produced in the private economy. In a position of equilibrium, the household would obtain the same increment of satisfaction from the last dollar it spent on elementary education as from the last dollar it spent on secondary education. Moreover, the increments from these last dollars paid for schooling would themselves be equal to the additional satisfactions received from the last dollars spent for ice cream, television, books, etc. No household calculates marginal utilities closely, but it is surely fair to say that most households try to

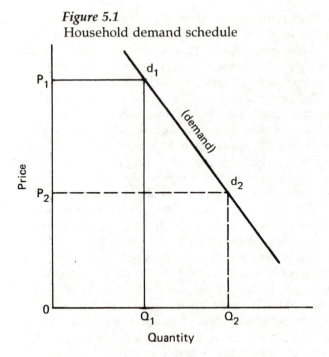

Figure 5.1
Household demand schedule

spend their income in ways that do afford them satisfactions. With greater or less assiduousness, they try to reach approximately the position of equilibrium that we have described.[2]

The Household Demand Schedule

Let us now establish the form of one of the fundamental relationships in economics, namely, the relationship between the *price* of a commodity and the *quantity* of the commodity demanded by a household. (Here, the term *demanded* refers to the willingness of the household to purchase a specified number of units of a commodity at a stated price in the present period; it does not refer to desire for the article, independent of financial ability and willingness to purchase units of it.) The relationship postulated in economics is this: The quantity of a commodity demanded by a household increases as the price falls and decreases as the price rises, other factors remaining constant. This can be shown in diagrammatic form, as in Figure 5.1, or in tabular form, as in Table 5.1.

[2] Of course, the act of spending money carelessly may afford satisfaction in itself.

Table 5.1
Quantity of books demanded by hypothetical
household at varying prices

Price	Quantity demanded
$ 6.00	18
7.00	15
8.00	12
9.00	9
10.00	6
11.00	3

In Figure 5.1 the relationship is called a *demand curve*. In tabular form it is called a *demand schedule*. The presentation of the curve or schedule shows that the phrase "demand for commodity x" should be interpreted, not in terms of a single quantity, but in terms of a set of quantities, the members of which show an inverse relationship with price.

Why does the quantity demanded show an inverse relationship with price? Let us recall our earlier statements about the equilibrium position of the household. We said that households seek to adjust their expenditures among the various goods so that no gain in utility can be achieved by spending less on one commodity and more on another. Suppose that the price of a single commodity—call it x—goes up. Often there will be another good (or goods) that serve the same function in the household. That is, some goods are *substitutes* for each other. (Butter and margarine are good examples.) Let commodity y be a close substitute for x. When the price of x increases (with the price of y remaining unchanged), households can be expected to substitute y for x in some degree.[3] Thus, the purchases of x decrease when its price rises, and its demand curve will have the shape shown in Figure 5.1.

However, commodities x and y are not perfect substitutes. If so, by definition, they are the same commodity. Since they are not perfect substitutes, we can consider changes in their utilities separately. The marginal utility of y will fall as the household buys more of it. Likewise, the marginal utility of x will increase, because the family is now purchasing fewer units of it. At some point, household equilibrium will be restored, with the family continuing to purchase

---

[3] When the price of, say, butter goes up, people can be expected to buy margarine.

some units of *x*: Its rise in price does not drive it completely from the market.

In summary, the *substitution effect* operates when a household adjusts its purchases to conditions of changing price: It buys less of goods that have become dearer and buys in their place other goods of similar function. What is important is a change in the price of one commodity *relative* to the prices of others.[4]

A second effect of a price change is that the level of real income in the household has fallen or risen (corresponding to whether the price of the commodity has gone up or down). Part of the resulting change in *expenditure* will be applied to the good whose price has changed. For example, if the price of milk rises drastically, households have become poorer in the real sense and will have to restrict their consumption of commodities in general. But part of this belt tightening takes the form of smaller purchases of milk itself. This, too, serves to explain the shape of the demand line in Figure 5.1. This *income effect* will be the greater as the item in question represents a substantial portion of the household budget. On this last point, let us recognize that a 20 percent increase in college tuition is likely to have a much greater impact on family consumption patterns that is a 20 percent increase in the price of salt. The substitution and the income effects ordinarily operate in the same direction, with both influencing a household to restrict its purchases of goods that have increased in price.

Subject to the peculiarities of public-sector decision making to be noted in the concluding sections of this chapter, it is appropriate to draw an analogy between responses of households and local school districts to price change. If salaries of teachers rise, school districts are subject to a substitution effect and an income effect. In the usual case, both effects would operate to encourage the school districts to economize on the use of teachers' time. School districts, like households, would seek to reestablish a position after a price change under which the last dollars spent on any given school input offered equal yield in terms of the districts' objectives as last dollars spent on all other known school inputs.

Elasticity of Demand

Having considered the underlying reasons for postulating an inverse relationship between price and quantity demanded, we have still to discuss the means of describing, or classifying, demand schedules.

---

[4] Under inflation, that is, with an equal rise in price of all commodities (or almost all), the allocation of household purchases will not necessarily show any change.

The device used is the measure of *elasticity. Price elasticity of demand* indicates the degree of responsiveness in quantity demanded to a small change in price. If a small price increase leads a household to make a large reduction in quantity demanded, then the demand schedule in the neighborhood of the initial price is called *elastic*. If, on the other hand, a small increase in price has very little influence on quantity demanded, the demand is *inelastic*.

Elasticity is commonly measured by a numerical coefficient of the following order:

$$E_p = \frac{\text{relative (percentage) change in quantity demanded}}{\text{relative (percentage) change in price}} \qquad (5.1)$$

Let us distinguish three cases of elasticity:

1. Elastic demand: The percentage change in quantity demanded is greater than 1 percent for a 1 percent change in price.
2. Inelastic demand: The percentage change in quantity demanded is less than 1 percent for a 1 percent change in price.
3. Unit elasticity: The change in quantity demanded is equal to 1 percent for a 1 percent change in price.[5]

If demand is elastic, a rise in price will cause a family to spend less money, in total, on the commodity, and a fall in price will lead it to spend more. If demand is inelastic, a rise in price will cause a household to spend more, in total, on the article and a fall in price, less. In the case of unit elasticity, expenditure is constant as price changes. It is convenient to think of *flat* demand curves as elastic and *steep* demand curves as inelastic. However, having made such a statement, we hasten to warn the reader that slope and elasticity are *not* the same thing; furthermore, a straight demand line does not have constant elasticity throughout its length. To see this, let us rewrite expression (5.1), the statement of elasticity, to read

$$E_p = \frac{\dfrac{\Delta Q}{Q}}{\dfrac{\Delta P}{P}} \qquad (5.2)$$

[5] Suppose, for example, the price of a given article, call it a record turntable, falls from $100 to $95 and suppose that the quantity demanded rises from 10,000 to 11,000. Demand is elastic, as a 10 percent rise in quantity demanded is associated with a 5 percent fall in price. Sales revenue would rise from $1,000,000 to $1,045,000. As seen by the seller, if demand is elastic, total sales revenue rises as sales price falls. If demand is inelastic, revenue falls as price falls. If demand is unit elastic, revenue is constant under change of sales price.

since $\Delta Q/Q$ can be regarded as an alternative way to state "relative (percentage) change in quantity demanded," etc. Now let us consider Figure 5.1 again. At point d_1, Q_1 is relatively small, so the ratio $\Delta Q/Q$ for any small change ΔQ will be relatively large. Just the opposite holds for the ratio $\Delta P/P$ at d_1. E_p, when measured at the upper, or left-ward, part of the demand schedule, will take on elastic value, regardless of the actual slope of the demand line (excluding cases when the line is absolutely vertical or flat). Using the price and quantity relationships at point d_2, we might, as an exercise, convince ourselves that elasticities measured at the lower points of conventional demand schedules tend toward low absolute values.

Why should demand schedules for some commodities be generally elastic and those for others generally inelastic? Behind any given demand schedule there are the factors of substitution and income effects. In explaining the degree of elasticity, however, it is customary to concentrate on the substitution effect.

Substitution will operate more strongly as there are available to the household other commodities closely related to the one in question. To use the familiar example, butter and margarine are close substitutes. We should expect a price change for either commodity separately to be followed by a substantial change in the quantity that is demanded—demand is elastic. And the large degree of response occurs because the household can easily shift between the two commodities to take advantage of buying more of the one that has become relatively cheaper. On the other hand, for certain drugs (insulin, at least until recently) there are no close substitutes. A price change in insulin would be expected to have almost no effect on the quantity demanded by a household. If the price rises, there is no other good one can drop—or use less of—in favor of the now relatively more costly insulin.

Before leaving the concept of elasticity, it is important to consider two additional measures: cross elasticity of demand and income elasticity of demand. (Both are distinct from price elasticity, which we have been discussing to this point.) *Cross elasticity of demand* is the measure of the responsiveness of quantity demanded of commodity x to a change in the price of commodity y:

$$E_c = \frac{\text{relative change in quantity demanded of commodity } x}{\text{relative change in price of } y} \qquad (5.3)$$

Whereas price elasticity of demand generally has a negative sign (an *increase* in price of a commodity—positive—is ordinarily accompanied by a *decrease* in quantity demanded—negative—etc.), cross elasticity is positive or negative, depending on whether the two commodities are in a competitive or complementary relationship with each other. Silk and nylon are competitive commodities: An increase in the price of one would be expected to lead to an increased amount of purchases of the other. Thus cross elasticity is positive. An example of complementary commodities—or commodities in joint demand—is automobiles and gasoline: An increase in the price of cars would lead to less consumption of gasoline. In this case, cross elasticity is negative. In many instances, two commodities are not closely linked in either a competitive or a complementary way, for example, oranges and neckties. Here the value of cross elasticity is quite low, and the question of sign is not especially important.

Income elasticity of demand is the measure of the responsiveness in quantity of a commodity demanded to a change in level of household income:

$$E_y = \frac{\text{relative change in quantity demanded of commodity } x}{\text{relative change in household income}} \quad (5.4)$$

Income elasticity refers only to the effect of a change in income. Relative prices (the price of one commodity as compared with the prices of all other commodities) are held constant, theoretically, in measuring income elasticity. Like cross elasticity of demand, income elasticity takes on both positive and negative signs. When the sign of income elasticity is negative, the commodity in question is classified as an *inferior good* with respect to the household under consideration. The negative sign means that less of the commodity is demanded by the household as its income rises. The household might buy less potatoes and more wild rice, less beer and more wine over the period when the level of income was increasing. Potatoes and beer would then be classed as inferior goods. What are *normal goods*, or goods with a nonnegative income elasticity of demand, for the great majority of households may be inferior goods for the very rich households.

For practically any household, however, the value of E_y for a large range of commodities will be equal to or greater than zero. A zero value indicates that the household does not seek to change its amount of purchases of a given commodity as its income varies. Zero is the dividing line between normal and inferior goods. The value 1 is also a dividing line. At 1, the changes in quantity demanded and in income are equal. Hence, the family is spending the same proportion of its income on the commodity both before and after the change in its level of income. Between zero and 1, a household seeks to increase its purchases of the article as its income goes up; but the relative change in quantity demanded is less than the relative change in income. The proportion of income spent on the article—or on the household's budget—declines as income rises. Finally, a value greater than 1 indicates that the commodity will account for a larger and larger share of the household's budget under successive gains in level of income.

We can describe, either in analytical or empirical terms, the responses households make to the uses of income; but such description does not tell us how household tastes are formed in the first place. Surely, however, we may recognize that educational systems exist to help people improve their tastes, along with improving their work skills. The general direction of educational impact on tastes is to change the household's *time discount rate,* in the sense that members of households become willing to use some of today's time to increase the level of satisfaction they can get from tomorrow's use of time. Learning to play a musical instrument is an example. Thus, education's influence on taste stands in opposition to the intended influence of much of television advertising, in which instant satisfaction is stressed, and the expenditure of income on items that do not require much time, either in learning to use them or in their consumption itself.

Before leaving this discussion of elasticities, we should make a clear distinction between price elasticity and cross and income elasticities. Price elasticity refers to the responsiveness in quantity demanded to a small change in price in an *existing demand* schedule (or curve). We are measuring movement in and along a schedule or curve. This is illustrated in Figure 5.1 as price moves from P_1 to P_2 and quantity demanded changes from Q_1 to Q_2. When another commodity changes in price (an effect measured by cross elasticity) or when there is a change in household income (an effect measured by income elasticity), we have to deal with a new schedule of demand. There is a *shift in demand,* so that more (or less) is demanded at every price than was true under the former schedule.

Figure 5.2 shows a shift in demand from D_1 to D_2, a higher level of demand. The process of moving from a demand curve D_1 to a demand curve D_2 is called an *increase in demand.* With price constant at P_1, the quantity of the article that people seek to buy increases from Q_1 to Q_2. This is distinct from the kind of change that occurs with price elasticity, which is called a *change in quantity demanded* (the change from Q_1 to Q_0 in Figure 5.2, which results from the change in price from P_1 to P_0).

An increase in demand can occur (1) as income in the household goes up (except in the case of inferior goods, where a decline in income would lead to an increase in demand) and (2) as the price of a competing good rises (or as the price of a complementary good falls). A shift in demand can also occur through a change in household

Figure 5.2
Shift in demand

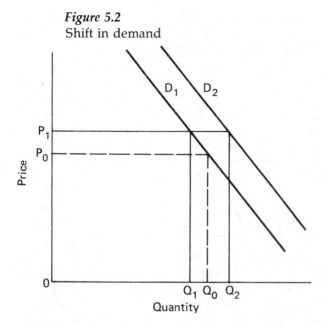

tastes or through the operation of a government regulation affecting household demand. The growing public feeling in the 1960s (now largely dissipated) of the importance of education in fulfilling the country's commitment to the objective of social mobility surely served to increase the demand for this service.

So far, we have been considering points in the theory of household demand. Individual household demand schedules can be totaled into schedules for all households of a region—called a *market demand schedule.* The basic concepts of elasticity relate to the market demand schedule as they do to the household demand schedule. Price elasticity is used to describe a *given demand curve. Shifts in demand* will more often than not reflect the operation of either income or cross elasticity of demand.

As manufacturers have acquired power in their markets to set—within limits—their selling prices, the process of estimating elasticities has become more than theoretically interesting. If a manufacturer is on that part of a demand schedule that is price inelastic, a cut in price will put the firm in the position of having to produce more units to obtain a smaller gross revenue. A rise in price, however, would yield the firm larger gross revenue for a smaller output. The opposite holds if demand for the firm's product is elastic with respect to price.

Likewise, manufacturers are interested in the relationship between changes in disposable income and the quantity of their industry's product that consumers buy. Thus, many manufacturers do attempt to make estimates of income elasticity of demand. It is generally assumed that income in the United States will rise year by year on the average. Will, for example, households spend the same proportion, a larger or a smaller proportion of their larger income on automobiles? The answer to this question is extremely important to the automobile industry. The strength of the drive in the households to spend their income on consumer's goods affects, in turn, the proportion of national income that is made available for education.

Indifference Curve Analysis

One major analytical device in economics is called the *indifference curve*. We shall want to use this mental construct when we discuss household preference for public versus private goods. But it is most easily explained in the context of how households respond to changes in the price of a commodity. Let us start with some simple algebra.

Recall that households, given the level of their incomes, seek to adjust their expenditures among the various goods and services in such fashion that no gain in utility can be achieved by spending less on one commodity and more on another. This is equivalent to saying that the ratios of marginal utility to price for all commodities are equal:

$$\frac{MU_x}{P_x} = \frac{MU_y}{P_y} = \frac{MU_z}{P_z} \ldots \tag{5.5}$$

where MU stands for marginal utility; P represents price; and the subscripts x, y, and z designate different commodities.

Now, let us assume that there are only two commodities, x and y, purchased by a household, and that the household spends all its income on these two commodities, that is, family income $= P_x \times X + P_y \times Y$. What happens when the price of x goes up while the price of y remains unchanged? Let us stipulate that the household continues to buy the same amount of x as before the price change. In equilibrium position we had

$$\frac{MU_x}{P_x} = \frac{MU_y}{P_y} \tag{5.6}$$

Since the household is still buying the same amount of x, MU_x has not changed. But P_x has increased. Even if it were possible for the household to continue to buy the same amount of y, we know that the real situation has become

$$\frac{MU_x}{P_x} < \frac{MU_y}{P_y} \tag{5.7}$$

To restore the equality between the two ratios, the household, under rational behavior, would buy less x than before the price changed; it would do this in order to raise the value of MU_x, for P_x is beyond its control. This is the operation of the substitution effect.

Moreover, it is impossible for the household to continue buying the same amount of x and the same amount of y, as the household's income previously was completely absorbed in buying certain amounts of the two commodities at the old prices. Hence, the household will probably have to sacrifice some units of y in order to maintain its purchases of x at an appropriate level. The household has become poorer in the real sense because the price of x has risen. But notice that as the household gives up units of y, the marginal utility of y increases. This is, once again, the operation of the principle of diminishing marginal utility. The rise in the marginal utility of y would further increase the magnitude of the ratio MU_y/P_y relative to MU_x/P_x.

In summary, the substituion effect is the procedure under which a household adjusts its purchases under conditions of changing prices to buy less of goods that have become more expensive by using in their place other goods that are similar in function. A second effect of a price change is that the level of real income has fallen, or risen (corresponding to whether the price of the commodity has gone up or down). Part of the resulting change in expenditure may be expected to fall on the good whose price has changed. Ordinarily the substitution and the income effects operate in the same direction, with both influencing a household to restrict its purchases of goods that have increased in price.

So much for the statement of the substantive argument. Now we note that expression (5.6) can also be written[6] as

$$\frac{MU_x}{MU_y} = \frac{P_x}{P_y} \tag{5.8}$$

The two-commodity equilibrium position of the household can thus be described as one in which the ratio of the marginal utilities of the two commodities is equal to the ratio of their prices. At this point, we are ready to discuss indifference curves.

[6] Multiply both sides of (5.6) by P_x and then multiply both sides by $1/MU_y$.

Figure 5.3
Indifference curve for two commodities

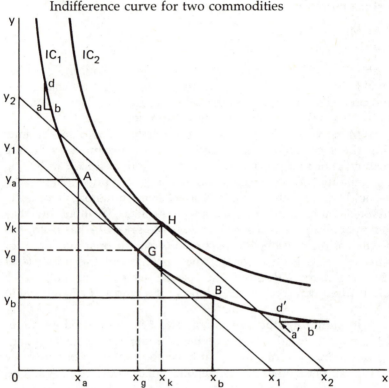

Consider Figure 5.3. The y-axis represents quantities of commodity y, and the x-axis measures quantities of commodity x. The
curved line, IC_1, is an *indifference curve* showing all combinations of
quantities of commodities x and y that afford the given household
equal satisfaction. That is, between the combinations y_a and x_a, on the
one hand, and y_b and x_b, on the other, the household is indifferent.
Why should this line bow in toward the origin? The principle of
diminishing marginal utility tells us that it must. On IC_1, note the
small triangles *dab* and *d'a'b'*. Let *da* = *d'a'*. When the household gives
up *da* of commodity y, starting from *d* (a point at which it has a
relatively large amount of y) a comparatively small amount of x, *ab* (of
which it has little), serves to compensate. But when the household
gives up *d'a'* of y, starting from *d'*, a much larger amount of x, *a'b'*, is
needed to compensate; now y is in short supply and x is abundant.

The slope of IC_1 (and of any indifference line to be drawn on Figure 5.3) represents $-MU_x/MU_y$, because IC_1 represents a relationship between marginal utilities sacrificed and gained as the household swaps small quantities of one commodity for another, under the condition that total utility remains constant.[7]

Consider now the straight line y_1x_1. This is called the *price line*, or the *budget line*. It represents the different amounts of x and y that can be purchased for a fixed sum of money—call it total income of the household. If the household spent all its income on y, it could obtain y_1 units. If it spent all its income on x, it could obtain x_1 units. Or it can obtain any combination of units along the line y_1x_1. (The line is straight because it is assumed that the single household has no measurable influence on market price. Hence, the prices of x and y do not vary when the household shifts its purchases from one of the goods to the other.) The slope of y_1x_1 is $-P_x/P_y$, since these two prices measure how many units of x must be sacrificed to obtain the additional units of y, under the condition that total expenditures on the two commodities are constant.

With an indifference curve of IC_1, at what combination of x and y will the given household be in equilibrium? Our previous analysis shows that it will be at the point G—the point of tangency between IC_1 and y_1x_1, that is, the point where

$$\frac{MU_x}{MU_y} = \frac{P_x}{P_y}$$

which is, of course, expression (5.8). At this point, y_g of y is consumed and x_g of x.

It is true, of course, that any other point on IC_1 would afford the household the same amount of utility, but *no other point on IC_1 is attainable under the budget y_1x_1*. Another interpretation is to say that we seek tangency between a given budget line and the indifference curve that is highest—or farthest to the right—with the idea that people are always happier with more of both commodities. By contrast, IC_2 shows a point of tangency with $y_2 x_2$ at H, representing a larger budget. A line drawn between a series of points such as G and H shows the response of the household to purchase of different goods in the market place when its income changes but prices do not.

How can we use an indifference curve to distinguish between the substitution and income effects of a price change? Consider Figure

---

[7] The slope of the indifference curve can be derived from the following relationship:

$$\Delta \text{ total utility} = MU_x \cdot \Delta X + MU_y \cdot \Delta Y = 0$$

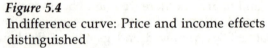

Figure 5.4
Indifference curve: Price and income effects
distinguished

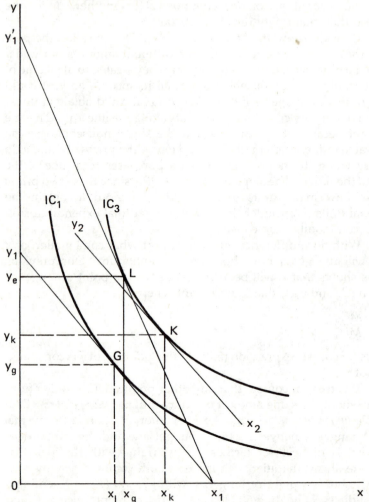

5.4. The lines IC_1 and y_1x_1 are the same as in Figure 5.3, as is equilibrium point G. The line y'_1x_1 represents a fall in the price of y. The
household can now obtain $y_1y'_1$ additional units of y for the same
budget total (the line pivots from x_1, and we see that only the price of
y, not x, has changed). The equilibrium position of the household
shifts from G to L. This shift can, however, be regarded as consisting

of two parts: an income effect, G to K, where $y_2 x_2$ is drawn parallel to $y_1 x_1$; and a substitution effect, K to L, moving along to a new indifference curve IC_3 to recognize the relative cheapness of y. The reader might wish to draw the corresponding cases of a fall in the price of x and, say, a rise in the price of y.[8]

Prices and the Concept of Marginal Cost

Households maximize utility when they arrange their budgets so that the last dollar spent on any given type of commodity or service is as useful as anything else they could get for that dollar. This kind of behavior on the part of households is a necessary but not a sufficient condition for drawing the maximum total utility from any set of resources. The sufficient condition is that prices themselves be related to costs of production and, more specifically, to costs of production at the margin of output.

Suppose that two items, call them sailboats and campers, each consumes resources in their production valued at $6,000. That is, to make one more sailboat or one more camper, manufacturers need labor, materials, etc., valued at $6,000. For some reason, be it monopoly control or whatever, let sailboats be priced at $7,500 and campers at the true resource costs, $6,000. The $7,500 price for sailboats indicates that some households are willing to spend that much for a sailboat. But the situation represents a misallocation of resources, in that $6,000 shifted from the production of campers to the production of sailboats gives people more of what they more strongly desire and should thus be able to get. In the situation described, some resources, in particular some of those being employed in making campers, are not being put to their highest valued use. As A. P. Lerner has said,

> One could say that the function of prices is to discourage consumers from using up things and to encourage producers to produce them. Consumers should be discouraged from using up available goods and services to the degree to which it is important that they be left for others to consume. This is indicated by the degree to which other consumers bid up prices. If there is a very small supply of an item which is in great demand, its price will be very high, which induces

---

[8] We may again draw an analogy between the household depicted in Figure 5.4 and a school district. The district's budget could be represented by the lines $y_1 x_1$ and $y_1' x_1$.

consumers to use it sparingly. If an item is plentiful, the price will be low, which will discourage consumption very little, and if the item is superabundant so that it becomes a completely free good (the price is zero) then there is no discouragement at all to its consumption. . . .

But . . . prices [should also give] the proper degree of encouragement to producers so that the proper quantities of the different products have been made available by them. As long as it is possible to benefit consumers by producing less of one product and, with the resources set free, producing something else that the consumer would rather have had instead, the different products have not been produced in the proper proportions. But in a competitive economy any price greater than marginal cost of a product encourages the producer to expand output, and any price below marginal cost is an inadequate encouragement so that the producer responds to it by contracting output. Such contractions set free productive resources to be used by the expanding producers to make more of the items with prices above marginal cost—and the high price is the indication that the product is preferred by the consumer. When the gaps between marginal cost have all disappeared, no future shifting of resources to preferred products is any longer possible. The producers have been given just the right degree of encouragement. . . .[9]

Decision Making in the Public Sector

Private activities—the activities of privately owned enterprises—are not responsible for supplying all the goods and services we consume. *Government purchases of goods and services*, equal, approximately, to the value of government services to households and to businesses, amounted to $339.0 billion in 1975; and *government transfers*—social security payments, veterans' benefits, food stamps, relief, etc.— added another $168.9 billion to government's bill. Together these sums represented 33.5 percent of GNP in that year.[10]

It is now time to see how households relate to government, in contrast to the way they relate to private business firms. The first essential point is to note that government services, in the main, are essentially different from the outputs of private firms. There are

[9] A. P. Lerner, *Everybody's Business* (New York: Harper & Row, 1964), pp. 15–16.
[10] U.S. Department of Commerce, *Statistical Abstract of the United States* (Washington, D.C.: U.S. Government Printing Office, 1976), pp. 393–398.

several ways to describe the contrasting characteristics of public and private outputs. We will consider those offered by Richard A. Musgrave and Carl Shoup.

Richard Musgrave on Social Goods

According to Musgrave, we distinguish public outputs by the existence of *market failure*. Markets can function only when the *exclusion principle* applies—when one person's consumption is strictly dependent on his or her having paid a price for some service or commodity and when that payment grants the person exclusive control over consumption of the service or article. If, for example, you want an automobile for your private use, you expect to pay a price for it. Once having paid the price and obtained the automobile, you would not take kindly if a stranger obtained a duplicate set of keys and drove it about. Indeed, the police stand ready to protect your right to control exclusively the uses of the car you have bought.[11] In addition, it is in the nature of private goods to offer benefits that flow naturally to the particular consumer who has paid the price; these benefits are not, at the same time, available to another consumer. Private consumption in this sense is *rival*. As Musgrave says, "A hamburger eaten by A cannot be eaten by B."[12]

When the exclusion principle should not or cannot be applied, markets cannot function and public provision may be sought. To take a useful, albeit improbable example, suppose it came to pass that people felt anybody's automobile was available for their use and that the police acquiesced in such behavior. People would no longer pay the large sum necessary to buy new cars because they would know that their neighbors would feel free to use them at any time. The private market for cars would collapse. People might agree that government could levy a tax to buy cars and establish car pools, where cars might be available on a sign-up or book-ahead basis.

Under what circumstances do we find that exclusion cannot be applied? Musgrave gives the following example:

> Consider for instance travel on a crowded cross-Manhattan street during rush time. The use of available space is distinctly rival and exclusion (the auctioning off, or sale of the available space) would be efficient and should be applied. Use of crowded space would then go to those who value it

---

[11] Richard A. Musgrave and Peggy B. Musgrave, *Public Finance in Theory and Practice* (New York: McGraw-Hill, 1973), chap. 3.
[12] Ibid., p. 52.

most and who are willing to offer the highest price. But such exclusion would be impossible, or is too costly at this time. We have here a situation where exclusion *should* but *cannot* be applied. [13]

The stage is thus set for public intervention to ameliorate the problem of cross-town traffic tie-ups, though the proper form of that intervention is yet to be discovered.

From our point of view, the more interesting cases are those when consumption is *nonrival,* that is, when one person's partaking in consumption benefits in no way reduces the benefits available to another person. As we shall soon see, education produces nonrival consumption, and this is the chief argument for public, as distinct from private, support of educational services.

When consumption is nonrival, exclusion *should not* be applied. Quoting Musgrave again,

> Consider, for instance, the case of a bridge which is not crowded. A's crossing, therefore, will not interfere with B's. Charging a toll would be quite feasible, but so long as the bridge is not crowded, it would be inefficient to do so since it would curtail the use of the bridge. [14]

That is, the marginal cost of an extra car using the bridge is zero. The marginal cost of finding some other crossing, say, a ferry, can be assumed to be positive. Efficiency in the use of resources demands that the bridge be utilized by all comers, at least up to the point that the bridge becomes crowded.

In the case of certain types of services, both conditions apply. That is, exclusion is not feasible and, since consumption is nonrival, undesirable as well. National defense is an example. There is no feasible way to exclude any group of U.S. citizens from the protection against external forces that is offered by the various agencies of the Defense Department. And, since my being protected in no way diminishes the protection offered to you, there is no reason for anyone to seek to exclude any group of citizens from the benefits of protection.

When the exclusion principle cannot or should not be applied, we cannot rely upon voluntary payment to finance the service. Presumably national defense is important to all of us. Yet few of

[13] Ibid., p. 53.
[14] Ibid., pp. 53–54.

us would make a voluntary contribution for defense. We can all perceive that the amount of protection we receive is not measurably affected by the contribution any single one of us would make. Therefore, if I as an individual make no payment, I receive no less defense; thus I have no positive incentive to contribute. Knowing that my neighbor sees things in the same light, I do not expect him to pay, and I certainly would not want to contribute if he does not. And so on. This is known as the *free rider* problem. When the exclusion principle is not applicable, governments, representing all the people, resort to taxation to finance the specific services. We willingly vote to tax ourselves to support services toward which we would not voluntarily contribute, because taxation implies that each of us bears an appropriate share of costs.

Carl Shoup and Group Consumption Goods

A somewhat different analysis of public activity has been presented by Carl Shoup.[15] He draws a distinction between *marketable* goods and *group consumption* goods. The former are those toward which the exclusion principle applies. The latter are those that can be supplied *more cheaply* in a nonincludable form (even, presumably, when the service could be subject to exclusion). He gives the following as an example:

> we may suppose that mosquitoes afflicting a certain group of households can be destroyed by draining pools and swamps, or alternatively by stationing men with sprayers and swatters in and around each of the households that would pay for this service. In this case, the per capita cost of the service is almost certain to be lower under the group consumption, non-marketing technique. . . .[16]

Shoup draws a further distinction, between group consumption and *collective consumption* goods. The general definition is as follows: A collective consumption good is one that, if supplied to one person, can be supplied to additional persons at zero incremental cost.[17] Many collective consumption goods are marketed—theater performances are an example—so the collective consumption quality of a good does not itself establish a case for public intervention.

[15] C. S. Shoup, *Public Finance* (Chicago: Aldine, 1969), chap. 4.
[16] Ibid., p. 67.
[17] Ibid., p. 68.

For group consumption goods, the contrary generally applies; that is, when goods possess the characteristics of group consumption, it is generally preferable to supply them outside the market. Because of the free rider problem, we must expect them to be paid for by a system of taxation.

As a last point, Shoup admitted that some goods are by their nature nonexcludable—the "cannot exclude" category of Musgrave. Shoup states,

> for a few services the physical characteristics of the service are indeed decisive regardless of the level of service, the size of the group, or the area covered, they cannot be distributed by a marketing technique . . . no matter how much one might be willing to spend to put them on this basis. One notable example is exploration of space. . . . Another example is the improved cultural milieu that the community enjoys from the education of the members of that community. This improved milieu is a product distinct from the education itself, and it cannot be rationed or priced in a manner to exclude any particular individual in the group.[18]

Social Benefits of Public Education

It should now be clear that the chief economic justification for public support for elementary and secondary schools is that the schools yield nonexcludable goods, commonly called *social benefits*, or *externalities*. What, then, are the social benefits of education?

Education is a branch of the "knowledge industry." As defined by Fritz Machlup of Princeton, "knowledge is anything that is known by somebody," and the "production of knowledge" is "any activity by which someone learns of something he has not known before even if others have."[19] Clearly, schools are the major instrument for passing knowledge from one generation to the next and, hence, comprise an activity within the knowledge industry.

The knowledge industry—and specifically the schools—contributes to political democracy. "In a free society, education helps to develop greater awareness of, and ability to participate effectively

---

[18] Ibid., p. 72.
[19] Fritz Machlup, *The Production and Distribution of Knowledge in the United States* (Princeton, N.J.: Princeton, 1962), p. 7.

in, the democratic process."[20] This point can be documented by studying, for example, the relationship between voter participation and level of education. Further, as Shoup noted, educated people find it good to live in a society in which they can share insights with other educated people and engage others in discussions to challenge their ideas, etc. Education supports the development of the arts, and this offers a contribution to the aesthetic environment. These are important, possibly overriding, social benefits of school services.

There are other likely types of social benefits. Simple comparative observation among the nations of the world suggests an association between a country's willingness and ability to support education and the state of its technology. (In old-fashioned terms, we might say that education promotes inventiveness in the population.)[21] Moreover, in Chapter 2 we noted that the sorting, or talent identification, function of educational systems provides benefits to all. In general, social benefits associated with elementary and secondary education are described as habits of orderliness, punctuality, willingness to accept hierarchical relationships in the workplace—in general, "good citizenship." At higher levels of education, inventiveness, initiative, and related habits of mind constitute the main social benefits. Thus, social benefits are different at different levels of schooling, as we noted in Chapter 4.

The reader may be curious about why there has been no comment about the contribution education makes to the quality of the labor force and, hence, to national economic growth—the subject of Chapter 3. The reason is that most such benefits are claimed by members of the labor force themselves and thus represent "private" benefits of schools. That is, when people use their education to obtain a better job than they otherwise might have, they are the primary beneficiaries of that education.[22] The social benefits, on the other hand, are broadly diffused and largely nonquantifiable.

---

[20] Burton Weisbrod, "Investing in Human Capital," *Journal of Human Resources*, 1, no. 3 (Summer 1966): 16.

[21] As the great English economist Alfred Marshall wrote, "the economic value of one great industrial genius is sufficient to cover the expenses of education of a whole town, for one new idea, such as Bessemer's chief invention, adds so much to England's productive power as the labour of a hundred thousand men." (*Principles of Economics* [London: Macmillan, 1920], p. 216.)

[22] There are, however, particular groups that receive benefits from GNP growth. If one is unemployed or handicapped, it is probably better to live in a rich country like the United States than in a poor one like India. One's absolute standard of living is likely to be higher, anyway.

However, in its basic nature, education is plainly subject to the exclusion principle. That is, it is perfectly feasible to charge fees for school attendance; it is perfectly feasible to rely entirely or mainly on the private sector to provide education services. In Indonesia, parents are charged fees to enroll their children in government primary schools. Until the latter part of the nineteenth century, England relied primarily on the private sector to provide educational services. Such practices are not unknown.

In the United States, we assume that the social benefits of education are significant and that, if parents are left on their own to pay for the education of their children, the flow of educational services so purchased will be too small to provide the necessary standard of those social benefits that schooling yields. Hence, we have established a system of elementary and secondary education supported by taxation and free of parental or student fees. So far, neither of these basic propositions to defend public support can be grounded on convincing empirical evidence.

Consumer Satisfaction in the Public Sector

We have seen that households are free to maximize their satisfactions in the private sector. This is not to say that all households are equally happy or that some might not feel a desperate need for higher incomes. It does say, however, that any given household is free to distribute its disposable income among the various goods and services laid before it in the marketplace in such a way as to *maximize its satisfaction* from whatever amount of purchasing power it has. This was the subject of the first half of this chapter.

In the public sector, households are not generally able to maximize their satisfactions. The argument is intuitively straightforward. Consider a school district comprising 1,000 families, of which 500 have school-age children. It is reasonable to suppose that the families with children will, on the average, place a different valuation on the school services offered by the district than will families without children. The latter group will likely prefer smaller school budgets, and the former group, larger ones. Families with children receive both private and social benefits from education; those without receive only the social. It is also eminently reasonable to suppose that the 500 families with school-age children will display differences in tastes about education. Some will think education very important; others will feel that their children will make out about the same regardless of how much money the school district spends on them. Yet, there will finally be only one level of school budget. Obviously, when there are differences in tastes and only one level of school budget, some households will be dissatisfied.

Imagine, instead, that education were to be put in the private sector. Those families without children would not be required to contribute. Families that gave education a high priority of expenditure would presumably be able to find expensive schools in which to enroll their children, and conversely for families that ranked education low. At their given levels of income, families would be better able to maximize satisfactions, now including education within their private budgetary decisions.

It is intuitively clear that the public school budget actually chosen will most likely be a middle ground. Those families who want high expenditures are likely to be in a minority, and similarly for those who want very low. Neither group is likely to poll a majority of votes for their spending proposals. In the typical case, only a middle budget will gain a majority of votes.

When several functions are to be controlled by one vote, the problem of attaining a reasonable degree of satisfaction in the public sector is compounded. Consider, with respect to national policy, a family that has the following three preferences: low defense budget, high environmental protection, and a major federal role in financing education. Suppose it is voting for a U.S. senator. Of two candidates, one may be against defense, for environment, and against a federal role in education. The other may be for defense, against environment, and for federal involvement in education. One vote covers all, so there is no way the family can vote to allocate public resources in accordance with its full set of preferences.

Technical Note on the Consumer in the Public Sector

We have suggested that public-sector operation produces irreconcilable differences in fitting resource uses to the tastes of different households. This can be described in a diagram, as shown in Figure 5.5. Consider the two households, *A* and *B*, as they decide how to distribute their incomes between private goods (vertical axis) and public goods (the two horizontal axes). [23] Point *D*, which is halfway between points A and B, indicates that the income of the two households is

[23] M. C. McGuire and H. Aaron, "Efficiency and Equity in the Optimal Supply of a Public Good," *Review of Economics and Statistics*, 51, no. 1 (February 1969): 31–39.

Figure 5.5
Divergent preferences in the public sector

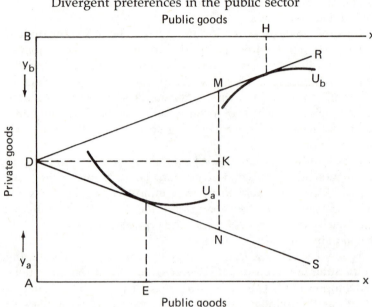

Source: Adapted from M. C. McGuire and H. Aaron, "Efficiency and Equity in the Optimal Supply of a Public Good," *Review of Economics and Statistics,* 51, no. 1 (February 1969): 32. Reprinted with permission of North-Holland Publishing Company, Amsterdam.

equal. If *A* spends all its income in the private sector, it will have *AD* goods; if *B* does the same, it will have *BD*. The two lines *DR* and *DS* show the amounts of private goods that must be sacrificed to obtain additional amounts of public goods. We might think of *DR* and *DS* as tax lines. The two indifference curves, U_a and U_b, reveal preferences in the two households for a mix of private and public goods. *A* prefers relatively few public goods and would be happiest with an amount of public goods equal to *AE*. Household *B* is more inclined toward the public sector and prefers an amount equal to *BH*. If there is only one level of public provision, imagine it to be *DK*, then clearly neither household is fully satisfied.

Just how many public goods are to be provided would presumably be determined by a process of bargaining. We can bracket the amount, however. It will not be greater than *BH*, for not even *B*, the big public spender, wants more. It will not be less than *AE*, for not even *A*, the economy-minded voter, wants less.[24]

[24] Figure 5.5 can be manipulated in interesting ways. Changing the height of point *D* changes the distribution of income between the two parties. Pointing the cone formed

Local Government and Choice in the Public Sector

Is there nothing to be done to improve the fit between households' tastes and the provision of public services? Charles M. Tiebout advanced a set of theoretical ideas to suggest that the answer is affirmative.[25] At the same time, he established the main argument in economic theory for the existence of local government.

The basic ideas are these:

1. Local governments offer households arrays of public services that are significantly different in type and quality.
2. Households are thus able to "vote with their feet" and pick the locality that most closely conforms, in its provision of services, to their particular preference patterns.
3. Hence, choice of residence becomes equivalent to consumers' making decisions in a supermarket among private goods that compete for their pocketbook.

In Tiebout's words:

> Consider . . . the case of the city resident about to move to the suburbs. What variables will influence his choice of a municipality? If he has children, a high level of expenditure on schools may be important. Another person may prefer a community with a municipal golf course. . . . The consumer-voter may be viewed as picking that community which best satisfied his preference pattern for public goods. This is a major difference between central and local provision of public goods. . . . The greater the number of communities and the greater the variance among them, the closer the consumer will come to fully realizing his preference position.[26]

In the next chapter we will examine in much greater detail the question of households' choice in education. We will consider the

---

by the lines *DR* and *DS* upward or downward shifts the relative costs of government between the two parties. Compressing the cone, that is bringing the lines *DR* and *DS* closer together, indicates a reduction in unit cost of public goods, or, to put it another way, higher productivity in the public sector.

[25] C. M. Tiebout, "A Pure Theory of Local Expenditures," *Journal of Political Economy*, 64, no. 5 (October 1956): 416–417.

[26] Ibid., p. 418.

strengths and weaknesses of the Tiebout position. We will also note recent proposals, such as education vouchers, designed to improve upon the Tiebout position.

Summary

We assume that, in the United States, individual households exercise a degree of control over allocations of resources. In the private sector, households give signals to suppliers of goods and services that reveal their preferences. These signals are the households' responses to offers of suppliers, whether to buy or not to buy at the preferred prices. Households maximize satisfactions by so adjusting their budgets that last dollars spent on any one item afford equal satisfactions to those gained from last dollars spent on other items. Purchasing patterns shift in response to changes in price, household income, and tastes. We may reasonably say that education plays a major part in forming tastes.

In the public sector, households influence resource allocations by the voting process and, in the case of local government, by moving residence. However, compared with the private sector, allocations of public resources are difficult to fit to the preferences of individual households. How to improve the process of resource allocation in the public sector is the general subject of the next three chapters.

Selected Bibliography

Baumol, William J. *Economic Theory and Operations Analysis.* 4th ed. Englewood Cliffs, N.J.: Prentice-Hall, 1977.

Becker, Gary S. *The Economic Approach to Human Behavior.* Chicago: University of Chicago Press, 1976.

Burkhead, Jesse, and Jerry Miner. *Public Expenditure.* Chicago: Aldine-Atherton, 1971.

Gwartney, James D. *Economics: Private and Public Choice.* New York: Academic, 1977.

Shoup, Carl S. *Public Finance.* Chicago: Aldine, 1969.

Singer, Neil M. *Public Micro-economics.* Boston: Little, Brown, 1976.

Chapter Six

Household Choice and Distributing Educational Resources

At the end of Chapter 5 we discussed the idea that political decentralization, that is, the delegation of decision-making powers to local governments, is a means of maximizing satisfactions of households. To put the point more accurately, it could be viewed as such a means if certain conditions are met. Before we examine the particulars of the case for "voting with one's feet," let us place the issue of centralization versus decentralization in a broader context, namely, the provision of educational services.

Centralization Versus Decentralization in the Public Sector

The first thing to note is that we have a mixed system of educational finance and control in the United States. Though substantial powers are held at the local level—enough to allow school districts to afford parents' choices in Tiebout's sense (which we discuss later in this chapter)—it is also true that state and federal governments pay part of the bill for services that are administered by local authorities. (In 1975–76 the local authorities provided 48.3 percent of revenue receipts, the state governments 43.7, and the federal 8.0 percent.) Furthermore, state and federal governments apply pressure to influence administrative decisions of local authorities. This raises the question of *why* we have a mixed system. Why not, for instance, turn over completely such services as education to local finance and control? There would seem to be a number of reasons for not doing so.

1. Services like education offer benefits that spill over from one geographical area to the next. Under complete decentralization some local authorities will be better situated to finance and administer educational programs than others. Inadequate programs in laggard authorities may represent a loss of welfare in the nation as a whole. For example, the welfare of any nation is affected by its success, as we noted earlier, in identifying and nurturing highly talented members of the rising generations. If half the young people of a country are poorly served by local educational authorities, we may be reasonably sure that about half the potentially high-grade scientists, business managers, political leaders, and poets will never have as good a chance as they should to offer their talents to the nation.

But why should decentralization lead to major inadequacies in educational programs? In theory, it need not. If all local authorities are of sufficient size to exploit economies of scale,[1] if they are all enlightened about the nature of educational production functions (if they know, that is, how to spend their resources in such a way as to maximize production of desired educational outcomes), if they all have adequate financial resources relative to the prices they must pay for educational inputs (inputs such as teachers, materials of instruction, etc.), and if they all are willing to direct and maintain effective educational programs, then a decentralized system could conceivably maximize net present value of educational outcomes.

In the real world, however, those conditions are seldom met. Many local authorities are too small to receive the economies of scale offered by properly sized secondary schools and properly sized programs for diagnosis and treatment of the physically handicapped. Knowledge of educational production functions is poorly developed

---

[1] *Economies of scale* exist in industry when costly but highly specialized techniques or machinery are employed that are exceedingly productive, with the result that unit costs fall as output reaches high levels in any given firm. Smaller firms, not using the costly, high-output processes, have higher unit costs and are likely to fail. This leads to the *natural monopoly* argument to defend exclusive franchises given to utility companies. One telephone company can serve a given geographic area more cheaply than 100 companies can because duplication of telephone lines (and of telephones in the home) is avoided. In education it is hard to discover economies of scale in elementary education, once enrollment is equal to an acceptable class size in each grade level (six grades, say, times 25 students = 150 students). At the high school level, however, the costs per student of offering specialized courses drop substantially as enrollment in a particular high school increases—a case of economies of scale in secondary education. For discussion of economies of scale in general, see Richard S. Eckaus, *Basic Economics* (Boston: Little, Brown, 1972), pp. 469–475.

(see Chapter 7), but what knowledge is available is shared between any given local authority and the central educational institutions. Local authorities ordinarily differ with respect to both taxable wealth and the prices they face in the marketplace for educational resources. Indeed, poverty and high prices are sometimes positively correlated, creating an unfortunate situation. For example, rural communities may be unable to raise money for paying teachers because households in the area are too poor; at the same time, qualified teachers may be unwilling to work in such towns at the same wage rate they would accept in the suburban ring of the metropolis. To be willing to teach low-income rural youth, that is, teachers may demand "hardship" increment in salary.

What can we say, finally, about the willingness of local authorities to direct and maintain high-grade educational programs? Certain progressive ones may express such willingness, but we cannot count on all to do so, even if limiting financial resources was no particular problem. As we noted, benefits of education may spread from the local authority over the whole nation. This can readily be seen when superior graduates of a rural school system leave home to work in metropolitan areas. Some part of their contribution to the life of the nation may return to their rural counterparts. But no greater benefit will be received, on the average, by the people who live in their (former) home town than by rural people generally. Yet, the cost of providing superior education must, under a completely decentralized system, be borne wholly in the locality. Because benefits are likely to be spread widely in the geographic sense and because costs are likely to be geographically concentrated, to offer superior educational services is not necessarily a good bargain for the residents of a given community. Hence, decentralization may result in a general, widespread underfinancing of education, relative to its marginal benefit-cost ratio with respect to national development.

2. Complete decentralization of education may be inconsistent with the national policy for income redistribution. Admitting that determining who really pays tax of a given type—that is, assessing *tax incidence*—is an unsettled and controversial matter in economics, it is reasonably certain that taxes employed by central and state government fall less severely on poor households than do taxes levied by local governments.[2]

---

[2] It is not contended that poor households in any case would have higher tax bills, as measured in dollars, than rich ones. To anticipate some of the discussion in Chapter 9, what is important is the size of tax bill relative to household income. A levy is *progressive* if richer households are required to pay a higher proportion of their income in tax than are poor households. A tax is *regressive* if poor households are taxed at a

More importantly, decentralization reduces, when it does not absolutely forestall, the capacity of central and state governments to shift resources from richer geographic areas to poorer ones. There are short-run and long-run consequences. Educational systems, as we saw at the beginning of Chapter 2, are major employers of labor power. If a government shifted from a completely decentralized system of educational finance to a completely centralized one, the consequences are likely to be that the number of teachers employed in poor districts would rise and the average level of pay of all teachers in those districts would go up. This is a short-run effect; and because of the magnitude of educational employment, it is not to be ignored. The long-run effect is to be found in the following process: As educational resources are redistributed from rich regions to poorer ones, the life chances of children in the poorer places should improve so that they are able to enter higher paying and higher status occupations than otherwise. Social mobility is the long-run aspect of the shift of resources that might occur in moving from complete decentralization to complete centralization.[3]

3. Decentralized control implies that the power of central and state governments to exercise political control of instructional processes is checked. This may be regarded as an advantage in that it reduces the possibility that a dictatorial central government might use the educational system for purposes of political indoctrination. But local governments can also be nefarious. We shall see in a later section that localism is substantially synonymous with the clustering of households by social class. It is thus not beyond imagining that some communities exist in which there is substantial consensus on social issues. This could conceivably result in oppression of minorities on, say, racist grounds. Federal and state governments in our country today are reasonably effective in preventing overt kinds of racist behavior by local boards.

---

higher percentage of income than the rich. In general, the types of taxes used by central and state governments are more likely to be progressive than the kinds used by local governments. This is only one side of the matter. The distribution of public-sector benefits may be progressive or regressive, depending on whether poor households or rich are the primary receivers. See Carl A. Shoup, *Public Finance* (Chicago: Aldine, 1969), pp. 23–37.

[3] This statement is made despite the findings in recent literature, for example, the *Coleman Report,* which might be interpreted to mean that shifts in educational resources are relatively powerless to affect the life chances of children. The question of the effects of educational expenditures is explored in Chapter 7.

4. The economic efficiency of the educational system is heightened when schools and colleges channel students into those particular career lines that are most likely to offer employment opportunities in the future. Thus, the educational system should function to protect the country against the twin problems of educational unemployment, on the one hand, and critical bottlenecks in the supply of skilled labor power, on the other. Partly to recognize this necessity, institutions of higher education are seldom placed under the control of small local governments; to regulate the number of student places in college on the basis of labor power planning requires that educational authorities be able to forecast future labor power needs and enforce the results of such analysis on students and faculty. Complete localism is not amenable to such tasks. In the first place, local authorities lack the analytical tools to make labor power forecasts and to provide them with those tools would represent wasteful duplication. In the second, with respect to control of numbers of student places, progressive and effective local authorities would see their labors and sacrifices undercut by careless and weak authorities, and the pressure on progressive authorities to abandon attempts at control would become undeniable. Though this reason for intervention by federal and state authorities in policies of educational institutions applies mainly at the college and university level, it has relevance for local school authorities in terms of their activities in the field of vocational guidance.

Those, then, are some reasons why we may prefer to avoid complete decentralization of control and finance of education. May we, thus, conclude that complete centralization is the appropriate policy? There are arguments against taking such a step, and in some cases the arguments against complete centralization look surprisingly like those advanced against complete decentralization.

1. Centralization does not abolish the need for regional and local administrators: It simply restricts their power to control more than the smallest details of day-to-day operations. All major decisions must be referred to a central point for discussion and resolution. When a service must be distributed very widely—and education is such a service—but when all effective power is retained at the center, two unfortunate results are likely to follow: Decisions will be made slowly, sometimes so slowly that answers to yesterday's problems, when applied to today's conditions, only serve to compound today's difficulties; and knowledge of local conditions, needs, and resources, which any alert local administrator possesses in generous measure, will be little utilized. Central administrators, lacking such detailed

knowledge, will be reluctant to promulgate orders that establish new departures in one area, no matter how appropriate, for fear that other areas will demand similar or related changes—or protest if the first area's changes are imposed on them by fiat. Consequently, for the central administrators, the future becomes hard to predict and the safer course is to maintain the status quo.[4]

2. But the difficulties go beyond institutional rigidities. Knowledge about the educational needs and interests of different types of students is limited and so is knowledge about the technological requirements to meet those interests and needs. It is hard to say what types of teaching behavior best suit a given student or how much time the student should spend in pursuing different types of instruction or what sorts of materials are best for the student to have, given whatever incentives the particular student has to learn. This limited knowledge is common to both central and local administrators; but the point is that complete centralization might serve to make educational development—the improvement, that is, of the functioning of the service—dependent on a rather static stock of knowledge not built up and renewed by findings from locally initiated experiments. Complete centralization might not be conducive to local innovation and experimentation. Given the distressingly inadequate lack of knowledge for making decisions about educational resource allocations, local actions in trying out ideas is very much to be desired.

3. Knowledge is also deficient for making close judgments about the quality of educational resources, most particularly for assessing teacher competence.[5] Unless close judgments can be made about the quality of educational resources, it is difficult if not impossible to measure differences in supply-price schedules of school inputs in different local areas. Under complete centralization, this problem could rebound to the disadvantage of children who attend school in big cities and thus to the loss of the majority of low-income children in the country. Why? Complete centralization implies that

[4] For a discussion of information flows under decentralized control, see Manfred Kochen and Karl W. Deutsch, "Toward a Rational Theory of Decentralization: Some Implications of a Mathematical Approach," *American Political Science Review*, 63, no. 3 (September 1969): 734–749; and Frank Levy and Edwin M. Truman, "Toward a Rational Theory of Decentralization: Another View," *American Political Science Review*, 65, no. 1 (March 1971): 172–179.

[5] The difficulties of constructing teacher cost indices are described in W. Norton Grubb, "Identifying Teacher Supply Functions and Constructing Cost Indices: Methodological Explorations with California Unified School Districts," Childhood and Government Project, University of California at Berkeley, 1976.

the central authority determines teacher salary schedules for use in the various geographic areas in its charge. For example, suppose we say that the government of the State of New York takes complete control of public education K–12 in that state. The state government would then determine what salaries would be earned by teachers who work in different places in the state. Quite probably the state would establish a salary differential for New York City teachers (in excess of salaries paid to teachers who work in the suburbs) to reflect the assumed extra difficulties of teaching in city schools. But the differential might be inadequate to attract to the city teachers of competence equal to those who apply for jobs in the suburbs.[6] However, in the absence of reliable measures of teacher competence, it is impossible to know how badly the city is being deprived, if it is, and how much money is needed to rectify the situation. In the meantime, the suburban teachers would contend that the New York City differential reflected only historical standards of pay, which had been determined as a bad political bargain between city officials and the teachers' union.

4. Some degree of local autonomy in education is consistent with maintaining those types of political freedom we enjoy in the United States. Although we might wish to see a central authority intervene in the affairs of local school districts when the rights of minorities are offended, we might be equally reluctant to see local authorities deprived of all rights to determine the values imbedded in the curriculum and in the instructional processes. This would simply open the door too wide for the indoctrination of the young toward a single ideology, such ideology being under the absolute control of the standing government.

5. Complete centralization of finance and control at the state or federal level could result in a reduced flow of revenues for schools. This is not a prospect that educational interest groups can enjoy. And, at first look, this concern may appear inconsistent with what we have said about the financial consequences of complete decentralization, namely, that some school districts would spend too little on their services to maximize the net present value of their contributions to society. Actually, there is no contradiction. Under decentralization *some* school districts may spend too little and some, *demonstration effects* aside, may spend too much. The demonstration effects, however, can be important in pushing the overall level of

---

[6] Of course, it could turn out that the city receives too generous a differential; we have simply chosen what we see as the more likely possibility.

spending ahead.[7] The idea is that progressive, wealthy districts, free to choose their levels of expenditure, *demonstrate* to the rest of the educational community the characteristics of superior education and create a demand for such superior programs on the part of the ordinarily endowed school district. Another way to put it is that decentralization fosters competition among school districts to put up programs as good or better than are known to exist in neighboring areas. The result of the competition is likely to increase the rate of advance in educational spending over what it would be in the total absence of such competition. Complete centralization implies that interdistrict competition to offer superior educational programs is restricted to finding better ways to spend a given budget, and competition can no longer be directed to raise the size of the budget of the individual district.[8]

What it comes to is that neither complete centralization nor decentralization appears appropriate as a guiding principle in United States education. Local authorities require substantial powers to establish curricular values, in part as an ultimate check to the development of a totalitarian state. At the same time, federal and state

[7] For discussion of the operation of the demonstration effect on household budgets, see James S. Duesenberry, *Income, Saving and the Theory of Consumer Behavior* (Cambridge, Mass.: Harvard, 1949), pp. 26–27, 105. Also see Seymour Sacks, *City Schools/Suburban Schools: A History of Fiscal Conflict* (Syracuse, N.Y.: Syracuse University Press, 1972).

[8] That the operation of the local government stimulates educational spending has been observed in Nepal, a culture very different from our own. A Nepalese ministry of education report states: "Some evidence on the relationship between localism and financial support is available. . . . Formerly, Nepalese schools were administered by local committees. At the beginning each local committee would be self-appointed and would establish a single school. Rather quickly a new local committee would apply for government grant, but as late as 1970, 60 percent of education revenues were locally raised. Around the year 1970 an educational reform began to be implemented under which administrative powers were to be held by district [regional] committees, with members appointed by central government officials. The proportion of local funds in total education support has now begun to fall. . . . Local resentment over the shifts in financial authority from the village to the district level was . . . presumed to play a role in the declining willingness of people to support education. This did . . . turn out to be a very significant factor. When asked in a . . . questionnaire to explain the decrease in local support, by far the largest number of questionnaire respondents . . . identified the 'centralization' of educational authority as the single most important factor. . . . In interviews as well, it was clear that distrust of the new mechanism of financial decision-making was widespread. Villagers were not enthusiastic about raising money over which they had no control. . . . This sense of loss of control . . . was accentuated by the fact that the District Education Committee was seen as a body made up largely of appointees of central government officials" (*Local Contribution to Education* [Kathmandu, Nepal: Ministry of Education, 1974], p. 26.

authorities should intervene if local values stray too far from our democratic and pluralistic ideals. If geographic or other conditions indicate the need for small school districts, they should exist; but state and federal authorities should try to see that students are not adversely affected by programmatic shortcomings. (Possibly regionalizing those services subject to economies of scale is the appropriate solution in this case.) Local authorities should have sufficient autonomy in designing programs to encourage experimentation and new ideas, but federal and state authorities should finance educational research and analyze and publish the research results. In other words, local, state, and federal agencies should all seek new knowledge and share it when it is found. Local authorities might continue to hold revenue-raising powers, but state and federal government should continue to distribute grants, particularly to poorer districts and to those in which student achievement is low. Such a system is not tidy, but it is what has evolved in the United States and apparently for good reason. We can certainly expect, however, to witness conflicting drives toward greater decentralization and toward tighter centralization over a long period.

In the meantime, we can be assured that households will have opportunities to express some degree of choice in the field of education. Our task is to explore the nature of choice mechanisms, what is to be said for them, how they operate, how new mechanisms might be expected to operate.

The Tiebout Arguments

At the end of Chapter 5 we observed that the existence of local government units, assigned responsibility to provide certain social services, allows households to make choices about the type and quality of the services they prefer. They make the choice simply by finding that community in the area that offers the most closely approximate pattern of preferred social services and settling down there. Some households may prefer academic schools and some vocational; some families may be relatively indifferent toward schools for their children but be interested in extensive community recreation programs; some families may display great concern for protective services and the privacy that goes with them. Whatever the preferences, some communities will come closer to satisfying certain households than other communities, as long as all communities are not ordered by a central authority to provide exactly the same types and qualities of social services.

Private markets assume differences in tastes among households and, within certain limits, private entrepreneurs seek to cater to those differences in taste. Economists conclude that such activity on the part of private entrepreneurs raises the level of human satisfaction. If I like Trollope and you like Tolstoy, we are both happier if we can find our favorite authors in the bookstore than if one central publisher decides the only novels published this month are those by Dickens. Charles M. Tiebout, in his classic article of 1956,[9] extended this idea to the public sector. Under centralized delivery of social services, what we get is what the central government decides to offer. And we, as citizens, would have little recourse should we want a different pattern of services, except to vote for a new package. But in Chapter 5 we saw that decisions reached by voting are likely to be those least offensive to the typical voter. Persons who have strong feelings—positive or negative—toward some particular public program are not likely to be well satisfied: They will find themselves provided with either too little of it or too much.

According to Tiebout, things operate differently when service responsibilities are assigned to local governments:

> The consumer-voter may be viewed as picking that community which best satisfies his preference pattern for public goods. This is a major difference between central and local provision of public goods. . . . The greater the number of communities and the greater the variance among them, the closer the consumer will come to fully realizing his preference position.[10]

The essence of the argument has been restated by James M. Buchanan and Charles J. Goetz as follows:

> Tiebout tried to demonstrate that so long as local government units are appropriately assigned the tasks of providing certain public goods and services and so long as individuals retain freedom of personal migration among jurisdictions, there are efficiency-generating processes at work, despite the "publicness" of the goods provided.[11]

[9] Charles M. Tiebout, "A Pure Theory of Local Expenditures," *Journal of Political Economy*, 64, no. 5 (October 1956): 416–424.

[10] Ibid., p. 418.

[11] James M. Buchanan and Charles J. Goetz, "Efficiency Limits of Fiscal Mobility: An Assessment of the Tiebout Model," *Journal of Public Economics*, 1, no. 1 (1972): 25–26.

What does Tiebout's argument imply about the distribution of educational services among households? In the first place, it clearly means that types and quality of educational services will be different, one group of students compared with another. Tiebout asserted that his model for satisfying household preferences in the public sector is more effective "as the number of communities" in a given commuting area is larger and the "variance" in service levels among them is greater. To make matters simpler, let's say that we divide schools into categories by quality, such that some are classified as superior, some ordinary, and some inferior (the actual gradations, presumably, would be much finer than this). The question to raise about Tiebout's model and, finally, about our system of local government that the model defends, is this: How is it decided which children are to attend the superior, the ordinary, and the inferior schools. Given that not all children at the same time can attend the best schools, how are places in the best schools *rationed?* The answer given by Tiebout is that, as nearly as it can be practically done, the rationing process should imitate the rationing process of the private market economy, in order to maximize household satisfactions.

Rationing occurs in the private economy through the operation of the *pricing system.* Suppose two services, education and recreation, are supplied wholly in the private market. Imagine that household *A* has extreme preference for education and low regard for recreation, while household *B* has just the opposite tastes. At a given moment, suppose household *A* is consuming low-grade educational and high-grade recreational services and that household *B* has much educational and little recreational services. Obviously, things are out of kilter, and the two services are improperly rationed between the two households. Indeed, we may say that *A*'s consumption of recreation is wasteful because the family is using high-grade services for which it actually has low regard; similarly, *B*'s consumption of education is wasteful. As we saw in the last chapter, the satisfactions, or welfare, of both families can be improved if family *A* will shift its dollar from recreation to education, thereby releasing superior recreational services for the use of family *B*, that treasures them highly. If *B* would shift spending from education to recreation, it would release the superior school services to use of families like *A*. Under Tiebout's argument, when education and recreation are provided, not in private markets, but in the local public sector, the same process described above occurs when family *A* moves from a community that stresses recreation in its package of services to one that emphasizes education and as family *B* moves in the opposite direction. *A* would release its command of superior recreational services to families like *B* and, in exchange, acquire access to the better schools being released from the use of families like *B*. If differences in tastes are complex, then it is intuitively clear that the process of fitting services to tastes works best, as Tiebout said, when there are a multiplicity of local governments within a given commuting area and when there is substantial variance in service standards among them.

But it does mean, finally, that some children are offered better school services and some worse. This may seem incongruent with the ideal of equal educational opportunity, but we surely must accept that there are going to be different standards among schools and teachers: Not every child is going to have educational services that fit his or her needs ideally. Given this, we return to the main question: Does household choice in the local public-sector reinforce or diminish the prospects of getting as close as we can to the ideal of equal educational opportunity?

The argument of the last chapter informs us that we can predict reasonably well the expenditure decisions of a household if we know their *tastes* (establishing price and cross-elasticities of demand for particular articles of consumption) and *income* (establishing income elasticities of demand).

Exercise of Household Choice with Respect to Tastes

The Tiebout argument establishes the conclusion that households will cluster in accordance with their preferences for local government services. Since it is the adult members of households who typically make choices about residential locations, we would expect parents who hold education in high regard to move to those geographic zones in which school services are reported to be good. Initially, we may imagine that this sorting-out process has nothing to do with household income, just parents' estimation of the importance of good education to their children. We may also assume, for the sake of the argument, that parents' tastes for the education of their children has no relationship to their own levels of schooling. The Tiebout rationing procedure would, even in this case, assure the following result: Children whose parents had strong drives toward education would be grouped together in certain schools, and children whose parents were relatively indifferent toward education would be situated in other schools.

That is the logical consequence of household choice in the field of local public services. Whether such classification of children by parental tastes for education impedes, facilitates, or is neutral with respect to equalizing educational opportunity is not known. However, when parents who are keen to see their children receive a good education manage to locate themselves in a reportedly good school district, the children of such parents are likely to receive educational reinforcement in the home to match the extra stimulus provided by teachers in the superior school districts. Government action might thus be seen to strengthen the school prospects of the child who has educational advantages in his home rather than to compensate for the lack of such advantages on the part of other children.

So far we have been arguing as if the only differences in education that matter to parents are generalized differences in quality. This is not necessarily the case. Some parents may seek schools that emphasize basics and close classroom discipline; others may wish to enroll their children in what are called open schools. Some may seek programs of skill development or schools with a scientific bias, while others may look for schools that emphasize culture and art. Yet others may want a school of a particular ethnic orientation. Insofar as schools can be identified in terms of such characteristics and parents choose residential locations to reflect their preferences, there is no necessary connection between exercise of parents' tastes and the equity of distribution of educational resources. However, we must still say that the process of exercising educational choice is cumbersome. The kind of school that fits a child at one point of time is not necessarily the type the child will need when he or she is older; but should the family have to sell a house, buy another, and move to accommodate itself to such a shift in educational tastes? Likewise, the kinds of schools available in a given attendance zone may fit the needs of some of the children in the family but not necessarily all. Yet, surely the family cannot be expected to establish residence in several different attendance zones to obtain the particular types of educational experiences its different children require.

Exercise of Household Choice under Income Inequality

We have noted that the distribution of income in the United States is quite unequal.[12] When a poor family and a rich family purchase goods and services in the private market, each may well seek to allocate its income such that the last dollars spent in different items

---

[12] See Chapter 2.

afford the same increment of satisfactions—each may be equally careful in budgeting, that is. But it remains true that the rich household can have more of everything.

When we say that the existence of local governments allow households to purchase public services in accordance with their individual preferences, we may be including in the Tiebout analysis that other aspect of the private distribution of goods and services, namely, that the rich are allowed to acquire—even encouraged to acquire—more services than the poor. Certain evidence is consistent with this proposition, as we shall see in later sections. And it follows that, with regard to the distribution of educational resources in the short-run, the structure of local government in its basic design is antithetical to that kind of distribution consonant with achieving equal educational opportunity, namely, making available at least equal amounts of educational resources to poor as well as to rich children.

The visible form of income-based discrimination in the public sector is suburbanization. Particular geographic areas have advantages for residential use: A view, good air, separation from industrial noise and pollution, access to shoreline or large parks are examples of such advantages. The price of land, even from the beginning of development is likely to be high in such places. This expensive land can, in principle, be used either for high-density or low-density housing. However, it is reasonable to expect that rich families will take over some of the attractive land for their estates. Once a set of contiguous estates has been established, it behooves the owners to make sure that they fall within a separate unit of local government.[13]

The reasons are multiple. On the side of local public services, the well-to-do inhabitants are easily able to put up the money for handsome school facilities, libraries, and so on. They are easily able to bid for services of well-trained teachers. And, though they are likely to offer those teachers high salaries, rich communities enter the market for teachers' services with the additional advantage of attractive working conditions: small classes, well-behaved children to teach, a relatively high proportion of academically motivated students, a relatively low proportion of physically and mentally handicapped children, and so on. Once hired, the teachers would be able to spend most of their working time on the serious business of teaching and not on maintaining order; this is of obvious advantage to the parents of the town.

---

[13] In California the rich community of Beverly Hills is completely surrounded by the city of Los Angeles and the rich community of Piedmont is entirely surrounded by the city of Oakland.

Though local public expenditures in well-to-do communities are likely to be high per capita, compared with local expenditures in the state generally, most of the local budget will be devoted to purposes important to the local residents, for example, college-preparatory school programs, summer music camps, cultural and artistic events. The local budget will not be strongly directed toward the kinds of needs many residents of central cities have: protection (police budgets in the suburbs, though they are of considerable size, typically do not represent as large a proportion of total budget as do police budgets in large cities), drug abuse treatment and prevention, compensatory education, health and welfare costs, and the like.

On the financial side, the great amount of taxable wealth per capita allows the local budget in rich communities to be financed at a low local tax rate.[14] This is not to say that per capita local tax *payments* are small—indeed, in such a community they are typically quite large—just that the tax *rate* is low. This has a particular consequence, as we shall see later.

If a low-income household could find a cheap apartment in the town or if it could buy a small piece of land and put a cheaply constructed house on it, it would receive notable benefits: good schools; quiet, safe streets; recreational opportunities; clean air, a low tax rate, and so on. But the older residents would face disadvantages. On the service side, programs might be required to meet the special needs of low-income families; if so, the priorities of the local budget would no longer be closely in tune with the tastes of the high-income households.[15]

---

[14] In 1965, this author wrote, "the thing to realize is that some communities, the rich ones, are able to provide high-quality school programs at quite low tax rates. Beverly Hills [California] has an enviable reputation both for the amount of money it spends on education and also for the wisdom with which the funds are spent. Yet, the 1962–63 budget brochure stated, 'The new tax rate [for Beverly Hills' schools] still is the lowest in the state for a unified school district with an enrollment exceeding 600.' And Beverly Hills' school taxes were 27 percent lower than those of any other authority in Los Angeles County" (*The Cheerful Prospect* [Boston: Houghton Mifflin, 1965], p. 27). It was from arguments such as this that the landmark case of school finance reform, *Serrano* v. *Priest*, was developed. See Chapter 11 for further discussion of this point.

[15] To some extent this problem is solved by state and federal grants of a type that break the connection between size of tax base and tax rate. In this case, for example, if the state had established a district-power-equalizing (DPE) grant-in-aid system, the community should be indifferent about whether the incoming families brought with them a lot of children to educate or whether they chose to live in a cheap house. (See Chapter 11.) However, even under DPE the community would be adversely affected if the incoming children individually were expensive to educate. Also, most municipal services are not subject to the degree of financial equalization that education is; and incremental nonschool costs would fall mainly on the local tax base.

In principle, this problem is not insurmountable. The new residents could possibly be taxed to pay for the extra costs they impose on the community.[16] But here is where the local government financial system imposes a difficulty. In a suburb of great estates, the local tax rate is likely to be low, because even a low rate levied on houses of $500,000 to $1,000,000 will provide ample yield for the local budget. But a low tax rate levied on an apartment house of small flats or a modest single-family house will not produce much revenue. Indeed, the revenue for the local budget generated by the new residents will be less per capita than that paid by the older residents. Not only do the new residents not meet any extra costs they impose on the town, they also do not even pay a pro rata share of the costs of existing programs. On the other hand, it would be unconscionable to adopt a set of differential local tax rates such that the cheaper the house a family lived in, the higher the tax rate for that property.[17]

[16] Buchanan and Goetz ("Efficiency Limits of Fiscal Mobility," p. 30) suggest that equilibrium in household mobility exists when

$$MVP_x^i + (B_x^i - T_x^i) + \left[\frac{\partial(\Sigma B^j)}{\partial N_x} - \frac{\partial(\Sigma T^j)}{\partial N_x} \right]$$

$$= MVP_y^i + (B_y^i - T_y^i) + \left[\frac{\partial(\Sigma B^j)}{\partial N_y} - \frac{\partial(\Sigma T^j)}{\partial N_y} \right],$$

$$i, j = 1, 2, \ldots, M, \qquad i \neq j \tag{1}$$

where x and y refer to pairs of locational alternatives; i and j designate persons (or households); MVP refers to marginal private goods value produced by a location in a given locality (distance to work, charm of the neighborhood, and so on); N represents the number of persons in the community; B stands for the benefits of personal services; and T stands for tax payments. For all residential choices, the individual household would seek

$$MVP_x^i + (B_x^i - T_x^i) = MVP_y^i + (B_y^i - T_y^i) \tag{2}$$

That is, the house search has reached the point where any private market advantage of living in x are exactly compensated by a fiscal surplus in y, that is, excess of public benefits over taxes, or conversely. The bracketed terms in equation (1) indicate the effect, positive or negative, of family i's living in x or y on the older residents of x and y. The individual household ordinarily will not take account of the bracketed terms in making its choice of location. Thus equation (1) extends Tiebout's argument to say that household mobility may be helpful or harmful to the older residents of any given community but will be neutral only accidentally. Accordingly, the analogy Tiebout makes to utility-maximizing expenditures of income in private markets is inherently imperfect—what is good for one household may be bad for the other households in the neighborhood to which the given household enters or from which it leaves.

[17] The assumption that rich households seek to bar the poor from their communities has been stated as follows: "On the importance of keeping out the poor, particularly ethnic minorities, a virtual consensus exists. The poor would bring with them the very problems suburbanites left the city to escape: crowding, increased crime levels, environmental decay, the fear of which has now emerged as a full-blown 'no growth'

We thus see that entry of poor families into a well-to-do community is likely to cause an increase in level of local tax rates. Again, this is not a terrible thing for the rich residents to bear, except for the probability of *tax capitalization*.[18] Local tax rate, and the expected direction of change in tax rate, is a component of house value. A new arrival to a metropolitan area who is rich might see that in town X, houses are attractive, local public services are good, and local tax rates are low. In town Y, assume that houses are similar to those in X, as are services, but that tax rates are high. Other things equal, the new arrival would bid less for a home in Y than in X to avoid assuming larger costs to live in Y than in X with no offsetting advantages. If tax rates in Y had gone up as a consequence of Y's accepting low-income families, then the older residents have received a capital loss. They, and they alone, bear this cost, not the prospective purchaser. Since the capital loss could easily be in the order of $100,000, even rich families cannot face the prospect of any substantial rise in local tax rates with impunity, unless tax rates in all similar communities of the region are increasing in step.

But this latter possibility implies regional control in housing distribution. Until such time as public control of housing distribution is established, it pays rich householders to keep low-income families out of their neighborhoods. In order to be able to do so, it helps to live in a smaller town. In the smaller town, it is more likely that the older residents can control zoning ordinances to see that undeveloped land is not made available for low-income housing. In a smaller town, when a house comes up for sale, it is more likely to be sold to a friend of someone in the neighborhood or to a business acquaintance, thus lessening the possibility that anyone would allow several families to

_____

movement in suburbs across the country" (Kenneth F. Phillips and Michael A. Agelasto, II, "Housing and Central Cities: The Conservation Approach," *Ecology Law Quarterly*, 4, no. 7 [1975]: 821). At the same time, the courts are beginning to press suburban communities to provide suitable land for low- and moderate-income housing. For example, on May 4, 1976, a New Jersey trial court struck down as unconstitutional zoning ordinances of 11 communities in Middlesex County (Urban League of Greater New Brunswick v. Burrough of Carteret, Sup. Ct., Middlesex County, Chan. Div. No. C-4122-73). The complaint was treated by the court as one of economic rather than racial discrimination. Recent judicial decisions involving the low-income housing provisions of the Housing and Community Development Act of 1974 may, in fact, lead many suburbs to reject federal aid in lieu of compliance.
[18] For a discussion of capitalization of differences in school tax rates, see Robert Reischauer and Robert Hartman, *Reform of School Finance* (Washington, D.C.: Brookings, 1974), pp. 51–53.

live in the same house. (The smaller the town, the fewer the houses that come on the market in any period of time, and the more likely is it to arrange a private sale.) Thus, the financial structure of local government and the process by which differences in local tax rates are capitalized lead naturally to preference on the part of rich households for small units of local government.

So far we have considered the case of the very rich, but the pressures toward social-class isolation affect the middle-income family in precisely the same way. The magnitude of possible loss in wealth through tax capitalization would be smaller in the absolute sense, but then the middle-class family has less wealth to lose than the rich. What we are led to expect, then, is a hierarchical pattern of housing by social class, with really poor families being segregated in central cities and in certain low-income towns, often of an industrial type.

The process of creating such a pattern of housing was not inevitable. Through the nineteenth and early twentieth centuries, central cities grew by the process of annexing newly developed areas. Annexation allowed families who had moved to the outskirts of a city, possibly seeking cheap land, to obtain access to the public services of the city. During the 1920s however, annexation slowed down and the process of suburbanization took over. Urban spread apparently reflects the desire of American families, especially those with young children, to live in ground-level, detached housing. Urban spread has been substantially underwritten by the federal government's highway programs and mortgage insurance.[19] However, spread does not necessarily imply suburbanization (nor, alas, would continuation of the process of annexation necessarily have implied the creation of socially mixed neighborhoods). Just why suburbanization took over is not altogether clear, but we can point to three possible explanations:

1.   Beginning in the 1920s, state governments encouraged county and regional authorities to supply public services to independent suburbs (water, sewer, roads, lights, etc.) that previously the neighborhoods would have obtained for themselves by annexation to a city.

2.   The existence of small local governments is consistent with American ideas of pluralism and the participation of residents in community affairs (the New England town meeting ideal).

3.   Suburbanization allows rich and middle-income families to avoid, or to pay a smaller share of, certain social costs, such as

[19] See William Alonso, "Problems, Purposes, and Implicit Policies for a National Strategy of Urbanization," in *U.S. Commission on Population Growth and the American Future: Population Distribution and Policy,* 5 (1972): 631.

protecting central city properties and providing central city residents with at least minimum standards of education, health, food, and housing.[20]

Some Evidence of Social-Class Isolation

We turn from general argument and discussion regarding the matter of social class isolation to evidence. What we present here is a kind of case study. We do not claim that rich and poor families never live side by side nor that conditions in certain parts of the United States are not different from those of others. All the material in this section is intended to convey is that it is possible to find a situation that corresponds closely to what we would predict from the preceding theoretical analysis of residential segregation.

The site of the evidence is California, and we will progress from statewide data (of an earlier vintage) to data on San Francisco and its immediate environs. California would seem to be an interesting state to study for several reasons. First, among the states of the country, it has been settled and developed in rather recent times. Housing development, that is, should not have been as strongly influenced by European ideas of class and caste as the Eastern seaboard. Indeed, California schools traditionally have exerted themselves to ease ethnic labels, at least among the white populations.[21] Second, California is politically progressive, especially around San Francisco; and we might think that blatant attempts to achieve social-class isolation would be distasteful to a majority of the population.

Table 6.1 shows simple correlations among a set of socioeconomic variables of California school districts as of 1960.[22] The

[20] These arguments are developed in Ann R. Markusen, "Class and Urban Social Expenditure: A Local Theory of the State," mimeographed, 1976.
[21] For discussion of this point, see Guy Benveniste and Charles Benson, *From Mass to Universal Education: The Experience of the State of California and Its Relevance to European Education in the Year 2000* (The Hague: Martinus Nijhoff, 1976), chap. 1.
[22] The values in the body of the table indicate a degree of *association* between two variables, not causation. All values fall between zero and 1. The closer to zero is a value, the less the degree of association between the two variables. The value of 1 indicates that the association is perfectly close; in measuring change, the value of one variable could be substituted for the other. For a discussion of correlation techniques, see John C. G. Boat and Edwin B. Cox, *Statistical Analysis for Managerial Decisions* (New York: McGraw-Hill, 1970), chap. 13. The data from the *1960 Census of Population* were prepared for a report of the California Senate Fact Finding Committee on Revenue and Taxation, *State and Local Fiscal Relationships in Public Education in California 1965*, by this author; see especially pp. 41–48.

Table 6.1

Correlation coefficient matrix showing the socioeconomic variables in 392 elementary and unified school districts in California, 1960

Variable		X_1	X_2	X_3	X_4	X_5	X_6	X_7	X_8	X_9
A.D.A. per sq. mile	X_1	1.000	−0.126	−0.170	0.125	0.415	0.396	0.352	0.269	0.435
Percentage employed in professional jobs	X_2		1.000	−0.126	0.299	0.111	0.482	0.405	0.534	0.388
Percentage unemployed	X_3			1.000	−0.455	−0.223	−0.549	−0.569	−0.490	−0.487
Children under 18 living with two parents	X_4				1.000	0.311	0.435	0.345	0.297	0.348
Percentage of housing units owner-occupied	X_5					1.000	0.519	0.340	0.306	0.374
Median income of households	X_6						1.000	0.815	0.827	0.766
Median school years of adults	X_7							1.000	0.804	0.813
Median house value, owner-occupied	X_8								1.000	0.767
Median rent, renter-occupied	X_9									1.000

Source: Bureau of the Census, U.S. Department of Commerce, *1960 Census of Population* (Washington, D.C.: U.S. Government Printing Office, 1962).

sample consisted of all elementary and unified school districts having 300 or more students in the 17 counties included in the U.S. Census Bureau's definition of standard metropolitan statistical areas: In short, the sample consists of California's urban area school districts, excluding the smaller ones. There were 392 such districts.

The correlation coefficient matrix is consistent with residential segregation. For example, household income is highly correlated with education level of adults. That is, if we know that median household income of a school district is high, we have strong reason to expect that the population of the district is, on the average, well educated. Both education and income of households are closely related (separately) to house value and level of rent; house value and level of rent are closely related to each other. In other words, a person of low income, who is probably a person of low education as well, *might* find it hard to find a place he can afford to live in if the average levels of income (and education) in a given community are high.

Table 6.2 is a somewhat similar correlation coefficient matrix, in that several socioeconomic variables are identical with those of Table 6.1. However, the unit of analysis in Table 6.2 is the census tract (a small geographic area containing about 4,000—or fewer—persons) and the date is 1970. Moreover, the geographic locus of Table 6.2 is the San Francisco Bay Area, specifically the cities, towns, and unincorporated places in the counties of San Francisco, San Mateo, Marin, Santa Clara, Alameda, and Contra Costa—the counties that ring the Bay. As we can easily see, the basic relationships of Table 6.1 are repeated in Table 6.2, even though the unit of analysis in Table 6.2 is smaller, even though a 10-year period separates the two tables, and even though Table 6.2 refers to a particular region of the state, not to the state's metropolitan areas generally. Education and income variables are each related to house value and rent level of census tracts; so is type of occupation of head of household ("white collar" in Table 6.2, "professional" in 6.1). In general, for variables of overlap between the two tables, the values of the correlation coefficients are the same in sign and are of roughly similar magnitude.

We have stated that Tables 6.1 and 6.2 are consistent with a pattern of residential segregation by social class, but we do not claim that they provide wholly convincing evidence of it. Indeed, we could say that the tables simply show that people with higher levels of education have higher incomes, on the average—this we already know—and that richer people live in more expensive houses than poorer people—again, this is hardly news. But there is actually more to it. The tables both show that home ownership and income are positively related. Thus, richer people are more likely to own their

Table 6.2
Correlation coefficient matrix showing the
socioeconomic variables by census tracts in the San
Francisco Bay Region, 1970

Variable		X_1	X_2	X_3	X_4	X_5
Percentage white (excluding Spanish surname)	X_1	1.000	0.715	0.199	−0.029	−0.128
Percentage of families with income over $10,000	X_2		1.000	0.064	−0.280	−0.462
Median age	X_3			1.000	0.833	0.395
Percentage of population over age 65	X_4				1.000	0.538
Percentage of population over 18, single	X_5					1.000
Percentage of families with children under 18	X_6					
Percentage of population enrolled in school	X_7					
Median school years of adults	X_8					
Percentage of employed in white-collar jobs	X_9					
Median house value, owner-occupied	X_{10}					
Median rent, renter-occupied	X_{11}					
Percentage of housing units owner-occupied	X_{12}					
Average number of persons per housing unit	X_{13}					

Source: Bureau of Census, U.S. Department of Commerce, *1970 Census of Population* (Washington, D.C.: U.S. Government Printing Office, 1972).

homes and poorer people to rent. Given the difficulties that poor people have establishing credit worthiness, this makes sense. It would theoretically be possible that upper class suburban communities—those in which, inter alia, the values of owner-occupied houses are high—could contain *low-income rental housing* as well. Thus, residential isolation by school district or census tract would be ameliorated. But we see that the evidence points the other way; house values and rents are positively correlated in both tables.

X_6	X_7	X_8	X_9	X_{10}	X_{11}	X_{12}	X_{13}
−0.096	0.060	0.655	0.661	0.500	0.576	0.417	0.041
0.180	0.310	0.628	0.652	0.663	0.800	0.754	0.379
−0.778	−0.669	0.093	0.349	0.209	−0.028	−0.157	−0.666
−0.768	−0.691	−0.108	0.120	−0.047	−0.283	−0.419	−0.726
−0.638	−0.447	0.017	0.107	−0.104	−0.369	−0.710	−0.765
1.000	0.678	−0.093	−0.280	−0.089	0.205	0.464	0.878
	1.000	0.246	0.028	0.162	0.336	0.542	0.730
		1.000	0.824	0.701	0.596	0.333	0.008
			1.000	0.741	0.610	0.239	−0.165
				1.000	0.605	0.322	0.046
					1.000	0.622	0.373
						1.000	0.675
							1.000

Given, however, that Tables 6.1 and 6.2 tell us nothing *in detail* about the distribution of housing values in communities, let us pursue the matter further by referring to the central city of San Francisco and the suburban communities of its two most adjacent counties, San Mateo and Marin.[23] The city (which is also a county) and the two adjacent counties contain a large number of poor

[23] Total families of the three counties in 1970 was 364,136. We are indebted to Gary Hoachlander, Childhood and Government Project, University of California at Berkeley, for assistance in this section of this volume.

families: 25,213 with incomes of $3,000 or less in 1969. These families are the unskilled, the elderly, those headed by a single adult, and the general welfare community. Frequently, one finds that poor families need access to a central city, either during the entire work week (for central cities remain a repository of low-skilled jobs) or periodically (to go to the hospitals and clinics, to attend vocational schools, to visit relatives, and so on). [24] Hence, we can imagine that there is a set of poor families who look to San Francisco for work, service, or support of some kind and who would find it extremely difficult to live beyond the southern border of San Mateo county or beyond the northern border of Marin: Transport costs and transport time so dictate.

Let us then consider the following question: If a family in 1970 had had, at most, $100 a month to spend on rent or if it could, at most, afford a house valued at $20,000, where in the three-county area would it likely be found living? [25] Table 6.3 provides information on this point. There were in the three-county area 56,134 occupied rental units at $100 a month or less. Of these, 48,913, or 87.1 percent, were in San Francisco. Only 7,221, or 12.9 percent, were in the suburbs. There were 23,968 occupied houses valued at $20,000 or less; 11,409 (47.6 percent) in San Francisco and the rest outside. So far, then, we can say that if a family must rent—and most poor people in metropolitan areas do rent—the chances are the poor family would live in the city.

If the family can live in its own home, the chances of a suburban existence improves greatly—over half of the $20,000 and below houses are outside the city. But are the cheaper houses distributed evenly over San Mateo and Marin counties? Not very. Column (5) of Table 6.3 shows that in San Mateo County seven cities— Burlingame, Daly City, East Palo Alto, Menlo Park, Redwood City, San Mateo, and South San Francisco—contained 6,226 of the county's 9,944 low-priced houses (62.6 percent), while all six cities of the county in which median house value exceeded $37,500 included, as a group, only 176 low-priced houses out of a total of 17,199 occupied housing units. Thus, the communities of high house value had only

---

[24] San Francisco stands at the very top of a narrow peninsula separating the Pacific Coast from the waters of the Bay. Immediately to the south of the city is the suburban county of San Mateo and, at some distance below, the county of Santa Clara. Immediately to the north of the city, across the Golden Gate Bridge, is the suburban county of Marin. Marin, San Francisco, and San Mateo counties are the main land areas to enclose the Bay on its western side. We do not deal with East Bay communities and the central city of Oakland.

[25] An annual rent of $1,200 indicates a household income of $4,000, assuming that 30 percent spent on rent is a rough maximum a family can tolerate.

1.0 percent of their housing units in the "occupied homes of $20,000 value or less" category. The corresponding group of communities in Marin had only 88 low-value houses out of a total of 7,400 housing units. Accordingly, even if our hypothetical poor family could own its own home (in the $20,000 or less value range), and even though this improved its chances of living in the suburbs, it still had a very small chance of being in a place where house values—and presumably amenities in general—were of a high standard.

With respect to renting a cheap unit in the suburbs, the small supply of low-rent units was itself substantially confined to certain communities, as column (4) of Table 6.3 shows. The communities of high house value in San Mateo contained only 199 low-rent units and in Marin, 244.

The question about availability of housing to the poor can be put another way: Suppose a poor family moved to the Bay Area for the first time in 1970 and sought shelter. Columns (6) and (7) of Table 6.3 show the situation: Most of the low-rent units that were available were in the central city; some relatively cheap housing for sale was available in the city and outside. But neither purchasable nor rental units were available in the generally high-value communities like Atherton, Hillsborough, Belvedere, and so on.[26]

What we have seen in detail for San Francisco and its environs extends over the whole Bay Area (population 4,174,233 in 1970). There is a statistically significant positive relationship between income level of household and income homogeneity of neighborhood. That is, the richer the families are, the more tightly they cluster together. And at any given income level, families that pay an unusually large proportion of their incomes on housing tend to inhabit communities that are white and, for the given income level, of relatively high social status (as measured by education level and occupation). Those variables count for more in sorting people out than local government service levels or tax rates.[27]

[26] For other references to this topic, see A. Thomas King and Peter Mieszkowski, "Racial Discrimination, Segregation, and the Price of Housing," *Journal of Political Economy*, 81, no. 3 (May-June 1973): 590–606; G. Alan Hickrod and Daniel Jaw-Nan Hou, "Social and Economic Inequalities Among Suburban School Districts: Observations from a Two-Decade Study" (Paper delivered at the annual meeting of the American Educational Research Association, Chicago, Ill., April 1974).

[27] In the United Kingdom there has been a major shift in educational policy, as we noted in Chapter 1. Formerly, students earned entitlement to attend superior secondary schools, called grammar schools, by getting high scores on competitive scholastic examinations. The examinations were given to students at about age 11; they were administered by the local authorities. Since 1965 the general policy has become one of providing secondary education in comprehensive schools, and the "11+" selection

Table 6.3
Distribution of low-income housing, city of San Francisco and adjacent counties

County	Median house value (1)	Number of occupied housing units (2)	Occupied rental units (3)	Occupied rental units at $100 per month or less[a] (4)	Units of owner-occupied houses, $20,000 or less (5)	Units for rent, $120 per month or less (6)	Units for sale at $25,000 or less (7)
San Francisco	$23,780	295,174	198,274	48,913	11,409	4,305	230
San Mateo, total	31,940	185,028	71,180	4,830	9,944	411	253
Low to moderate house values							
Burlingame	36,990	11,263	5,591	451	215	46	0
Daly City	26,980	21,618	8,320	720	1,251	49	29
East Palo Alto	18,375	6,026	3,484	203	1,643	35	58
Menlo Park	34,920	9,812	4,639	271	802	30	38
Redwood City	27,380	20,560	10,425	629	832	74	22
San Mateo	32,280	28,683	13,679	684	703	40	13
So. San Francisco	26,260	14,075	4,643	672	779	35	0
Subtotal		112,037	50,781	3,630	6,225	309	160
High house values							
Atherton	56,060	2,316	176	17	36	0	0

Portola Valley	52,170	1,364	283	14	44	0	0
Woodside	50,775	1,488	242	14	9	0	0
Subtotal		17,199	3,483	199	176	5	0
Marin, total	34,570	67,266	26,427	2,391	2,615	255	77
Low to moderate house values							
Fairfax	26,880	2,915	1,352	119	308	28	0
Novato	29,055	8,280	3,474	129	411	33	4
San Anselmo	29,225	4,651	1,574	207	394	0	25
San Rafael	35,185	13,629	6,380	691	278	81	3
Sausalito	35,385	3,089	1,982	120	46	4	0
Subtotal		32,564	14,762	1,266	1,437	146	32
High house values							
Belvedere	54,960	896	236	8	0	0	0
Larkspur	40,855	3,529	1,803	116	70	9	0
Ross	49,500	814	158	15	8	0	0
Tiburon	47,180	2,162	899	105	10	0	0
Subtotal		7,400	3,096	244	88	9	0
Grand total		547,468	295,881	56,134	23,968	4,971	560

[a] San Mateo County contains 20 recognized communities and Marin, 11. The sample of county places displayed here was chosen in the following way: The first group in San Mateo, Burlingame through South San Francisco, are those containing 200 or more low-rent units (monthly rental $100 or less); the second group, Atherton through Woodside, are those in which average house value was $47,500 or more. In Marin, the same procedure was followed, except that the first group, Fairfax through Sausalito, are communities containing 100 or more low-rental units.
Source: Bureau of the Census, U.S. Department of Commerce, 1970 Census of Population (Washington, D.C.: U.S. Government Printing Office, 1972).

Does Social-Class Isolation Affect Education?

We have established a general argument to explain the phenomenon of social-class isolation in the United States. We have also examined evidence in a major state, California, which supports the theoretical conclusions. The next question, then, is this: Does social-class isolation affect educational processes in our schools, or does it make no difference in the quality of schooling children receive?

The first thing to recognize on this topic is that many poor families are bottled up in central cities and the second, that central city educational authorities have difficulty in coping with the schooling requirements of low-income youth. For one example, in 1971 average 12th-grade reading scores in San Francisco stood at the 32nd percentile in California statewide ranking and in 1975, at the 18th percentile statewide. Third-grade scores in 1971 were at the 21st percentile and 6th-grade scores in 1974 stood at the 13th. Since the 6th graders were presumably mainly the same as the 3rd graders three years earlier, some classes of "San Francisco's students dropped further behind their peers throughout the state the longer they stayed in school."[28]

Insofar as low-income households find it difficult to obtain housing outside the central cities of metropolitan areas, the argument so far suggests that these households are not free to exercise choice in terms of local public services in the sense that Tiebout postulated. The situation is especially painful for those low-income households confined to the central city that want their children to receive high quality education. Such families are virtually forced to enroll their children in schools in which the average level of accomplishment of students in basic learnings is far below that of suburban areas.

---

process has been abolished. In the main, rights to attend a given secondary school are established by location of family residence, that is, under the same system of geographic entitlement used in the United States. This basis for regulating attendance rights has, in turn, led to some clustering of families by social class and educational interests. However, the Scottish educational authorities, traditionally egalitarian, are trying to minimize the effects of residential clustering by readjusting secondary school attendance boundaries from time to time. See "Flitting No Guarantee of Place in School," *The Scotsman*, September 4, 1975, p. 7. The term "flitting" refers to a family changing its residence from one school attendance zone to another.

[28] James W. Guthrie, "The Fiscal Future of the San Francisco Public Schools, Part 3: Expenditure Patterns and Organizational Productivity" (Paper prepared for the San Francisco Public Schools' Commission, University of California at Berkeley, April 1976, p. 19. The figures cited in the above paragraph are from the same source, p. 18.

Low-income parents might wish to have their children placed in predominantly middle-class schools for many reasons—less disruption and violence, access to well-trained and experienced teachers, and so on—but they might also expect that their children's achievement levels would be higher than if they attended "ghetto schools." Otherwise, the attainment of social-class integration in education would be, in the final analysis, an empty gesture. Several thorough studies indicate that achievement levels of low-income youth are higher in an integrated setting than they would otherwise probably be. We will discuss the methods of these kinds of studies in Chapter 7. Here we will discuss the findings of three such reports.

Alan Wilson's report to the U.S. Commission on Civil Rights (1967), based on intensive study of 4,100 students in the Richmond, California, school district, contains the following results:

> Allowing for individual differences in personal background, neighborhood context and mental maturity at the time of school entry, variations in elementary school context make a substantial and significant difference in subsequent academic success at higher grade levels. . . .
>
> The social class composition of a school—indicated by the proportion of students whose parents are unskilled laborers, unemployed, or welfare recipients—affects the academic development of both . . . [black] and white students in either racially-integrated or racially-segregated situations. . . .
>
> Social class segregation of students, through its effect upon the development of academic skills, has ramifying consequences for students' subjective sense of competence and belief that they can plan and control their futures.[29]

Donald R. Winkler, in a major restudy (1975) of the Richmond school situation, using longitudinal data, obtained the following results:

> the coefficient on socio-economic status composition is statistically significant and indicates that reducing the proportion of low SES peers by 10 percentage points would improve student achievement by 3.33 percentile points. The null

---

[29] Alan B. Wilson, "Educational Consequences of Segregation in a California Community," in U.S. Commission on Civil Rights, *Racial Isolation in the Public Schools*, (Washington, D.C.: U.S. Government Printing Office, 1967), II, 202, app. C3.

hypothesis of "no effect" of peer group is rejected for the white sample as well as for the black sample.[30]

Anita A. Summers and Barbara L. Wolfe, in a study (1975) sponsored by the Federal Reserve Bank of Philadelphia, accumulated data in the following manner.

> The exceptional cooperation and data facilities of the Philadelphia School District enabled us to develop a rich data base. Detailed pupil histories, as of 1970–71 or 1971–72, were constructed. We looked at 627 students in 103 elementary schools between the end of the third and the sixth grades, 553 students in 42 schools between the end of the sixth and the eighth grades, and 716 students in five senior high schools between the ninth and twelfth grades. . . . In many ways, they provided us with a better basis for analysis than other researchers have been able to obtain; pupil histories were extremely detailed, following students over time was possible, the number of schools covered was large, and individual pupils were matched with the teachers they had and with the characteristics of those teachers.[31]

The authors reached, inter alia, the following conclusions:

> In the elementary school, when all other school characteristics are unchanged, black and non-black students appear to have the largest growth in achievement when they are in schools with a 40 to 60 percent black student body, rather than in schools that are more or less racially-segregated. The stimulative effect seems to be true both for black and non-black pupils in the sample. *In short, all elementary school students in the sample benefited in terms of achievement when they were in schools where the percentage of blacks about equalled the percentage of non-blacks.* . . .[32]

This statement, on the face of it, says nothing about social-class integration, only racial; but given the existing correlation, as of the

---

[30] Donald R. Winkler, "Educational Achievement and Student Peer Group Composition," *Journal of Human Resources,* 10, no. 2 (Spring 1975): 201.

[31] Anita A. Summers and Barbara L. Wolfe, "Which School Resources Help Learning? Efficiency and Equity in Philadelphia Public Schools," *Business Review,* Federal Reserve Bank of Philadelphia, February 1975, p. 7.

[32] Ibid., p. 16.

time of this writing, between social status and race, the statement is largely equivalent to our argument for social-class integration. Moreover, the authors also concluded:

> Elementary school students in the sample who are at grade level or lower perform distinctly better when they are with more high achieving students. Students performing above their grade level are not particularly affected.[33]

From our discussion of household choice in the public sector, these conclusions seem obvious (with which, of course, the reader is free to differ):

1. There is a substantial amount of social-class segregation in the distribution of housing in the United States.
2. The systems of local finance and the system of geographic entitlement to local public services perpetuate social-class isolation of neighborhoods.
3. Income homogeneity of neighborhoods and the consequent concentration of low-income housing in central cities and larger suburbs seriously impair the operation of Tiebout-type utility maximization for lower-middle- and lower-income households.
4. Social-class isolation is peculiarly significant in depriving children from lower income families of high quality education.

The Voucher Alternative

Concluding that the present arrangements in distributing education among households is not working too well does not necessarily lead us to the position that centralization of services, or some greater degree of it, is the appropriate policy alternative. Indeed, for two decades respected economists, lawyers, and the like, have contended that further decentralization is the better course. The intent is to increase, not decrease, the power of the individual household in making educational choices for its children. Writing in 1955 Milton Friedman, a leading economist from the University of Chicago, stated that while public support of elementary and secondary education could, in his opinion, be justified by the social benefits generated

---

[33] Ibid., p. 17.

(which he called "neighborhood effects"), he could find no compelling argument to defend public administration of schools. The government, then, might be well advised to raise a sufficient sum of money through taxation to assure maintenance of social benefits, but it could well turn the money over to households to purchase educational services from private schools. Friedman stated:

> We have seen that both the imposition of a minimum required level of education, and the financing of education by the state can be justified by the "neighborhood effects" of education. It is more difficult to justify in these terms a third step that has generally been taken, namely, the actual administration of educational institutions by the government, the "nationalization," as it were, of the bulk of the "education industry." The desirability of such nationalization has seldom been faced explicitly because governments have in the main financed education by paying directly the costs of running educational institutions so that this step has seemed required by the decision to subsidize education. Yet, the two steps could readily be separated. Governments could require a minimum level of education which they could finance by giving parents vouchers redeemable for a specified maximum sum per child per year if spent on "approved" educational service. Parents would then be free to spend this sum *and any additional sum* on purchasing educational services from an "approved" institution of their own choice. The educational services could be rendered by private enterprises operated for profit, or by non-profit institutions of various kinds. The role of the government would be limited to assuring that the schools met certain minimum standards such as the inclusion of a minimum common content in their program, and as it now inspects restaurants to assure that they maintain minimum sanitary standards.[34]

Friedman admits that there are certain arguments against his plan. (1) It might be difficult to provide the "common core of values deemed requisite for social stability" in a democracy. This concern arises from the possibility that "schools run by different religious groups" would instill "sets of values that are inconsistent with one another" and with the prevailing values taught in nonsectarian schools. Friedman is inclined to give this argument short shrift:

[34] Milton Friedman, "The Role of Government in Education," in *Economics and the Public Interest*, ed. Robert A. Solo (New Brunswick, N.J., Rutgers, 1955), pp. 127–128.

Under greater freedom to choose a school for one's child, it is possible that the "final result may therefore be less rather than more parochial education." (2) The opening up of greater choice among schools might serve to accentuate class distinctions. In a way this is the same argument as in (1); but the problem is here viewed in terms of class, as distinct from religious, distinctions. Again, Friedman tends to brush this argument aside. At present, the attendance areas for particular public schools are "peopled by children with similar backgrounds thanks to the stratification of residential areas." Only a very few people can send their children to nonparochial private schools, which serves to accentuate class distinction. Then, he concludes, "The widening of the range of choice under a private system would operate to reduce both kinds of stratification." This is a conclusion with which we will shortly take issue. (3) In some rural areas it is practical to have only one school of reasonable size. Perforce, parents cannot have the satisfaction of choice, that is, a "natural" monopoly exists, and the school might as well be run by public authorities, the only other real choice being such a degree of state regulation of a private monopoly—to insure that no social or religious group gets unfair treatment, for instance—that the inspectors might almost outnumber the inspected. Though Friedman places little weight on the first two opposing arguments, he nonetheless modifies his original proposal to arrive at this final statement:

> The arrangement that perhaps comes closest to being justified by these considerations—at least for primary and secondary education—is a mixed one under which governments would continue to administer some schools, but parents who chose to send their children to other schools would be paid a sum equal to the estimated cost of educating a child in a government school, provided that at least this sum was spent on education in an approved school. This arrangement would meet the valid features of the "natural monopoly" argument, while at the same time it would permit competition to develop where it could.[35]

What advantage does Friedman himself claim for his scheme of elementary and secondary education? There is first a special advantage, having to do with the problem of racial segregation. At first glance it might appear that Friedman's scheme would be offensive to those who favor desegregation, because it plainly offers financial aid to those who want to send their children to private, segregated

[35] Ibid., p. 130.

schools. To Friedman, however, forced segregation and forced non-segregation are both evils. The plan outlined offers a third alternative, namely, the existence at the same time of exclusively white schools, exclusively black schools, and mixed schools. If the people in the country are willing to give more than lip service to their ideals, presumably over time the mixed schools would grow at the expense of the nonmixed.

> So long as the school system is publicly operated, only drastic change is possible; one must go from one extreme to the other; it is a great virtue of the private arrangement that it permits a gradual transition.[36]

The general advantages that Friedman mentions are these: (1) A wider range of choice with respect to schools for their children would be open to parents. (2) The greater amount of private enterprise in education would—through competition—act to make the schools more efficient and promote a "healthy variety" of schools. (3) Educational enterprise would become more "flexible"; in particular, salaries of school teachers would become responsive to market forces.

In the form suggested by Friedman, educational vouchers have not received serious attention in the United States. Basically, the scheme appears not to meet justifiable stands of equity. Rich parents in high-wealth districts would have a double advantage: (a) property wealth would allow them to provide themselves with vouchers of substantial dollar value at low local school tax rates, and (b) household private wealth would allow them to add on to the value of the voucher a sum to pay for extra school services. Poor parents in low-wealth districts would likely receive vouchers of modest value only and be quite unable to add on much to those sums from their private resources. All told, the Friedman voucher plan would likely increase social-class isolation in schools over the degree to which we experience it today.

By the mid-1960s, however, a number of "regulated voucher schemes" had been proposed, intended to provide households greater choice in education while softening the inequities of the original Friedman proposal.[37] We will consider two of these: the Coons-Sugarman plan for *"family power equalizing"* and Jay Chambers' *"Compensation principle and price competition voucher plan."*

[36] Ibid., p. 131.
[37] See Center for the Study of Public Policy, *Education Vouchers* (Cambridge, Mass., 1970); T. Sizer and P. Whitten, "A Proposal for a Poor Children's Bill of Right," *Psychology Today*, August 1968, pp. 58–63.

Family Power Equalizing

The intent of family power equalizing[38] is to provide educational choice to families while at the same time assuring that—insofar as possible—low-income households have equivalent conditions of access to various schools as do rich households. One requirement is that households be forestalled from adding on to the amounts of their vouchers; this is accomplished by forbidding schools to spend in excess of their total of voucher receipts (capital funds, endowments, and borrowing are also closely controlled under the plan) in any given year. However, it is implicit that parents be able to choose schools of different levels of expenditure per student—otherwise we would have one flat level of expenditure (in the absence of local variations in voucher values and parental add-ons, which were provided for in the Friedman plan).

Coons and Sugarman suggest that there should be four levels of educational expenditure (the number is arbitrary but a smaller one does not make much sense) and that schools in both the public and private sectors would be established—or establish themselves—in each geographic area. Parents would thus have a range of expenditures from which to choose; a choice of public or private administration; and presumably, a choice of curricula emphasis. At the elementary level, the expenditure pattern proposed at one time was the following: lowest, $600 per student; low-middle, $900 per student; high-middle, $1,200 per student; and highest, $1,500 per student. Dollar expenditure levels for secondary schools were somewhat higher; but, in each case, the schools were enjoined to spend each year precisely the given sum of dollars per student, no more, no less.

State and federal grants would continue under the Coons-Sugarman proposal, but local taxes for schools would disappear. In their place, parents or guardians (but not childless families) would contribute to the cost of educating their children. The school tax rate would vary positively with the cost of the education the parents chose—low in a $600-a-year school and high in a $1,500 one—and also with the level of household income. In its latter aspect, the school tax resembles a progressive personal income tax. As Coons and Sugarman state:

> Basically, the model would create an educational market offering products (schools) at several distinct levels of per-pupil cost. At each of these levels, proprietors—public and private

---

[38] Family power equalizing is a concept developed by John Coons and Stephen Sugarman, Boalt Hall School of Law, University of California at Berkeley.

(the system could be made exclusively public or private)—
would compete for the custom of buyers (parents) all of
whom have been made substantially equal in their power to
purchase admission. To establish that equality the model
would condition access to any school upon an equivalence of
economic sacrifice for every family choosing that school, irrespective of family income. Accordingly, each family's selection of a school from among schools of varying per-pupil cost
would represent also a choice among varying rates of a
special tax to be levied upon the family's income; but the tax
burden on families of different incomes choosing schools
of the same per-pupil cost would, in economic terms, be
rendered equivalent by means of a progressive rate structure.
For example, upon enrolling its children in an elementary
school which receives—and is effectively limited in spending
to—the statutory minimum tuition credit of $600, a family
with an income of $4,000 would become subject to a tax of
$16.50. Access to a $1,500 school would cost that same family
$54.50. Enrollment in these same two schools by children of
richer families would create correspondingly greater tax
liabilities. For example, a $20,000 income family would pay
$440 and $1,218 for the respective schools. Not only would
the tax be proportionately larger for the wealthier family; the
rate would also be adjusted to account for diminishing marginal utility.[39]

A second equity feature of family power equalizing is open
access. As long as a child is of appropriate age, he or she is intended
to have the same chance of admission to any school his or her parents
select as any other child. When a given school is oversubscribed—
when more children wish to attend than there are places for them—
selection would be made on a random basis, as in a lottery. Some
versions of family power equalizing allow a school to select a certain
number of students by its own criteria—though a reasonable number
of places are to be left for random entrance—and other versions allow
preference to children who already have siblings in the given institution. Once a child is enrolled in a school, however, the child is
entitled to remain there until he or she completes the course

---

[39] John E. Coons and Stephen D. Sugarman, *Family Choice in Education: A Model State
System for Vouchers* (Berkeley: Institute of Governmental Studies, University of
California, 1971), pp. 10–11.

(graduates), if educational performance is satisfactory, or until parents elect to withdraw the child and place him or her in another institution.[40]

Compensation Principle and Price Competition Voucher Plan

Jay Chambers, an economist at the University of Rochester, has suggested a more flexible voucher plan than the Coons-Sugarman model. Chambers' plan is intended to afford families even more choice; increase the degree to which educational institutions are subject to forces of competition; and, at the same time, assure that access of low-income families to superior educational institutions is preserved.[41] The essential features of the plan are the following:

1. Each family is provided a minimum valued voucher, Vo, for each of its school-age children (Chambers uses $500 as the hypothetical value of Vo).

2. Educational institutions are free to charge "whatever tuition they desire,"[42] except that none, obviously, would charge less than $500.

3. For families selecting institutions charging more than Vo—and this would be most families—vouchers for extra tuition will be available from the state. The size of the voucher "varies inversely with family income and directly with the absolute level of the tuition charged at the school chosen by the family."[43] The value of the voucher is inverse to family income in order to subsidize more completely the educational expenditures of poor families than of rich families. The value rises with school costs so that all families having high demand for educational services can consider putting their children in superior institutions. However, it is a feature of the plan that higher quality education costs every family more than lower quality; this feature is intended to encourage all families to pay serious attention to what they are getting for their money from educational institutions. Finally, the rate of

[40] Ibid., p. 55.
[41] Jay Chambers, "An Alternative Voucher Plan: The Compensation Principle and Price Competition," School of Education, Stanford University, Occasional Papers in the Economics and Politics of Education, no. 72-1 (Stanford, Calif., 1972).
[42] Ibid., p. 13.
[43] Ibid.

Figure 6.1
Relationship between net school costs and family
income in compensation principle and price
competition voucher plan

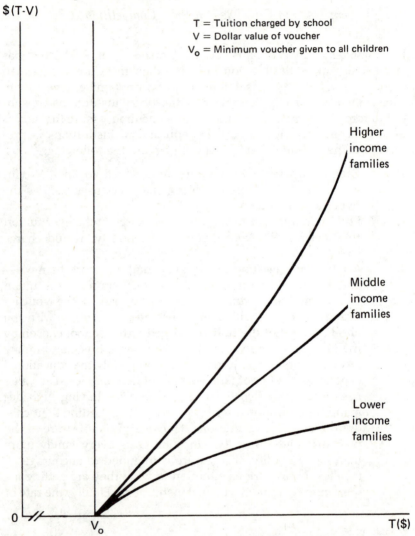

$(T-V)

T = Tuition charged by school
V = Dollar value of voucher
V_o = Minimum voucher given to all children

Higher
income
families

Middle
income
families

Lower
income
families

0

V_o

T($)

Source: Adapted from Jay Chambers, "An Alternative Voucher Plan: The Compensation Principle and Price Competition," Occasional Papers in the Economics and Politics of Education, School of Education, Stanford University, 1972, p. 16.

change in the absolute difference between tuition and value of voucher becomes progressively larger for rich families and progressively smaller for poor as tuition rises.[44] (See Figure 6.1.)

According to Chambers, his proposal for compensation principle and price competition is likely to offer greater gains in educational efficiency than family power equalizing:

> The major difficulty with the Coons plan [FPE] is that it may not provide for the full benefits of competition. While the plan does allow for competition on the basis of quality, and type of educational services offered, it stifles any possibility of price competition between schools. The Coons plan sets up arbitrary expenditure classes of schools. This, however, assumes implicitly that a particular educational technology can be produced efficiently at one of these expenditure levels. But a particular educational technology could be produced efficiently only within a very narrow range of expenditure not covered by the expenditure classes of the Coons plan. For

[44] Ibid., p. 16. On page 17 Chambers provides a table to show how the financial relationships would work:

Absolute amounts and proportion of tuition charges per student paid by the family

Family income	$500 Vo		$750		$1,000		$1,250	
$3,000	$0	(0%)	$25	(3.3%, 10%)	$30	(3%, 6.0%)	$35	(2.8%, 4.7%)
7,500	0	(0)	150	(20.0, 60)	200	(20, 40)	250	(20.0, 33.0)
12,000	0	(0)	200	(27.0, 80)	425	(43, 85)	675	(54.0, 90.0)

Source: Jay Chambers, "An Alternative Voucher Plan: The Compensation Principle and Price Competition," School of Education, Stanford University, Occasional Papers in the Economics and Politics of Education, no. 72-1 (Stanford, Calif., 1972), p. 17. Reprinted with permission.

The figures are illustrative only. The relationship in actual practice would be continuous, that is applying to each dollar figure between Vo and any maximum tuition charge. The income figure of $7,500 was intended (as of 1972) to refer to middle-level income of a family of four persons. The figures in the table show family charges per student for each level of tuition. The first percentage figure in each set of parentheses shows the percentage the family pays of gross tuition ($25 for the low-income family is 3.3 percent of a tuition charge of $750); and the second percentage figure is the proportion the family pays of tuition, less minimum voucher (for the $3,000 family, $25 equals 10 percent of $750 tuition, less $500 minimum voucher, or 25 equals 10 percent of $250).

example, suppose a particular educational technology could be produced within the range of $800 to $900 a student. Given four expenditure classes, $500, $750, $1,000, $1,250, a school choosing to provide this type of technology would have to operate at a minimum at the $1,000 level to remain solvent. The result is that schools providing such a technology will either reap excess profits or be less inclined to operate efficiently.[45]

By avoiding fixed expenditure classes, Chambers' plan encourages educational institutions to compete on the basis of actual costs of the instructional programs offered to students.

A second possible advantage of Chambers' plan over Coon's and Sugarman's is that the state is freed from having to fix classes of expenditure levels and then police them. In almost any state there are bound to be regional cost differences in providing educational services. If the state ignores these differences, it establishes unearned increments of profit (to private suppliers) or the opportunity to supply extra services to students (in public agencies) in the favored regions, while the disadvantaged areas would be unable to meet explicit standards of quality. On the other hand, if the state establishes a set of regionally differentiated expenditure standards, it is likely to embroil itself in controversy about whether the exact regional expenditure differences reflect true assessment of cost differences or some political reality. Teachers' unions would possibly find the differentials to be an issue for action. Chambers' plan allows the differential to be established by market forces; and, when competition rules, evidence provided by market forces is hard to dispute. In any case, the state would not be a direct party in any argument because it would be free of responsibility for establishing those differentials that came to exist.

Vouchers Pro and Con

The following arguments may be advanced in favor of educational vouchers.

Pro: Children Are Each Different We may assume that children differ in their interests and tastes. One child may like music and another, sports. The first child, let us suppose, is about to enter

---

[45] Ibid., p. 12. The four expenditure levels specified in the quotation are not exactly equal to those suggested by Coons and Sugarman; but all such figures are illustrative only and minor differences among the authors do not affect the argument.

junior high in a small, suburban school district. She might prefer to attend a junior high school in which, once she had attended classes in the basic subjects (English, history, mathematics, and so on), the rest of her day could be spent with teachers who shared her main interest, who were performing musicians themselves, or who had deep knowledge of musicology, the history of music, and so on. For this student, it would be nice if the principal was a musician, for principals can do much to establish the atmosphere and shape the intellectual interests of a given school.

However, the American educational system has difficulty in responding to such specialized interests. In a small suburban district, it is likely there will be one, or at most two, junior high schools. Since a majority of students are likely to have interests other than music, and since there are one or two junior high schools to offer the only "free" education that is available to the households of the district, and since attendance at some approved school is compulsory for all healthy children, it would hardly be fair to the majority of students to establish a strong curricular bias in one field, music, which is of main interest to only a minority.

On the other hand, in any large metropolitan area, we might find enough musically inclined children within a given commuting area to justify establishing a junior high school for that specialty. And similarly for other specialities. Once such specialized institutions had been established, parents could exercise choice in education and thus bring to bear their most intimate knowledge of what is good for their child in selecting a school for him or her. After all, the parents have more knowledge of their own children than any teacher or guidance counselor is likely to have. Since parents bear the consequences in their daily lives of successful or unsuccessful educational choices, we might reasonably suppose that parents would be conscientious in exercising educational choice.

Pro: Breaking Down the Monopoly In any particular school district, the local school board is in position of a near monopolist. Most parents cannot afford private independent schools, and many parents do not wish to enroll their children in religious institutions. The only way, then, to meet the requirements of compulsory attendance laws is to use public schools. To exercise choice within the public sector requires a change of residence, a cumbersome process at best. Hence, any given school system is effectively protected at present from private competition and substantially protected from competition from any other public school system.

Voucher plans would increase competition on both counts: Private schools would spring up to receive parental vouchers, and entitlement to attend any given public school would no longer be a function of parents' address. Schools that had half empty classrooms would be forced to re-examine and improve their practices or go out of business. Schools that had long waiting lines could establish branches to more fully satisfy consumer demand. In short, efficiency in education would be increased.

Breaking up the educational monopoly should also serve to reduce the incentive of richer families to cluster together in closely bounded neighborhoods. When the school one's child is entitled to attend no longer has anything to do with where one lives (in a given metropolitan area), there is somewhat less reason for the well-to-do to isolate themselves residentially from less well-endowed families, and, of course, from their children and the costs attendant upon the schooling of poorer children.

Similarly, arguments can be advanced against voucher plans.

Con: The Administrative Nightmare Regulated voucher plans require a lot of regulation. Under family power equalizing, the state would be pledged to assure that parents did not add on sums to the value of their vouchers. Since parents do such things as run cake sales, volunteer their time to school enterprises, and so on, the state would either involve itself in tedious accounting of such endeavors and produce much frustration among good-hearted parents in the process or see the "no-add-on" provision dissolve into nothing. The state would also have to see that the class of less well informed parents was not taken advantage of by slick, seedy educational operators and that the open admissions rule was honored in actual practice. It would also have to assure itself that schools did not depart too far from basic American values—did not, for example, hire a majority of teachers of racist or fascist persuasion. The administrative complexities would appear to be enormous and of dubious worth in the end. (Of course, Chambers' plan does not require the state to police the no-add-on stricture; and, in this sense, it requires less administrative oversight. But the absence of the no-add-on rule leads us to the second main objective to vouchers.)

Con: The Increase of Social Isolation in School Voucher proposals would seem to do little to reduce social-class isolation of the large poverty populations in central cities, unless, that is, children in urban ghettoes are not to spend enormous amounts of time commuting to school in the suburbs. As Henry Levin has written,

It is important to note that schooling must be consumed at the point of purchase; therefore, geographical location of schools becomes a salient feature of the market place. But if previous experience of the slums can be used for prediction, few if any sellers of high quality educational services at competitive rates will locate in the ghetto. Not only is there no Saks Fifth Avenue in Harlem; there is no Macy's, Gimbel's, Korvettes, or Kleins.[46]

In the suburbs, on the other hand, vouchers might easily lead to increased social-class isolation. Though the plans initially might be designed to make it very costly for richer parents to enroll their children in the highest quality institutions, over time the rich might use their political power to lessen their relative disadvantage in the educational marketplace. Thus, practically all rich children might attend high-quality schools simply because their families were accustomed to "buying the best" for them. Other families, not being rich, might easily feel the financial strain, particularly, if they had several children enrolled, of buying the most expensive schooling available. The most disadvantaged child of all, it would seem, would be the one whose parents were not interested in education and paid only the minimum amount, because that child would most likely find himself in a class full of such other disadvantaged youth. This is the most extreme form of isolation in an educational setting one can imagine.

Little confidence, finally, should be put in open admission guarantees. Any school principal is likely to see that the quickest way to improve the reputation of the school is to improve the quality of the students. Under open admissions the principal may have little control of the intake of students, but he or she probably can control which students are "flunked out." Even more difficult for the state to detect and proscribe, students could be so selectively discouraged by teachers and administrative staff that they voluntarily leave and enter other institutions. Open admissions, in other words, does not remove all power from administrators to control characteristics of clientele.

Advocates of vouchers sometimes argue that we shall not know whether vouchers are good or bad until we experiment with them.[47] Unfortunately, limited experiments may provide us with limited information about what the results of widespread adoption of voucher schemes would be. In this writer's view, the dismantling of the public education system is a matter to be approached with the greatest caution.

[46] Henry M. Levin, "The Failure of the Public Schools and the Free Market Remedy," *The Urban Review*, 2, no. 7 (June 1968): 34.
[47] Stephen D. Sugarman, "Family Choice: The Next Step in the Quest for Equal Educational Opportunity?" *Law and Contemporary Problems*, 38, no. 3 (Winter-Spring 1974): 554.

Two topics we raised in this chapter require further treatment.

1.   Assuming that social isolation is essentially harmful to the education of children, can this problem be addressed by greater state involvement in the provision of educational services? We consider this topic in Chapter 10.

2.   Assuming that greater family choice in education is desirable and that the adoption of a full-fledged voucher plan is, for various reasons, possibly undesirable, what opportunities for exercise of greater choice lie unexploited with the public sector? We turn to this question in Chapter 8.

Summary

We seek in the United States a system of education that preserves advantages of local decision making and that, at the same time, is fair in its distribution of opportunities among different types of students. These two objectives do not appear to be easily reconcilable in practice. Distribution of educational opportunities traditionally is regulated by the principle of geographical entitlement: The neighborhood in which a family lives establishes the school to which the family is entitled to send its children. We have in our country a pattern of housing that displays social-class isolation; hence, our schools are similarly subject to social-class isolation. Evidence is available to indicate that social-class isolation in schools is, on balance, harmful to children from low-income homes. One major proposal to reconcile decentralization with equitable treatment of children is the voucher plan. We examined the arguments for and against the use of educational vouchers in this chapter.

Selected Bibliography

Benson, Charles S., Paul M. Goldfinger, E. Gareth Hoachlander, and Jessica C. Pers. *Planning for Educational Reform: Financial and Social Alternatives.* New York: Harper & Row, 1975.

Buchanan, James. *Public Finance in Democratic Process.* Chapel Hill: University of North Carolina Press, 1967.

Carnoy, Martin, and Henry M. Levin. *The Limits of Educational Reform.* New York: David McKay, 1976.

Downs, Anthony. *An Economic Theory of Democracy.* New York: Harper & Row, 1957.

Fromm, Gary, and Paul Taubman. *Public Economic Theory and Policy.* New York: Macmillan, 1973.

Juster, F. Thomas, ed. *Distribution of Economic Well-Being.* New York: Columbia, 1976.

Chapter Seven

Public Rationality in Educational Decision Making

An objective in American educational policy is to see that, insofar as possible, all children have a fair start in their educational careers. The argument of the last chapter suggests it would be inappropriate to rely in any major degree on a market-based distribution of educational resources to achieve that objective. Public control is required; otherwise the inequalities present in our society will reproduce themselves in the educational marketplace. In short, low-income children would end up with lower quality schooling, on the average, than that received by high-income children.

Public control, however, implies that public authorities make decisions about which children receive what kinds of services; that is, the allocation process cannot be left to the blind operation of market forces. But public agencies can be expected to make appropriate decisions only when they are able to define objectives in fairly precise terms and when they know which sets of educational resources will be effective in reaching those objectives. For example, suppose a city school board decides that at least 85 percent of high school students should acquire basic skills at 9th-grade level or higher by the time they leave high school. We can argue about whether the figure of 85 percent is too high or low, what learnings constitute "basic skills," what tests to use to measure "9th-grade level," and so on. Indeed, we might argue about whether the stated objective is as important as some other objective, such as "building citizenship"; but these kinds of questions are subject to resolution, for the time being, by reasoned debate.

What is much more difficult to know is how to accomplish educational objectives within the constraints public school authorities face. There are limitations in quantity and quality of resources available to any district. There are limitations in the amount of time that students are willing to devote to learning and there are differences among students in their willingness to use time devoted to learning in an intensive way. Ideally, school authorities would have information to guide them to maximize student learning (of various specified kinds) within whichever constraints are binding at a given point of time.

During the 1960s considerable optimism developed that resource allocation decisions of public authorities could become rational and scientific. The general framework of analysis was called *program budgeting*. Though the concept of program budgeting was perhaps oversold, it is important to examine the fundamental ideas of the plan because the introduction of the concept stimulated a considerable body of policy analysis that continues to this day. The major intent of this chapter, then, is to describe certain major types of policy analysis and to see how far such analysis presently can take us toward improving resource allocations of public school authorities such that the city school district we mentioned above might know which types of teachers to assign to which students in which sized groups, and which types of instructional supplies and equipment to employ, in order that it could have the best chance at the given time of meeting its objective that 85 percent, say, of high school students had at least 9th-grade-level basic skills.

The Concept of Economic Program Budgeting

Charles L. Schultze of the Brookings Institution, Washington, D.C., has presented possibly the clearest description of the planning, programming, and budgeting system (PPBS).[1] He states,

> PPB[S] can be viewed as both a set of goals and objectives and as a system of achieving those goals. . . . [The first aspect of PPBS is] careful identification and examination of goals and objectives in each major area of governmental activity. . . .

[1] Charles L. Schultze, *The Politics and Economics of Public Spending* (Washington, D.C.: Brookings, 1968).

PPB[S] attempts to force government agencies to step back and reflect on the fundamental aims of their current programs.[2]

In education, for example, school boards might undertake to decide what characteristics of teachers were important to the task of instructing the young and what were unimportant, in order that their teacher recruitment procedures might recognize the former set of characteristics more fully than the latter. At a higher level of government, state boards of education might attempt to find out which kinds of teachers school districts were seeking to hire and to increase the supply, using such measures as influencing schools of education in *their* recruitment of people to the profession and in encouraging the establishment of certain types of retraining programs.

The second step of program budgeting is to investigate the outputs of particular programs, relative to their stated objectives. As Schultze says,

> the effectiveness of various manpower training programs can only be determined in relation to a particular set of objectives. "Creaming off" the manpower pool by concentrating training resources on unemployed white high school graduates may prove highly effective when measured by the proportion of trainees subsequently employed at steady jobs and higher wages. But, if the objective is to improve the lot of the hard-core unemployed or underemployed in the ghetto, comparing alternative programs on the basis of such measures of effectiveness would be inappropriate and misleading.[3]

In education, school boards might conceivably establish as one of their objectives raising the proportion of high school students from low-income homes who enter four-year colleges. According to Schultze's statement, the board should look not just to figures on total high school graduates going to college, but to the socioeconomic status (SES) distribution of those who enter college. It would also be appropriate, as an ancillary matter, to consider the SES distribution of those who enter college from the district's high schools and drop out. If teachers are put under pressure to see that more low-income youth are made eligible for college, they may do that but at the same time fail to help the students be able readily to succeed in college, once

[2] Ibid., p. 19.
[3] Ibid., p. 20.

admitted. Thus the attainment of the objective would be rather empty.[4]

The third step in implementing program budgeting is measuring costs. This process should be as comprehensive as possible. Here is an example. In California it is now a matter of educational policy that high school students can obtain diplomas at age 16 by passing an examination in basic subjects. This should represent a cost saving to the state, but prediction of its magnitude is not easy. In the early years of operating this California High School Proficiency Examination, few students would be expected to participate, simply because it takes time to distribute information about the plan and for students to assess the gains and losses of leaving school early. Initially, then, operating the plan might not decrease enrollment enough to allow reducing high school staffs. But we should not conclude that no reductions will ever take place. The procedure, then, is to formulate a set of assumptions that allows prediction of cost consequences over a period of years, not just in the current year. And as the future unfolds, the assumptions themselves can be corrected in the light of experience.

On the other hand, certain budget items may be quite inflexible with respect to decline in high school enrollment—central office administrative salaries, for example, and even library expenses in the high school. Some costs might rise—on a per-student basis: teaching costs in specialized courses that, for one reason or another, must continue even in the face of enrollment declines. Careful budget analysis must recognize these different kinds of budget impacts. From the state's perspective, leaving high school early may result in an *increase* in the education budget when and as early leavers enter public institutions of higher education sooner than they otherwise would.

The fourth step of program budgeting is to formulate objectives in multiyear terms. In the words, again, of Charles Schultze:

> The long-term nature of most public programs calls for long-range planning. In practice, an equally important *tactical* aspect of multi-year planning becomes evident. In the short

---

[4] It might thus be construed that the effectiveness of any educational program can only be assessed on the basis of the kind of life an individual had during his entire lifetime. In a way, this is true. But the longer the time between some event in an individual's life and the close of his formal schooling, the more powerful, presumably, will be the force of noneducational variables on that event and the harder it becomes to isolate the influence of formal schooling itself.

run, . . . agencies are captives of the past. Prior commitments, inertia, promises . . . the need to "educate" interest group constituents . . . often cause rigid constraints on yearly budget decisions. In any one year, therefore, the impact that an agency head can have on his operating bureaus is limited. By concentrating solely on what can be done in each annual budget, he can achieve very little. Major changes in objectives, operating practices, and budget allocations must be accomplished in the light of longer-range goals.[5]

The fifth and crucial step of program budgeting is analysis of alternative means to accomplish given ends, of reaching, that is, program objectives. Program budgeting assumes that the evaluation of alternative means should be based on costs: The least costly means of reaching a given program objective is always preferred to the most costly. For example, suppose a school board established an objective of reducing early reading failure from an initial level of, say, 40 percent to 15 percent in five years' time. Two means of accomplishing the objective (not the only two, of course) are reducing class size and hiring more highly qualified teachers. (Sophisticated forms of program budgeting allow for combinations of such educational resources, but the idea remains that there are alternative *combinations* to evaluate on cost grounds.) In evaluating the alternative means, the district would prefer the one that allowed it to reach its objective at the least dollar cost. The techniques of making *cost-effectiveness studies* will be noted later in this chapter.

The sixth and final step in program budgeting is "to establish these analytic procedures as a systematic part of budget review."[6] Alas, this has not generally been done.

On the face of it, program budgeting is an eminently logical procedure. It suggests that public agencies should figure out what their short- and long-run objectives are and then, by using cost-effectiveness analysis, determine how best to meet those objectives. We might wonder how public agencies have ever operated otherwise. Yet, when the concepts of program budgeting were introduced in the early 1960s, they were heralded as an innovation.[7] More puzzling

---

[5] Ibid., p. 22.

[6] Ibid., p. 23.

[7] On August 25, 1965, President Lyndon B. Johnson announced the following: "This morning I have just conducted a breakfast meeting with the Cabinet and with the heads of Federal agencies and I am asking each of them to immediately begin to introduce a new and very revolutionary system of planning and programming and budgeting

still, the popularity of the innovation waned almost overnight. Writing in a report to the Joint Economic Committee of the U.S. Congress in 1969, Paul Feldman appeared to represent a consensus with respect to results of federal government application of PPBS when he said:

> In the three and a half years since the system was instituted, analytic staffs have been created, program structures have been defined, and program memoranda and financial plans have been presented. Despite adherence to the formalities of the system, however, the predicted revolution has not taken place. Presentations purporting to be analyses are often no more than poetic rewarding of old style budget submissions. Where attempts have been made to present real calculations of costs and outputs, the conclusions have been rejected on the grounds of political irrelevance. . . . That visible changes in the budget decision process and in budgets have not taken place is commonly acknowledged, and observers of government who have an interest in PPBS, either as critics or as supporters, recognize that dissatisfaction with the system is widespread. . . .[8]

What went wrong?

In the first place, PPBS was vastly oversold. Its advocates early on seemed to imply that the system would generate almost automatically a welfare-maximizing set of public operations. But there actually is nothing in the system that will enable us to choose

---

throughout the vast Federal Government, so that through the tools of modern management the full promise of a finer life can be brought to every American at the lowest possible cost.

"This program is designed to achieve three major objectives: it will help us find new ways to do jobs faster, to do jobs better, and to do jobs less expensively. It will insure a much sounder judgement [sic] through more accurate information, pin-pointing those things we ought to do more, spotlighting those things we ought to do less. It will make our decision-making process as up-to-date, I think, as our space-exploring programs." (Taken from transcript of the president's news conference on foreign and domestic matters, *New York Times*, August 26, 1965, as quoted in David Novick, ed., *Program Budgeting: Program Analysis and the Federal Budget* [Cambridge, Mass.: Harvard, 1965], p. v.)

[8] "Prescription for an Effective Government: Ethics, Economics, and PPBS," in *The Analysis and Evaluation of Public Expenditures: The PPB System*, A compendium of papers submitted to the Subcommittee on Economy in Government of the Joint Economic Committee, Congress of the United States (Washington, D.C.: U.S. Government Printing Office, 1969), III, 866–867.

among competing objectives. As William Gorham, a leading advocate of PPBS, stated:

> We have not attempted any grandiose cost-benefit analysis designed to reveal whether the total benefits from an additional million dollars spent on health programs would be higher or lower than that from an additional million spent on education or welfare. If I was ever naïf enough to think this sort of analysis possible, I no longer am.[9]

Another aspect of overselling was the assumption made that PPBS could be adopted quickly by all federal agencies and departments and by state and local governments as well. Opportunities for analysis vary greatly among different programs in the present state of the art: relatively easy in highways and water resources; relatively hard in health, welfare, and education. To some extent, successfully applying PPBS depends on the existence of a critical mass of analysts available in a given department or, say, big city school office, at a given point of time. The demand that PPBS be widely adopted under such differing conditions led too many government offices to go through the motions of the analysis, not the content, and this gave the system a bad name.

But there are also political difficulties. PPBS assumes a flexibility that is frequently not present in public bureaucracies. When the acceptance of PPBS requires radical changes in methods of providing a service, those whose status or jobs are threatened can be expected to try to thwart the shift, even while proclaiming the worth of the new ideas. Various means of preventing change are available. Assigning work by rules of seniority is the most easily noted, but there are certainly others.

Moreover, PPBS assumes the acquiescence of public interest groups affected by major changes in the way services are provided. Once a group has become accustomed to the operation of any program, it rarely wants to yield its favored position to increase the technological efficiency of the service for the whole population. Affected public interest groups are likely to use political influence to see that some changes recommended by advocates of PPBS are not implemented.

If the promise of PPBS was less than the actuality, this does not deny the need for rational decision making in the public sector,

[9] U.S. Congress, Joint Economic Committee, *The Planning Programming-Budgeting System: Progress and Potential*, 90th Cong., 1st sess., 1967, p. 5.

including education. And, in fact, interest generated by advocates of PPBS toward that system has accelerated the development of analytical tools, even though these tools do not yet take us all the way toward welfare-maximizing allocations of public resources. In this chapter we shall discuss two main analytical devices in the field of education: production function studies and cost-benefit and cost-effectiveness studies.

Educational Production Function Studies

In this section we will describe the methods, results, criticisms, and potentiality of *educational production function studies*. But first we will discuss the kinds of policy illuminating questions these sorts of studies seek to answer. The studies attempt to relate the production of certain measurable and, presumably, important educational outcomes to the consumption by school districts of certain defined school resources—such as teachers' time, instructional materials and equipment, and so on—subject to certain conditions of the student (SES characteristics) and of his or her peers in the classroom. When successfully conducted, the studies inform school districts on *what* to spend money: whether to spend incremental budget sums on reducing class size or on hiring more highly qualified and expensive teachers or on teacher retraining; whether to spend money on lengthening the school year or to save it by shortening the school day; whether to support busing to reduce social-class isolation or to provide additional health services for students. The questions are framed, of course, not in either-or terms—for example, every dollar on busing and no dollars on health or vice versa—but in terms of, say, how much on busing and how much on student health, just as we might ask how much on conventional instructional materials, textbooks, and the like, and how much on new technology, such as computer-assisted instruction.

To serve both local and state budget officers, production function studies also are intended to help answer the question on *whom* to spend money. In arranging for the distribution of state grants to education, in which types of districts—rural, upper class suburban, working-class suburban, central city, and so on—will there appear the greatest gain in learning of students per additional dollar of aid? Do the dollars spent in bilingual education produce high achievement gains or only moderate gains? Are gifted-student programs highly productive or only moderately so? The answers to these questions could help guide resource allocation to different students.

An even more sophisticated question considered by production function studies is, On whom should money be spent and when? For students of different backgrounds and interests, at what point in their educational careers should we seek to concentrate educational resources? For some students, are the earliest educational years the most important in determining their ultimate educational development? Is it the prenatal and postnatal nutritional status of the child that should receive priority of resources in some instances? Or, for other students, are the high school or college years the most educationally important, and thus should they receive the heaviest input of resources? These, then, are some of the questions with which educational production function studies seek to deal.

Methods of Analysis

Production function studies in education typically have assumed that there is a significant relationship between something that happens to a student—called *outputs*—and three main sets of variables to characterize conditions of learning—called *inputs*. One main set of input variables is intended to describe the home or out-of-school environment of the student; another set describes important characteristics of the given student's fellow students; and a third set describes components of the schooling environment.[10] In symbols, production function work then becomes a study of the following statement:[11]

$$A_{it} = g(F_i^{(t)}, P_i^{(t)}, S_i^{(t)}) \tag{7.1}$$

where A_{it} = quantitative measures of attainment of the ith student at time t

$F_i^{(t)}$ = set of family or neighborhood characteristics of ith student cumulative to time t

---

[10] The best known of the production function studies is James S. Coleman et al., *Equality of Educational Opportunity* (Washington, D.C.: U.S. Government Printing Office, 1966). This author conducted one of the earliest of the studies—see Charles S. Benson et al., *State and Local Fiscal Relationships in Public Education in California* (Sacramento, Calif.: Fact Finding Committee on Revenue and Taxation, State Senate, 1965). The 18 production function studies that had been completed by the early 1970s are critically analyzed in Harvey Averch et al., *How Effective Is Schooling: A Critical Review and Synthesis of Research Findings* (Santa Monica, Calif.: Rand Corporation, 1971), chap. 3 and app. A. One outstanding study is Eric A. Hanushek, *The Value of Teachers in Teaching* (Santa Monica, Calif.: Rand Corporation, 1970).

[11] This statement follows the discussion in Eric A. Hanushek and John F. Kain, "On the Value of *Equality of Educational Opportunity* as a Guide to Public Policy," in *On Equality of Educational Opportunity*, Frederick Mosteller and Daniel P. Moynihan, eds. (New York: Random House, 1972), p. 123ff.

$P_i^{(t)}$ = set of student body characteristics (peer influences) cumulative to time t

$S_i^{(t)}$ = set of school inputs received by the ith student cumulative to time t

Logically, there is little in this general statement with which we might take issue; the learning of a student is almost certainly influenced to a significant degree by his or her upbringing, his or her classmates in school, and the characteristics of the school itself. Disputes arise when efforts are made to go from the general statement toward empirical models that assess the relative significance of the different sets of presumably independent variables. As we shall see, there are difficulties with the quality of data and with the theoretical basis of the statistical analysis.

However, considering the general statement for a moment, we note that the independent variables are listed in a certain order, that is, in effect, policy-oriented. The set of variables considered last is $S_i^{(t)}$, the school variables. And the reason is that these variables are thought to be most readily subject to change, once a reason for change is indicated. For example, suppose (contrary to fact) production function studies consistently show a strong negative relationship between student achievement and class size. Assuming that parents and other voters would prefer schools to deliver high student achievement rather than low, it should not be too difficult for school districts to hire additional teachers, reduce class size, and raise student achievement.

Student achievement might also be modified by changing the peer composition of classrooms. Indeed, in the last chapter we noted studies that show achievement rises as social-class isolation is reduced. $P_i^{(t)}$ as a set of variables is introduced before $S_i^{(t)}$ to indicate that changing $P_i^{(t)}$, though not impossible—this is what certain busing programs are all about—is more difficult and possibly slower to accomplish than changing the school variables, $S_i^{(t)}$. The first set of variables introduced, $F_i^{(t)}$, might be taken as given, under the idea that public policy does not invade privacy of the home and, except in extreme instances, public authority does not mandate particular types of behavior on the part of parents and other child custodians or parent surrogates. (Actually, some components of $F_i^{(t)}$ are relatively easy to change for the better: consider prenatal and early postnatal nutritional status of mother and child, day care centers to relieve school-age children of the need to tend their younger siblings after school while the mother works, and so on).

This is the train of argument, then: Accepting family background characteristics *and* peer compositions as given, what *school variables* are relatively effective in raising levels of student attainment? (Or, accepting $F_i^{(t)}$ as given, what changes in $P_i^{(t)}$ and $S_i^{(t)}$ are relatively effective on student attainment?) Intuitively, we can readily see one of the major difficulties with production function studies in education. Suppose, as is not unlikely, that the three sets of independent variables are related to each other. For example, take a group of children of upper income parents. These children are likely to attend school with children who are above average in motivation to study: $P_i^{(t)}$ is favorable to stimulate the ith student. These students also are likely to attend schools staffed by well-trained and experienced teachers, schools in which there is a generous amount of instructional materials and supplies, and so on. Assume it to be true that children of high-income parents, other things equal, are likely to do better in school than children of low-income parents. Then, given relationships among the sets of independent variables, the policy-oriented ordering we discussed becomes a crucial matter. When we take account of differences in family background first, we are likely to attribute to its influence those aspects of peer composition and school input variables that are related to family background. Under available statistical techniques, the true influence of family background is likely to be overstated, and the influence of variables, such as $S_i^{(t)}$, that are entered into the analysis later is likely to be understated—some unknown part of the influence of $S_i^{(t)}$ will have already been included in $F_i^{(t)}$. If upper class children have initial learning advantages for reasons of family background and if they also receive instruction from superior teachers, it is practically impossible to know how much of their overall learning advantage is related to family and how much to teachers. Consequently, when we say that we will consider teacher effectiveness only after we have distributed as much learning differences as we can to family influences, we are really only dealing with that part of teacher influence which is uncorrelated with family factors.

We might argue, of course, that we should arrange experiments such that certain children of identical family background are exposed to teachers that are thought to be superior and other children of these same identical family backgrounds are put before teachers thought to be inferior, in order to isolate the effects of S variables from F variables. Or, we might try to hold fixed the F and S variables and allow P to vary, so that we might isolate the effects of peer groups on learning. However, in the absence of operational theories of learning, such experimentation on young children could only be described as wilful. We are thus left with natural experiments and the statistical techniques of multiple correlation.[12] *Natural experiments* have been described by Henry Averch in the following way:

> By a natural experiment we mean a situation created by chance or coincidence . . . in which basically similar individuals have been subjected to different stimuli. By analyzing their responses, the researcher hopes to discover how individuals in general will respond to the various stimuli. In education, for example, a natural experiment would occur if students at the same grade level from identical backgrounds and subject to identical peer-group influences were to attend different schools and thus receive different amounts of various school resources. An analysis of this situation might reveal whether differences in the students' outcomes were systematically related to differences in the amount of resources they received. Another natural experiment would occur if students from differing backgrounds were to attend the same school at the same grade level, be subjected to the same peer-group influences and receive identical amounts of every school resource. Analysis of this situation could show the extent to which differences in their outcomes systematically varied with the differences in their backgrounds.[13]

In practice, analysis of education production functions by means of natural experiments requires collecting data on a large number of students, for example, the Coleman report analyzed data of 645,000 students.[14] What types of data are commonly collected?

Educational Outputs   The measures of outputs most commonly used are achievement test scores, reading tests in the first instance and mathematics scores in the second. Other output measures used from time to time are educational aspirations of students, length and regularity of school attendance, and proportion of graduates of given high schools going on to college.

[12] Techniques of multiple correlation are described in any number of comprehensive, basic statistics texts. See, for example, John E. Freund, *Modern Elementary Statistics* (Englewood Cliffs, N.J.: Prentice-Hall, 1952), chap. 17.

[13] Averch et al., *How Effective Is Schooling*, p. 37.

[14] James S. Coleman et al., *Equality of Educational Opportunity* (Washington, D.C.: U.S. Government Printing Office, 1966), chap. 1.

Educational Inputs Measures of educational inputs fall into the three categories we previously mentioned: family background, peer group, and school resources. For family background, certain standard input measures are the following: occupation of father and mother, educational level of father and mother, household income, number of siblings, house value, and possessions in student's home. Peer-group inputs are ordinarily measured by percent of minority students in the classroom, proportion in college preparatory curriculum, proportion of fast and slow learners, and student transfers. School resources are commonly identified as instructional expenditures per student, science laboratory facilities, library volumes per student, teacher's verbal achievement, teacher's degree level, quality of teacher's own education, teacher's experience, and teacher's perception of student's quality.

By means of *multiple regression analysis,* the researcher seeks to convert these kinds of data into an equation of the following form:

$$O = a + b_1 f_1 + \ldots + b_n f_n + c_1 p_1 + \ldots + c_n p_n$$
$$+ d_1 s_1 + \ldots + d_n s_n \tag{7.2}$$

Where O = one or more measures of a student's output

a = a normalizing constant of no special concern in the analysis

f_i = the amount of the ith family background factor

p_i = the amount of the ith peer composition factor

s_i = the amount of the ith school resource received by the student

b_i = the unit contribution of the ith family background factor to student's output

c_i = the unit contribution of the ith peer composition factor to student's output

d_i = the unit contribution of the ith school resource factor to student's output

It is thus seen that the student's output is determined by the *addition* of a whole series of contributions from the three main sources: family, peers, and school resources. Each separate source of output is a product of a parameter, b_i, c_i, and d_i, times a certain amount of an input variable. This kind of linear production function assumes that each unit of a particular school resource (for example, years of teacher's experience) or of a particular family background factor (for example, each $1,000 of household income) adds a constant amount to the student's output. And the unit contribution, as adjusted, or weighted, by the values b_i, c_i, and d_i, does not change regardless of how much of the given input the student receives and regardless of how much or little the student receives of the other inputs. For example, one student may come from a home of immense wealth and another from a home of dire poverty. Equation (7.2) says that both students would be equally affected in educational attainment by an equal change in, say, teacher's verbal score.

Particular interest is attached to the values of the coefficients b_i, c_i, and d_i, as determined by regression analysis. On the one hand, the sign of the coefficient is of importance. Commonly we assume that a student's output is likely to be greater in smaller classes than large. If s_1 is class size and d_1 is positive, this would challenge the assumption about the positive effects of reducing class size, in that $d_1 \times s_1$, with d_1 positive, indicates that student's output rises as class size gets bigger, not smaller. On the other hand, the size of b_i, c_i, and d_i is important (with size of coefficient being considered relative to the units of measurement of the inputs f_i, p_i, and s_i). If one of the coefficients is zero, then the given input contributes nothing at all to student's output. If the value of the coefficient is large, then, subject to the qualifications about units of measurement of inputs, the given input is substantially influential on student's output, that is, it has power. Standard statistical procedures are available to separate coefficients into two classes: (A) In the first class are coefficients that, in terms of probability, are almost certainly different in value from zero. This is the class of those that are different in value from zero and are, for practical purposes, sufficiently immune from measurement error to be unable to show the nonzero values they possess if their true value were zero. (B) In the second class are coefficients that are not sufficiently immune from such measurement error. Only *statistically significant* variables—those whose coefficients pass the test of probability on having a nonzero value—are ordinarily regarded as being of interest for policy purposes. Even within this group, some may be nonmanipulable by society, and some of those that are manipulable may lack power (even though their coefficients pass the test of statistical significance).

Here is an example of a relatively simple production function. Elchanan Cohn set out to study the effects of a small set of school variables on the quality of Iowa public high schools (family and peer influences are not dealt with explicitly).[15] The measure of high school quality is $Y = T_{12} - T_{10}$, where T_{10} equals the average composite score on Iowa Test of Educational Development of 10th-grade students,

[15] Elchanan Cohn, "Economies of Scale in Iowa High School Operations," *Journal of Human Resources*, 3, no. 4 (Fall 1968): 422-434.

and T_{12} equals the average composite score on Iowa Test of Educational Development of 12th-grade students. One of the equations Cohn estimates is:

$$Y = 4.197 - 0.0178s_1 - 0.276s_2 + 0.00019s_3 + 0.0047s_4 .$$
$$+ 0.000005s_5 - 0.0002s_6 + 0.0034s_7 - 0.00008s_8 \qquad (7.3)$$

Where Y = output as defined

s_1 = average number of college semester hours per teaching assignment (level of teacher training)

s_2 = average number of different subject matter assignments per high school teacher

s_3 = median high school teachers' salaries

s_4 = number of credit units offered in the high school

s_5 = building value per student

s_6 = bonded indebtedness per student

s_7 = class size

s_8 = average daily attendance

Only the coefficients for median teachers' salary and the number of assignments were statistically significant. All other coefficients were not significantly different from zero. The teacher salary variable can be interpreted in the following way. Gains in 12th-grade achievement over 10th-grade achievement in Iowa public high schools will rise by 0.19 points for each $1,000 increase in median teachers' salaries ($1,000 $\times s_3$ = $1,000 × 0.00019 = 0.19).

The sign of the teacher training coefficient is negative. This indicates, at first glance (though we must add that the value of the coefficient is not statistically significant), that school quality diminishes the more highly trained the teachers are. Cohn comments:

> The coefficient of college hours per teaching assignment turns out to be negative. This conclusion is somewhat surprising; however, *if* the number of college hours is negatively correlated with teaching experience and *if* experience is positively correlated with Y (output), the negative sign may not be so distressing.[16]

Results and Criticisms of Production Function Studies

The policy conclusions of production function studies (with the possible exception of the Summers-Wolfe study, to be noted below) are

[16] Ibid., p. 426.

conflicting and ambiguous. The Coleman report[17] found that peer-group composition variables were relatively important in determining student achievement, while Marshall Smith's re-examination of the Coleman data did not.[18] Hanushek's results on teacher effectiveness indicated that teacher's verbal facility was significant in raising achievement of white students but not of black, while teacher's training and experience were insignificant in the case of both blacks and whites.[19] Several studies—Coleman, Levin, [20] Hanushek, Benson,[21] Burkhead[22]—have indicated that, among school variables, teacher characteristics are relatively important. But the existing studies hardly give confidence that the measures used to describe teacher characteristics—salary, level of training, experience, verbal facility—are anything more than proxies for what matters in the face-to-face interaction of teacher and student—nor that characteristics reported to be significantly important in one educational setting will turn out to enhance productivity in another.

Overall, the explanatory power of the studies is weak—typically, they explain on the order of 25 percent of achievement variations among students. That set of variables regarded as being least amenable to manipulation by social policy is family background, and it is the most powerful set in virtually all production function studies, ordinarily accounting for at least half of the variations in student achievement. These facts about the results of educational production function studies have led Harvey Averch to observe

> the production functions estimated thus far enable us to use information regarding a student's background and the services he received from his school to predict his outcome somewhat more accurately. However, this improvement in accuracy comes . . . from our ability to take account of the student's background in making our prediction. Knowledge of the [school] resources the student received has proved to be of minor value. . . . [And] almost every study finds one or two or three school resources to be significantly related to

[17] Coleman et al., *Equality of Educational Opportunity.*

[18] Marshall Smith, "Equality of Educational Opportunity: The Basic Findings Reconsidered," in Mosteller and Moynihan, *On Equality of Educational Opportunity*, pp. 230–342.

[19] Hanushek, *Value of Teachers in Teaching.*

[20] Henry M. Levin, "A New Model of School Effectiveness," in *Do Teachers Make a Difference?* U.S. Department of Health, Education, and Welfare, Office of Education (Washington, D.C.: U.S. Government Printing Office, 1970), pp. 55–75.

[21] Benson et al., *State and Local Fiscal Relationships.*

[22] Jesse Burkhead, Thomas G. Fox, and John W. Holland, *Input and Output in Large-City High Schools* (Syracuse, N.Y.: Syracuse University Press, 1967).

student outcomes. But these studies generally examine a large number of school resources. Along with the two or three resources that are found to be significant, many are found to be insignificant . . . [and] when we compare the results of various studies, we find that the same resources do not appear among the lists of significant variables.[23]

The latter observation might be restated: Production function studies in education have not yet commenced to build a *cumulative and reliable* body of information to guide allocation of school resources toward attainment of measurable outcomes.

In view of the considerable efforts that have been expended by economists and sociologists, we may reasonably inquire why the results are so meager and uninformative. One problem is that the various sets of independent variables are related each to the other. We have already discussed this problem of *multicollinearity* at some length. The general effect of multicollinearity is to lessen the confidence we may place in the relative importance of one variable, as compared with other variables in explaining some event. If, for example, household income of student and teacher's experience are correlated—this is often observed to be the case, when and as teachers use seniority to gain a place in a school serving the middle and upper classes—and if the two variables are entered one after the other in an estimating equation, the variable entered first—family income, say—will explain not only the variance in student achievement attributable to income independently of teacher's experience but also the variance in student achievement that is attributable to that part of teacher's experience which is correlated with family income. When teacher's experience is entered later in the estimation equation, on the other hand, it picks up only that part of the remaining variance in student achievement that is attributable to variation in teacher's experience that is uncorrelated with family income—and this could be a very small proportion, indeed. If, alternatively, the variables were entered in reverse order, the share of student achievement attributable to teacher's experience might be overstated.

There is no wholly satisfactory statistical technique to deal with multicollinearity, but certain procedures are sometimes used. One is to *partition* the data. We might, for example, examine productivity relationships in education separately for children from different social classes: For children who are more or less uniformly rich or uniformly poor, does teacher experience make any important difference in educational achievement?

[23] Averch et al., *How Effective Is Schooling*, pp. 45, 46.

Secondly, we could simply compute the relationship between percentage changes in student achievement and percentage changes in expenditures on different school resources. If we might reasonably suppose that the relationship would be different for children of different social classes, then separate computations could be made for different classes of children. However, one problem with such an attempt to finesse the existence of multicollinearity—to force the data, that is, to reveal policy preferences for purchase of school inputs even when true relationships between independent variables and dependent are unknown—is that production function studies give only average effects, not marginal. Over a given set of schools, for example, the studies show the average effects of changing class size. They do not reveal the effects of a small change in class size in any given school, a school, for example, in which class size may already be abnormally low.

A second major problem with production function analysis if *simultaneity*. When a single equation is used to establish a relationship between a set of independent and a set of dependent variables, we assume that the independent variables are determined *outside the system*, or are *exogenous*. But it is possible that the so-called dependent variable can have an influence on one or more of the independent variables. For example, achievement gains are commonly dependent variables, and student's attitude is one of the independent. The basic idea is that a student's attitude affects his or her achievement. But changes in achievement may affect student's attitude. Such feedback can produce biased estimates of production parameters. The method to deal with the problem of simultaneity is multiple regression analysis based on a set of simultaneous equations; the technique is called *two-stage least squares*. [24] Studies employing this more sophisticated technique represent better research, but the results are not substantially different from single-equation models.

A third problem with educational production function studies is that they have been executed largely as fishing expeditions. The process is nothing more than obtaining different kinds of data on large numbers of school children and feeding these into a large computer, hoping all the while that at least some of the variables classified as independent will turn out to be statistically significant in determining student attainment. [25] There are not sufficiently accurate

[24] The study by Harvey Averch and Herbert Kiesling, *The Relationship of School and Environment to Student Performance: Some Simultaneous Models for the Project TALENT High Schools* (Santa Monica, Calif.: Rand Corporation, 1970), is an example of two-stage least-squares analysis.
[25] This is not to say that educational production function studies are confined to the additive, linear model of equation (7.2). It is quite possible to use nonlinear, multiplica-

and useful descriptions of the learning environment to justify radical experiments with educational programs for children. If we could justifiably conduct actual experiments in a clinical setting, we could presumably test hypotheses about how children of different ages, sex, and backgrounds respond to major changes in the learning environment. Quite possibly, such knowledge would be cumulative in that new, more powerful hypotheses would replace older ones in the research process.

But policy researchers in education have been confined mainly to the use of natural experiments, with which there is a major difficulty. Suppose we were studying productivity relationships in a competitive branch of the private economy. We could reasonably assume that the owners and managers of the firms had a common objective: profit maximization. Competitive forces should assure that the owners and managers, over a given period, had made reasonably accurate assessments of productivity relationships in each of their particular cases. Input prices would, of course, vary from one firm to the next. Recognizing such differences, firm *A* might use a lot of skilled labor but not the newest machinery. Firm *B* might have very advanced machinery that allows it to economize on skilled labor. In the private sector, we can assume that these differences in processes reflect input prices and that firm *B*, in installing new equipment, added the amount of equipment and released the amount of skilled labor needed to maximize output for the given size of its operating budget—or, alternatively, to minimize costs for a given volume of output. All firms, then, operate on or close to the production possibility curve, and we can be reasonably certain that data obtained from such firms would reflect true marginal rates of substitution of factors of production. We could rely upon data from the field to tell us how much a given piece of equipment saved in skilled labor and vice versa.

In education, things are quite different. There is not agreement on a common objective: Some principals may encourage their teachers to emphasize preparation for college; other may stress acquisition of vocational skills, and others may stress athletics. Moreover, school districts are not under strong pressure to maximize output relative to cost. And we therefore cannot assume that schools are making allocations of resources that place them on or near their

---

tive relations. See Stephen Michelson, "The Association of Teacher Resourcefulness with Children's Characteristics," in *Do Teachers Make a Difference?* U.S. Department of Health, Education, and Welfare, Office of Education (Washington, D.C.: U.S. Government Printing Office, 1970), pp. 120–168.

production possibility curve. Let us take a hypothetical example. Suppose two districts are spending $1,000 per student on teachers. In district A, let experienced teachers be scarce and newly trained ones plentiful; let the opposite condition prevail in district B. Suppose class size in A is 15, with staffing mainly inexperienced; suppose B has class size of 30, with mainly experienced staff. Can we suggest with confidence to district C that one experienced teacher is the productive equivalent of two inexperienced? Hardly. Because schools lack a common objective and are not pushed by competitive forces to their production possibility curve with respect to any objective, education production functions describe average practice, not true relations of input substitutability.[26] As Jesse Burkhead has said,

> On the estimation of production functions in the private sector, it is assumed that the factory manager . . . has reasonably good knowledge of the marginal productivity of the factors that he utilizes and, thus, he is able to optimize factor combinations to maximize profits. But in elementary and secondary education there is no reason to assume that a school principal, or district superintendent, or board of education has knowledge of . . . the marginal productivity of resource inputs. Even if these were known, it could not be assumed that it would be possible to secure least-cost combinations, given the institutional rigidities of mandates and conventional practice. Neither is there a reasonable substitute for the objective function of profit maximization. Thus the optimization rationale that underlies production functions in the private sector is inapplicable for elementary and secondary education.[27]

Finally, there are serious problems with the quality of data in educational production function studies. Data are generally by-products of administrative requirements. For example, to predict replacement demand for teachers, state governments require data regarding age and experience of teachers. These data, in turn, are entered in production function studies to describe characteristics of

---

[26] Suppose that student achievement scores in districts A and B are the same. Does this establish the productivity equivalent of one experienced to two inexperienced teachers. Not necessarily, because the inexperienced teachers in district A might really be interested, for example, in the athletic prowess of their students, not their academic attainment. Hence, we have no measure of what the level of academic attainment in A would be if teachers were interested in stimulating it.

[27] Jesse Burkhead, "Economics Against Education," *Teachers College Record*, 75, no. 2 (December 1973): 198.

teachers. But, assuming that experience is an important independent variable, a count of years in the classroom is hardly adequate. On a priori grounds, we could suggest that the *nature* of experience is what is important: Where was experience gained, in what types of schools and working with what types of students, and how was teaching experience related to preservice and in-service training? Such detailed observations are seldom available.

Data are also, ordinarily, aggregated to show observations for schools as a whole—and, in some cases, school districts. A lot of potentially useful information is lost by averaging out through such aggregation. For example, suppose there is a true positive relationship between teacher experience and student attainment. Let the production function studies be based on schools as the unit of analysis. Since we would seldom find a school in which *all* teachers were either highly experienced, or of minimum experience and in which student background characteristics and peer composition were approximately equal, the relationship between experience and student performance could not come strongly to light. The high productivity of the experienced teachers would be averaged with the lower productivity of the inexperienced in any given school.

Data are also, ordinarily, accumulated for one year's schooling only. That is, the studies do not trace the accumulation of educational and other inputs over any substantial period of the student's educational career (we may, for example, know something about the 5th-grade teachers of a given body of 5th-grade students, but we know nothing about what sort of 2nd-grade education they had; some may even have been in a different school). Because home environments may be more stable than educational environments, at least in terms of influence on student attainment, the fact that most educational production function studies are not *longitudinal* may serve to downgrade the true influence of school variables on output.[28]

Hope for the Future

It is entirely possible, of course, that a second generation of production function studies will be more successful than the first. An example is provided by the Summers-Wolfe study conducted by the

---

[28] Hanushek and Kain in "Value of *Equality of Educational Opportunity*," p. 131, state that "individual and family characteristics are more in the form of stocks and, hence, are subject to less intertemporal variations than are school inputs, which more closely approximate flows. Thus, use of cross sectional measurements of contemporaneous school factors clearly tend to understate the total effect of educational inputs on achievement."

Federal Reserve Bank of Philadelphia.[29] In the first place, the study offers considerable improvement over previous ones in quality of data, which are longitudinal to the extent of accumulating records on student achievements and educational inputs over two years (and in some cases, three). The data are not aggregated—each student is a separate case.[30] Some rather novel independent variables are the following: teacher's score on the National Teachers' Examination, academic rating of teacher's undergraduate college, federal funds expenditure per student, and expenditure on instruction in basic skills (elementary schools only).

The Summers-Wolfe study is also notable because it avoids some of the theoretical problems—such as multicollinearity—that plagued earlier educational production function studies. The reason is that the study is explicitly policy-oriented. It is based in one large school district, Philadelphia. The prices of educational inputs are common to all schools of the district. The study addresses a specific question: If school authorities in Philadelphia wished to improve the distribution of educational opportunity, as measured by reducing the relationship of social class on students' achievement, what shifts in resources would they be best advised to make? This is a more straightforward question than to determine the shares of educational achievement that are contributed by home, peers, and school, which is the basic question of the conventional production function study. The Summers-Wolfe analysis returns production function work to its original policy focus.

Some illustrative results of the Summers-Wolfe study are:

1. The effect of school inputs on achievement is very different for students of different home backgrounds.
2. Teacher's experience "has a very different impact on high— and low—achieving pupils. High achieving pupils do best with more experienced teachers, but these teachers lower the learning growth of low achievers—these students do best with relatively inexperienced teachers, who, perhaps, have an undampened enthusiasm for teaching. . . ."[31]
3. Teachers who are graduates of highly-rated colleges and universities are distinctly more successful than teachers from

---

[29] Anita A. Summers and Barbara L. Wolfe, *Equality of Educational Opportunity Quantified: A Production Function Approach* (Philadelphia: Department of Research, Federal Reserve Bank of Philadelphia, 1975).

[30] The study dealt with 627 elementary students in 103 schools, 553 junior high students in 42 schools, and 716 students in 5 senior high schools.

[31] Ibid., p. 12.

low-rated institutions and they are especially helpful to the low-income student.

From such findings, the authors suggest a redistribution of teachers' services within the Philadelphia district in order to raise the performance of low-achieving students. We will consider these recommendations further in Chapter 11.

Cost-Benefit and Cost-Effectiveness Analysis

Another set of research techniques that can be used to inform resource allocation processes in the public sector is that of *cost-benefit* and *cost-effectiveness* analysis. We group these two procedures together because they are closely related.

Cost-Benefit Studies

Cost-benefit studies proceed from a definition of a program or project to be evaluated, ordinarily of a long-term nature. Connected with any project or program are *costs,* at least some of which are measurable in quantitative terms. Likewise, the project or program will provide outcomes called *benefits.* For cost-benefit analysis to be successfully applied, at least some of the major benefits must be susceptible to quantitative measurement. The streams of cost and benefits are discounted to the present, using an appropriate rate of discount. If present discounted value of benefits exceeds discounted costs, then, theoretically, the given program or project qualifies for funding. An agency could select among such projects to maximize net benefits for any given sum of investment. Even when discount costs exceed discounted benefits, the agency might still fund a given project. What the agency obtains by conducting cost-benefit analysis in such a case is an estimate of the costs of obtaining the nonquantifiable benefits yielded by the given investment.

As is probably clear, cost-benefit analysis is very similar to the rate-of-return studies we described in Chapter 4. The same problems of choosing an appropriate rate of discount apply to both. Both seek to guide decision makers as they deal with the future but on the basis of data from past events and conditions. The difference between rate-of-return and cost-benefit analysis is that the former applies to regional or economywide investments in, say, major educational programs, and the latter applies to discrete projects or programs, such as the introduction of a new vocational program in a given school district.

The general questions to be answered in conducting cost-benefit analysis are:

1. Which cost and benefits are to be included?

2. How are they to be valued?

3. At what interest rate are they to be discounted?

4. What are the relevant constraints?[32]

We will illustrate the process by examining an early, classic application of cost-benefit analysis by Burton Weisbrod to an educational situation, and we will then describe some more recent studies.

Weisbrod's application of cost-benefit analysis dealt with a program to prevent high school dropouts.[33] Benefits, the measurable ones, that is, were computed as the present value, discounted at a rate of 5 percent, of differential lifetime median income of high school graduates versus dropouts. These data were drawn from the U.S. census. Different estimates were made for males and females and for white and nonwhite, and both of these categories were further identified by residence (Non-South or South), though the residency classification was not employed in the final analysis.

Costs of dropout prevention were estimated from data of an experimental program in St. Louis, Missouri. A group of potential dropouts was identified (as of the early 1960s) and was then divided into a control group and an experimental group. The experimental group received extra educational services, such as special counseling and assistance in finding and keeping jobs—part-time jobs; summer jobs; and, once high school was completed, full-time jobs. Of the 429 students in the experimental group, 189 (44.1 percent) dropped out of high school in spite of the dropout prevention program. However,

---

[32] The list is taken from the comprehensive article by A. R. Prest and R. Turvey, "Cost Benefit Analysis: A Survey," *The Economic Journal*, 75, no. 300 (December 1965): 686. We should note that constraints may be budgetary, legal, or moral. With regard to moral constraints, certain potentially high-yield educational projects might be judged not suitable because they involve invasion of the privacy of the family.

[33] Burton A. Weisbrod, "Preventing High School Dropouts," in *Measuring Benefits of Government Investments*, ed. Robert Dorfman (Washington, D.C.: Brookings, 1965), pp. 117-149. See also Weisbrod's, "Income Redistribution Effects and Benefit-Cost Analysis," in *Problems in Public Expenditure Analysis*, ed. Samuel B. Chase (Washington, D.C.: Brookings, 1968), pp. 177-209.

Table 7.1
Computation of present value of additional lifetime income per average dropout prevented

Race and sex (1)	Percentage of dropout prevented (2)	Present value per dropout prevented (3)	Weighted present value (4)
White male	30.0%	$3,420	$1,026
White female	10.5	4,600	483
Nonwhite male	33.8	1,750	592
Nonwhite female	25.7	2,500	642
Total	100.0		2,743

Source: Burton A. Weisbrod, "Preventing High School Dropouts," in *Measuring Benefits of Government Investments*, ed. Robert Dorfman (Washington, D.C.: Brookings, 1965), p. 142. Copyright © 1965 by The Brookings Institution. Reprinted with permission.

52.0 percent of the control group dropped out, and the difference of 7.9 percentage points between the two groups is statistically significant. Extra expenditures *per student* in the experimental group over a two-year period was $460. However, when account is taken that of any 100 students in the program, only a small proportion could be claimed as successes—derived from the percentage point difference between the control and experimental group of 7.9—we must expand the cost per student by pro rata to recognize program failures, and we must also add the expenditures of the normal program for the previous two years of high school. The cost *per dropout prevented* then comes to $6,500.

The benefits of the program are computed as shown in Table 7.1. Column (3) shows values by race and sex of the excess of lifetime income of high school graduates over dropouts, discounted at 5 percent. Column (2) represents the percentage share of dropouts prevented in the St. Louis program, that is, 30 percent of the dropouts that were prevented were white males. (It is thus assumed that 30 percent of dropouts that *could be prevented* would be white males.) The weights of column (2) are applied to the estimated benefits in column (3) to obtain the weighted present value in column (4). The total weighted present value of the dropout prevention program is thus $2,743 or, as a rounded number, $2,750.

The final comparison of benefits and costs of dropout prevention is given in Table 7.2. Costs per dropout prevented exceed benefits by $3,800. This is the price society might be said to pay for the nonmeasurable benefits that are listed in the table, such as decreased costs of welfare programs.

Table 7.2
Summary of benefits and costs per high school dropout prevented, St. Louis program[a]

Resource costs per dropout prevented	
Direct prevention costs	$5,815
Additional instructional costs[b]	725
Total	6,540
Internal benefits per dropout prevented	
Increased present value of lifetime income	2,750
Improved self-esteem of student	(+)
External benefits per dropout prevented	
Increased productivity of cooperating resources[c]	(+)
Increased social and political consciousness and participation	(+)
Decreased social costs (e.g., of crime and delinquency)	(+)
Decreased social costs of administering welfare programs	(+)
Intergenerational benefits[d]	(+)
Total cost per dropout prevented not covered by measured benefits	3,800
Distributional effects	(XX)

[a] The symbol (+) refers to an unmeasured, positive benefit; (XX) refers to a quantity that is not commensurable with costs and benefits.
[b] The additional costs borne by the school district in providing regular instruction in the last years of the high school program for students who might otherwise have dropped out.
[c] Related to the assumption that more highly educated workers stimulate their fellow workers to higher levels of productivity.
[d] Related to the assumption that more highly educated parents will stimulate their children to higher levels of educational attainment.
Source: Burton A. Weisbrod, "Preventing High School Dropouts," in *Measuring Benefits of Government Investments*, ed. Robert Dorfman (Washington, D.C.: Brookings, 1965), p. 148. Copyright © 1965 by The Brookings Institution. Reprinted with permission.

A second example of cost-benefit analysis in education is provided by Walter I. Garms, who undertook to assess the economic worth of the Upward Bound Program. He describes the program as follows:

> The Upward Bound Program [exists] to find able high school students who would be unlikely to go on to college because of poverty or because of low perceptions of probable success. . . . Typically, the program has attempted to identify these students in their sophomore year in high school. They are given an intensive program at a local college during the ensuing summers until college enrollment, and during the school year there are occasional Saturday sessions at the college. The work is designed to introduce these students to skills and attitudes that are helpful in college and to remedy the subject matter areas in which the student is weak.[34]

Garms obtained a sample of 7,236 students who entered the program in the period 1966-1968. Their records of educational attainment, particularly whether they continued in college, were accumulated and compared with the educational attainments of their older siblings of the same sex who had not participated in Upward Bound (the control group). The extra educational attainments of the Upward Bound students were translated into lifetime earnings differentials and were discounted at rates of 5 and 10 percent, alternatively. Garms also employed data on Upward Bound stipends and grants and on costs borne by the student in attending college.

The computation of benefits and costs to an individual member of the Upward Bound Program is illustrated in Table 7.3 (data are for white males; the original article also offers data on white females and nonwhite males and females). It is estimated, on the average, that Upward Bound participants spend something less than one year in college over the time spent in college by their older siblings. This difference produces a raw lifetime income differential in favor of Upward Bound participants. The figures $5,209 and $770 shown in Table 7.3 are such differentials discounted at rates of 5 and 10 percent. Before discounting, however, two adjustments had been made: The raw income differentials were reduced by (1) 25 percent to reflect that extra pay requires a person to pay extra taxes and (2) an additional 25 percent to recognize an assumption that only 75 percent

[34] Walter I. Garms, "A Benefit-Cost Analysis of the Upward Bound Program," *Journal of Human Resources*, 6, no. 2 (Spring 1971): 206-220 (quote is on p. 206).

Table 7.3

Benefits and costs of Upward Bound Program to
individual members, white male participants

5 percent discount rate	
Benefits	
Lifetime income differentials (after taxes)	$5,209
Upward Bound stipend	210
Scholarship and grants	454
Total	5,873
Cost differentials	
College tuition fees	370
Fixed living costs of attending college	260
Total	630
Net benefits	5,243
10 percent discount rate	
Benefits	
Lifetime income differentials (after taxes)	770
Upward Bound stipend	202
Scholarship and grants	373
Total	1,345
Cost differentials	
College tuition fees	308
Fixed living costs of attending college	215
Total	523
Net benefits	822

Source: Walter I. Garms, "A Benefit Cost Analysis of the Upward Bound Program,"
Journal of Human Resources, 6, no. 2 (Spring 1971): 216. Reprinted with permission.

of income differentials can be attributed to education, as compared
with the contribution of other factors such as inherent ability, health,
and so on. Table 7.3 shows plainly the significance of choice of
discount rate. At 10 percent, extra earnings barely cover total costs;
and the benefit to the participant lies substantially in the stipend or
grant he receives.

Table 7.4 examines the worth of Upward Bound to society as
a whole (again, we confine our attention to the case of white males).
The importance of choice of discount rate is once more illustrated
dramatically. Social benefits per enrollee are high and positive at the 5
percent rate and high and negative at the 10 percent rate.

Table 7.4
Benefits and costs of Upward Bound Program to society as a whole, white male participants

5 percent discount rate	
Benefits	
Lifetime income differential (before taxes)	$7,020
Cost differentials	
Upward Bound cost to government	1,811
Upward Bound cost to college	260
Cost of regular college program	1,057
Extra living costs in attending college	260
Total	3,388
Net benefits	3,632
10 percent discount rate	
Benefits	
Lifetime income differentials (before taxes)	1,066
Cost differentials	
Upward Bound cost to government	1,737
Upward Bound cost to college	249
Cost of regular college program	852
Extra living costs in attending college	215
Total	3,053
Net benefits	−1,987

Source: Walter I. Garms, "A Benefit Cost Analysis of the Upward Bound Program," *Journal of Human Resources*, 6, no. 2 (Spring 1971): 219. Reprinted with permission.

Garms summarized his assessment of the Upward Bound Program as follows:

> From the economic viewpoint, Upward Bound is at best a marginal program, and the justification for its continued existence must be sought in presumed benefits which are not accounted for here. . . . [T]he data point out the possibility that the Upward Bound Program is primarily a device for identification of students who would be rather likely to go to college anyway. If this were its only function, all social benefits would . . . be eliminated, and private benefits would be limited to the value of the Upward Bound stipend.[35]

[35] Ibid., p. 220.

The third example on cost-benefit analysis we will discuss is not the result of an investigation but, rather, a statement of procedure. The problem is to make an economic evaluation of a program of vocational training. The procedure has been suggested by Manuel Zymelman.[36]

The first step is to determine the probability of employment for graduates of the given program. This requires a multifaceted investigation. Census data may be used to establish broad trends in employment in particular industries. Special surveys may be made of graduates of similar vocational programs to see what their employability record has been. Managers and owners may be interviewed to search out their criteria for hiring new workers and to see how well qualifications established in the given vocational programs will be received in the job market. Once these data are assembled, an estimate should be made, according to Zymelman, of the earnings during the first five years of the working life of the graduates of the given program. Also, an estimate should be made of earnings of people otherwise similar to graduates in terms of age, sex, and previous educational background but who do not attend the program.

Costs of the given vocational program are stated to be:

$$TC_j = PC_j + EC_j + MC_j + FC_j \tag{7.4}$$

where TC_j = total cost of program j
    PC_j = personnel costs of program j
    EC_j = equipment cost of program j
    MC_j = cost of materials for program j
    FC_j = cost of facilities for program j

Let us illustrate the computation of personnel costs. These are stated to be

$$PC_j = ADM_j + LP_j + CLP_j \tag{7.5}$$

where ADM_j = costs of administrators allocated to program j
    LP_j = cost of laboratory personnel allocated to program j
    CLP_j = cost of classroom personnel allocated to program j.

Costs are then assigned to program j on the basis of student hours of instruction for that given program as compared with total student hours in all programs of the institution. That is:

$$ADM_j = TCA \times \frac{HRS_j}{\sum_{i=1}^{n} HRS_i} \tag{7.6}$$

[36] Manuel Zymelman, *The Economic Evaluation of Vocational Training Programs* (Baltimore: Johns Hopkins, 1976).

where TCA = total cost of administrators and
HRS_j = student hours in program j

And

$$LP_j = \sum_{k=1}^{m} CLI_k \times \frac{HRSL_{kj}}{\sum_{i=1}^{m} HRSL_{ji}} \qquad (7.7)$$

where $\sum_{k=1}^{m} CLI_k$ = total personnel costs of instruction for laboratory
type k
$HRSL_j$ = student hours of laboratory instruction in program j
m = number of laboratories of type k

And

$$CLP_j = TCCLI \times \frac{HRSL_j}{\sum_{i=1}^{n} HRCL_i} \qquad (7.8)$$

where $TCCLI$ = total personnel costs of instruction in classrooms
(related work in the vocational program)
$HRSCL_j$ = student hours of classroom instruction in program j

Similar procedures are used to allocate equipment costs, facilities
costs, and so on, to the given vocational program. Then costs and
benefits are brought together in the following way:[37]

$$I_t = \frac{E_{t1} - E_{w1}}{(1 + r)} + \frac{E_{t2} - E_{w2}}{(1 + r)^2} + \ldots$$

$$+ \frac{E_{t5} - E_{w5}}{(1 + r)^5} + \ldots + \frac{E_{tn} - E_{wn}}{(1 + r)^n} \qquad (7.9)$$

where I_t = costs of the vocational program, as determined above
$E_{t1}, E_{t2}, \ldots,$ = average earnings in the given years of
graduates of vocational program
$E_{w1}, E_{w2}, \ldots,$ = average earnings in the given years of similarly placed persons who are not graduates of
the given program

It is assumed that the earnings differentials remain constant after five
years.

[37] Ibid., p. 74.

Cost-Effectiveness Studies

Cost-effectiveness studies in education are similar to cost-benefit studies in that they deal with some particular educational program, project, or type of expenditure, rather than assessing economywide aspects of schooling. The difference is that cost-effectiveness analysis does not specify an objective function, such as maximizing income differentials. Hence, to undertake cost-effectiveness analysis we are not required to estimate benefits attributable to an educational program; rather, we can specify some educational objective and show how it can be met at least cost. Some examples follow.

Using data from the Coleman report, Henry M. Levin sought to answer the question of how to recruit and hire teachers in such a way that salary expenditures are spent most effectively in raising achievement scores of students.[38] The method of multiple correlation was applied to obtain the (average) effects on student achievement of a change in teacher's verbal scores (based on a test of teacher's verbal ability administered in connection with the Coleman report) as compared with a change in length of teaching experience. For white students, it turned out that each additional point of teacher's verbal score was associated with an increase in the student's own verbal score of .179 points and that each additional year of teaching experience raised student's verbal score by .060 points. Levin then investigated the relationship between teachers' salaries, on the one hand, and teacher's verbal scores and experience, on the other:

> What is of particular interest . . . is that the approximate annual cost to schools of obtaining a teacher with an additional year of experience was about $79 and that of obtaining a teacher with an additional point on the verbal score was about $24.[39]

Thus, experience is more costly to the district than teacher's verbal score; yet, we saw that experience is less powerful in influencing student achievement than teacher's verbal score. Putting these two findings together, Levin concludes that the relative cost to a school district of increasing students' verbal achievement is far cheaper by hiring teachers with higher verbal ability than by hiring teachers with greater experience (for white students). Levin concludes:

---

[38] Henry M. Levin, "A Cost-Effectiveness Analysis of Teacher Selection," *Journal of Human Resources*, 5, no. 1 (Winter 1970): 24–33.
[39] Ibid., pp. 30–31.

The over-riding implication of this analysis is that school salary policies should provide financial incentives that will attract and retain teachers with greater verbal skills. . . . On the other hand, it is suggested that the schools grant too large a reward for experience. The result of reducing salary increment for experience and implementing them for verbal performance would appear to attract a more capable teaching staff with regard to the production of student achievement.[40]

Cost-effectiveness studies can also be the case-study, or descriptive, type. In 1973 the Office of Education Performance Review of the State of New York undertook a study of two inner city elementary schools in New York City, matched by poverty neighborhood, student transiency, ethnic distribution, and parental income, to see why one school was relatively successful in promoting educational achievements of students and one was not. The contrast in achievement was described as follows:

40 percent of the children in school A were reading at or above grade level compared to 20 percent for school B. The results indicate that school A fared better than school B on the functional reading measure at each of the three grade levels, i.e., school A had a higher percentage of students reading at or above grade level and a lower percentage of students reading two or more levels below grade.[41]

Data collection consisted of testing students and, more important, observations and interviews relating to instructional practices and classroom atmosphere:

Qualitative rather than quantitative techniques were emphasized. The opinions of school personnel, community members, and students were elicited both formally and informally. School processes and climate were assessed through frequent observations.[42]

---

[40] Ibid., p. 32.
[41] Office of Education Performance Review, State of New York, *School Factors Influencing Reading Achievement: A Case Study of Two Inner City Schools* (Albany, N.Y., 1974), p. 9.
[42] Ibid., p. 8.

The results were as follows:

> The findings of this study suggest that the differences in pupils' reading achievement in these two schools were primarily attributable to administrative policies, behavior, procedures and practices. Effectiveness of teaching, training and experience of teachers, appropriateness and availability of materials, and approaches to teaching reading did not differ significantly between the schools. . . . Administrative policies . . . were a major determinant of school, classroom, and community climate. Teachers' job satisfaction, parents' regard for the school, and children's willingness to participate in the school could be traced to the stability, fairness, and flexibility of the administrative team. . . . The leadership provided by principal A was not particularly charismatic . . . rather his competency lay in his skill in getting things done through people and he had built an administrative team with diverse skills. . . . The coherence of the reading program at school A stemmed from the efforts of the assistant principal in charge of reading.[43]

The third type of cost-effectiveness study we will discuss has to do with educational technology. The government of Mexico in 1969 began planning for a system of radio instruction of elementary students:

> *Radioprimaria* was intended . . . to allow a school with four teachers to offer all six grades of primary schooling. Three teachers would handle the first three grades in the traditional manner; the fourth teacher would have the fourth, fifth, and sixth grades in one classroom and would instruct with the assistance of radio lessons. Some instructional programs would be grade-specific while others would be directed to all three grades in common. When grade-specific lessons are broadcast, the students in the other two grades are supposed to engage in work on their own. It should also be noted that the above structure implies that students may be directed to listen to the same common broadcast each year for three years. . . . Each radio lesson lasts 17 minutes and about five programs are broadcast each school day. . . . [After a considerable exercise in testing of students, it was judged that]

[43] Ibid., p. 20.

Table 7.5
Comparison of annual cost per student, *Radioprimaria*
versus traditional instruction (in dollars)

Components	Radioprimaria	Traditional instruction
Traditional		
Administration	$50.00	$50.00
Classroom teacher	32.00	96.00
Facilities	6.10	18.29
Subtotal	88.10	164.29
Radio instruction		
Production	11.53	—
Transmission	1.44	—
Reception	.15	—
Subtotal	13.12	
Total annual cost		
per student	101.22	164.29

Source: Dean T. Jamison, Steven J. Klees, and Stuart J. Wells, *Cost Analysis for Educational Planning and Evaluation: Methodology and Application to Instructional Technology* (Princeton, N.J.: Educational Testing Service, 1976), p. 164. Reprinted with permission.

Radioprimaria had produced scores that are comparable to those of the children in direct teaching schools.[44]

However, costs per student differ markedly. Fixed costs are generally low because existing broadcasting facilities are used. The equation for total cost is

$$TC = 0.13N + 125.09h \qquad (7.10)$$

where TC = total cost in U.S. dollars, N = number of students the system serves, and h = number of hours the system broadcasts. As of 1972, 2,800 students were served and 280 hours were broadcast, yielding a cost per student hour of approximately $0.05.[45] The average cost of traditional and radio instruction is shown in Table 7.5. Assuming the finding that student achievement results between

[44] Dean T. Jamison, Steven J. Klees, and Stuart J. Wells, *Cost Analysis for Educational Planning and Evaluation: Methodology and Application to Industrial Technology* (Princeton, N.J.: Educational Testing Service, 1976), pp. 155, 157.
[45] Ibid., p. 162.

216 Public Rationality in Educational Decision Making

direct and radio instruction are approximately the same, then cost-effectiveness analysis indicates that radio instruction is the better buy.

The Educational Testing Service, which analyzed the Mexican radio experiment, concludes:

> The *Radioprimaria* is an interesting attempt at meeting the problem of the lack of sufficient educational opportunities in rural areas [in] Mexico and most other developing nations . . . [T]he unique configuration of the system, which combines several grades in one classroom with one teacher, results in considerable cost savings over the traditional direct teaching system.[46]

Observations on Cost-Benefit and Cost-Effectiveness Analysis

Cost-benefit analysis faces serious problems. First, as we have seen, the results of the analysis turn in large measure on the choice of discount rate. The argument in Chapter 4 about the arbitrariness of any such choice applies equally to cost-benefit and rate of return analysis. Second, cost-benefit analysis—up to this point at least—reaches its conclusions based on market criteria, for example, income differentials as determined in labor markets. Unmeasured outputs and consequences of educational programs, such as social cohesiveness and income redistribution, may actually be more important than market criteria in judging the relative worth of those educational programs.

Cost-effectiveness analysis is the more straightforward technique. It is relatively value-free, and its results are easier to interpret than are those of cost-benefit work—at least in a policy context. The only real drawback with cost-effectiveness analysis in education is that, when there are experiments and programs to evaluate, there is often little gain in effectiveness of educational activities to report upon. And the exercise tends to degenerate into cost-analysis only, as was the case of the Mexico experiment.

Summary

Substantial effort has been made to establish a rational framework for resource allocation in the public sector. The earlier, possibly overoptimistic, attempts to introduce the planning, programming, and

[46] Ibid., p. 163.

budgeting system (PPBS) into all civilian governmental activities have spawned a new interest in assessing evidence and using such evidence in making judgments about public policies, including educational policies. Calculating cost-benefit and cost-effectiveness ratios is now common practice in public agencies. Educational analysts have further developed methods for analyzing correlates of a child's school performance—how much of the difference in achievement from one child to the next is associated with his or her home background, the characteristics of his or her classmates, and the school program itself. As these studies become more sophisticated, they should help us greatly to see how to achieve educational objectives within, of course, the prevailing time and budgetary constraints. Up to the present, however, educational production function studies do not give us final results on the issues. There is no unanimity among the analysts on how to account for the different variables that influence educational output nor how to interpret the results of studies that have been made. Up till now, there is little basis for generalizing results from one school setting to another. Yet, the fact that the studies are underway and are showing improvements in methods is encouraging.

Selected Bibliography

Averch, Harvey, et al. *How Effective Is Schooling: A Critical Review and Synthesis of Research Findings.* Santa Monica, Calif.: Rand Corporation, 1972.

Burkhead, Jesse, Thomas G. Fox, and John W. Holland. *Input and Output in Large-City High Schools.* Syracuse, N.Y.: Syracuse University Press, 1967.

Cohn, Elchanan. *Input-Output Analysis in Public Education.* Cambridge, Mass.: Ballinger, 1975.

Coleman, James, et al. *Equality of Educational Opportunity.* Washington, D.C.: U.S. Government Printing Office, 1966.

Dorfman, Robert, ed. *Measuring Benefits of Government Investments.* Washington, D.C.: Brookings, 1965.

Katzman, Martin T. *The Political Economy of Urban Schools.* Cambridge, Mass.: Harvard, 1971.

Mosteller, Frederick, and Daniel P. Moynihan. *On Equality of Educational Opportunity.* New York: Random House, 1972.

Schultze, Charles L. *The Politics and Economics of Public Spending.* Washington, D.C.: Brookings, 1968.

Chapter Eight

Household Choice, Efficiency, and Equity

It is now time to draw together some of the main arguments from earlier chapters. Let us start with household choice. To increase the power of parents to decide what educational activities their children shall participate in is probably a worthy objective. This assertion is grounded on two assumptions: Tastes, including tastes for educational services, differ among individuals; and, to fit services to tastes, parents have information about their children not generally available to teachers and counselors and an expected commitment to the welfare of their children exceeding that of teachers and other school personnel. Indeed, we might argue from those assumptions that students, as well as parents, should have greater power to choose educational programs; if tastes differ, students know more about their own tastes for educational services than their parents do.[1] By what means should powers of choosing be increased? To grant choice in education by shifting the provision of services into the private market (as could be accomplished in a full-fledged voucher scheme—see Chapter 6) carries substantial risks. Hence, the problem we consider in this chapter is how to increase choice *within the public education sector.*

---

[1] We do not mean to suggest that students should be encouraged to establish minimum standards of learning for themselves or should elect to engage in trivial learning activities.

In considering efficiency, we recognize that educational resources are limited relative to the demands placed on our educational system, and we should strive to improve the efficiency of that system. But, alas, we lack clear, powerful guidance from analytical studies about how to accomplish that objective. Our ability to identify problems in the allocation of educational resources has exceeded our ability to analyze the complexities of learning processes. In light of this situation, we shall suggest structural changes to bring the *teacher's role* in educational development to the fore.

In terms of equity, the practice of geographic entitlement to school services, given the present degree of social isolation of neighborhoods, results in an uneven distribution of educational resources that favors the well-to-do. Yet, strong attacks on this problem run the risk of damaging the social fabric by impinging on what dutiful parents see as just rewards for good parenting. In Chapters 10 and 11 we will examine what can be done to ameliorate the unjust distribution of educational resources by reforming the system of educational finance. In this chapter, on the other hand, we will examine how the *out-of-school environment of young people* may affect the learning prospects of children in different social classes.[2] Also, we will examine students' incentives to learn and how they might be enhanced.

Educational Choice in the Public Sector

Let us see what choices have been discovered in public education to offer households.

Pace and Content of Learning in Secondary Schools

Secondary education in the United States has been described as *lock-step learning*, in which students proceed at one fixed pace through an ordained sequence of courses tied to the award of a diploma.[3] How did this system arise?

The overall regulation by government of educational outputs in this country can be said to date from 1647, when the General Court of Massachusetts decreed: "each Town with 50 families to provide a schoolmaster to teach all children who 'shall resorte to him, to write

---

[2] I am indebted to Elliott Medrich, Childhood and Government Project, University of California at Berkeley, for help on this particular topic.

[3] See Charles S. Benson, James W. Guthrie, and Brenda M. Archibald, "Lock-Step Learning," *The Andover Review*, 3, no. 1 (Spring 1976): 76–88.

and read.'"[4] Note that the objective was stated in acquired skills—in this specific case, the skills of literacy. By 1852, however, educational objectives had been translated into attendance for a *specified period of time* when the Commonwealth of Massachusetts passed the first compulsory attendance law to be found in the United States.[5] By 1918, 48 states, together with the District of Columbia, had compulsory attendance laws in force. Twenty states required attendance from ages 7 to 16 and 10 other states required that children attend school from ages 8 to 16. At the other extreme, 5 states—Georgia, Louisiana, North Carolina, South Carolina, and Texas—required attendance only to what was then the national minimum age of 14.

Connecticut specified that a year of schooling equalled 38 weeks. Eight states defined a year of schooling as nine months, while 18 other states defined it as eight months. The shortest specified length of school year, three months, was found in Oklahoma, though Alabama declined to define the length of school year altogether in its early compulsory attendance statute.[6]

A practically universal pattern of compulsory attendance had become set by the end of World War I, under which children were required to attend school during certain ages and the minimum length of school year was also generally defined. Moreover, elaborate provisions requiring teachers and administrators to report truancy, as well as legal penalties for failure so to report, were established; and the powers and duties of truant officers were clearly laid down.

> The test of efficiency of any compulsory education system may be fairly shown by the answers to two questions, which are: First, what percent of the total school population does it get into school, or otherwise reach? Secondly, how well does it keep them in school, or in training elsewhere? Generally speaking, the law which scores satisfactory in this test is a satisfactory law.[7]

Shortly after compulsory attendance was effectively standardized, a similarly mechanical procedure for determining when a person could be judged to have completed high school was established. High school graduation was determined by the accumulation

---

[4] Bureau of Education, Department of the Interior, *Laws Relating to Compulsory Education,* bulletin 1928, no. 20 (Washington, D.C.: U.S. Government Printing Office, 1929), p. 2.
[5] Ibid., p. 4.
[6] Ibid., pp. 6–7.
[7] Ibid., p. 29.

of a specified number of credits: "Amount of credit is most commonly referred to in terms of the unit. The unit is variously defined in different sections, but in general it represents approximately one fourth of a year's work as performed by a student of average ability."[8] Another common accounting measure was semester credit, with two semester credits equal to one unit. By 1928 all states except Massachusetts expressed graduation requirements in terms of semester credits or in units, requiring between 29 and 36 semester credits for the diploma. The school day had then to be arranged to assure that, one way or another, students could acquire the required numbers of credits for graduation:

> The average length of the school day . . . is slightly less than six hours. In the average school the typical pupil spends three hours and 40 minutes in class, slightly more than 1-½ hours in study, and 24 minutes in extracurricular activities. An average of 19 minutes of each day is consumed by intermissions between periods. . . . [However] the length of the class period has no consistent influence upon the total amount of time spent in work on various courses. . . . In schools with short periods the pupils spend more time at school and at home in studying the various subjects than do those in schools with long periods. The larger amount of time spent in study by pupils in schools with short periods is compensated for by the longer time spent in the classroom by pupils in schools with long periods.[9]

Now, we do not contend that compulsory attendance laws failed altogether to promote learning in recalcitrant students or that the laws did not serve to put pressure on low-income parents to allow their children to attend school beyond the ages at which they acquired capacity to work (at least within the household). Nor do we contend that the requirement to take—and pass—a specified number of courses fails altogether to establish minimum standards of student performance in high school. Our concern is that the policy gave

[8] Bureau of Education, Department of the Interior, *Requirements for High School Graduation*, bulletin 1928, no. 21 (Washington, D.C.: U.S. Government Printing Office, 1929), pp. 2–5.
[9] Office of Education, Department of the Interior, *The Program of Studies*, bulletin 1932, no. 17, monograph no. 19 (Washington, D.C.: U.S. Government Printing Office, 1933), pp. 330, 335.

virtually no attention to the problem of maximizing the uses of the time of all students, the fast, the average, and the slow.

However, there are departures from lock-step learning that have offered—and still offer—means for students, presumably acting with the advice and consent of their parents, to exercise choice about the pace and content of their high school programs. We will describe an early program in Little Rock, Arkansas, and then we will consider an experiment in student choice being conducted in California.

In 1929–30 Little Rock Senior High had a 6-3-3 form of organization and enrolled 2,200 students. The superintendent described the essential features of his plan to maximize the use of student time as follows:

> The plan for securing economy of time for the more able pupils in the secondary school grades of the Little Rock system consists essentially in setting up uniform subject matter requirements in each field of study, and in providing arrangements by which pupils may fulfill these requirements at various rates of speed. Unusual attention is given . . . to securing in the case of each pupil as rapid progress as the pupil's individual ability may permit, so that each pupil may form the habit of working at a high degree of effort and efficiency.[10]

Junior high school students who secure A's and B's in courses could take extra courses or "rapid progress sections":

> Pupils whose previous work meets the required standard and where health, maturity, and general ability make rapid progress desirable, may be assigned at the beginning of any semester to one of these [rapid progress] sections. During each semester the sections cover two half-years of work in one of the major subjects. A different subject is "doubled" each half-year.[11]

In the senior high school, students were encouraged to sign up for additional courses; they were also encouraged to take correspondence work from the state university:

[10] Office of Education, Department of the Interior, *The Reorganization of Secondary Education,* bulletin 1932, no. 17, monograph no. 5 (Washington, D.C.: U.S. Government Printing Office, 1933), p. 337.
[11] Ibid., p. 338.

> The senior high school is inclined to give full allowance . . .
> for credits transferred from other institutions, *on the assump-*
> *tion that its own obligation is to gauge the ability of its pupils by*
> *their performance rather than by more arbitrary credit standards.*
> . . . The foregoing arrangements apply to pupils enrolled in
> the junior and senior high schools for full-time study. The
> senior high school offers courses also for students who can
> devote only part time to school work, at hours at which these
> students can take advantage of such courses.[12]

The Little Rock system offered, as well, summer sessions for advanced work and for make-up work. College preparatory students
were encouraged to take vocational courses in the summer. Administration of the Little Rock plan called for special effort.

> [E]ach major subject field throughout the system has been
> put in charge of a special supervisor, who has been made
> responsible for appropriate grade placement of materials and
> for the general integration of the course of study. The super-
> visors have devoted particular attention to establishing grade
> standards in terms of particular goals for each semester's
> work, so that the requirements for advance credits may be
> defined with reasonable accuracy . . . arrangements have
> been made through which, when the need arises, pupils may
> take both junior and senior high school courses at the same
> time.[13]

Moreover, the superintendent stated that the district took pains to
advise students and their parents of opportunities to accelerate study
programs. Special notice was given at commencement to students
who had completed their high school program early.

Students could advance their program by one full year by the
time of graduation. In 1929–30, 74 students were graduated from
Little Rock Senior High at least one-half year early. And this number
represents approximately 1 in 6 in a graduating class of 435.[14]

It may be assumed that some students, at least, wish to
complete their junior-senior high studies at a faster rate than normal.
The Little Rock plan allowed these desires, within limits, to be
fulfilled. It economized in scarce resources: the time of students and

[12] Ibid., p. 339 (italics added).
[13] Ibid., p. 341.
[14] Ibid., p. 343.

teachers. The most noteworthy feature of the plan, perhaps, is the encouragement given to students to study and obtain knowledge— and eventually credits—in settings outside the Little Rock school system.

In passing, we observe that a few other school systems also sought to allow students who wished to do so to speed up their progress toward diplomas. In the 1920s, Newark, N.J., Omaha, Nebraska, and Nashville, Tennessee, were making "all-year schools" available to their students.[15] The superintendent in Salt Lake City, Utah, in 1926 reported the establishment of a 6-3-2 plan, stating that

> the large majority of our young people should graduate from high school in 12 years from the time they enter kindergarten, and thus be ready for college or for practical life at 17 or 18 years of age. We are convinced that all the essentials of the subject matter now taught in the longer course can be as thoroughly mastered with the shorter course, and that much dawdling can be prevented as well as loss of time from giving attention to irrelevant or useless subject matter.[16]

The second example of a departure from lock-step learning is one that has recently begun in California, but even it has its historical roots. The California plan is based in the first instance on a *proficiency test*. Students aged 16 and over may elect to take the test; if they pass it they are entitled to receive a certificate of high school completion that is legally equivalent to a high school diploma. But the idea of a proficiency test was introduced in California by statute in 1918. The state required the establishment of evening school programs in places where 20 or more persons aged 18 to 21 were illiterate and the state required illiterate persons to attend such programs until the age of 21 or until they could "read, speak, and write the English language with the proficiency required for completion of 6th grade."[17]

The program we will discuss commenced under California Senate Bill 1112, which was signed into law by Governor Ronald Reagan in 1972 and directed the State Education Department to draw up a high school proficiency examination. The examination, first

[15] Bureau of Education, Department of the Interior, *Biennial Survey of Education, 1922–24*, bulletin 1926, no. 23 (Washington, D.C.: U.S. Government Printing Office, 1927), p. 41.
[16] Bureau of Education, Department of the Interior, *Biennial Survey of Education, 1924–26*, bulletin 1928, no. 25 (Washington, D.C.: U.S. Government Printing Office, 1928), p. 70.
[17] Bureau of Education, *Laws Relating to Compulsory Education*, p. 8.

administered on December 20, 1975, is offered three times each year. Those who pass are given a certificate that is legally the same as a regular high school diploma. Parental permission is not required to take the examination.

The examination itself is *norm-referenced,* meaning that it is intended to yield scores that serve only to describe the performance of a single individual relative to that of other individuals. Passing mark is set at the median score of second semester high school seniors: "The norm-referenced exam is a screening device to 'let through' the median-or-above and to retain those below the median within the secondary school system."[18] It follows that educational choice as provided by the California High School Proficiency Examination is limited to the average or above average student.

The examination purports to reveal the student's grasp of basic educational skills, such as solving mathematical problems relating to household income and expenditures; writing, including sentence structure and punctuation, and the like. It is not designed to screen students for college success. The questions in the test were derived from many sources—National Assessment of Educational Progress, Wisconsin Test of Adult Basic Education, New York State Basic Competency Tests, and tests developed by local districts in California, among others.[19] Students are informed of results on a pass or fail basis. The State Department of Education assures students that if they take the test and fail, no one is so informed. Hence, bad results on the test should not prevent students from getting into college later if they become eligible otherwise.

Students who pass the examination face a number of options.

1.   They may leave high school, provided they obtain permission of their parents, and enter the job market as 16- or 17-year olds, or travel, or engage themselves in strictly independent study.

2.   They may continue their education at a community college. The award of the Certificate of High School Proficiency guarantees their admission.

3.   If their transcripts and test scores (in addition to the school leaving examination) warrant it, they may enter public or private four-year colleges or universities.

4.   They may undertake study in a proprietary vocational school.

[18] Ellen Polgar, "State of California High School Certificate of Proficiency," (manuscript, Department of Education, University of California at Berkeley, 1976), p. 5.
[19] Ibid.

5.   They may continue to study in their local high school free of requirements to accumulate course credit for traditional graduation.

It is the fifth possibility that is attracting the most interest in California educational circles. Under a law passed in 1975, the California State Board of Education is required to specify rules for *independent study* under which students can acquire high school credits for activities that the students themselves can help design and that need not be conducted within the grounds and building of the high school itself. Examples are building solar-heated houses, studying wilderness survival, covering local events that commercial TV and radio news would not deal with and broadcasting them, and so on.[20] Under California law, each high school student in attendance represents a substantial financial resource to the local school district, because the main forms of state aid to education are based on a student count and because the legal limits for raising funds for education through the local property tax are also related to student enrollment. Hence, school districts have an incentive to help students design educational programs of interest, especially those students who have passed the high school proficiency examination and are eligible to leave school early with the legal equivalent of a high school diploma.[21]

Curricular Choice in the School Program

Without going all the way to a market-oriented educational voucher system, it is possible to provide choice to parents regarding curricular emphasis, teachers, and staffing pattern overall. This has been demonstrated in the Alum Rock (California) Voucher Project, which began operating in the 1972–73 school year. First, we should point out that the Alum Rock experiment is not a voucher system as such

[20] I am indebted to David Stern and John Harter, Department of Education, University of California at Berkeley, for discussion of this point.

[21] It might be contended that the California High School Proficiency Examination does not represent an innovation for two reasons: Many high schools since the late 1950s have been offering college level work to those students who were ready for it; and, under Carnegie Corporation sponsorship, many colleges and universities have accepted students who managed to accelerate their high school program—that is, have early admissions programs. For discussion of such alternatives, see *The Fleischmann Report on the Quality, Cost, and Financing of Elementary and Secondary Education in New York State* (New York: Viking, 1973), II, 65–77. However, these modifications of the secondary program did not envisage awarding a certificate of high school completion on the basis of a standard, statewide examination in basic skills nor do they provide for students to remain in high school after they completed the formal requirements for a diploma. In these latter respects, the California program has a claim to novelty.

systems were described in Chapter 6. There are no private educational institutions included in the plan. Consequently, the chance to test the effects—for good or evil—of interschool competition for students is limited to a set of institutions that is subject to the full set of controls and constraints embodied in the California Education Code. Were private institutions to have been included in the experiment, the opportunity to see how parents would respond to curricular innovation would probably have been greater because private institutions are not as rigidly bound as are public ones to follow traditional practices in education. Second, teachers in the Alum Rock experiment retain whatever measure of job security they would otherwise have had. Thus, if a particular program does not find favor with parents or their children and enrollment declines, teachers do not, on that account, lose their jobs.

However, the degree of choice is considerably greater than we find in the typical school district. As of 1974–75, parents were asked to select among 55 "minischools," each one of which offered a particular program emphasis and pattern of staffings.[22] These minischools existed in 14 "voucher schools" out of a district total of 24 schools. One minischool stresses "fine arts for creative expression"; another is bilingual and bicultural; another provides a "down-to-earth program" giving "opportunity for a great deal of direct experience learning—down-to-earth, direct-feel, sight, smell, sound observation and absorbing of the world"; another emphasizes math and science, offering "individual approach to science in a laboratory setting experimentally-oriented"; and so on.[23]

Faculty in the minischools are expected to submit their program descriptions to the district offices by March of each year. These descriptions are compiled in a booklet and distributed to parents, along with a voucher, or certificates of preference, for each child in the family. Parents indicate first, second, and third choices; and students are assigned to schools on a first-come, first-serve basis. The program description indicates curricular emphasis; it also gives information about parental participation, class size, experience and instructional specialities of staff, and methods to be used in evaluating the work of students. One of the strengths of the Alum Rock approach is that teachers are allowed to sort themselves in small, compatible groups; they are then encouraged to devise a program they think might appeal to a certain number of parents and their

[22] Jim Warren, "Alum Rock Voucher Project," *Educational Researcher*, 5, no. 3 (March 1976): 13.
[23] Sequoia Institute, Alum Rock Union School District, *Educational Choices for Your Child: Voucher Program Alternatives, 1973–74* (Alum Rock, Calif., 1973), pp. 31, 39.

children. Rarely in recent times in America have teachers been able to play so direct a role in designing school programs. Evidence indicates that teachers in Alum Rock enjoy the experience; their morale, indeed, appears to be high at a time when teachers in other districts are feeling oppressed by budget retrenchment, school closings, and adverse parental reaction to these conditions.[24]

Enrollment determines budget in a given minischool: "In Alum Rock, elementary children are worth $574 each and middle school children $778 each. An additional $275 is added for each child who is eligible for the free lunch program."[25] Parents may choose any minischool in any voucher school, regardless of intradistrict attendance zones. Busing is provided when a child attends a non-neighborhood school. In 1974–75, 1,000 children went out of their neighborhoods; this is a matter to reckon with in evaluating the American parent's attachment to the concept of the "neighborhood school." Fears that offering choice to parents would lead to increased social-class isolation in schools of the district have not been realized.

Evaluation of the project in its first half decade has been favorable. With respect to the teachers in the project, the following has been stated,

> [T]he most striking outcome of the project has been its ability to mobilize teacher enthusiasm and commitment. Teachers feel that the programs they have designed are "theirs" and, consequently, they feel a vested interest and professional pride in making them successful. Teachers have been working longer hours and extra days of their own volition to improve their mini-schools. Peer pressure has been mobilized frequently by teachers in a program when they have felt that one of their members was not doing his or her share.[26]

As for parental attitudes toward the Alum Rock voucher project, it is perhaps sufficient to note that student enrollment in

---

[24] For major evaluation of the Alum Rock Project, see Daniel Weiler, *A Public School Voucher Demonstration: The First Year at Alum Rock—Summary and Conclusions* (Santa Monica, Calif.: Rand Corporation, 1974).

[25] Warren, "Alum Rock Voucher Project," p. 14.

[26] Ibid. There is some evidence, however, that the Alum Rock District in the later 1970s was reverting toward more centralized control of teacher assignments, finances, and curriculum. The problem seemed, in part, to be that teachers found it difficult to expand the size and reach of those programs that were unusually popular with parents and students. But the retrogression from the ideal of decentralization seems to have been brought on mainly by financial distress in the district. See Eliot Levinson, "The Alum Rock Voucher Demonstration: Three Years of Implementation," Rand paper no. P-5631 (Santa Monica, Calif.: Rand Corporation, 1976), pp. 20–31.

minischools increased from approximately 4,000 in 1972–73 to 9,000 in 1974–75 (out of a district total enrollment of approximately 15,000 in both years). But there is more to it: It is almost certainly true that parental frustrations are lessened when they can play a role in picking programs and teachers for their children, instead of having to accept the particular teacher who is assigned to instruct their children because sometimes, for whatever reasons, a given teacher and a child will simply not get along. Frustrated parents no doubt impede the work of their children, though not intentionally, by criticizing the teacher in the privacy of the home, exacerbating the hostility between teacher and child. The Alum Rock project should help avoid much of this problem.

Parental choice of public schools did not begin in Alum Rock, however. From the mid-1960s, the city of Milwaukee, Wisconsin, has followed a policy of open enrollment.[27] Parents can seek to enroll their child in practically any school in the city district which is appropriate for the child in terms of grade level. Whenever parents wish their child to attend a school outside their immediate attendance area, the parents fill out a simple, single page form. The parent need give no reason for the transfer, and the form requires no information about the socioeconomic characteristics of the family. Transfers are ordinarily made routinely and impersonally. As of 1974, some 20,000 students, or about 15 percent of total enrollment at elementary, junior and senior high levels, were transfers. Transfer students are expected to provide for their own transportation to school, though public transportation is available to them at a discount rate.

A considerable amount of information about schools is provided to parents by the city of Milwaukee school district and is published in two newspapers. The information includes the following items: average student achievement scores in reading and mathematics, average class size, stability of student enrollment, percent of new students, truancy, percentage of overage pupils, training level of teachers, and experience of teachers.

An econometric study has been conducted to determine if Milwaukee's open enrollment was functioning in accordance with economic criteria.[28] *Economic criteria* were defined to relate to the following questions: (1) Do parents seek out schools for their children in which the level of perceived educational quality is high and avoid

[27] Other cities that had open enrollment plans in 1976 were Minneapolis, Minnesota; Cincinnati, Ohio; and Eugene, Oregon.

[28] James Moody, "Open Enrollment: A Study in Revealed Preferences for Educational Outcomes in a Big City School System" (Paper delivered at a meeting of the Econometric Society, San Francisco, California, December 29, 1974).

schools in which quality is seen as low? (2) Does distance of school from home have an adverse effect on transfer enrollment (increasing distance to school is seen as the equivalent of a rising price for educational services and, by conventional ideas of price elasticity of demand—see Chapter 5—should have such an adverse effect)? (3) Is selection of school substantially unrelated to ethnic factors?

By and large, the questions were answered in the affirmative. In opting for transfer and in selecting an out-of-district school, parents appeared to respond strongly to reported levels of student achievement. Interschool differences in teacher characteristics did not seem to have much influence on parental selection, but the reason may be that parents do not draw a close relationship between average level of teacher training and experience and educational quality. Distance had a negative effect on transfer enrollment, but its effect was not as strong as the positive effect of achievement scores in determining enrollment patterns. Lastly, in the words of the study's author, "no strong support for racial prejudice controlling educational purchases of either race could be found."[29]

Finally, on the topic of parental-student choice in regular day public schools, we note that large high schools, if they are well financed, can extend the range of course selection in great measure. The Evanston (Illinois) Township High School, for example, enrolling nearly 5,000 students, offers separate programs for the academic student, for the student interested in the fine and performing arts, and for the student who is attracted to physical education and practical arts. In 1972–73, the high school provided 39 courses in foreign language, 20 in science, 17 in mathematics, 22 in music, 15 in art, 16 in business, and 25 in industrial subjects.[30] In other words, the Evanston model provides considerable choice within the given institution, making transfers not particularly necessary.

Curricular Choice Outside the School Program

With the exception of certain large, well-endowed high schools, the capacity of regular day public schools to offer diversified instruction programs is quite limited. The main justification of public school budgets is in the role that tax-supported schools play in developing vocational skills, that is, in maintaining the quality of the work force over the generations and in promoting qualities of good citizenship. If a course is judged to serve mainly nonvocational interests and if, at

[29] Ibid., p. 19.
[30] Evanston Township High School, *Annual Report* (Evanston, Ill., 1973), p. 61.

the same time, it is expensive—because it appeals to a small number of students only—then it is unlikely to find a place in the public school curriculum. The vocational-cum-citizenship-building function of public schools can apparently be satisfied with a fairly standardized set of courses in language, numbers, science, and government. The possibility exists that the American educational system fails to help students develop sufficiently their capacity to use nonwork time in active, creative ways. Since it is in uses of nonwork time that people are best able to express individuality—in an industrial or postindustrial society, that is—this failing of our educational system, if it exists, is serious.

The problem appears to affect some students more than others. Whatever is provided in American education toward the development of nonwork skills and interests is commonly provided as a joint product with development of vocational skills. Hence, those students who are selected to continue their education for a prolonged period have greater access to both types of schooling. Education must create certain academically meritocratic distinctions, and those students who are chosen for the higher forms of vocational training, such as medicine, law, the sciences, and so on, must be selected, as far as possible, on the basis of their aptitudes for work in various technical fields and professions. Otherwise, our educational system would be accused of wasting scarce talent. Distributing training for avocational interests *need not* follow the same meritocratic criteria as for vocational, nor need it be as intensive and concentrated in time as vocational (though if students so desire, it might be). Actually, we would argue that the distribution of avocational training in America is possibly perverse. To see why, let us consider a simple parable.

Take a young woman (it could just as well be a young man) who attends a private secondary school and then goes to Harvard and then to Yale Law School. She attains in the process a vocation of the highest monetary worth and, unless she is unusually slovenly, irascible, or of a socialist bent, proceeds to a position in a metropolitan law firm specializing in corporate law, where she prices her services in at least three figures by the quarter hour. At the same time that this fortunate person is acquiring her entry qualifications for her vocation, she is made aware, on the most agreeable terms possible, of the world's literature, music, ancient and modern art, and so on. In addition, she has access to excellent facilities and instructors and coaches for all imaginable physical sports. While acquiring her vocational prowess, she is as well equipped as America can make her to lead a life full of culture and approved exercise.

Let us make a contrast between that woman's preparation for adult life and a more ordinary case. Consider a young man who

attends a public secondary school of no academic or social preten-
sions; who proceeds to a two-year community college, taking a
specialization in basic engineering, or machine shop; and who completes his formal training by enrolling in a proprietary school for
instruction in aircraft maintenance. In his entire academic career, the
man is unlikely to see a teacher or professor who has written a book of
literary criticism, analyzed a classical musical score, or made a serious
visit to an archeological site. His sports program, like his cultural, will
be similarly deficient.

Yet, this man is more likely than the woman to spend his
working life in routinized activity, serving under close direction. He
will probably have long evenings and week-ends free for leisure
activities, and he will probably spend many weeks of his life in
short-term unemployment. The Yale law graduate, on the other
hand, will probably feel pressed for work time during much of her
career; she will reach home quite often late at night in a mentally
exhausted state. She is unlikely ever to know periods of involuntary
unemployment. Thus, she probably will display, at best, a dilettante's
interest in the cultural heritage to which she was so richly introduced.

In short, the person who has both the time for and the need
to develop a rich life outside the work place is introduced during his
or her formative years to the possibilities in a relatively meager fashion; the person who will find his or her fulfillment primarily in work
is made aware of the possibilities to use nonwork time in measures far
beyond his or her capacity to participate. This is why we might say
that the distribution of educational opportunities for the use of nonwork time is perverse.

In part, the difficulty arises because the same screening
mechanism is used to regulate the distribution of both vocational and
avocational education. No one should deny the importance of
meritocratic selection procedures to control entry to training for the
most demanding occupations. But such importance does not necessarily establish an argument that the same selection process also be
used to deny high-grade avocational training to those passed over for
high-grade vocational training. Just the contrary would be in order.
What we then need is a vast opening up of the cultural resources of
institutions of higher education.

This implies that the joint production aspect of vocational and
avocational education can be severed, and some might deny the
possibility. It might be said, for example, that Harvard has first-rate
musicologists on its faculty because some Harvard students intend to
be musicians. If intending lawyers take the courses given by the
musicologists, no one minds, as long as there is space in the
classroom. But the music faculty is not hired by Harvard primarily to

serve the cultural enlightenment of intending lawyers, medical doctors, and engineers. One person's cultural enrichment is thus another person's vocational development. Harvard—to use it as an example of a superior educational establishment—serves the combination of interests well, not because it is elite, though it is, but because it is highly specialized.

This argument about the difficulty of separating vocational and avocational education may be correct so far as it goes. But it does not explain why the Harvard musicologists' instruction (regular day instruction, that is), insofar as it is made available to nonmusicians, should be confined in the main to people labeled as "Harvard students," why certain students have exclusive rights to the whole range of services of highly specialized institutions. Laws of probability suggest that some students in, say, a nearby technical institute have a keener avocational interest in music than some Harvard undergraduates who are enrolled in music courses. The fact that one screening system divides us into sheep and goats for vocational and avocational instruction is an artifact of excessive identification of students' entitlements with particular academic institutions.

We have already alluded to a second part of the problem, namely, that our public schools are constrained from offering highly diversified courses in their own enrollments, while junior and senior high students do not have the opportunity to find alternative sources of instruction. One possibility is that regional school authorities could serve specialized needs while holding within prevailing cost parameters, by exploiting economies of scale. If a given high school has only 10 students who are seriously interested in astronomy, that school could hardly justify the purchase of a large telescope and cameras, and hiring a Ph.D. in astronomy to give instruction. But in all the high schools of the metropolitan commuting area, there might well be 400 students a year who had a keen interest in the subject. Such a number could justify the purchase of the equipment and engaging an astronomer-teacher on a part-time basis. Clearly, such instruction would be supplementary to regular school work and would take place in afternoon, week-ends, and holiday periods. As the *Fleischmann Report* suggested,

> the Board of Cooperative Educational Services (i.e., "BOCES," the regional educational authorities at elementary-secondary level in New York State) could offer a number of services funded directly by the state. Among these would be innovative or specialized courses of such limited appeal that they could not be offered in any of the separate school

districts participating. Each BOCES superintendent might prepare an annual "spring catalogue" of such courses similar to college course catalogues. Provided adequate enrollments were obtained, such courses should be financed through an annual state appropriation made available to the various BOCES in proportion to their enrollments in the programs.[31]

Opening up higher education to serve the avocational interests of young people is no adequate solution to the problem of the adverse distribution of opportunities for nonwork education in the absence of attempts to provide more specialized courses at junior and senior high students. Unless the avid curiosity of the younger persons is served, it cannot be fully rekindled by the time they are of college age.

The Teacher's Role in Educational Productivity

As we saw in Chapter 7, several educational production function studies have indicated that teacher characteristics rank high, as compared with other school variables, in determining students' achievements. Since education is labor intensive and since the teacher is the human agent most substantially involved in the instruction of the young, the production function studies appear to confirm common sense. Our task in this section is to see how the teacher's contribution to productivity might be further enhanced. Because scientific knowledge about effectiveness of teaching is quite limited, we offer observations that are grounded in the rudimentary logic of the professional work place—nothing more. We take up three points: the introduction of the teacher *to* his profession; the opportunities of teachers to advance *in* their profession; and the opportunities teachers have to contribute to the advance *of* their profession.

Teacher Apprenticeship

Teachers ordinarily prepare themselves for their work by earning a bachelor's degree in a four-year liberal arts program (very few

---

[31] *The Fleischmann Report*, III, 34–35. The Soviet Government has had considerable experience along this line, and the "Pioneer Palaces" it created to provide instruction in depth through specialized courses in the arts and sciences, serving students in substantially large catchment areas, have been highly successful. See W. K. Medlin, W. M. Cave, and F. Carpenter, *Education and Development in Central Asia: A Case Study on Social Change in Uzbekistan* (Leiden, Netherlands: Brill, 1971), chap. 7.

graduates of M.I.T. go into teaching; many graduates of Boston University do), followed by a one- or two-year program of teacher training. Satisfactory work in a graduate department of education may or may not lead directly to award of a master's degree, but it does earn teaching credentials in any case. The graduate programs are commonly differentiated in content depending on whether the intending teacher expects to work in an elementary or a secondary school. Most of the time spent in teacher training is taken up by classroom work in the college or university. A few hours a week are ordinarily devoted to practice teaching, that is, in credit courses in which the prospective teacher works in a classroom of a cooperating school district under joint supervision of a teacher in that district and a faculty member of the college or university attended.

Prospective teachers rarely get any practice in highly specialized fields, since the number of students enrolling in a specialized course in any given college or university would likely be too small to justify the expense of setting up the course and of the faculty time spent on supervision. Indeed, we may well suspect that the practical work of prospective teachers is generally inadequate. Yet, if colleges and universities tried to increase the practical content of their teacher training programs radically, the costs would probably be quite high.[32]

Too often new teachers enter their first full-time assignments inadequately prepared to practice independently or to manage a classroom effectively. Indeed, they often do not know where to find instructional materials for their classes or how to handle the large volume of paperwork that confronts them. In spite of these handicaps, the new teacher must frequently teach students with serious learning problems.

Managing a classroom for the first time is not easy, even under the best circumstances. There is initially the problem of arranging instruction in an orderly manner, and then the problem of winning the interest and cooperation of the students. Beyond these obvious requirements, the effective teacher must constantly be listening to the students to offer the response and encouragement that carries a student over hurdles in learning. Unless the teacher is always sensitive to signals that students, sometimes unconsciously, are giving, he or she will be unable to help some students learn, since

[32] *The Fleischmann Report,* III, 186, shows that as of spring 1970 in Brooklyn College, the cost per student of student-teaching courses ranged from $103 to $2,906, while the average cost of all teacher education courses in the college was $87.

young minds often lose interest if questions are not answered when asked or if misunderstandings are not cleared up when they first arise.

Because learning in most subjects is sequential, lifetime damage can be inflicted by teachers who cannot sense what is going on in the minds of students. The teacher must accurately feel when certain students are ready to deal with a given topic—a particular concept in mathematics, say—and must know, judging from their questions, precisely *how* a concept can be made intuitively plain to a given set of students. Moreover, the teacher must display this sensitivity hour after hour, day after day, while dealing with between 15 and 30 students of widely differing interests and real abilities, all at one time.

New teachers frequently speak of the "sense of shock" that overwhelms them when they first find themselves holding sole responsibility for managing a classroom. Obviously, a new teacher cannot be expected to manage a classroom well before acquiring experience in that setting. Most human activities that involve high risk to the client, whether medical patient or airline passenger, provide thorough apprenticeship opportunities for the new practitioner. By definition, apprenticeship is participation as a junior partner in the actual work process. Education is an activity that carries high risk to the client—the student—but present apprenticeship arrangements are not at all well developed.

The distinguished critic of American educational policy, James Bryant Conant, has suggested that school districts should assume substantial responsibility for apprenticeship arrangements:

> In my judgement, no kind of preservice program . . . can prepare first-year teachers to operate effectively in the "sink or swim" situation in which they too often find themselves. Many local school boards have . . . been scandalously remiss in failing to give adequate assistance to new teachers. I recommend, therefore, that during the initial probationary period, local school boards should take specific steps to provide the new teachers with every possible help in the form of (a) limited teaching responsibility; (b) aid in gathering instructional materials; (c) advice of experienced teachers whose own load is reduced so that they can work with the new teacher in his own classroom; (d) shifting to more experienced teachers those pupils who create problems beyond the ability of the novice to handle effectively; and (e) specialized instruction concerning the characteristics of the community,

the neighborhood, and the students . . . [the teacher] is likely
to encounter.[33]

Similarly, William R. Odell proposed that the boards of education
establish *portal* schools, which he described as follows:

> The central purpose of a portal school would be to train new
> teachers and long-term substitutes to take their place as fully
> contributing members of the teaching force by associating
> them for the period of one year with senior teachers who
> represent models of teaching excellence. . . . The portal
> schools would operate on two basic principles: first, system-
> atic turnover of beginning personnel; second, the influence of
> powerful teacher models on neophytes in the profession.[34]

We shall return later to further consideration of such an institutional
innovation.

Teacher Advancement

In economic analysis, labor productivity is linked to specialization.
People differ basically in their skills. To such inborn differences in
specific capacities are added the influence of acquired skills. Ordinarily, people differ in their interests so that some are led to acquire skills
or knowledge in one branch of human inquiry and some in another.
Some teachers, for example, are gifted in verbal tasks and extend
their knowledge into fields of language, literature, and history. Other
teachers excel in analyzing quantitative relationships and study such
fields as mathematics, pure science, and applied technology. But
beyond these natural and acquired specialities, there are attributes of
energy, ambition, and commitment. If the system allows and rewards
it, some people will seek to undertake the harder, more demanding
tasks that others shun. Given these differences, it makes no economic
sense to distribute teaching assignments in literature and mathematics among all secondary teachers equally; nor does it make sense to
hold all teachers, including the most energetic and committed, to the
level of work output that the average teacher can provide.

[33] James Bryant Conant, *The Education of American Teachers* (New York: McGraw-Hill,
1963), pp. 70–71.
[34] William R. Odell, *Educational Survey: Report for the Philadelphia Board of Public Education* (Philadelphia: Board of Education, 1965), pp. 128, 387.

Specialization provides opportunities for teachers to capitalize on their strengths, whether these lie in dealing with certain types of instruction or with certain types of students. Teachers should be able to develop their individual talents and then spend a large part of each working day performing specialized duties. To some extent, this is encouraged by local school administrations. By and large, teachers can choose the grade level at which they work and the subjects they are to teach at secondary level, provided, of course, the market is not over supplied with their particular specialty. By choosing the school district in which they seek employment—and possibly by seeking work in a particular school of the district—teachers can exercise some degree of choice with regard to the types of students they serve.

Yet, as the Rockefeller Brothers Fund said in 1958, and it is still largely true today, "perhaps no profession has suffered such a general neglect of specialized abilities as that of the teacher."[35] How so? First, accepting that some teachers are no doubt better than others at training new teachers, there are limited opportunities for exercising such skills because the function of teacher training is held almost exclusively by the faculties of education departments in colleges and universities. Second, given that some teachers are better than others at applied research in education, there are few opportunities for exercising such skills because, as we shall note below, practically all research in education is done outside the public school system—most of it is done in colleges and universities and a bit is done in the private firms that market educational technology.

The third indicator of the lack of appropriate specialization in education is somewhat harder to describe. Though some teachers teach younger children and some older ones, and some teachers teach literature and others mathematics, specialties are not hierarchically arranged, priced by market criteria, or systematically rewarded. This applies as long as, but only as long as, the person continues to have teaching responsibilities in the public school classroom. This statement can be illustrated by examining standard salary arrangements for teachers.

The standard salary plan for classroom teachers is as shown in Table 8.1. Differences in pay are ascribed almost wholly to two factors, "seniority" and "level of training," meaning courses successfully completed in an institution of higher education. (Some

[35] *The Pursuit of Excellence: Education and the Future of America* (New York: Doubleday 1958), p. 24.

Table 8.1
Standard form of pay schedule for classroom teachers
(in dollars)

Years of experience (seniority)	Level of training		
	B.A.	M.A.	M.A. plus 30 semester hours
0	x_1	y_1	z_1
1	x_2	y_2	z_2
2	x_3	y_3	z_3
3	x_4	y_4	z_4
4	x_5	y_5	z_5
5	x_6	y_6	z_6
6	x_7	y_7	z_7
7	x_8	y_8	z_8
8	x_9	y_9	z_9
9	x_{10}	y_{10}	z_{10}
10	x_{11}	y_{11}	z_{11}

where $x_n > x_{n-1}$; $y_n > x_n$, and $z_n > y_n$.

additional increments of pay may be awarded for extracurricular duties of teachers, though, except for head football coach, these ordinarily are rather small.) The justification is that somehow experience and training improve the capacity of teachers to do their work. But the relationship between experience, on the one hand, and training, on the other, and the tasks the teacher is expected to perform is left quite vague. Gaining additional training and experience does not elevate a teacher to a *new position of teacher* in which the person is relieved of the routine chores that inexperienced teachers are well able to perform and assigned the specialized, demanding tasks that only experienced, highly trained teachers could successfully perform.

Yet, until a separation is made between what is expected of an experienced teacher and what is expected of an inexperienced one and between what is expected of a highly trained teacher and a minimally trained one, school boards will have difficulty in establishing salary schedules that offer *large* rewards for training and experience. Suppose a district has a single highly experienced, superbly trained, and much loved teacher who is to retire at the end of the school year. By whom will that teacher be replaced? Quite possibly by a person who has never done a day of teaching beyond the practice teaching classes in college and whose academic qualifications do not extend beyond a B.A. plus one year's teacher education. To satisfy the parents of the children who attend the given school, the administration must pretend that an equal replacement has been found for the retiring teacher.

But if the replacement is approximately equal, experience and training must count for little in determining the actual performance of the teacher in the classroom. And if differences in experience and training are assumed to count for little, they cannot logically justify major differences in pay. The pay level of the highly experienced and trained teachers of a given school district are thus bound inexorably to the pay level of beginning, relatively untrained, teachers. If the entry-level pay of teachers itself is at a high standard, we might say that recruitment to the field of education operates under no handicap. But the beginning pay level is modest, being roughly equal to the starting pay of the current group of all college graduates. Since entry to the profession of teaching is not as competitive as entry to, say, law, medicine, or engineering—nor is it based on as rigorous a training period—we could hardly expect beginning pay of teachers to stand at any high mark.

Beginning pay for teachers, then, is approximately average for newly hired college graduates and maximum pay is closely linked to the beginning level, seldom exceeding it by a factor of more than two. As things have stood in the past, classroom teaching as an occupation limits itself to persons who have modest desires toward earning income. Surely teaching as an occupation can accommodate hundreds of thousands of persons who are not income-acquisitive, many of whom are no doubt splendid teachers. It could be unfortunate, however, if the teaching profession excluded from its membership a seeding of persons who are aggressive in pursuit of material rewards, for often it is such persons who display high levels of energy in setting standards of work performance, in finding new and better ways to do things, and, in the case of education, in seeing how far the child who does not immediately take to learning can be brought along.

Not, of course, that the entire profession of education operates independently of status rewards. School districts employ large numbers of administrators, administrative aides, curriculum specialists, student personnel specialists, counseling specialists, and the like. These positions carry salaries at considerably higher levels than does that of classroom teacher. And those positions offer other benefits as well: secretaries to handle routine and other chores, travel expense accounts, private offices, time off to make lunch time speeches at Rotary Clubs, and the like. By and large, the administrative and related positions are filled from the ranks of classroom teachers. By and large, administrators, curriculum specialists, and the like, are relieved entirely of classroom teaching responsibilities. Suppose, then, that a young man joins a school district, works hard and successfully in the role of classroom teacher and thereby attracts attention to himself. Let him be promoted to an administrative position. The end result is that successful teaching leads, not to expanded opportunities (admittedly, yet to be defined) in the activity of classroom teaching, but to the single opportunity of giving it up and not doing it any more. Since this process seems to convey the meaning that administrators are persons who "have proven themselves too good to be just teachers," it would appear to demean the role and responsibilities of the classroom teacher.

We seem to have stated two general problems regarding the teaching profession. First, the profession of teaching should appropriately be raised in status. Taken seriously, teaching is hard work, and the quality of teaching received is of vital importance in the lives of many young people. One step to raise the status of teaching would be to require administrators and all other nonteaching certificated personnel to carry part-time assignments of classroom teaching.[36] Second, ambitious and successful classroom teachers should be granted more interesting and challenging *career ladders* than they now have. Just what expanded opportunities should be made available is not entirely clear, though we believe that training neophyte teachers and applied research in education should surely be among them. New institutional settings are probably required to work out this problem, and new administrative arrangements certainly are.

To speak, however, of establishing categories of superior duties within the field of teaching raises a special problem to which we have barely alluded—distributing the services of advanced teachers among different student populations. Parents cannot be expected to take it lightly if their child is being taught by a "regular classroom teacher" while their neighbor's child is being taught by a "master teacher category III" or some similarly classified person, *unless there is a sensible reason for the difference in standard of service provided.*

---

[36] This was recommended by the *Fleischmann Report,* III, 174–175: "All certified persons qualified to teach should be required to assume classroom teaching responsibility amounting to at least 20 percent of a full-time teacher's work load. . . . Aside from the cost savings that could result, we consider this proposal worthwhile because it allows administrators, supervisors, and specialists to keep in touch with the interests, capabilities, and attitudes of today's young people, and because it helps counteract the tendency of teachers and administrators to think that classroom teaching is less important or less difficult than management and supervision."

Building a career ladder for teachers requires establishing a rational basis for the distribution of differentiated teaching services among client populations.

The Teacher's Role in Applied Research

In Chapter 7 we saw that we lack solid, well-grounded information about which educational techniques best meet specific learning objectives. For example, it is impossible to estimate accurately the amount, type, and dollar cost of the educational resources needed to overcome the initial learning disadvantage of certain students. As another example, it is not possible to know how to identify the points in a student's educational career where he or she can make most productive use of various incremental resources. Most distressing of all, there are no means, aside from intuition and folklore, by which the practicing teacher can judge how to improve his or her own effectiveness. This lack of information is appalling when we remember that public expenditures on education are exceeded only by expenditures for national defense.

The problem is not a total lack of educational research but that such research has failed to build over the years. This year's study of the effects of ability grouping may contradict last year's, and frequently no one is able satisfactorily to explain why the two investigations yield opposite results. In such circumstances, education cannot claim to have a basis in science, at least not yet.[37]

The bulk of educational research is carried out by graduate students for their doctorates and by faculty in departments of education.[38] Inevitably, many of these efforts are inadequately financed; some are carried out by relatively inexperienced persons; and practically all are done by persons who lack day-to-day involvement with the work of the classroom teacher. Because of the large number of variables that affect education, which must be controlled to give a good chance that research results will be vigorous and valid, educational research conducted outside a controlled laboratory setting is unlikely to be, and indeed has not been, cumulative.

[37] Steps toward solving this problem are suggested in an article by Richard S. Light and Paul V. Smith, "Accumulating Evidence: Procedures for Resolving Contradictions Among Different Research Studies," *Harvard Educational Review*, 41, no. 4 (November 1971): 429–471.

[38] It is perhaps instructive that of the 1,133 papers presented at the April 1976 meeting (in San Francisco) of the American Educational Research Association, only 105 (less than 10 percent) appeared to have been written by, or in collaboration with, classroom teachers.

Schools then might well accept guidance in this matter from the medical profession. Before the advent of highly scientific computer-based medical research, there was a slow but effective process of accumulation of knowledge that occurred as doctors reported on interesting cases to local, state, and national medical societies. (Only the more interesting case papers filtered up to state and national levels; and often in that process several doctors interested in the same type of case would collaborate on a single paper.) These medical papers offered the best description that the doctor could make of the patient and the patient's problem, described accurately the steps the doctor took in the treatment, and portrayed in some detail the later condition of the patient, dead or alive. A causal relationship between treatment and final condition of the patient was not generally claimed by any single doctor. But when several cases indicated similar findings, a more thorough examination of the treatment process and the results was usually conducted. The locus of this more thorough type of research was the *teaching hospital*, a large number of which were established early in the modern history of the medical profession. These were generally located in areas of high population density. In collaboration with the medical faculties of universities, these teaching hospitals became centers for three important functions: high-grade medical service to clients (often free of charge); on-the-job instruction of young practitioners; and applied research.[39]

From the analogy of the early beginnings of modern medical research, it may be appropriate for teachers, corresponding to medical general practitioners, to take a more active role in applied research, and record, discuss, and publish statements on their own more interesting teaching experiences, along with their professional insights on those experiences. It might also follow that establishing a new type of institution to correspond to the teaching hospital would advance the science of education.

Related to the point about teachers' contribution to the development of their field of work is a problem in the continued professional growth of the teacher. As things stand now, most in-service professional growth that is recognized for salary awards is accomplished by taking courses, often in evenings and during week-ends, at a nearby college or university. The faculty of the college or university, by giving the teacher a passing mark in the course, makes legitimate the teacher's receiving an increase in pay.

[39] For a discussion of the development and present role of the teaching hospital, see John Knowles, ed., *The Teaching Hospital* (Cambridge, Mass.: Harvard, 1966).

There seem to be several things wrong with this procedure. The school district in many cases has little control over the content of in-service education; and neither do the teachers because they are often limited to whatever the college or university is offering at the time they attend. Accordingly, there may be little relevance of the content of in-service education for the actual work of the teacher in the classroom. Further, the process is somewhat invidious: University faculty do not receive salary increases when and as they get passing marks in evening courses; they are assumed to know what they need to study and to be able to pursue it.

It would seem preferable if in-service training were brought more closely under the control of the professionals who work in a given district. The process of collective bargaining could be used to establish procedures to determine which activities are legitimate as in-service training and which are not. It should even be possible to negotiate the length of a "professional work week," specifying how much time should be devoted to classroom teaching, class preparation, tutorials, parent conferences, and professional development.

A Policy Proposal: Professional Schools in Central Cities

The problems we cited in this chapter about teachers' careers and teachers' contributions toward developing the education service might possibly be solved by establishing a new kind of institution. Such an institution is identified as a "professional school" in the *Fleischmann Report*.[40] These schools would be located in central city areas and would serve the complementary functions of exemplary teaching, teacher training, and applied research. The schools would provide services to a large geographic area; hence, the school should be funded fully by either the state or the federal government.

However, professional schools could be administered (subject, of course, to performance review by the funding agency) jointly by a local university and the local school board. The reason for dividing administrative responsibility is to try to assure that the schools do not fall into the pattern of university-model or laboratory schools. If universities alone had responsibility for these schools, they might appoint only faculty members from a given department of education to senior staff positions: a permanent staff recruited from a wider set of disciplines is preferable. Though a university

[40] *The Fleischmann Report*, III, 188–190.

connection is important to insure access to qualified research specialists, it would be unfortunate if research energies were directed largely to the specific interests of faculty members rather than to the effectiveness of instructional strategies as defined by the city's school authorities. The fusion of universities and local school districts in the administration process might direct the energies of university scholars toward solving school problems.

University faculty members assigned full- or part-time to the professional schools would be joined by educators. Teaching and training functions would be carried out by exceptionally competent master teachers, serving, in some cases, on a two-year rotating basis (though some master teachers might spend a stated number of days in the professional school and their remaining time in a regular school of the district).

Ideally, the professional schools would be the sites for *internships* of all newly graduated, intending teachers in the state, giving improved training. First, new teachers would no longer be thrown into full-time classroom responsibilities but would assume such duties gradually over a one- or two-year period. Second, new teachers would have ample opportunity to observe master teachers at work in classrooms and learn from their examples. Third, because the size of professional schools would presumably be large, new teachers could acquire highly specialized teaching skills.

Professional schools would also be centers of applied research, in the tradition of the teaching hospital. Tentative hypotheses about instructional effectiveness developed and reported by regular teachers could be fed into the professional schools for rigorous scrutiny.

Last, differentiated career roles of teachers could well be developed at the professional schools. Master teacher, educational researcher, and intern are three roles suggested so far, but there could be more.[41] Because the schools would be located in central cities and would presumably enroll many children from low-income families, the concentration of teaching talent in them should not raise an equity issue. But if differentiation of teacher roles became an important part of the school scene, then the question of equity in the assignment of master teachers would have to be addressed.[42]

[41] We do not discuss the question of how master teachers would be chosen from the general body of classroom teachers, though *The Fleischmann Report*, III, 191-194, contains suggestions about this.

[42] We recognize that the magnet schools of Boston and a few other cities have features in common with the professional school described here.

The Child's Role in Educational Productivity

It is a known fact that not all children perform well in school. The Coleman report and related studies[43] have shown that a low level of a child's school attainment is associated, to a statistically significant degree, with the poverty level of the child's family. Based on findings of production function studies, Harvey Averch's conclusion was, "the socioeconomic status of a student's family and community is consistently related to his educational outcomes."[44]

The point can be illustrated by data from the Summers-Wolfe study of the Philadelphia public schools.[45] Table 8.2 indicates that average score for the group of 6th graders on the Iowa Test of Basic Skills was 5.32. For children from homes of less than $7,000 annual income, the average score was 4.77; for children from homes with incomes in excess of $9,000 (not a terribly high level, of course), the average score was 5.88. Of the lowest income group, 67.62 percent of the children scored less than 5.0; for the highest income group, the corresponding figure was 29.86 percent. Nearly a quarter (24.18 percent) of the highest income group of 6th graders obtained scores of over 7.0; only 4.55 percent of the lowest income group of children got marks that high. A similar pattern of performance by income class is revealed for the 8th-grade students.

The association of school performance with a family's SES has been a matter of concern, and major public policy efforts have been launched to reduce that association. The larger scale efforts, notably compensatory education (Title I of the Elementary and Secondary Act) and Headstart, have been closely tied to the in-school environment of the child. Title I is almost wholly so and Headstart, even when not administered by local school authorities, is strongly influenced by nursery school and kindergarten models. These programs, with exceptions, do not appear to have been notably successful.[46] Thus, we may reasonably consider whether there are conditions in the life of the poverty child outside the school that impede his or her educational development, and whether public policy could be directed successfully to eradicate or ameliorate those conditions.

---

[43] See Chapter 7.

[44] Harvey A. Averch et al., *How Effective Is Schooling?: A Critical Review and Synthesis of Research Findings* (Santa Monica, Calif.: Rand Corporation, 1971), p. 45.

[45] This study was discussed on pages 201–203.

[46] For a balanced discussion of this point, see J. M. Hunt, "Has Compensatory Education Failed? Has It Been Attempted?" *Harvard Education Review*, 39, no. 2 (Spring 1969): 278–300.

The policy issue is not to abandon compensatory education and related school-based efforts but, rather, to seek a complementary, reinforcing relationship between compensatory education and adjustments in the out-of-school environment of the poverty child. As Marcelo Selowsky has written, "two independent questions would seem appropriate: First, to what extent are we over-investing in schooling vis-à-vis preschool age types of investment? Second, what are the types of investment in preschool age that can be manipulated by public policy and what is the 'productivity' of such invest-

Table 8.2
Percentage distribution of scores of 6th- and 8th-grade students, Philadelphia public schools, in Iowa Test of Basic Skills, by income groups, 1972

Scores	Percentage breakdown for entire class	Less than $7,000	$7,000–$9,000	More than $9,000
		Household income class		
6th grade				
Less than 3.0	1.27	1.14	1.81	0.95
3.0–3.9	12.30	21.59	9.04	7.11
4.0–4.9	34.00	44.89	37.95	21.80
5.0–5.9	22.06	16.48	26.51	23.22
6.0–6.9	17.00	11.36	15.66	22.75
7.0–7.9	9.04	3.41	7.23	15.17
8.0 and over	4.34	1.14	1.81	9.01
Average	5.32	4.77	5.20	5.88
8th grade				
Less than 4.0	5.42	7.95	4.82	3.79
4.0–4.9	16.28	26.14	17.47	7.11
5.0–5.9	24.23	31.25	28.31	15.17
6.0–6.9	16.09	14.20	13.86	19.43
7.0–7.9	14.11	10.80	13.86	17.06
8.0–8.9	13.20	6.82	15.06	17.06
9.0–9.9	5.97	2.27	4.22	10.43
10.0 and over	4.70	0.57	2.41	9.94
Average	6.49	5.72	6.32	7.27

Source: Anita A. Summers and Barbara L. Wolfe, *Equality of Educational Opportunity Quantified: A Production Function Approach* (Philadelphia: Department of Research, Federal Reserve Bank of Philadelphia, 1975), p. 38.

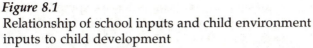

Figure 8.1
Relationship of school inputs and child environment
inputs to child development

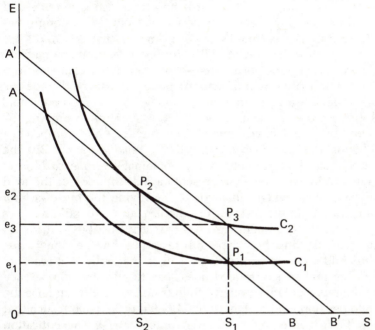

Source: Adapted from Marcelo Selowsky, "A Note on Preschool Age Investment in Human Capital in Developing Countries," *Economic Development and Cultural Change,* 24, no. 4 (July 1976): 710. Copyright © 1976 The University of Chicago. Reprinted with permission.

ments?"[47] This puts the point well. But we will see later in this chapter that it may not be only the preschool life of the poverty child that needs attention—though that is very important—but also his or her life through adolescence.

The point can be restated graphically, using a type of indifference curve (see Chapter 5), as shown in Figure 8.1. Let the isoquants C_1 and C_2—that is, lines representing a single magnitude of

[47] Marcelo Selowsky, "A Note on Preschool Age Investment in Human Capital in Developing Countries," *Economic Development and Cultural Change,* 24, no. 4 (July 1976): 708.

some kind—represent stages of competence acquired by a representative poverty child, with "competence" standing for an index of cognitive skills, noncognitive skills, and physical energy. Because the competence curves bend inward toward the origin, school imputs and child environment inputs are not perfect substitutes (although, because C_1 and C_2 are assumed to exist it implies that the inputs are limited substitutes). Let the line *AB* represent a distribution of a fixed dollar sum on two types of inputs: school (including compensatory education) and child environment. At point P_1—assumed to be the present situation—a large amount of money, $0S_1$, is spent on school inputs and a relatively small amount, $0e_1$, is spent on improving the child's out-of-school environment. The highest child competence level obtainable under *that distribution of expenditure* is C_1. But the highest possible child competence level obtainable for *the fixed budget* is C_2, tangent to *AB* at P_2. P_2 represents a redistribution of the total child development budget in favor of improving the out-of-school environment and to the disfavor of school-related expenditures.

So far the argument assumes that it is possible to make an absolute reduction in school expenditure and to shift the money thus saved to child environment outlays. This is, naturally, not realistic. But suppose that society indeed does seek to raise the competency level of the representative poverty child from C_1 to C_2. It can raise the total child development budget from $0A$ ($=0B$) to $0A'$ ($=0B'$), such that the new budget line crosses the C_2 contour at P_3. The education budget would be held constant, and all of the new money would be spent on trying to improve the out-of-school environment of the poverty child. This is not an efficient solution but, because the educational outlays cannot be cut for political reasons, it is a least-cost approach to reach competence level C_2.

Are there means now available to estimate the relationship between change in the out-of-school environment of poverty youth and rates of growth in their competence? Unfortunately no. But we can build a case for the relationship on a priori grounds. Further, at least in the field of early nutrition, scientific evidence on the relationship is emerging. In the opinion of this author, the a priori case alone is sufficiently convincing to warrant experimentation.

Early Nutrition and Human Competence

A number of thorough studies on human development have established strong evidence that mild malnutrition—not severe—of the mother during pregnancy and of the child in his or her first two to three years has biological consequences.[48] Rates of infant mortality are higher under mild malnutrition, as are rates of succumbing to infectious diseases. The child is likely to be smaller than a well-nourished child, both in height and in size of muscles, and head circumference tends to be smaller.

There is also now presumptive evidence that nutritional deficiencies of the mother during pregnancy and of the young child result in psychological liabilities.[49] Children whose mother was not well nourished and who have been underfed as infants do less well than normal children in tests of object associations, rudimentary logic, measurement, memory, and so on. This finding appears to be independent of family's SES. Another factor that seems to affect psychological development is the amount of mental and social stimulation given to an infant by adults or by older siblings. Malnutrition may work in consort with stimulation, in that the malnourished child, being apathetic, fails to stimulate the adult members of the family to pay attention to him or her—he or she "turns off" older persons by dull behavior.

Insofar as continuing research confirms these conclusions, the obvious policy step is to provide nutritional supplements to families with pregnant women and young children. England, for example, provides free milk and vitamins to expectant mothers in low-income families and to their children who are under school age. Even at age three, it may be possible to reverse previous harmful effects. Selowsky states that

> research undertaken in Cali, Colombia—attempts to identify the types of intervention (nutritional supplementation as well as behavioral stimulation) necessary to overcome specific mental deficit in preschool children (age 3) from the lowest economic level families of that city. The importance of the research stems from the facts that (a) the children analyzed are not characterized by extreme malnutrition, the kind of case usually studied in the pure nutrition studies; they tend to represent a more typical situation of low-income families in urban areas . . . and (b) particular emphasis is being given to

---

[48] J. J. Cravioto and E. De Licardie, "The Effects of Malnutrition on the Individual," in *Nutrition, National Development, and Planning*, ed. A. Berg (Cambridge, Mass.: M.I.T., 1973).

[49] Robert E. Klein et al., "Is Big Smart? The Relation of Growth to Cognition," *Journal of Health and Social Behavior*, 13 (September 1972): 219-225.

analyze the separate effects of particular types of stimulation interventions on specific mental tasks of the child relevant for future learning. The preliminary findings showed that particular stimulation and nutritional interventions at age 3 can boost certain mental capabilities over and above the performance of well-nourished children from similar income groups.[50]

It might seem that the United States is so rich a country that even its poor people obtain adequate nutrition but this is not so. First, income is quite unevenly distributed. In 1971, for example, there were 5,303,000 families below poverty income threshold (defined for 1971, as an income of $4,113 for a family of four); the average income deficit was $1,446.[51] Second, not all food sold in stores has good nutritional content. Third, even those families who are at or slightly above the poverty income threshold are not necessarily protected. As President Richard M. Nixon's Commission on Income Maintenance Programs stated:

> The food budget [of the poverty threshold income level] requires more than a third of the poor family's income. . . . A family can buy a nutritionally adequate diet for this amount, using the Department of Agriculture's food plan, but it must eat considerably more beans, potatoes, flour and cereal products, and considerably less meat, eggs, fruits and vegetables than the average family. Each member of the poor family may consume less than one-quarter pound of meat a day. . . . Unfortunately, the Department's food plan, the basis of the poverty index, is not very realistic. It is estimated that *only about one-fourth of the families who spend that much for food actually have a nutritionally adequate diet.* The plan calls for skills in meal-planning and buying that are rare at any income level. . . . Moreover, the Department's plan assumes the shopper will buy in economical quantities and take advantage

---

[50] Selowsky, "Preschool Age Investment in Human Capital," p. 718. The research was undertaken by H. McKay, A. MacKay, and L. Sinisterra and was reported in a paper presented at the Western Hemisphere Conference on Assessment of Tests of Behavior from Studies of Nutrition, Puerto Rico, October 1970, entitled "Behavioral Interventions Studies with Malnourished Children."

[51] Office of Management and Budget, Executive Office of the President, *Social Indicators* (Washington, D.C.: U.S. Government Printing Office, 1973), pp. 173, 186.

of special bargains, but this is particularly difficult for a poor family with inadequate storage and refrigeration facilities.[52]

Fourth, recognizing that malnutrition of expectant mothers and infant mortality are closely associated, probable evidence of malnutrition is afforded by the fact that infant mortality rates in poverty areas are two to three times as high as in middle income areas.[53] Finally, a Health and Nutrition Examination Survey conducted by the National Center for Health Statistics in 1971–72 shows that the black individuals below poverty income threshold had a median caloric intake of 1,519 per day, compared to 1,924 for white individuals above the poverty threshold. For poor blacks, median protein intake was 56.23 grams, while the corresponding figure for nonpoor whites was 74.81. Poor blacks consumed 78 percent of standard requirement of iron; nonpoor whites consumed 101 percent of standard requirement of iron.[54]

Household Work Requirements

On the average, children in low-income households have duties to the household exceeding those of children in middle-income families.[55] These consist of cooking, cleaning, shopping, and, more distressingly, care of sick parents and other incapacitated persons. Also, poor children are frequently called upon, as they pass out of infancy, to take care of young siblings, nieces, nephews, and so on. The children of the poor have more work to do in the home, and they

---

[52] President's Commission on Income Maintenance Programs, *Poverty Amid Plenty: The American Paradox* (Washington, D.C.: U.S. Government Printing Office, 1969), pp. 15–16 (italics added).

[53] Office of Management and Budget, *Social Indicators*, p. 32; and *Report of the National Advisory Commission on Civil Disorders* (New York: Bantam, 1968), pp. 269–270.

[54] U.S. Department of Commerce, *Statistical Abstract of the United States* (Washington, D.C.: U.S. Government Printing Office, 1975), p. 91.

[55] In preparing this and the following two sections of this chapter, I am indebted to Elliott Medrich and his associates in the Childhood and Government Project, University of California at Berkeley (funded by Ford Foundation and Carnegie Corporation) for preliminary material drawn from a study of the child's use of time. The material was obtained from in-depth, intensive interviews of a cross-section of youth in Oakland, California, in 1976. Actual results of the survey will be published in 1977 and 1978. The observations on these pages are my interpretations of the material based primarily on conversations with interviewers and a thorough reading of a sample of the parents' questionnaire returns. Medrich and his group are in no way responsible for my interpretations.

have to do the work under difficult conditions: cleaning up rat-infested quarters, cooking in the absence of proper cooking implements, washing in the absence of places to hang the wet clothes, and so on.

These extra requirements come about from several causes. Many poor families are single-parent families, and when the single parent can find work, even temporary work, the child must assume a part of parental duties. Unless a public day care center is at hand, there is seldom a place for a poor parent to leave a child when he or she goes to work. And day care centers seldom serve through the full range of years when a young child needs supervision. In these cases, it falls on older siblings to take care of the younger. Even when the family has two parents, both work frequently, with the father having a day job and the wife working in a night custodial job. Strictly speaking, the father might take care of the young children when he gets home from work, but realism cautions that the burden is likely to fall on the adolescent members of the family.

A second reason for poor children having to take up adult duties is that the adult members of poor families are more prone to debilitating illnesses than are adults in middle-income households.[56] When sickness strikes, the low-income family is ordinarily unable to hire nurses, baby sitters, and the like; and the extra burdens fall on younger members of the household. These conditions may well exist in a setting of mild nutritional deficiencies, and the attendant ills of low energy and irritability. In a low-income household, it may take the child and adult members *longer* to accomplish any given household task than it takes well-fed, healthy persons. Thus, the distribution of household work duties by income class places the most onerous burdens on children who have the least stamina to carry them out.

Every child wants to spend a certain amount of time "playing." And, because poor children have to spend time doing extra household tasks, we might expect them to hold time available for play in special regard. The end result may be that they subtract the time spent in doing household work almost entirely from time available for homework, independent study, and participation in lessons and

[56] *National Advisory Commission on Civil Disorders,* p. 269, states that as of 1968 "about 30 percent of all families with incomes less than $2,000 per year suffer from chronic health conditions . . . as compared with less than eight percent of the families with incomes of $7,000 or more." With inflation, all income classes receive more dollars today, on the average; but given the deterioration of central city areas, it is probable that the health disadvantage of low-income groups is still what it was in 1968.

other group activities complementary to the child's intellectual development.

Physical Confinement to the Home

Low-income neighborhoods are characterized by relatively high rates of violent crime.[57] Younger adolescents are also often subject to physical harassment by older adolescents, and playgrounds and recreation centers do not always have enough adult supervision to prevent such abuse. These conditions, plus the lack of money to purchase fares on public transport lines, serve to confine children up to the age of early adolescence to their houses and apartments after school hours. There are two unfortunate consequences at least: The houses are crowded and noisy and do not offer quiet places for retreat and study that the academically inclined low-income child might find at a library or well-run children's center; and the children are not able to get enough physical exercise to relieve nervous tensions.

Absence of Intellectual and Artistic Stimulation

Middle-income youth have access to a great variety of activities outside the regular school program, provided their parents are willing to seek them out. There are music lessons, dancing lessons, science instruction, visual arts instruction, individual sports (swimming, tennis, horseback riding), drama, woodworking, foreign language, printing—the list is almost endless. From the child's point of view, the activities are sometimes too generously provided. But they do serve to keep the mind active and they reinforce, to some degree, the interest that the child shows toward his or her school work.

The low-income child has few such opportunities, if any at all.[58] First, the places of instruction are likely to be far from the home; and for the reasons cited, the child has difficulty getting out of the house. Second, participation in such activities often demands prerequisites, that is, learnings acquired in the regular school program. Low performance in school thus bars the child from out-of-school activities that might serve to stimulate his or her interest in school. Third, in certain cases, participation in a given program is allowed only if a parent contributes time to the activity. Plainly this is not possible for most low-income parents.

[57] Office of Management and Budget, *Social Indicators*, p. 67.
[58] Ibid., pp. 214–22, provides data showing that nonwork activities are strongly income-related, especially, it appears, with respect to outdoor recreation.

Policy Implications

The conditions we have described make the development of competence in low-income youth difficult. And school and school-related programs, even compensatory types, are inadequate to overcome the deficiencies in the out-of-school environment of children and young people. What, then, are the policy implications?

The policy implications of nutritional deficiencies are obvious and have already been alluded to: nutritional supplements for expectant mothers and young children. As for home and neighborhood conditions, it might appear that only broad solutions could suffice: income redistribution (based on full employment and welfare reform, as a start) and the rebuilding of central city areas. Ideally, this is correct, but whether the United States is prepared to advance on such goals under any short time horizon is of doubt.

In the meantime, those aspects of the poverty environment that are especially inimical to the child's development might be pinpointed and then changed. Some progress could be made within present budgetary limits if the poverty environment was examined from the special view of child welfare. For example, to reduce requirements on low-income children to take care of sick adults and their siblings, additional nursing care could be focused strongly on households with young adolescents and after-school centers could be provided to serve children at older ages than day care centers ordinarily accept. To reduce the confinement of children to their homes, additional adult supervision of play areas and recreational centers could be provided, along with additional police protection in low-income neighborhoods from the time of school closing until, say, nine in the evening. Public transport could be made free to children and extra police protection of the routes could be put on at times when children were likely to be using them. Additional centers for study and for supplementary educational programs could be established in low-income areas, along with indoor and outdoor recreation facilities. Indeed, providing vouchers for out-of-school instructional and recreational programs would appear to be an ideal use of the voucher concept, for several reasons. First, the natural difficulties of public schools in providing highly specialized programs could be overcome by allowing children of similar interests from different attendance areas to meet together, thus bringing costs per student down to tolerable levels. Second, the imbalance in providing out-of-school lessons between rich children and poor children could be rectified. And third, quite probably the cause of social-class integration would be served, as children of similar intellectual and recreational interests use their vouchers to cross class lines. These actions and others like them would represent no extraordinary demand on the public sector—all that is required is an acceptable priority toward helping the young of the poor.

A Further Measure of Educational Equity

We now can understand how questions of efficiency and equity in education are intertwined. Efficiency in education is heightened as the number of low achievers is reduced. But low achievement is associated with low income. One likely route toward reducing the incidence of low achievement is to improve the out-of-school environment of poverty children. Yet, such steps toward this end as we have discussed could be justified on equity grounds alone. Let us turn now to another topic in equity.

The conventional ideas about fairness in the functioning of an educational system center on several questions. One is the distribution of educational resources to different social classes, whether these distributions are equal on a per-student basis or weighted in favor of low-income youth. Another is the question of the distribution of places in institutions of higher education and whether children of lower socioeconomic groups obtain a proportional share of places in highly regarded colleges and universities and so on. These are all important matters, but they do not exhaust the subject of fairness in the operation of an educational system. A further object of inquiry is the distribution of the "products" of an educational system, especially with regard to the distribution of the services of the professional and scientific elite.

One person's income is another person's price, and the educational system legitimates setting high prices for human services in such fields as law, financial management, medicine, and the performing arts. One result of these high prices is that lower income households do not, for example, obtain top quality legal service: "There is broad agreement in the law profession that many people cannot get the legal help they need."[59] There is also a two-class system of medical service. Poorer patients are "passed on to the public hospital system, the traditional haven for the indigent sick . . . while rich patients much more conveniently obtain what is probably the best medical service available in the world."[60] Even if a low-income

[59] Lesley Oelsner, "Lawyers and Ethics: How Much Help to the Poor?" *New York Times*, August 22, 1976, sec. 4, p. 18.
[60] H. Jack Geiger, "How the Hospitals in New York Got That Way," *New York Times*, August 22, 1976, sec. 4, p. 5.

household manages to save a bit of money, it will not have access to the best financial advice about how to invest it. The services of performing artists are not generally available to low-income households, except on television; nor is attention often paid to the interests, tastes, and realities of experience of low-income families in the creative work of writers, designers, choreographers, and the like. We are all closely affected, for good or ill, by the results and applications of scientific research, but the selection of research priorities is by no means a democratic process. Consequently, in viewing the equity of our educational system, we can conclude that it may be of at least equal importance to any given set of newborns to know how fairly the products of that system are distributed, as it is to know how fair access is to places within that system.

The situation exists even though the educational system is largely supported by tax dollars—even prestigious private universities obtain roughly half their revenues from the federal government. So the poor are taxed, along with all other citizens, to support an educational system, the more competent graduates of which are allowed to price their services at levels the poor can no way meet. This is not an inevitable condition. It is possible to imagine that the legal profession could be nationalized—lawyers, just like doctors in Great Britain and judges in the United States, would receive their incomes from government. Then, in the distribution of legal services, we might accept the philosophical point of the progressive income tax that marginal dollars of income of rich households represent less utility, or worth, than the marginal dollars of poor households. For a local case of a given type, household entitlement to a lawyer's time would then be set as an inverse function of household income. This is simply an example of how distribution of services of highly educated people could be made more equitable.

Summary

In the absence of a well-developed body of scientific knowledge about how to improve educational opportunities for students, we turn to recommendations drawn from simple observation and experience. Students and their parents reasonably demand more choice in selection of educational activities. Past and present innovations in school districts spread across the country show that substantially greater opportunities for selection among a set of curricular activities can be provided within the public sector. In similar vein, we have noted a series of possibilities that would allow teachers to have a more satisfying and intellectually stimulating career.

But neither of those arguments addresses directly the problem of the relative concentration of low-achievers who live in low-income neighborhoods. Many studies, as we saw in Chapter 7, indicate that socioeconomic status is a major correlate of school failure; yet, it is generally assumed in educational policy that home (and neighborhood) environment must be taken as given. In this chapter we attempted to describe certain conditions of poverty life that could be changed through public policy, even while that policy respects the privacy of family life.

Selected Bibliography

Chase, Samuel B., Jr., ed. *Problems in Public Expenditure Analysis.* Washington, D.C.: Brookings, 1968.

The Fleischmann Report in the Quality, Cost, and Financing of Elementary and Secondary Education in New York State, 3 vols. New York: Viking, 1973.

Knowles, John H., ed. *The Teaching Hospital.* Cambridge, Mass.: Harvard, 1966.

Levin, Henry M., ed. *Community Control of Schools.* Washington, D.C.: Brookings, 1970.

Machlup, Fritz. *The Production and Distribution of Knowledge in the United States.* Princeton, N.J.: Princeton University Press, 1962.

Marmor, Theodore R. *Poverty Policy.* Chicago: Aldine-Atherton, 1971.

Chapter Nine

Revenue Sources for the Public Schools

The operation of public schools relies mainly on revenues drawn from taxation. Our chief task in this chapter is to see what the tax structure is in the United States and to see how economists distinguish "good" taxes from "bad." In the next two chapters we shall examine the grant-in-aid arrangements by which state and local government are linked together in the support of schools. Together they provide about 92 percent of school revenue.[1] The special topic of federal aid to education is deferred until Chapter 12.

Public Revenue Structure

The federal government collects more revenue than state and local governments combined, but not by a wide margin. In 1974 federal revenues were $289 billion, or 59.6 percent of total public revenue. Not counting monies paid to them by the federal government, the states collected $108 billion (22.2 percent of total revenues), and local authorities on their own behalf collected $88.4 billion (18.2 percent of total).[2] Though the federal government is not itself a large source of

[1] Bureau of the Census, U.S. Department of Commerce, *Statistical Abstract of the United States* (Washington, D.C.: U.S. Government Printing Office, 1976), p. 138.
[2] Ibid., p. 261.

funds for schools, the central authority's influence on the overall system of taxation is significant, and we need to know how it raises its money. Table 9.1 indicates the major sources as of 1976 and how the use of the major sources has changed since 1960. The largest single source of federal revenue in modern times is the individual income tax. In 1976 it brought in 35.7 percent of total federal revenue. The estate and gift taxes and customs duties, with which middle-income and high-income families have to deal, had a combined share in 1976 of only 2.5 percent and from the point of view of aggregative economic policy can safely be ignored. Federal excise taxes are levies on such items as cigarettes, liquor, electric light bulbs, jewelry, and the like, and are presumably passed along to the consumer. They represent about 10 percent of federal receipts.

The big message of Table 9.1 is the dramatic reduction in the share of receipts from corporate income taxation and the equally dramatic increase in the share drawn from social insurance levies. These latter are collected chiefly as payroll taxes and are used mainly to finance the federal social security and unemployment insurance schemes. As we shall see later, there is cause to be concerned over what is happening to the equity distribution of tax burden because of the federal shift toward payroll levies: Payroll taxes are generally regarded to be "less fair" in incidence than, say, progressive personal income taxes. Like with the corporate tax, there has been a reduction in the use of individual income tax at the federal level.

At the state level, as shown in Table 9.2, general sales taxes, together with various forms of excises on gasoline, alcohol, and tobacco, make up roughly half of tax revenue. However, the use of individual income taxes has become more important over the last decade and a half, and they now represent approximately one quarter of state tax revenues. It should also be noted that Table 9.2 applies to *tax revenues* of state governments only. In 1974 states received over $30 billion in grants from the federal government, approximately half of which was intended for the support of public welfare programs.[3]

Table 9.3 shows that levies on property are the major source of tax revenue of local governments, accounting for over 80 percent of local tax revenue in all the years shown. The strong reliance on the property tax dates from before the turn of the century. But like states, local governments obtain substantial funds in the form of grants-in-aid. In 1974 local governments received $54.8 billion from federal and state agencies, an amount in excess of what they raised by property taxation.

---

[3] Ibid., p. 266.

Table 9.1
Federal budget receipts, by source, for fiscal years
1960, 1970, and 1976 (in billions of dollars)

Source	1960 Amount (in billions)	1960 Percent	1970 Amount (in billions)	1970 Percent	1976 Amount (in billions)	1976 Percent
Individual income taxes	$40.7	44.0%	$ 90.4	46.7%	$106.3	35.7%
Corporate income taxes	21.5	23.2	32.8	16.9	47.7	16.0
Social insurance taxes	14.7	15.9	45.3	23.4	91.6	30.8
Excise taxes	11.7	12.6	15.7	8.1	32.1	10.8
Estate and gift taxes	1.6	1.7	3.6	1.9	4.6	1.5
Customs duties	1.1	1.2	2.4	1.2	4.3	1.4
Miscellaneous receipts	1.2	1.3	3.4	1.8	10.9	3.6
Total[a]	92.5	100.0	193.7	100.0	297.5	100.0

[a] Totals may not add to 100% because of rounding.
Source: Barry M. Blechman, Edward M. Gramlich, and Robert W. Hartman, eds., *Setting National Priorities: The 1976 Budget* (Washington, D.C.: The Brookings Institution, 1975), p. 10. Copyright © 1975 by The Brookings Institution. Reprinted with permission.

Table 9.2
State tax collections, by type of tax, for fiscal years
1960, 1970, and 1974 (in millions of dollars)

Type of tax	1960 Amount (in millions)	Percent	1970 Amount (in millions)	Percent	1974 Amount (in millions)	Percent
General sales	$ 4,302	23.9%	$14,177	29.6%	$22,595	30.5%
Excise on motor fuels	3,335	18.5	6,283	13.1	8,207	11.1
Excise on alcohol and tobacco	1,573	8.7	3,728	7.8	5,159	7.0
Individual income	2,209	12.2	9,183	19.1	17,015	23.0
Corporate income	1,180	6.5	3,738	7.8	6,015	8.1
Motor vehicle and operator's licenses	1,468	8.1	2,728	5.7	3,759	5.1
Other taxes and licenses	3,969	22.0	8,024	16.7	11,385	15.4
Total[a]	18,036	100.0	47,961	100.0	74,135	100.0

[a] Totals may not add to 100% because of rounding.
Source: Bureau of the Census, U.S. Department of Commerce, *Statistical Abstract of the United States* (Washington, D.C.: U.S. Government Printing Office, 1976), p. 273.

Table 9.3
Local government tax collections, by type of tax, for fiscal years 1960, 1970, and 1974 (in millions of dollars)

Type of tax	1960 Amount (in millions)	1960 Percent	1970 Amount (in millions)	1970 Percent	1974 Amount (in millions)	1974 Percent
Property	$15,798	87.4%	$32,963	84.9%	$46,452	82.2%
Sales and gross receipts	1,339	7.4	3,068	7.9	5,542	9.8
Individual and corporate income	254	1.4	1,630	4.2	2,413	4.3
Other	692	3.8	1,173	3.0	2,108	3.7
Total	18,083	100.0	38,834	100.0	56,515	100.0

Source: Bureau of the Census, U.S. Department of Commerce, *Statistical Abstract of the United States* (Washington, D.C.: U.S. Government Printing Office, 1976), p. 258.

265

To summarize these data on the tax structure of the United States: Each level of government has a single preferred tax source—at the federal level, the individual income tax; at the state, the category of sales and excise taxes; at the local, the property tax. Should any of these levels expand its fiscal responsibilities at the expense of another? If, for example, the federal government takes over full fiscal responsibility for the welfare system or a state government takes over full financing of its public schools, then two possibilities emerge. First, the government that is assuming the greater financial responsibility might use its chief tax instrument more intensively. If the federal government relieved states and large cities of the requirement to pay a share of public welfare, it might obtain the additional revenues by raising tax rates on personal income. The states and large cities would now need to raise less revenue on their own and might reduce rates in sales and excise tax schedules. The whole tax structure would be shifted toward greater reliance on personal income taxation. As we shall see later in this chapter, this would make the overall tax structure of the country more progressive. Alternatively, the government that assumes greater fiscal responsibility might adopt a tax presently used by another government. For example, it has been suggested that the federal government establish a tax on *value added*.[4] We will discuss value-added tax shortly. For the present, it is sufficient to note that the value-added tax and the general sales tax, the mainstay of state government finance, are practically identical in their impact on household budgets. Thus, if the federal government took over welfare entirely and at the same time imposed a value-added tax, the overall tax structure would be little changed. The welfare money would all come from the federal government, but the extra money from the federal level would be raised in practically the same way that it is now raised by state governments—and by those large cities, such as New York, that hold fiscal responsibility for welfare.

Likewise, if state governments should take over full responsibility for financing schools, they might use the sales taxes more intensively—or they might take over the administration of part of the property tax from local government.[5] The latter step would produce little change in tax structure. However, whether or not assuming the costs of a service by a superior level of government produced a

---

[4] Value-added tax is popular among the governments of Western Europe, and it figures prominently in the tax structure of the United Kingdom. See Carl S. Shoup, *Public Finance* (Chicago: Aldine, 1969), pp. 250–251.

[5] See Charles S. Benson et al., *Final Report to Senate Select Committee on School District Finance* (Sacramento: California State Senate, 1972), I, 77–83.

change in tax structure, such action would almost certainly produce a more even geographic distribution of benefits.

Brief Description of Certain Taxes

We are all familiar with the nature of the individual income tax, as that tax is employed by federal and state governments.[6] Likewise, most of us have day-to-day experience in paying general sales and excise taxes, the simplest levies in design. But we should understand the property tax because of its importance for school support. And we should consider the value-added tax, not yet generally familiar in the United States but a levy suggested by tax experts for possible use by the federal and state governments.

Property Taxation

As the name implies, the property tax is a levy on property or wealth. Conceivably any form of wealth, including stocks and bonds or cash value of insurance policies, could be subject to tax under the levy. But in actual practice the property tax is imposed on physical assets, chiefly real estate.[7] Homes, factories, commercial buildings of all types, farm structures, as well as land under and around all such properties, are its main targets.

The property tax is an old one, having been used in the reign of Queen Elizabeth I to provide money to support the poor of England. Its processes of administration have not changed greatly over time. The central task in administrating the tax is assigning a taxable value to different properties. In the case of ordinary single-family houses, this value is commonly computed by examining sales prices of similarly situated houses that have recently turned over in the market. For estates, apartment houses, office buildings, factories, and the like, there are two alternative procedures to sales-price comparison (these procedures come into play when the given type of property is infrequently bought and sold). One is to estimate the cost of reproducing the existing structure and then subtracting from the replacement value a sum to represent depreciation from all causes. To this net value of improvements is added an estimate of the land's

---

[6] More will be said about the income tax with respect to its *incidence* later in this chapter.

[7] It is also common to find that business investors are subject to property taxation. For householders, the tax is frequently levied on such consumer durables as automobiles, campers, and boats.

value if it were vacant (hypothetically). The alternative method is to assess value on the income-producing potential of the property.[8] Real estate appraisal is by nature highly judgmental, and state governments frequently oversee the work of the local assessment officer.[9]

Once the *assessment roll,* that is, the listing of values of all individual parcels (properties), is complete, a total is cast up for the given local community. In the meantime, let us say, an expenditure budget has been prepared. From the gross total of voted expenditures is subtracted the estimates of funds to be received as grants-in-aid from the federal and state governments. There is also a subtraction made for revenues from sales of permits, school lunches, and so on, to derive an amount to be raised by local taxation. The local tax rate is then computed as a ratio: amount to be raised by property taxation divided by amount of local tax base. For example, suppose the amount to be raised is $100 million. Let the local tax base be $10 billion. The ratio of $100 million to $10 billion is in the order of 1 percent. It would be appropriate to quote a local tax rate in the given locality of 1 percent of assessed valuation (this is the value established for tax purposes; it may or may not be the same as market value). For a house valued for tax purposes at $40,000, the tax bill would be $400 for the year. Actually, rates are commonly quoted as so many dollars per $100 of assessed valuation, or so many dollars per $1,000 of assessed valuation, called *mills.* In this example, the rate would be $1 per $100 of assessed valuation, or 10 mills.

To summarize: Local tax rate is determined under the following relationships:

$$L = E - S - F - O$$
$$L = tB$$
$$t = \frac{L}{B} \tag{9.1}$$

where E equals voted expenditure; L equals local tax funds; S equals state aid; F equals federal aid; O equals other local sources (for example, charges for school lunches); B equals local tax base; and t equals

---

[8] For a discussion of property valuation procedures, see Oliver Oldman and Ferdinand P. Schoettle, *State and Local Taxes and Finance: Text, Problems, and Cases* (Mineola, N.Y.: Foundation Press, 1974), pp. 137-243.

[9] Insofar as the size of the *local tax base*—that is, the sum of values of individual properties—determines the amount of aid a district receives from the state government, with more aid being directed to local districts that are low in wealth and have relatively limited means to support the necessary level of local services, assessors naturally have an incentive to take a pessimistic view of the worth of properties in their ken. State overseers of assessors attempt to monitor this problem.

local tax rate. The relationship between mills and a tax rate expressed as a percentage is, Y mills = 0.1 Y percent. Hence, a tax rate of 1 percent is equal to 10 mills.

One difficulty in using the property tax as the chief instrument for raising local government revenue is that the size of the property tax base, meaning taxable values per capita or taxable values per public school student, varies widely from one locality to the next. For example, in California in 1974–75, the taxable value per unit of average daily attendance in public elementary school districts (as a unit of local government) ranged from $476 in a low-wealth district to $1,299,577 in a high-wealth one.[10] Such variation is not easily accommodated in state aid schemes to equalize local fiscal capacity. The main reason for such disparity in wealth is that industrial and commercial properties are unevenly distributed among the taxing jurisdictions within a given state.

This disadvantage aside, the property tax has much to recommend it for use by local government. Indeed, the case for the property tax is essentially the case for a reasonable degree of autonomy in local administration of services. Property, once developed, cannot escape the laws, as can rich individuals, by moving from a high-tax to a low-tax jurisdiction. The property itself is security for payment; nonpayment can result in foreclosure by the local authority. The yield of the property tax, once the rate is fixed, is easily predictable from one year to the next. Finally, and most important, the rate of tax can be varied from year to year at no inconvenience in terms of compliance to the taxpayer.[11] Local government needs vary from one period to another because of changing requirements for capital goods and because federal and state grants are subject to substantial year-to-year fluctuations. Local sales and income taxes, where they are in use, require local businessmen to withhold sales tax receipts at fixed rates and to withhold payroll taxes at fixed rates, all on behalf of local government. They are inconvenienced, if called upon to perform this service, whenever tax rates are changed because an important part of their accounting system must be revised. The property tax is seen by the taxpayer as a single annual bill; if the property owner can find the money to pay it, the fact that the rate changes a bit, up or down, from one year to the next is of no special importance.

[10] California State Department of Education, "Fingertip Facts on Education in California" (Sacramento, Calif.: 1976), p. 2.
[11] That is not to say that a rise in property tax rates represents no hardship for low-income families, only that fluctuations in rates represent no inconvenience in the mode of payment.

Value-Added Taxation

In our discussion of national income accounting (Chapter 2), we noted that the final value of any physical product or service can be regarded as the sum of increments in value created by separate firms. For example, in making bread, the farmer sells wheat to a miller who hired labor to produce flour. The flour is sold to the baker who produces bread. The flour has a higher value than wheat, and the bread has higher value than the flour, and so on. A tax can be levied on these increments in value. The base of the tax could be defined as a firm's (any firm's) gross receipts, minus the value of all the purchases of *intermediate products*—goods and materials in process and services such as telephone, tax accounting, and the like—supplied to the given firm by other firms. Also subtracted would be the given firm's purchases of capital goods and equipment.

A tax imposed on value added as just described is the logical equivalent of a general retail sales tax. This follows from the fact that the sum of values added for any product equals the value of the product (sales price) at the point of final sale. Hence, it is always possible, in principle, to equate a given rate of tax on retail goods to some rate of value-added tax.[12] Coverage of the two taxes may, however, be different. As retail sales taxes are used in the United States, services are rarely included in the base, for example, services of travel agents, financial consultants, automobile repairs, and so on. Value-added tax (VAT) easily covers services as well as sales of goods. On the other hand, the retail sales tax commonly exempts prescription drugs and food bought in grocery stores. If VAT were actually collected from all firms (instead of at the point of final sales), it might be difficult to continue such exemptions, for any particular chemical company, for example, might not know how much of its output was being used in food processing or in, say, the production of paints.

Unlike most central governments, the United States federal government employs no broad based tax on consumption. If we are looking for a new, higher yield tax to use, either to finance improved services or reduce pressure on some old tax, VAT might seem to be the logical candidate. But because it is equivalent to the retail sales tax, in turn the mainstay of state government finance, it is not really a new tax at all. If VAT were to be imposed by the federal government,

[12] Richard A. Musgrave and Peggy B. Musgrave, *Public Finance in Theory and Practice* (New York: McGraw-Hill, 1973), p. 308.

it would need to be integrated in some fashion with the retail sales taxes of the states, and the end result might be taxation of consumption at very high levels indeed, especially in those states that now make intensive use of sales taxes.[13]

Criteria of Taxation

What is a "good tax"? There are four main criteria: equity, economic effects, administrative feasibility, and responsiveness of yield to economic changes.

Equity

The two main standards under equity are *benefit* and *ability to pay*. The benefit principle relates tax burden on the household to the amount of benefits received from government, while the principle of ability to pay relates tax burden to economic capacity. Under either principle, the tax instrument should provide "equal treatment of equals": Persons who are in relevant respects equal should be dealt with in approximately the same way. If a tax is levied on the benefit principle, then two households that receive the same amount of benefit should pay equal amounts of taxes. Similarly, if a tax is levied on the ability to-pay principle, then two households that have equal amounts of economic capacity should contribute in the same measure. In short, a good tax is not arbitrary in its *incidence.*

Treatment of Unequals Under the Benefit Standard The benefit standard is based on an analogy with consumption of goods and services in the private economy. There the output of firms is paid for according to the amount of product that a particular household buys and uses. This is the *commercial rule,* and it is strictly applied in allocating the costs of public enterprises (municipal power stations, waterworks, and so on) to the households of the area. The benefit basis is also used to a considerable degree in financing highways through the earmarking of gasoline taxes for this specific function.

[13] At the time (1971–1973) when school finance reform was in the national headlines, proposals were made that the state governments adopt VAT to replace property taxation for local schools. We have indicated that the use of the name VAT is the major difference between VAT and retail sales taxation. If the property tax for schools is to be phased out, it would be better for the states, on equity grounds, to find replacement revenue by making more intensive use of individual income taxes at progressive rates.

Those who uphold the benefit standard may say that it is the only fair basis of taxation. Any other schemes imply that some people will pay for what other people get. And advocates may point out that the benefit standard is least damaging to economic incentives. Whatever the arguments for the benefit standard, it appears to be unworkable over large portions of the public economy. The most important reason for public expenditures in the first place is the inability to allocate benefits of certain kinds, such as defense, to households. In certain other areas, such as education, it is roughly possible to measure—or to make comparisons with regard to—the flow of individual, as distinct from social, benefits. But, if costs were allocated on this basis, some large families in the lower income brackets would have to give up goods that are essential to a minimum standard of living. Pursued far enough, the basis of raising the revenue would defeat the ends of the public service the revenue is to support.

Treatment of Unequals Under the Ability-to-Pay Standard
In the United States of America ability to pay is accepted as the stronger criterion of equity in taxation. Ability is commonly defined in terms of current income, not wealth (though the two measures are related.)[14] This does not take us very far, however. If household *A* has $20,000 more income than household *B*, how much more in taxes should *A* pay? Even under a regressive structure, it is possible for *A* to contribute more dollars.

Now let us define terms. Since a tax is levied on income, it is appropriate to establish categories of tax burden *relative to income*. A *proportional tax* is one under which the ratio of tax paid to income is constant for all households. For example, if a $6,000 household pays $600 in tax, and a $10,000 household pays $1,000, both are taxed at 10 percent of income. A *progressive tax* is one under which the ratio of tax paid to income is larger for a higher income household than for one of low income. If a rich family contributes at a rate of 20 percent while a poor family pays at the rate of 10 percent, the tax is progressive. Finally, a *regressive tax* is one under which the ratio of tax paid to income is greater in poor families than in rich. These three categories are defined in terms of ratios of percentages—the criterion is one of *relative* tax burden.

---

[14] While some forms of wealth, like vacant land, may yield no current income, they may be increasing greatly in value. Thus wealth can increase while current income remains constant. If, for example, the land is sold, the proceeds may be subject to capital gains taxation, but only at special low rates. In short, wealth receives preferential tax treatment over income.

For many years economists tried to establish a ratio structure under the concept of *equal sacrifice*.[15] This included three distinct approaches. *Equal absolute sacrifice* would call for each household to give up an amount of dollars so that the same amount of utility was lost by all (this, of course, looks at the transaction only from the taxpaying side, since some utility is derived from the public programs the taxes support). *Equal proportional sacrifice* would require a $20,000 household to give up twice the amount of utility as a $10,000 household. There is no logical way to choose between these first two approaches to designing a progressive tax schedule. More damaging, there is no way to compare the utility of income in different households. Under the *minimum aggregate sacrifice* approach, levies are arranged to subtract the smallest total amount of utility from the society while meeting a given total tax bill. This calls for the government to meet its needs by taxing first the highest income in the country, then the next highest, and so on (suppose the highest income is $500,000,000 and the next highest $400,000,000; the government would take $100,000,000 from the highest income, then begin taxing both the first income and the second, until it had reached the third highest income, and so on), leveling increases down until it had got the total amount of money it required. In sum, the plan would call for taxation of *all income* over a certain level, say $18,000, and no taxation below that level. What such a plan would do to economic incentives is not clear. But if we accept the idea that marginal utility of income diminishes—the richer you are, the less your last dollars are worth to you—it has the advantage of logic.

In general, economists prefer a progressive rate structure for two reasons: First, taxation should not take dollars that are necessary for a minimum standard of living. As long as demands for government services are high and as long as there are several million very poor households in the country, it follows that taxes will have to be levied at higher rates on the rich than on the poor. Second, taxation should do something to reduce extreme inequality in disposable income. This, alas, does not offer a clear guide to the degree of progression in tax structure—that is, it does not inform Congress about the different rates of tax that should be applied to different levels of household income. And, obviously, a given amount of tax revenue can be raised under many different combinations of specific tax rates.

[15] They tried to give meaning to John Stuart Mill's nineteenth-century dictum that "the subjects of every state ought to contribute to the support of government, as nearly as possible in proportion to their respective abilities . . ." (*Principles of Political Economy* [New York: Appleton, 1893], II, 394).

But, to paraphrase the noted economist F. W. Taussig, it may be sufficient simply to know the direction in which we should be moving.[16] Taking account of income inequality in the United States, that direction would seem to be toward greater progressiveness.

Economic Neutrality

If a government has a choice between two tax instruments, it should logically prefer the one, other things equal, that has the least unfavorable effects on the private economy. The general criterion is that a good tax is neutral with respect to the allocation of resources. It does not distort consumers' spending patterns nor affect decisions of households with respect to savings and investments; it has neither positive nor negative effects on work incentives, choices of alternative means of production, and so on. Expenditures for such activities as education are recognized as having favorable effects on the private economy; these kinds of public services stimulate economic growth. What is desired is that the possible *unfavorable effects* of levying the taxes not cancel the good effects of the services the taxes support or lead to other damages to the private economy.

What happens, for example, when the government places a new excise tax on a particular commodity? Ordinarily, the retailer passes the tax along to the consumer: The price of the taxed article rises. Further, the total tax revenue of the government increases if households continue to buy at least some amounts of the commodity. This flow of funds to the government allows a shift in production from the private sector, and the intended effect of the new tax is to accomplish such a shift. But there is also an unintended effect. Let us recall from Chapter 5 that the price system is a signaling device channeling information between households and businesses. The excise tax creates a situation in which the households and businesses are no longer thinking in terms of the same price. The price as seen by the seller is net of tax, while the price to the buyer includes it: "The tax has driven a wedge into the price system. As a result, the private economy is misled into producing the wrong combinations of goods, underproducing those heavily taxed."[17] A completely neutral tax would provide the government with its money without causing such a distortion of economic activity.

One completely neutral tax is a *poll tax* (or *head tax*). In no way can a person's economic decisions affect the amount of tax that he or she must pay. No change in the person's rate of work or pattern of

[16] F. W. Taussig, *Principles of Economics*, 4th ed. (New York: Macmillan, 1939), p. 540.
[17] Otto Eckstein, *Public Finance* (Englewood Cliffs, N.J.: Prentice-Hall, 1964), p. 7.

investment or consumption alters the amount of tax due. However, the idea of a poll tax is that everybody must be liable to pay exactly the same amount; consequently, the amount levied per head must be so low that even poor people can pay it. It follows that poll taxes cannot be productive sources of public revenue. Another possibility is a tax on *economic surplus,* such as the rent of land (as distinct from rent on improvement on the land). Since the supply of land is fixed by nature, this tax is economically neutral. Yet another possibility is a tax on commodities for which the demand is inelastic, that is, on commodities that are bought in approximately the same quantity whether the price goes up or down. Taxation of price-inelastic goods, like salt, has been a practice of government at least since the Middle Ages. However, this kind of taxation is generally regressive in incidence. Hence, the search for an economically neutral tax in this case runs afoul of the criterion of equity.

When economists ask empirical questions about the economic effects of a particular tax provision, they are dealing basically with human motivation. Professionally, they are not equipped to analyze human motivations; there are also substantial problems in measuring the economic effects of a tax. The specific provisions of a levy do not exist in isolation from other forces that impinge on economic performance. An expected effect can be cancelled by other tax provisions or by other institutional changes in the economy. In some cases, the direction of the effects is uncertain. Do high income tax rates increase or reduce work incentive? If people feel that the money reward after tax becomes worth less and less as tax rates climb on the progressive scale, high rates can reduce incentive. But if people have fixed income goals for education of children, retirement, travel, and so on, the effect can be just the opposite, since a higher level of gross income is needed under the tax to reach the goals. This explains, in part, moonlighting, working wives, and the long hours of some self-employed lawyers and accountants.

Sometimes the effect is clear, but its implications for the economy are not. If the merging of business firms is promoted by corporation taxes and death duties, is this good or bad for the economy? In yet a third case, there may be agreement both on the direction of an effect and on its deleterious influence on the economy (the corporation tax, for example, restricts growth of new firms) but lack of agreement on whether the matter is serious enough to warrant a revision of the tax structure. In summary, assessing the economic effects of taxation is a troublesome area. It is fair to say, however, that the various tax instruments have *some* harmful effects (such as reducing the incentive to invest, consuming valuable human talent in tax litigation, and distorting household consumption patterns) and that these effects are somewhat different from tax to tax. Hence, we have an argument for using many different taxes; concentrating on one or a few would result in an excessive amount of their particular economic side effects.

Administrative Feasibility

A tax that may be administered successfully by one level of government may be utterly beyond the capacity of another level to handle. An individual income tax of highly progressive rates is readily employed by national government but not by lower levels. In a modern industrial state, economic affairs are extraordinarily complicated, and it is no easy matter to define "taxable income." A central government can assemble a team of highly professional accountants and lawyers to interpret revenue codes, and it can employ auditors who are competent to deal with extreme complexities of financial relationships. Because the private and corporate affairs of rich individuals are often closely intertwined, the same team of experts is also available to administer the corporate income tax. It would be wasteful in the extreme if local authorities attempted to duplicate such an agency (Internal Revenue Service) to administer local income taxes.

On the other hand, state governments process enough income tax returns to justify the existence of qualified administrative staff, and present practices of integrating federal and state administration of income taxes raises the calibre of state performance. But state income taxes are not highly progressive in rate structure. If they were, the effective level of federal government assistance to states would be raised because state income taxes are deductible in federal returns. And we cannot expect the federal government to encourage states to employ highly progressive rates. Moreover, state personal income taxes, though deductible, do not represent a credit on the federal tax—that is, they cannot be subtracted dollar-for-dollar from the federal tax liability. Hence, states are reluctant on their own account to employ highly progressive rates because if they tax rich people more heavily than neighboring states, or are perceived to do so, the rich will move away. The only way that states could use a highly progressive schedule of rates would be if they all agreed to adopt the same, or nearly the same schedule. In that case, they might as well ask the federal government to collect the tax for them.

A similar argument applies to use of sales taxes by local governments. If sales tax rates vary in a given commuting area by any noticeable amount to the retail shopper, consumers are likely to concentrate their purchases in low-tax districts. Localities then will be put under pressure by merchants, especially those localities that levy sales taxes at a high rate, to conform to some normal standard of rate. In that case, the sales tax might as well be collected on behalf of localities by state or county governments.

Somewhat the same argument applies to the use of property taxes by local governments. The real or implied threat of taxpayers' mobility makes it difficult for a locality to get far out of line from its neighbors in property tax rate. The problem is more serious with respect to taxation of commercial and industrial properties, because the owners often have no attachment to community other than as a geographic base for making profit. As seen by the town, such commercial parcels are often large. Though an empty factory is taxable, owners of empty factories often demand—and get—a reduction in taxable valuation. Home owners are less prone to move in response to local tax differentials because, generally speaking, they have chosen to live in the community for many reasons, of which tax rate (unless, of course, the differential becomes very large) is ordinarily a minor one. This argument suggests that localities are better able to administer a property tax on residential housing than a tax that is imposed on all real property, leaving taxation of commercial and industrial properties to statewide administration.

We thus see that the reliance of different levels of government on different types of taxes—progressive income taxes at the federal, sales and excise at the state, and property at the local—is grounded in consideration of administrative feasibility. A tax is administratively feasible when the given level of government can employ staff of sufficient competence to deal with technicalities and can control taxpayer mobility to reduce tax avoidance to a tolerable level. A good tax, then, is a tax that is administratively feasible for the level of government that needs to use it.

Responsiveness of Yield to Economic Changes

Taxes differ widely in terms of the total volume of funds they produce and the way their yields respond to changes in national (or regional) income. An excise tax on electric light bulbs would produce very little money, in total, for the government. And, since the demand for light bulbs, at least in a rich country like the United States, is inelastic with respect to *household income*, it is not to be expected that the yield from such an excise tax would be very responsive to changes in *national income*. An excise tax on automobiles would produce vastly more money, in total, than one on light bulbs because automobiles represent a far larger share of national output. Also, expenditures on automobiles reflect changes in household income rather closely. Hence, an excise tax on automobiles would show substantial changes in yield when national income went up or down. A general sales tax obviously has a large revenue potential. But its responsiveness to income changes is quite moderate because its yield reflects a kind of average of the income elasticities of all the various commodities consumed, some of which, like light bulbs, are sluggish in terms of income changes and others, like automobiles, display a stronger relationship.

The personal income tax is an interesting case. The total yield can be extraordinarily large. In 1976 the yield at the federal level was estimated as $106.3 billion (see Table 9.1), which was approximately 6.6 percent of GNP. And, the personal income tax is highly responsive to changes in income. Consider the following arithmetic example: Suppose the income of a household rises from $8,000 in one year to $10,000 in the second. Let the household consist of husband, wife, and two children, each person being entitled to a $900 exemption. Assume that the regular standard deduction is 15 percent of gross income, or $1,400, whichever is smaller. Let the rate of tax be 15 percent on the first $4,000 of taxable income and 20 percent between $4,000 and $6,000. Tax computation (simplified, of course) would be as shown in Table 9.4.

Note that a 25 percent increase in gross household income produces a 67 percent increase in tax yield.[18] Such an effect flows from two common features of individual income taxation: the use of exemptions and deductions to exclude a portion of household income from any taxation at all, and the use of a progressive rate structure. When national income is rising, many households will find their income tax liabilities increasing more than in proportion to their gross income, and the opposite occurs when national income is falling. As seen by governments, any given percentage increase in national (or regional) income produces a magnified percentage increase in income tax yield.

When economists discuss the responsiveness of tax yield to change in income, they ordinarily use the shorthand expression *income elasticity of yield,* which is defined as the ratio

$$E_t = \frac{\text{percentage change in tax yield}}{\text{percentage change in national (regional) income}} \quad (9.2)$$

If the elasticity coefficient has a value of 1, then the percentage changes in tax yield and income are equal. A 5 percent change in national income would lead to a 5 percent change in revenue from the

[18] Joseph A. Pechman, *Federal Tax Policy* (Washington, D.C.: Brookings, 1966), p. 60.

Table 9.4

Tax computation

	Year 1	Year 2
Gross income	$8,000	$10,000
Less: Exemptions	3,600	3,600
Less: Standard deduction	1,200	1,400
Equals: Taxable income	3,200	5,000
Tax at base rate of 15%	480	600
Tax at second bracket rate of 20%	0	200
Total tax	480	800

Source: Joseph A. Pechman and Benjamin A. Okner, *Who Bears the Tax Burden?* (Washington, D.C.: Brookings, 1974), p. 59. Copyright © 1974 by The Brookings Institution. Reprinted with permission.

given type of tax. Suppose the elasticity coefficient has a value of 1.5. Then a 5 percent change in national income would produce a 7.5 percent change in tax yield. A value of less than 1 would indicate that the relative change in tax yield is less than the relative change in national income and that the given type of tax offers a return that is relatively unaffected by change in income.[19]

In a highly developed country like the United States we can anticipate that the responsibility of governments to provide services will grow. But the rate of increase in the need to provide services appears to be different from one level of government to the next. In particular, the expenditure requirements of state and local governments seem to be advancing more rapidly than the peacetime responsibilities of the federal government. Because of its intensive use of the individual income tax, the federal government has a revenue structure that is income elastic. (The income elasticity of federal personal income tax is approximately 1.8.)

Generally speaking, the income elasticity of taxes used by state and local government averages out at a value of about 1.0.[20]

[19] Elasticity can also be written (more precisely) as

$$E = \frac{\dfrac{dT}{T}}{\dfrac{dY}{Y}} = \frac{dT/dY}{T/Y}$$

where T = tax yield and Y = national income.

[20] For a discussion of income elasticity of yield of different types of taxes, see Oldmand and Schoettle, *State and Local Taxes and Finance*, pp. 104–118.

Thus, expenditure requirements and elasticity of tax yield are mismatched by level of government. To make their tax systems more income elastic, state and local governments would need to concentrate their revenue sources on a highly progressive income tax, like the federal one. But we have seen that such a tax is not well suited for state and local use, on the ground that rich taxpayers would flee from any taxing jurisdiction that imposed higher rates than its neighbors.

There is another reason why such a tax is not well suited for state and local use. What goes up may come down; thus, a tax of high income elasticity of yield may be helpful to a government in prosperous times and it may be a disaster in an era of economic depression. State and local governments are not expected to borrow money long term to finance their current operations (though some have, for example, New York City); that is, they are not supposed to engage in *deficit financing*. Even if state and local governments had income elastic revenue sources readily available, they would be ill-advised to use them because the services they offer are not the type to be easily cut back in a depression.[21] In the absence of the alternative of deficit financing, cutting back would be inevitable. But, then, how does the federal government manage? By engaging very heavily in deficit financing, as do most other central governments in the world.[22]

We now see why money is available for defense and space exploration in good times and bad and why money is not available, not in the 1970s at least, for improving the quality of life in the large central cities: At given tax rates, federal revenues over the long run will expand much more rapidly than national economic growth, while state and local revenues will approximately keep pace.[23] The problem is mitigated but not fully solved by the federal government's practice of sharing some of its revenues with states and localities.[24]

---

[21] The difficulties faced by New York State in 1975 with regard to service cutbacks are discribed in Dick Netzer et al., "The New Politics of Less," *New York Affairs*, November 1, 1975, pp. 5–55.

[22] We discuss public borrowing briefly in Chapter 12.

[23] The problem is compounded by the tendency of unit prices of public services to rise more rapidly than prices in general. The underlying cause is the inability of public agencies to substitute physical capital for labor in the production of their outputs. Private firms make such substitutions all the time. With the new capital goods in place, output per hour of work goes up and so do wages. Public agencies must raise wages and salaries to keep pace with the dominant private sector of the economy, but they have little increased productivity to offset the higher per-unit labor costs. Hence, the higher rate of price inflation in the public sector. See William J. Baumol, "Macroeconomics of Unbalanced Growth: The Anatomy of the Urban Crisis," *American Economic Review*, 57, no. 3 (June 1967): 415–426.

[24] We discuss federal assistance to states and localities in Chapter 12.

Who Pays the Taxes?

Analysis of *tax incidence* is one of the most difficult and complex topics in economics. But in terms of equity in financing government (including equity in financing schools), it is a topic of central importance. Tax incidence as a concept draws a distinction between the statutory liability to make a tax payment to a government and the bearing of the ultimate burden. All taxes ultimately are paid by households. When a tax is imposed on a corporation, corporate officers will write out a check to government. But the corporation is not a household in the economic sense. Possibly the corporate tax will be paid by the households who are owners of the corporation. But the corporation may succeed in *shifting* the tax *forward* to the households who are purchasers of its products (by charging higher prices than it otherwise would) or *backward* to its workers or suppliers (by paying a smaller wage bill than it otherwise would do or by putting pressure on its suppliers to lower their prices).

Even when the tax is a statutory obligation of a single individual, that person may manage to shift it. Consider an individual who owns an apartment building. Let the town raise its property tax rate. If that allows the owner to raise rents or reduce maintenance and if, in the absence of the tax increase, the owner would not have seen fit to do either, then we can say the owner has successfully shifted the tax forward. If the existence of property tax on apartments serves to reduce the quality of their construction, for example, by limiting floor space, part of the tax is shifted backward to the construction industry.

Incidence is a matter of *relative prices* and *relative incomes:* "What is relevant is the effect of a tax on the distribution of *real* incomes that are available for private use, and this depends on the changes in relative product and factor prices and not on changes in absolute prices."[25] A major assumption of incidence theory is the following: Households, existing in a competitive, profit-maximizing economy, under conditions of extreme mobility of factors of production, are in a position to obtain the largest income of which they are capable. Hence, when a tax is first imposed or when the rates of a tax already in use are raised, the tax or tax increment can be shifted in the general case *only* if the tax change itself produces a change in the *supply* of some factor of production. Take the example of an increase in property tax on an apartment building. Under strict interpretation

[25] Joseph A. Pechman and Benjamin A. Okner, *Who Bears the Tax Burden?* (Washington, D.C.: Brookings, 1974), p. 27.

of incidence theory, we must assume that the landlord is extracting as much rent from the tenants at all times as he possibly can. If, at the time of an increase in property tax, the owner raises rents to shift the increase in tax to the tenants, they will leave and the property will stand vacant until the owner reduces the rent to the former level. Thus, the landlord cannot shift tax in the short run. But, because profits in the apartment-rental industry have fallen, capital will be attracted away from that industry and toward other activities that have not been adversely dealt with. New construction will slow down, old buildings will be abandoned and the total supply of rental apartments will fall. This happens *as a consequence* of the property tax increase. As supply diminishes, rents rise (for nothing has happened to the *demand* for apartments). And as rents rise, landlords' profits climb back toward their former level. The landlords thus successfully shift at least part of the property tax to their tenants. This is a shifting of tax in the long run. In industries where supply can respond more quickly to a tax change, the shifting process will occur over a shorter period.

The controversy about tax incidence arises from conflicting views about the extent to which purely competitive forces prevail in the real world and the extent to which factors of production are mobile. We will discuss some examples of the conclusions of incidence analysis, starting with types of taxes about which there is reasonable agreement on incidence and moving to those about which there is not.

Individual Income Tax

It is a matter of consensus that individual income taxes are not shifted, that is, they are paid out of the income of the person against whom the tax is levied: "[W]orkers and investors do not appear to change working hours or savings in response to changes in tax rates. . . . If total hours worked and savings are relatively fixed, a tax on incomes must be borne by those on whom the tax is imposed."[26]

---

[26] Ibid., p. 30. But this is not to say that changes in income tax rates have no economic effects. Suppose that the structure of rates is made more progressive, with total yield held constant. Almost certainly the demand for goods and services that appeal peculiarly to rich households will fall relative to demand for goods and services of mass appeal. Owners and workers in firms that cater to tastes of the rich would then suffer a loss in income. These economic effects are ordinarily ignored in incidence analysis.

Payroll Taxes

We have noted that payroll taxes represent a rising share of federal resources. There formerly was general agreement that payroll taxes are paid out of the wages and salaries of workers against whom they are levied: "The payroll tax is assumed to be borne by workers because lower take-home pay as a result of the tax will not induce wage earners to withdraw from the labor force."[27] But at the present time an alternative view, that when rates of payroll taxes are increased, unions succeed in their bargaining efforts to raise wages by a corresponding amount, is finding favor. However, unions are most likely to possess such strength in quasi-monopolistic industries, and such industries have sufficient economic power to pass the wage rise through to consumers in the form of higher prices for their products.

General Sales Taxes

It is widely agreed that the general sales tax is borne by consumers in proportion to their total expenditures on commodities and services subject to the levy. The tax does not produce any change in relative prices and, hence, does not affect consumption patterns. But when the tax is first imposed in a given state, the decline in overall purchases by consumers (as the tax is passed along, prices rise and quantity demanded falls) may reduce profits at the retail level and back through the chain of production. Capital may shift to untaxed services until rates of profits are equalized, and the final result is that the burden of tax is shared between consumers and factors of production. Also, when one state uses a sales tax and a bordering one does not, retailers in the state with the tax who are located along the border may pay part of the tax out of their profits.

Corporation Income Tax

There is no general consensus about who pays the corporation income tax. One view is that all business firms seek to maximize profits; that is, they have adjusted the sales and input prices of their goods, as closely as their knowledge allows, to the profit-maximizing price. When a corporation income tax is then imposed, there is no further action a given corporation can take to shift the tax to anybody. Profits in the corporate sector fall, and capital shifts to the noncorporate sectors. The influx of capital into the noncorporate sectors of the

---

[27] Ibid., p. 33.

economy reduces returns in that sector as well. Assuming the total supply of savings is fixed and that aggregate salaries and wages remain unchanged, the entire corporation income tax is borne by capital. The rate of return to capital drops in both corporate and noncorporate sectors, and the after-tax profit rate is presumably equal in both.

A second view of corporation tax incidence denies that corporations seek to maximize profits. It holds that corporate managers seek a desired rate of return to capital. And corporations are seen to shield themselves from the forces of competitive markets and to have sufficient economic power—as quasi-monopolists—to adjust their prices whenever the need arises. Thus, if government imposes a tax on corporations—or raises rates under an existing tax—they raise their selling prices just enough to maintain the desired rates of return. The tax, in other words, is built into the determination of selling price. The end result is that the tax is paid by consumers, not by owners of capital. There is not yet any resolution of these conflicting views about who pays the corporation income tax.

Property Tax

The question of who pays the property tax should be of special interest to educators because so much of school revenue is drawn from this particular levy. Unfortunately for logical neatness, the property tax is one about which there is considerable controversy. But first, a (minor) point about which there is general agreement: Property tax on vacant land is paid by the owners. There is nothing in the imposition of a property tax that affects the supply of vacant land or its worth.

Taxes on owner-occupied properties are assumed to be paid by the owners; there is little action a householder can take in the market to shift his or her property tax to anyone. Until the early 1970s there was general agreement that property tax on owner-occupied housing was regressive because expenditures on housing rise less rapidly than income. That is, rich households devote a smaller percentage of their income to housing than do poor ones.[28] Since the property tax ordinarily is imposed at a flat rate in the various localities, the result is that low-income families pay tax on their houses at a higher rate than do the rich. This view has been challenged. First, as an empirical observation, it is denied that rich

[28] Dick Netzer, *Economics of the Property Tax* (Washington, D.C.: Brookings, 1961), p. 57.

households spend a smaller proportion of their incomes on housing than do the poor—though this empirical question has not been satisfactorily analyzed.[29] Second, regardless of empirical investigation, it is suggested that it is wrong to relate property taxes paid by home owners to their *current* incomes. Better to look at taxes, it is said, in relation to lifetime incomes. If this were done, then almost certainly the property tax would appear to be less regressive than when it is judged on an annual basis.[30] When a household is young and first buys a house, it may well buy one that is rather too expensive; the household expects to "grow into it." Likewise, when the head of household retires and income drops, the remaining family members may choose to continue to live in their house even though they "can no longer afford it." (They are helped to afford it in many instances because the mortgage has been paid off.) At both ends of the life cycle, a given household is paying relatively large amounts of property tax compared with its current income. But this is offset, so it is claimed, by what happens during the middle years of the life cycle when property tax payments compared with current income are relatively small.

As for property taxation of buildings other than owner-occupied residences, the argument proceeds as in the case of corporation income tax. If we assume that competition prevails, that owners are charging rents to maximize profits, and that the supply of savings is fixed, then imposing a property tax reduces profits of ownership of buildings—capital flows to less heavily taxed sectors of the economy, that is, to those in which the use of capital in the form of real property is relatively less, causing a reduction in profits in those sectors as well. Finally, profits in all sectors are equalized but at a reduced level. Capital bears the tax; apartment dwellers and consumers in general do not.

If we drop or modify the assumptions, a different picture emerges. If owners of apartment buildings have a certain degree of monopoly power, that is, control of rents, and if they seek to maintain a conventional rate of return—which is not necessarily the highest rate of return at any moment of time—then property tax increases may be passed along to renters in the form of either rent increases or reduced maintenance. Given that many renters have low income, this latter result could give a regressive bias to the tax.

---

[29] Henry Aaron, "A New View of Property Tax Incidence," *American Economic Review*, 64, no. 2 (May 1974): 214.

[30] Richard A. Musgrave, "Is a Property Tax on Housing Regressive?" *American Economic Review*, 64, no. 2 (May 1974): 228.

Alternatively, we could assume that the supply of savings is not fixed:

> In these circumstances, the initial effect of imposing a property tax is to reduce the rate of return to owners of real estate; but this reduction will ultimately discourage new investment and reduce the supply of buildings. The result will be a rise in the prices of services that are produced by dwelling units. Thus, instead of resting on owners of real estate, the burden of the property tax on residential buildings will be shifted to tenants. . . . Similarly, the burden of the property tax on other buildings will not fall on their owners but will be shifted to consumers in general.[31]

Some Empirical Evidence on Tax Incidence

Joseph A. Pechman and Benjamin A. Okner, in their recent major study of tax incidence in the United States, base their analysis on data of 72,000 families, including information on income, deductions, exemptions, and taxes of various kinds paid. The data cover such variables as age of members of household, home ownership, place of residence, and so on. Sources of data are federal individual income tax returns for 1966 and a special survey of low-income households conducted in 1967 by the U.S. Bureau of the Census (Survey of Economic Opportunity).[32]

As we have seen indicated, estimates of incidence reflect assumptions economists make. For example, the question of whether to distribute the corporation income tax in proportion to capital owned by different households or, say, in proportion to their estimated levels of consumption is determined by whether the assumptions is that the tax is not shifted except as it is borne by all capital, not just that under corporate ownership, or that it is shifted and is paid by consumers. Pechman and Okner can advance no single set of preferred estimates of incidence. What they do offer is alternative estimates based on different assumptions. Table 9.5 (pp. 288–289) shows two such estimates, one based on assumptions that yield a progressive distribution of tax burden and one that yields a regressive distribution. The progressive assumptions include: individual income tax paid by households on which it is levied; sales and excise

[31] Pechman and Okner, *Who Bears the Tax Burden?* pp. 20–21.
[32] Ibid., pp. 20–24.

taxes paid in proportion to consumption of taxed commodities; corporation income tax distributed 50 percent in proportion to dividends received and 50 percent in proportion to property income in general; the property tax on land and improvements as distributed to property income in general; payroll taxes as distributed to wages. The regressive assumptions are the same for the individual income tax and sales and excise taxes. However, under the regressive assumptions the corporation income tax is distributed 50 percent to property income in general and 50 percent in proportion to consumption; and the property tax on land is distributed to landowners and, on improvements, to occupiers of shelters (the proportion of the tax levied on housing of all types) and to consumption (that is, the industrial and commercial properties).[33] That part of payroll taxes that is levied in the first instance on employers is assumed to be paid half out of wages and half out of price increase passed along to consumers.

Certain conclusions emerge. Regardless of the incidence assumptions, the individual income tax, in spite of complaints about its loopholes, is progressive in impact. The sales tax and excises are definitely regressive. The corporation tax is progressive, but if the burden falls on capital (progressive assumptions), it is far more so then if we assume half the burden falls on consumption. The property tax is unusual in that its incidence switches from progressive to regressive (the change in incidence is not simply a matter of being more or less progressive or regressive), depending on which incidence assumptions we make, that is, whether it falls on owners of capital or on homeowners, renters, and consumers.

Since the property tax is the single most important in school finance, the ambiguity in estimating its impact on different income classes is unsettling for policy analysis. However, as we shall see in the next chapter, there are several reform measures readily available to reduce the burden of the property tax on low-income households. This would seem to be a worthy objective, whatever the overall pattern of incidence of that levy is.

Summary

Each level of government has its preferred type of taxation: at the federal level, it is income taxation; at the state, sales and excise; and at the local, property. Such emphasis laid on a particular type of taxation is, in part, a matter of tradition. But it also reflects considerations

[33] Ibid., p. 38.

Table 9.5
Effective rates on federal, state, and local taxes, by type of tax, by adjusted household income class, under progressive and regressive tax incidence assumptions

Adjusted family income (in thousands)	Individual income	Corporation income	Property	Sales and excise	Payroll	Personal property and motor vehicle	Total taxes
Progressive assumptions							
$ 0–3	1.4	2.1	2.5	9.4	2.9	0.4	18.7
3–5	3.1	2.2	2.7	7.4	4.6	0.4	20.4
5–10	5.8	1.8	2.0	6.5	6.1	0.4	22.6
10–15	7.6	1.6	1.7	5.8	5.8	0.3	22.8
15–20	8.7	2.0	2.0	5.2	5.0	0.3	23.2
20–25	9.2	3.0	2.6	4.6	4.3	0.2	24.0
25–30	9.3	4.6	3.7	4.0	3.3	0.2	25.1
30–50	10.4	5.8	4.5	3.4	2.2	0.1	26.4
50–100	13.4	8.8	6.2	2.4	0.7	0.1	31.5
100–500	15.3	16.5	8.2	1.5	0.3	0.1	41.8
500–1,000	14.1	23.0	9.6	1.1	0.1	0.2	48.0
1,000 and over	12.4	25.7	10.1	1.0	—	0.1	49.3
All classes	8.5	3.9	3.0	5.1	4.4	0.3	25.2

Type of tax

Adjusted family income (in thousands)	Individual income	Corporation income	Property	Sales and excise	Payroll	Personal property and motor vehicle	Total taxes
Regressive assumptions							
$ 0–3	1.2	6.1	6.5	9.2	4.6	0.4	28.1
3–5	2.8	5.3	4.8	7.1	4.9	0.4	25.3
5–10	5.5	4.3	3.6	6.4	5.7	0.3	25.9
10–15	7.2	3.8	3.2	5.6	5.3	0.3	25.5
15–20	8.2	3.8	3.2	5.1	4.7	0.3	25.3
20–25	9.1	4.0	3.1	4.6	4.1	0.2	25.1
25–30	9.1	4.3	3.1	4.0	3.6	0.2	24.3
30–50	10.5	4.7	3.0	3.5	2.6	0.2	24.4
50–100	14.1	5.6	2.8	2.4	1.3	0.1	26.4
100–500	18.0	7.4	2.4	1.7	0.7	0.1	30.3
500–1,000	17.7	9.0	1.7	1.4	0.4	0.2	30.3
1,000 and over	16.6	9.8	0.8	1.3	0.3	0.2	29.0
All classes	8.4	4.4	3.4	5.0	4.4	0.3	25.9

Source: Joseph A. Pechman and Benjamin A. Okner, Who Bears the Tax Burden? (Washington, D.C.: Brookings, 1974), p. 59.

of administrative feasibility and elasticity of yield. Equity in taxation is extremely important, given the large requirements for public revenue. But judgments on the equity aspects of different tax instruments are marred by uncertainty about how tax burdens fall on different groups of households, classified by level of income. However, we do know that educational services are supported in major degree by yield of property taxes and that property taxes, whatever their whole pattern of incidence is, appear to deal harshly with low-income households. If progress is to be made in reforming educational finance, these two points must be recognized.

Selected Bibliography

Aaron, Henry J. *Shelter and Subsidies: Who Benefits from Federal Housing Policies?* Washington, D.C.: Brookings, 1972.

Break, George F., and Joseph A. Pechman. *Federal Tax Reform: The Impossible Dream?* Washington, D.C.: Brookings, 1975.

Kirp, David, and Mark Yudof. *Educational Policy and the Law.* Berkeley, Calif.: McCutchan, 1974.

Maxwell, James A. *Financing State and Local Government.* Rev. ed. Washington, D.C.: Brookings, 1969.

Musgrave, Richard A., ed. *Essays in Fiscal Federalism.* Washington, D.C.: Brookings, 1965.

Pechman, Joseph A., and Benjamin A. Okner. *Who Bears the Tax Burden?* Washington, D.C.: Brookings, 1974.

Chapter Ten

General-Purpose State Grants for Education

Another major source of revenue for public schools, second only to local taxation, is grants-in-aid from state government. We distinguish initially between two main types of grants: general purpose and categorical. *General-purpose* grants are given directly to local school districts for those expenditures the districts are legally authorized to make. Thus, general-purpose grants support the local school budget in the same way that, in general, local tax revenues do. (Of course, because the grants flow to school districts, we may contend that the grants are not general purpose at all because they are restricted essentially to providing educational services. Thus, the more precise description is *general purpose within the field of education*.) *Categorical grants*, on the other hand, are given to school districts with restrictions on the uses to which the money can be put. Examples are grants for special programs for handicapped children, grants to provide extra school services to low-income youth, and grants to finance transport of students. In 1975–76 the 50-state total of state educational grants was $28.5 billion, of which $23.7 billion (83.2 percent) were general purpose and $4.8 billion (16.8 percent) were categorical.[1] In

[1] Esther O. Tron, *Public School Finance Programs 1975-76*, Office of Education, U.S. Department of Health, Education, and Welfare (Washington, D.C.: U.S. Government Printing Office, 1976), pp. 14-15.

this chapter we will concern ourselves with the general-purpose grant, leaving discussion of categorical aids to Chapter 12.[2]

The Rationale of General-Purpose Grants in Education

The basis for the use of general-purpose educational grants was given at the beginning of Chapter 6. The first purpose of grants-in-aid is to expand the volume of public services. Such grants earmarked for education are meant to improve the quality and extend the quantity of school services. Why should it be necessary for a higher level of government to be concerned about the adequacy of services provided by some lower level? The units at the lower level—call them local government—base their decisions about the proper standard of service on the volume of private internal benefits generated, that is, they fail to recognize the volume of external benefits that may accrue to the society at large. Necessarily, in the absence of grants-in-aid, there will be an underprovision of local public services.

Let us think specifically of school services. We saw in Chapter 7 that the benefits of education can properly be divided into two categories, private and social. The decisions of local school boards and local electorates about tax rates for schools can be expected to reflect more closely the estimated private benefits than the estimated social benefits. Contrast, for example, the school's function of preparing young people to enter college, which is substantially a private benefit, with its function of promoting good citizenship, almost exclusively a social benefit. Success in the first task is of paramount importance to the people of the district, especially those who are parents. Unless the school performs well in this regard, there is an immediate and irremediable loss to the local citizens. How well the second task is done is much less a matter of local concern because the quality of citizenship in the country, state, and even the region is only slightly affected by how well this single school district performs. Hence, the voters might seek to finance schools up to the point where the college preparatory work was reasonably well done but to skimp on extending programs to the point where young people could be assisted in developing the moral, cultural, and political awareness

[2] The most general of all arrangements exist between the federal government and the states. First, there is *general revenue sharing*. Second, deducting state and local taxes from federal individual income tax returns is a form of grant arrangement; but there are no controls over what the monetary equivalent of the deduction is used for at the state and local levels. We discuss these matters further in Chapter 12.

that citizenship in the modern world calls for. Furthermore, even some of the private benefits generated by a school district may be lost to it under a brain drain. That is, suppose school district X taxes itself severely in order to maintain an exceptionally good program. Some of its graduates may move to other towns and offer the benefits of their superior education to the employers and civic leaders of those towns, while in their parent district their places as members of the adult population are taken, say, by immigrants from towns that offered poor-quality schooling. Furthermore, even if social benefits are all retained within the given taxpaying jurisdiction, they may be garnered more fully by future generations than the present; this may cause present taxpayers to regard educational outlays as onerous. Lastly, the type of tax instrument available to local authorities may not be sufficiently responsive in yield to maintain the real value of the local authorities' purchasing power. An objective, then, of educational grants-in-aid is to push school expenditures to where marginal social benefits are equal to marginal social costs, recognizing that local districts on their own resources will not generally reach this optimum point.

A second objective of grants-in-aid is to reduce interdistrict differentials in tax rates. If school districts were, for example, left completely to their own resources, tax rates would be very high in poor districts and modest to low in rich districts. (By "poor" and "rich" is meant the amount of assessed valuation per pupil—low in poor districts and high in rich; they do not refer necessarily to level of household income.) Extreme differentials in tax rates are regarded as unfortunate on several counts. First, it is by no means clear that equity is served. Probably local tax rate differentials increase the regressiveness of the property tax. Assume that in a certain (poor) school district the modal family has an income of $20,000 and lives in a $40,000 house. Let the tax rate be 15 mills on full value. The tax on the household is $600, or 3 percent of its income. In another (rich) district, let the modal family have a $40,000 income, let it live in an $80,000 house, and let the tax rate be 10 mills on full value. The tax on the household is $800, or 2 percent of income. Regressiveness exists, even though in this example house value stands in the same relationship to income (two to one) in both families. (Admittedly, in comparing residential suburbs with industrial tax havens, this situation could be reversed.)

But aside from concern with regressiveness per se, it is commonly regarded as inequitable for residents of one school district to have tax rates twice as high as those prevailing in a neighboring district, both rates being in support of essentially the same local public service. Even more distressing is to have a poor district, in spite of burdening itself with high tax rates, unable to provide anything above the cheapest of school programs, while a nearby rich district is able to have handsomely staffed and equipped schools at low tax rates. A basic concept of local government is that citizens, within limits, are free to choose the quality of the public services they desire. A reasonable corollary is that districts choosing to have high-quality services should also have above-average tax rates, and the converse should hold for districts choosing to have low-quality services. The tax rate, after all, is the price of local services, and quality of service and price are usually supposed to move in direct proportion to each other. Unfortunately, in American education, they often stand in inverse proportion.

An added reason for being concerned about interdistrict tax rate differentials is the effect they exert on the consumer's choice of place to live. Theoretically, as we have seen, one of the arguments given in support of decentralizating government is that the household can choose where to live on the basis of the type and quality of public services offered by different communities. Tax rate differentials, as far as school services are concerned, narrow the choice severely. Consider a household of $20,000 income that desires exceptionally good educational services for its children. The best school programs will no doubt appear to exist in upper income residential suburbs. More often than not, these suburbs will have low tax rates because they include a concentration of high-valued properties. Our hypothetical household will note, of course, that property tax payments per household are high; otherwise, their expensive school programs could not be continued. Suppose the household is eager, however, to pay double or triple the dollar amount of the school tax it is presently paying in order to enroll its children in the superior school system. As we saw in Chapter 6, the increase in taxes, unfortunately, is the smallest of what is required. Since the upper income suburb will ordinarily desire to maintain its position of superior-schools-cum-low-tax-rate, it will require newcomers to buy expensive properties that will yield large dollar amounts of tax at low tax rates.

A third major reason for the existence of general-purpose grants is that the needs of local authorities differ—some face large requirements to spend money on educational services and some small. One basis for the difference is the characteristics of the students. If, for example, one district has a high proportion of students who are low achievers and a second has a small proportion, the first likely district has extra requirements for money in order to reduce the number of low-achieving students.[3] Alternatively, differences in needs exist if some districts must pay prices for educational resources that are notably higher than average. It is often contended (see Chapter 12) that central cities must offer teachers salaries that are higher than those paid in suburban districts if they are to employ teachers of equal competence. If the facts so indicate, this would justify a state's establishing a general-purpose aid formula that directed additional funds to central cities over what was given to suburban districts—on a per-pupil basis, of course.

A fourth reason for using general-purpose grants is to allow state governments to exercise a measure of control over local operations. Why should higher levels of government interfere in the operations of local authorities? Basically, the higher levels of government, with greater or less explicitness, attach different values to the cost-benefit ratios of specific educational programs, say, than do the local administrations. Often state governments will have better or more complete information about alternative costs and yields than will the local authorities. (If they do not, then something has gone quite wrong because the higher levels of government have better means than the local to collect and analyze data.) In other cases, state interference in local decision making strengthens the local authorities against local political pressures that may be counterproductive. Sometimes state governments give categorical or specific grants. Sometimes a bonus or penalty is attached to a main grant. For example, small districts that agree to consolidate may receive a bonus expressed as a stated percentage increase in the general-purpose operating funds they receive from the state government. In any case, the existence of general-purpose grants establishes a psychological climate in which localities are more likely to listen to state officers than if, say, all the money they were spending was drawn from the local tax base.

Grants-in-Aid

There are three major types of general-purpose grants: fixed-unit equalizing, percentage equalizing, and weighted population. We

[3] It might appear that categorical grants would better recognize differences in student achievement levels among districts than general-purpose grants. Indeed, categorical grants are employed for this purpose. However, if low-achieving students are found primarily in districts of low property wealth, then any of the standard general-purpose grants recognize this form of special need.

shall consider the nature of the three in brief compass and then take up some historical justifications of the grant formulas.

The Fixed-Unit Equalizing Grant

It should be said right off that all modern educational grants seek to adjust the flow of funds to the recipient district under two broad criteria: the needs of the district to spend money on educational services and the ability of the district to meet these needs from its own fiscal resources. A properly functioning grant system distributes money in direct proportion to expenditure requirements and in inverse proportion to the amount of local resources.

Under the fixed-unit equalizing grant, the amount of subsidy that a school district receives is the difference between a dollar estimate of expenditure requirement and a dollar estimate of a reasonable local contribution in support of school service. One estimate is prepared of the costs of basic educational services in the district and another of how much local taxpayers should pay in meeting these costs. If the estimated expenditures exceed the estimated amount of local contribution, the gap in revenues is closed by state subsidy.

The estimate of expenditure needs is obtained by multiplying attendance in the local schools by a figure representing an "adequate level" of expenditure per pupil, which is called the *foundation program;* it stands for the amount of dollars per pupil required to purchase the basic elements of an educational program. The local contribution toward school costs is the product of a mandatory (or in some states computational) tax rate and the value of the local property tax base. For example, suppose the state determines that adequate education costs $400 per pupil and that citizens of all school districts should be willing to tax themselves for schools at a rate of 1 percent of the value of their properties. If a district has 2,000 pupils and a tax base of $24 million, the state subsidy is computed as (2,000 × $400) − (.01 × $24,000,000) = ($800,000 − $240,000) = $560,000. The locality contributes $120 per pupil and the state pays $280, yielding the foundation program of $400. If another district with the same number of pupils is twice as rich, that is, has a tax base of $48 million, its local contribution per pupil will be $240 and its state subsidy will be $160, again a total of $400. Though the two districts are different in wealth, they can both provide a $400 program at the same local tax rate, namely, 10 mills.

Theoretically, the mandatory local rate is set at that value that would yield the cost of the foundation program in the richest district of the state.[4] The formula for the foundation program plan, then, can be written as

$$A_i = N_i u - r Y_i \tag{10.1}$$

Where A_i = subsidy to the ith district

N_i = number of pupils in the ith district

u = dollar value of the foundation program

r = mandatory (or computational) local tax rate

Y_i = property tax base of the ith district

$$r = \frac{N_1 u}{Y_1}$$

Where N_1 and Y_1 refer to the number of pupils and tax base in the richest district of the state.

What are the equity features of this plan? First, for the elements of the educational program common to all districts, such as the provision of teachers' services, supply of materials, maintenance of buildings, and so on, each district, rich or poor, is able to provide the standard amount per pupil, as measured by the value of the foundation program, at equal local tax rates. Second, when one district has a higher local tax rate than another, the extra burden reflects either inefficiency in financial management or that the taxpayers are willing to provide an extra-high-quality school program for their pupils. These two causes of high tax rates are exactly those that local taxpayers, not the citizens of the whole state, should be made to shoulder.[5]

The Percentage Equalizing Grant

Under the percentage equalizing plan aid is distributed so that the state pays the local authorities a share, or percentage, of locally determined school expenditures. The share is larger in poor districts than rich; hence, the grant is said to have equalizing effects.

If the range in assessed valuation per pupil is not extreme, it can be arranged that any two districts, regardless of the difference in

[4] The foundation program plan, also known as the Strayer-Haig formula, was first suggested for educational grants in George D. Strayer and Robert M. Haig, *Financing of Education in the State of New York*, a report reviewed and presented by the Educational Finance Inquiry Commission under the auspices of the American Council on Education (New York: Macmillan, 1923), pp. 173–174.

[5] For a discussion of *necessary costs* and how they should be recognized in grant schemes, see D. S. Lees et al., *Local Expenditure and Exchequer Grants* (London: Institute of Municipal Treasurers and Accountants, 1956), chap. 4.

their wealth, can finance equal dollar expenditures per pupil at equal local tax rates. That is, if district *A* spends $400 per pupil and has a tax rate of $2.50 per $100 of assessed valuation, all other districts that spend $400 per pupil will also have a tax rate of $2.50. If district *B* spends $500 per pupil and has a tax rate of $3.00, all other districts that spend $500 will have the $3.00 rate. Expenditure per pupil and district tax rates move in a one-to-one relation. This is achieved when grants are distributed under the following formula:

$$A_i = \left(1 - x \times \frac{y_i}{y}\right)E_i \qquad (10.2)$$

Where A_i = grant to *i*th district
   x = arbitrary constant normally having a value between 0 and 1.
   y_i = assessed valuation per pupil in the *i*th district
   y = assessed valuation per pupil in the state
   E_i = school expenditure in the *i*th district

The constant x having a value between 0 and 1 represents approximately the total local share of school support; accordingly, $1 - x$ represents approximately the state share. The state share can be adjusted downward by assigning a higher value to x and upward by assigning a lower value. If the state wishes to meet half the cost of public education through its subventions, the value of x would be 0.5.[6]

Let the state set $x = 0.5$ and let the statewide assessed valuation per pupil be $10,000. Suppose that in district *A* assessed valuation per pupil is $15,000 and that the district is spending $500 per student and has an enrollment of 20,000. Its operating expenditures will thus be $10,000,000 and the formula for state aid will read

$$A_a = \left(1 - 0.5 \times \frac{15,000}{10,000}\right) \$10,000,000$$

$$= 0.25 \times \$10,000,000 = \$2,500,000$$

District *A* will receive $2,500,000 from the state and will itself pay $7,500,000 for its educational program.

Now, in the same state let district *B* also have 20,000 students to educate, let its expenditures be $600 per student, and let its per pupil valuation be $5,000. District *B* is poorer than *A* but nevertheless

[6] For further discussion of percentage equalizing grants, see Charles S. Benson, "State Aid Patterns," in *Public School Finance*, ed. Jesse Burkhead (Syracuse, N.Y.: Syracuse University Press, 1964), pp. 205 ff.

has decided to spend more money for the schooling of its students than *A* thought was necessary. For *B*, the state aid formula will read

$$A_b = \left(1 - 0.5 \times \frac{5,000}{10,000}\right) \$12,000,000$$

$$= 0.75 \times \$12,000,000 = \$9,000,000$$

District *B* would receive \$9,000,000 from the state and spend \$3,000,000 of its own money to support its school program. The tax rate in *B* will be \$3.00 per \$100 of assessed valuation (\$3,000,000 of local expenditure divided by a tax base of \$100,000,000) and in *A*, \$2.50 (\$7,500,000 of local expenditure divided by a tax base of \$300,000,000). Thus, the tax rate in *B* is 20 percent higher than in *A*, but then expenditures per pupil in *B* are 20 percent higher. This example illustrates the notion that under a percentage equalizing grant school expenditures per pupil and tax rate can move in a one-to-one relationship.[7]

The Weighted Population Grant

There are three essential concepts embodied in the weighted population grant. First, the grantor appropriates a definite and fixed sum in aid of a particular public service. The amount is determined solely by the granting government; it is not directly related to the size of the client population (for example, number of public school pupils) or to the level of local expenditures. Second, the amount appropriated is divided among the receiving governments in proportion to some measure of population. In the case of school districts, the grant might be divided on the basis of shares of pupil population: If district *A* had 10 percent of the pupils in the state, it would receive 10 percent of the appropriation. Third, the measure of population ordinarily is adjusted, or *weighted* to take account of local needs and resources. For example, kindergarten pupils might be multiplied by a factor of 0.50, pupils in grades 1–3 by a factor of 1.50, pupils in grades 4–8 by 1.00, and in grades 9–12 by 1.20 to reflect differences in costs at the various grade levels. To recognize relative differences in local resources, enrollment might be weighted by the ratio of statewide assessed valuation per pupil to district valuation per pupil.

---

[7] We leave discussion of the efficacy of alternative grant schemes in meeting the basic objectives of grants-in-aid, that is, maximizing social benefits, reducing interdistrict tax rate differentials, and so on, to the next two chapters. Here we seek simply to indicate the nature of the major formulas.

The possibilities for devising weights are practically unlimited.[8] Once a weighting formula is decided upon, the actual values of, say, weighted enrollment for each school district in the state would be computed and a grand total arrived at. Any district's share of the grant appropriation would be equal to its share of the statewide total weighted population. Suppose, for example, the state appropriates $10,000,000 to be distributed to the school districts. Let the statewide total of weighted enrollment be 50,000,000. If the weighted enrollment in district *A* is 5,000,000, it will receive 10 percent (5,000,000 as a percentage of 50,000,000) of the appropriation, or $1,000,000.

The weighted population grant's chief virtue is its flexibility. Any number of weights can be incorporated, and the only limitation is the availability of relevant data from which to devise and compute weights. The formula will distribute any amount of money that is appropriated. Hence, it is a good formula to use when the legislature wants to keep close control of annual appropriations and when it is suspected that the amount of appropriations will vary from one year to the next, as would be the case if school appropriations were expressed as a percentage (either stable or increasing) of the state's total budget.

However, from the point of view of the school district, the weighted population formula does not allow close and accurate predictions to be made of the amount of money that will be received from state sources. And the distributions cannot be described in terms of the effects on local tax rates in the sense such effects can be stated

---

[8] For example, the University of California Mission to the Colombian Higher Education Project suggested that the central government distribute part of its support to public universities under a weighted population formula using the following system of weights:

$$W = (E \times A \times B \times C) R$$

Where W = weighted student population

E = enrollment in the current year

A = ratio of net domestic product per student in the nation to net domestic product per student in the department (state)

B = ratio of three-year moving average of costs per student per year to three-year moving average of cost per graduate

C = ratio of the year's enrollment to enrollment in the second preceding year

R = regionalization bonus, equal to 1.0 if the university was not part of a regional system and to 1.2 if it was.

The intent was to recognize departmental difference in resources, to recognize growth in enrollment, and to encourage regionalization. Also, the amount of grant would vary directly with costs per student but inversely with cost per graduate, this last feature being intended to encourage universities to become more efficient in reducing student wastage and halting the proliferation of academic specialties.

under both the fixed-unit equalizing and the percentage equalizing grants. Partly for this reason, the weighted population grant, though it has had a place in the set of federal grants to states (see chapter 12), has never been very important in state and local financial relationships, and we shall not consider it further here.

History of State Grants for Educational Services

The modern approach to state aid for education dates from the work of the Educational Finance Inquiry Commission (1921–1924). As Paul Mort has written, two pages "almost hidden" toward the end of the commission's study for New York State, prepared by George D. Strayer and Robert M. Haig, contain the "conceptual basis" of much of the present-day practice in equalization.[9] Sometimes the basic idea is described as the Strayer-Haig formula; sometimes, as we have seen, it is called the foundation program plan, or a fixed-unit equalizing grant.

In describing the practices of New York State in the early 1920s Strayer and Haig stated:

> A precise description of the basis upon which federal and state money is apportioned among the localities is an elaborate undertaking. The present arrangements are the product of a long history of piecemeal legislation. The result is chaos. The standards used are so numerous, and are combined and conditioned in so many different ways, that a simple description is exceedingly difficult, and a precise appraisal of the relative importance of all the different standards is quite out of the question.[10]

The authors did provide, however, the following summary:

> Almost all of the state aid is distributed primarily on a per-teacher quota basis which varies with the classification of the

---

[9] The document Mort refers to is Strayer and Haig, *Financing of Education in the State of New York*, pp. 173, 174. See Paul R. Mort, Walter C. Reusser, and John W. Polley, *Public School Finance*, 3rd ed. (New York: McGraw-Hill, 1960), p. 203.

[10] Strayer and Haig, *Financing Education in the State of New York*, p. 94. The experience of seeing state aid programs become increasingly complex by the passage of piecemeal legislation has been felt for a century in England and for only slightly less in the Scandinavian countries. See Howard R. Bowen, *English Grants-in-Aid* (Iowa City: University of Iowa, 1939); and Kjeld Philip, *Intergovernmental Fiscal Relations* (Copenhagen: Ejnar Munksgaard, 1954).

school district and, in the case of one of the quotas, with the assessed valuation in the district. Approximately one-half of the state aid is entirely unaffected by the richness of the local economic resources back of the teacher, and the portion which is so affected is allocated in a manner which favors both the very rich and the very poor localities at the expense of those which are moderately well off.[11]

In short, New York State was failing by a considerable margin to provide equal financial treatment to students in different types of school districts.

Strayer and Haig give primary weight to equalization as the objective of state aid. But it was necessary first to define equalization:

There exists today and has existed for many years a movement which has come to be known as the "equalization of educational opportunity" or the "equalization of school support." These phrases are interpreted in various ways. In its most extreme form the interpretation is somewhat as follows: The state should insure equal educational facilities to every child within its borders at a uniform effort throughout the state in terms of the burden of taxation; the tax burden of education should throughout the state be uniform in relation to taxpaying ability, and the provision of the schools should be uniform in relation to the educable population desiring education. Most of the supporters of this proposition, however, would not preclude any particular community from offering at its own expense a particularly rich and costly educational program. They would insist that there be an adequate minimum offering everywhere, the expense of which should be considered a prior claim on the state's economic resources.[12]

With this general definition of equalization, the next step is to see how it can be established:

To carry into effect the principle of "equalization of educational opportunity" and "equalization of school support" as commonly understood it would be necessary (1) to establish schools or make other arrangements sufficient to furnish the

[11] Ibid., p. 162.
[12] Ibid., p. 173.

children in every locality within the state with equal educational opportunities up to some prescribed minimum; (2) to raise the funds necessary for this purpose by local or state taxation adjusted in such manner as to bear upon the people in all localities at the same rate in relation to their taxpaying ability; and (3) to provide adequately either for the supervision and control of all the schools, or for their direct administration, by a state department of education. [13]

Strayer and Haig replaced "equal educational facility" with the notion of "equality up to some prescribed minimum." They also suggested that some schools might be administered directly by state education departments. One of the most distressing features of American education is that a school that is grossly and obviously failing to meet the needs of its students is allowed to continue under the same staff and local district's management year after year. The authors' suggestion that such schools be put under state administration as a way to rectify the situation has not been acted upon.

The authors' proposal for implementing the system of state and local finance was given as follows:

The essentials are that there should be uniformity in the rates of school taxation levied to provide the satisfactory minimum offering and that there be such a degree of state control over the expenditure of the proceeds of school taxes as may be necessary to insure that the satisfactory minimum offering shall be made at a reasonable cost. Since costs vary from place to place in the state, and bear diverse relationships to the taxpaying abilities of the various districts, the achievement of uniformity would involve the following:

1. A local school tax in support of the satisfactory minimum offering would be levied in each district at a rate which would provide the necessary funds for that purpose in the richest district.

2. The richest district then might raise all of its school money by means of the local tax, assuming that a satisfactory tax, capable of being locally administered, could be devised.

3. Every other district could be permitted to levy a local tax at the same rate and apply the proceeds toward the costs of schools, but—

[13] Ibid.

4. Since the rate is uniform, this tax would be sufficient to meet the costs only in the richest districts and the deficiencies would be made up by the state subventions.[14]

This proposal leads directly to the formula for the fixed-unit equalizing grant shown in equation (10.1). Arithmetic illustrations of the workings of the formula are given in Tables 10.1–10.7.

Another development of thinking about state grants for school services derives from a report by Harlan Updegraff and Leroy King (1922), in which they urged the adoption of what we have called the percentage equalizing grant.[15] As we have already seen, this is a device under which the state government shares in supplying funds to meet a locally determined volume of school expenditure. It is like a matching grant except that the term *matching grant* is often interpreted to mean dollar-for-dollar matching; under the percentage equalizing grant, the state's share is different from one district to the next, being low in rich districts and high in poor (this is the wealth-equalizing feature).

In writing of the percentage equalizing grant, Erick Lindman has stated:

> The history of state support for education has many illustrations of "matching," "reward for effort," or "stimulation." This principle has been criticized because it has been frequently misused. If the state pays one-half the cost of a certain phase of the school program uniformly to all school districts throughout the state, two basic errors are committed:
>
> 1. There is a distortion of emphasis within the school program since the phase of the program which receives the fiscal rewards will draw local funds from the other phases of the program.
>
> 2. The less wealthy school district will be unable to make the required local contribution and hence will be denied the benefit of the aid.
>
> It is obvious, however, that the matching principle can be used without being subject to this criticism. If all phases of

---

[14] Ibid., pp. 174–175.
[15] Harlan Undegraff and Leroy A. King, *Survey of the Fiscal Policies of the State of Pennsylvania in the Field of Education* (Philadelphia: University of Pennsylvania, 1922), chap. 2.

the school program were subject to the same matching provisions, there would be no distortion of emphasis of the school programs. Furthermore, if the matching ratios are adjusted by an equalization formula so that relatively greater percentages of state aid are granted to the less wealthy school districts, the second criticism is avoided.

The advantage of the matching principle is that it assures continued local effort even though state support is provided.[16]

The workings of the percentage equalizing grant will be discussed in more detail later in this chapter. Now we will look at the last important idea in the development of state support practices, namely, the concept of complete state support. The chief advocate was Henry C. Morrison of the University of Chicago and his position was most fully developed in his book *School Revenue* (1930).[17] His views were unique for his time, and though they sound less strange to our ears today, they call for a somewhat extended discussion.

There are two central themes in Morrison's work: the limits of public responsibility and equality of educational opportunity. With respect to public responsibility, Morrison drew a sharp distinction between private and public schools. Private schools were extensions of instruction offered in the family and were directed toward the attainment of private, or household, objectives. Whether such schools were supported by fees or by taxation was irrelevant. The objectives of private schools were commonly centered on occupational and social ends. The children "shall become acceptable members of the social group to which the parents belong and if possible shall be able to rise into higher and the highest levels of social prestige."[18] But a school does not become a public school simply by being *open* to the public. It must exist for a public or social, as distinct from a private, purpose. Naturally, the financial interest of the state, ideally, is restricted to public schools.

To Morrison, the chief public purpose was the inculcation of attitudes conducive to good citizenship in a democracy. It was important to teach self-control and aggressive moral purpose. "If you are a democrat and progressive, you try to establish schools which will both discipline the younger generation and generate intelligence

[16] Erick LeRoy Lindman, *The Development of an Equalized Matching Formula for the Apportionment of State School Building Aid* (Seattle: University of Washington Press, 1948), pp. 7–8.
[17] Henry C. Morrison, *School Revenue* (Chicago: University of Chicago Press, 1930).
[18] Ibid., p. 9.

about the world."[19] He was thus dealing with the preservation of the fabric of a democratic society and with the transmission of culture.

Nowhere in *School Revenue* is the curriculum of the public school laid out, but we can draw conclusions about its nature. It was to run from 8 to 12 years, the longer period apparently being the more desirable. The subjects were to be general and not specifically vocational; this was a point Morrison stressed repeatedly:

> It is not intended to pay . . . for providing the individual with the means of livelihood, nor for furnishing the industrial corporation with a supply of specially trained labor. . . . [If] these things . . . [are] done and the training of youth in the ways of civic intelligence and sound discipline neglected . . . the result will be an orgy of civic incompetency and the growth of a body politic saturated with examples of personal infantilism.[20]

General education, indeed, was seen as providing the base on which specific vocational training could be added by employers. Moreover, Morrison foresaw that the economy would come to rely less and less on craftsman type skills; he concluded (perhaps erroneously) that there would be less and less call for specific training activities conducted by employers.

Citizenship training, on the other hand, is essential in the democratic state, and it is most urgently necessary for the lower classes. It is the children of the lower classes who fail to receive citizenship training in the family environment. When citizenship training is not provided, a Gresham's law of education will come into play, and bad schooling will drive out good. This will be most readily apparent in central cities. The aftermath is violence and the general breakdown of civic order, which are all too common in our cities today.

As we shall see, the topic of equality of opportunity was for Morrison closely allied with his treatment of the citizenship school. He noted that "one district will find so ample a sum of taxables behind each child to be schooled that with little effort it can raise abundant school revenue, while another district can support only the most meager schools under a burden of taxation which eventually

---

[19] Ibid., p. 14.

[20] Ibid., p. 85. Morrison raised an interesting point, which is still unresolved today. If the state pays for a large volume of specific vocational training, including the professions, can it, in equity, avoid adopting an *incomes policy*?—which Morrison regarded as repugnant to democratic principles.

proves destructive to the tax base." [21] Past efforts to devise grant-in-aid schemes represent nothing more than tinkering with the problem at best, and at worst, bribery of an arcane type. "We have a childish faith in 'plans.' When the inevitable disillusionment comes, we conclude that the plan 'did not work' and look for another. In the case of equalization schemes, the disillusionment is prone to come at a time when the original plan has been forgotten and equality is discovered all over again." [22] (For those who advise governments on school finance policies, this last comment cuts rather close to the nerve.)

If citizenship schools are crucial for the survival of the democratic state, then inadequacies in the poorer local districts—where the family environment is almost certain to be failing miserably—are, of course, intolerable. Thus, citizenship education is set off from other types of public activities, such as street cleaning, in which the standard of performance in one local district is of relative indifference to the citizens of neighboring districts.

But cannot some substantial revision of the state's fiscal responsibility in education allow the local district structure to be preserved? No, says Morrison. First of all, what sum of money is to be redistributed? "If the state attempted to describe equal opportunity in terms of the schools of rich residential suburbs, there would be an early exodus from the state of all movable capital." [23] So it is necessary to define realistically the costs of citizenship education; and, a priori, the cost per pupil will vary from one district to another and, indeed, from one year to the next. Only the state could provide such computations. In Morrison's view, the cost per pupil would be highest in slum schools and in isolated, sparsely populated rural areas; it would be lowest in rich residential towns. As long as the concept of localism is predominant, the citizens of rich residential areas will decline to pay that volume of state taxes necessary to support adequate schools in the slums and rural regions:

> Our people still largely think of public education as a purely individual and local benefit . . . poor school districts are looked upon as poor relations at best, and perhaps sometimes not even the relationship is acknowledged. Tales of destitute townships are assimilated rather to tales of suffering in the Near East. We are sorry—and glad we do not live there. [24]

[21] Ibid., p. 164.
[22] Ibid., p. 194.
[23] Ibid., p. 196.
[24] Ibid., p. 165.

The local district structure necessarily implies that a large share of taxable income—that of the residents of rich towns—is removed from the support of schools of the state.

It is thus necessary to place limits on the expenditures of rich districts in order that public funds shall not be diverted into "private schools," as distinct from "citizenship schools."[25] Having gone this far, we have arrived clearly at a state system of education. Taxes for schools are to be collected where taxable income can be found in the state, and school resources are to be distributed in accordance with local requirements to provide a uniform standard of citizenship training.

To show that a state system of education would be beneficial, Morrison cited the analogy of a progressive city system that had grown large through the process of annexation. Before annexation, the small local districts surrounding the central city probably varied in wealth, the quality of local leadership, and the quality of educational services provided. The rich unincorporated areas would have maintained handsome schools and had extremely low tax rates; that is, taxable resources were being removed from the areawide support of the educational services. Poor areas might have had shockingly inadequate schools; and, in some cases, these inadequacies might truly have reflected the educational aspirations of the residents. After annexation, all taxables of the rich areas—and poor areas as well—are placed at the disposal of city needs. Standards of education in the poor areas are raised to those enjoyed by the city resident generally. Inadequacies in providing educational services are removed, and equity of contribution is, at the same time, improved. Morrison put it this way:

> Localism grew out of ward lines at least . . . the poorer sections of practically all cities get better schools than the inhabitants of those sections either could or would vote. . . . The city district has thus acted as a device for equalizing schools throughout the local community. The board of education is expected to provide the schools which are needed in all parts of the city regardless of regional resources, and it is legally able to do so.[26]

The consolidation of local school districts into a state system would presumably have the same kinds of favorable effects.

---

[25] Ibid., p. 201. Also, it was important to see that the rich districts did not gobble up an undue proportion of the real educational resources available in the state.
[26] Ibid., p. 205.

For many years, it appeared that states chose to ignore Morrison's contention that the state governments should provide most of the money for schools. As late as 1966–67, only 6 states—Alabama, Delaware, Hawaii, Louisiana, New Mexico, and North Carolina—had chosen to provide as much as 60 percent of the revenue receipts of their local school districts. Only Delaware and Hawaii offered 70 percent.[27] But things now seem to be changing. In 1975–76, 18 states provided 60 percent or more of school revenue and 8 states—Alabama, Alaska, Delaware, Hawaii, Kentucky, Mississippi, New Mexico, and North Carolina—produced 75 percent or more of educational revenues.[28]

Arithmetic Illustrations of Major Grants-in-Aid

We shall now consider in some detail the basic features of the fixed-unit equalizing grant, using hypothetical arithmetic illustrations. We shall also note the main aspect of the percentage equalizing grant. These are the two main schemes currently employed for the apportionment of funds for the general support of school operations.[29]

Table 10.1, the first illustration of the fixed-unit equalizing grant, is based on the following assumptions:

1. There are in the state five school districts only.
2. Each district contains one household.
3. Each household has one child enrolled in the local public schools.

These assumptions are, of course, intended to simplify the analysis. What happens to the analysis when the assumptions are relaxed will be discussed shortly.

In Table 10.1, the fixed-unit of school expenditure to be recognized by the state is $1,000 per student; it is called by its other label, foundation program, in the table. The richest district, *A*, could produce the $1,000 at a rate of 3.33 percent on its income. Thus the local contribution rate for all districts is determined.[30] Each district levies a tax at this rate, and the results are shown in column (3). Each

---

[27] National Educational Association, *Rankings of the States, 1967* (Washington, D.C., 1967), p. 47.

[28] Tron, *Public School Finance Programs*, p. 11.

[29] In the next chapter we describe features of both plans as actually used by selected states as of the mid-1970s.

[30] For convenience, we assume that both state and local taxes are levied on household income. If the reader wished to interpret the figures in column (2) of Table 10.1 as taxable property value, this would represent no significant distortion.

Table 10.1
Illustration of basic fixed-unit equalizing formula, foundation program equaling $1,000 per student[a]

District (1)	Income level (2)	Local tax (3.33%) (3)	State aid (4)	State aid plus local tax (5)	State tax (1.67%) (6)	State tax plus local tax (7)	Excess (+) or deficiency (−) of state aid (4) over state tax (8)
A	$ 30,000	$1,000	$ 0	$1,000	$ 500	$1,500	−$500
B	25,000	832	168	1,000	418	1,250	−250
C	20,000	666	334	1,000	334	1,000	0
D	15,000	500	500	1,000	250	750	+250
E	10,000	333	667	1,000	167	500	+500
Total	100,000	3,330	1,670	5,000	1,670	5,000	0

[a] Individual figures and column totals have been rounded.

district receives the difference, if any, between the yield of the local tax and $1,000. These amounts of state aid are shown in column (4), and column (5) shows that the total of local tax plus state aid in each district equals the $1,000.

The total of educational expenditures is $5,000, of which state aid is $1,670, or 33 percent. That $1,670 must come from somewhere, and the only reasonable source is a state tax on the residents of the state. Let us assume that the state tax is proportional—in the absence of more precise results from studies of tax incidence, this is the most reasonable assumption to make. Since $1,670 must be raised and the total income of the state is $100,000, a state tax at the rate of 1.67 percent is called for. The results of levying the state tax are shown in column (6), and total taxes for schools—state plus local—are indicated in column (7). Column (8) reveals the amount by which state aid exceeds or falls short of the state tax paid in each district. The two districts of above-average income pay more in state tax than they receive back; district C (average income) breaks even; and the two poorer districts receive a net subsidy. Income redistribution works.

According to Table 10.1, not all state aid, even in the poorest districts, represents a net addition to their resources. These districts, as well as all others, contribute to the state revenues from which school aid is drawn. Furthermore, no district of average economic ability or above receives any net gain. These conclusions suggest that the same degree of equalization can be achieved with a smaller amount of state distribution.

Table 10.2 assumes that each district levies a local tax of 5 percent, which is the sum of state and local taxes levied in Table 10.1. If the receipts of the local tax exceed $1,000 (the value of the foundation program), the excess could be transferred to a state fund. If the receipts from the 5 percent local tax are less than $1,000 per student, the deficiency could be paid to thelocal districts from that same state fund. Comparing Tables 10.1 and 10.2 we see that the equalizing effects are the same in each case, but the total amount of state aid in Table 10.2 is 45 percent of that in Table 10.1

Let us return to Table 10.1. Suppose the state government finds it has additional money available for school aid. What are the effects on school support under the fixed-unit plan? Let the extra money represent a 20 percent increase over existing state appropriations. The answer is shown in Table 10.3. State aid is increased from $1,670 (Table 10.1) to $2,000, a rise of 20 percent. However, in order for this money to be absorbed under the fixed-unit plan, it is necessary that the foundation program be increased by 20 percent— from $1,000 to $1,200 per student—across all districts in the state.

Table 10.2
Equalizing by fixed-unit standards under minimum
state aid, foundation program equaling $1,000 per
student[a]

District (1)	Income level (2)	Local tax (5%) (3)	Transfer to state fund (4)	Withdrawn from state fund (5)	School support (6)
A	$ 30,000	$1,500	$500	$ 0	$1,000
B	25,000	1,250	250	0	1,000
C	20,000	1,000	0	0	1,000
D	15,000	750	0	250	1,000
E	10,000	500	0	500	1,000
Total	100,000	5,000	750	750	5,000

[a] Individual figures and column totals have been rounded.

This, in turn, forces a larger flow of local tax money, from $3,330 to
$4,000—an increase of 20 percent. Note, however, that the proportion
of state aid in total school expenditures remains constant when the
foundation program amount is raised; it holds steady at 33 percent.

The *amount*, not the proportion, of state aid is thus
functionally related to the value of the foundation program. On what,
then, does the *share* of state support depend? For the fixed-unit
equalizing scheme, the answer is given in Table 10.4: It depends on
the degree of inequality of local district financial capacity. Compared
with Table 10.1, only one variable has been changed in Table 10.4,
namely, the income level (financial capacity) of district *A*. Because
that this is now assumed to be $60,000, producing a less even dis-
tribution of income, state aid, even with the foundation program
value held constant at $1,000 (as in Table 10.1), rises from $1,670 to
$2,830, an increase of 69.5 percent. The increase in state aid pushes
the state share from 33 percent to 57 percent.[31]

Now suppose that the state wished to have a foundation
program of $1,000 but did not want to assume the fiscal burden of a 57
percent share of school support. The common solution is indicated in
Table 10.5, where the local contribution rate is set at a somewhat
higher level than is indicated by the relation $r = N_1 u / Y_1$.[32] In Table

---

[31] In Table 10.4, the income level of the richest school district is six times as great as
that of the poorest. The actual range among school districts in values of assessed
property per student can be much greater than this.
[32] See equation (10.1) for the explanation of this variable.

Table 10.3
Fixed-unit equalizing with higher foundation
program of $1,200 per student[a]

District (1)	Income level (2)	Local tax (4%) (3)	State aid (4)	State aid plus local tax (5)	State tax (2%) (6)	State tax plus local tax (7)	Excess (+) or deficiency (−) of state aid (4) over state tax (8)
A	$ 30,000	$1,200	$ 0	$1,200	$ 600	$1,800	−$600
B	25,000	1,000	200	1,200	500	1,500	−300
C	20,000	800	400	1,200	400	1,200	0
D	15,000	600	600	1,200	300	900	+300
E	10,000	400	800	1,200	200	600	+600
Total	100,000	4,000	2,000	6,000	2,000	6,000	0

[a] Individual figures and column totals have been rounded.

Table 10.4
Fixed-unit equalizing under greater inequality of
income distribution, foundation program equaling
$1,000 per student[a]

District (1)	Income level (2)	Local tax (1.67%) (3)	State aid (4)	State aid plus local tax (5)	State tax (2.18%) (6)	State tax plus local tax (7)	Excess (+) or deficiency (−) of state aid (4) over state tax (8)
A	$ 60,000	$1,000	$ 0	$1,000	$1,308	$2,308	−$1,308
B	25,000	418	582	1,000	544	962	38
C	20,000	334	666	1,000	436	770	230
D	15,000	250	750	1,000	326	576	424
E	10,000	167	833	1,000	218	385	615
Total	130,000	2,170	2,830	5,000	2,830	5,000	0

[a] Individual figures and column totals have been rounded.

Table 10.5
Fixed-unit equalizing at greater than theoretical local contribution rate, foundation program equaling $1,000 per student[a]

District (1)	Income level (2)	Local tax, (stated rate, 2.5%) (3)	State aid (4)	State aid plus local tax (5)	State tax (1.73%) (6)	State tax plus local tax (7)	Excess (+) or deficiency (−) of state aid (4) over state tax (8)
A	$ 60,000	$1,000 (1.67%)	$ 0	$1,000	$1,038	$2,038	−$1,038
B	25,000	625	375	1,000	432	1,057	−57
C	20,000	500	500	1,000	346	846	154
D	15,000	375	625	1,000	260	635	365
E	10,000	250	750	1,000	173	423	577
Total	130,000	2,750	2,250	5,000	2,250	5,000	0

[a] Individual figures and column totals have been rounded.

317

10.5 the local contribution rate is put arbitrarily at 2.5 percent (instead of the true Strayer-Haig value of 1.67 percent, as in Table 10.4), and the state share falls back to 40 percent—$2,250 rather than $5,000. This is, of course, higher than the 33 percent state share in Table 10.1, but that table assumed a more even distribution of income of districts than do Tables 10.4 and 10.5. (On this point the latter two tables are more realistic.) See, however, what happens to the required rates of local taxation. District A can now support its $1,000 foundation program at a rate of 1.67 percent, while a 2.5 percent rate is required of the other districts. Under foundation program plans, state governments do not require rich districts to tax themselves at the statewide local contribution rate if they can raise revenues at some lower rate. Thus, when the local contribution rate is raised above its theoretical value, it is no longer true that all districts can provide themselves with the foundation program at no higher local tax rate than that required of the richest school district.

It should be noted that districts B through E are "better off" in Table 10.4 than in Table 10.1, as can be seen by comparing column (8) in both tables. However, this results because district A has provided an increase in the tax base of the state. The true comparison of district welfare in terms of state aid distributions is between Tables 10.4 and 10.5; districts B through E should prefer full-fledged implementation of the Strayer-Haig formula in Table 10.4 to its partial implementation in Table 10.5. Indeed, Table 10.5 illustrates what happens when state governments allow such fragmentation of school district structure that some end up with vastly greater taxable capacity than others: Either the state must put up most of the school money or it may accept only partial equalizing. Consolidating poor districts with rich ones eases the problem and is itself an appropriate means of school finance equalizing.

With respect to interdistrict tax rate differentials, the problem is often made even worse by the state stipulating that no district, however rich, shall receive less than x dollars per student in support from the state government. These grants are often called *flat grants*, indicating that the amount distributed is independent of such variables as district wealth. In Table 10.6, it is assumed that the state has a law to the effect that no school district shall receive less than $200 per student in the form of general aid. Only the grant to district A is changed, but this change leads to a slight increase in the state tax rate levied on all districts. The most dramatic result, however, is that the local tax rate in A to support a $1,000 program falls at 1.33 percent, which approaches 50 percent of the rate (2.5 percent, still) in the other districts.

Table 10.6

Fixed-unit equalizing at less than theoretical local contribution rate, with minimum flat grant, foundation program equaling $1,000 per student[a]

District (1)	Income level (2)	Local tax (stated rate, 2.5%) (3)	State aid ($200 minimum per student) (4)	State aid plus local tax (5)	State tax (1.88%) (6)	State tax plus local tax (7)	Excess (+) or deficiency (−) of state aid (4) over state tax (8)
A	$ 60,000	$800 (1.33%)	$ 200	$1,000	$1,131	$1,931	−$931
B	25,000	625	375	1,000	471	1,096	−96
C	20,000	500	500	1,000	377	877	123
D	15,000	375	625	1,000	283	658	342
E	10,000	250	750	1,000	188	438	562
Total	130,000	2,550	2,450	5,000	2,450	5,000	0

[a] Individual figures and column totals have been rounded.

Finally, Table 10.7 shows the combined effects of setting the local contribution rate at an arbitrarily high level, using minimum flat grants, and variations in level of school expenditure. To support a $1,200 program, a tax rate of 4.5 percent (or 45 mills) is required in E, a poor district, while that same dollar-value program can be had at a rate of 1.67 percent (16.7 mills) in A, a rich district. All the figures in Table 10.7 are the same as in Table 10.6, except it is assumed that both districts A and E choose to spend $1,200 a student. In both cases, the extra $200 comes strictly out of local sources; but the base to finance the extra expenditures is far greater in A than in E. This latter situation is cumulated on top of the inequities previously laid out in Tables 10.5 and 10.6. This is what it comes to: The Strayer-Haig equalizing plan, as it is commonly put into practice, is perfectly consistent with a pattern of local school tax rates that stand in an inverse relationship to local financial ability; that is, there are high tax rates in poor districts and low tax rates in rich. There is nothing in either the benefit or ability-to-pay standards of tax justice to defend such an arrangement.

These arithmetic examples are intended to provide a better understanding of the foundation program plan. But they are based, as we said earlier, on a set of simplifying assumptions. What happens when we relax the assumptions? The number of school districts in the example is irrelevant to the analysis, except when there are *phantom districts*, districts without children. Residents of phantom districts escape local school tax, and the burden of a fully implemented foundation program plan will no longer be proportionate with respect to income over the whole state. What of the assumption that the population of each district consists of one household? If the income of households within districts is each equal, burden of school tax will remain proportional, even though the local tax is regressive (or progressive). But realistically households within school districts have unequal incomes. If the local tax is regressive, the burden of school support will be regressive on the households of the state, even though the burden is proportional with respect to school districts under the Strayer-Haig formula. What if local tax is levied on property, not income? Property-rich districts are favored under the Strayer-Haig formula. If high-income families live in property-rich districts, the state and local educational financing system is pushed toward regressiveness; the opposite applies if property-rich districts are inhabited by low-income families.

We assumed in our examples that each household has one child in school. If the proportion of school-age children to total population is different among school districts, the strict Strayer-Haig formula no longer assures proportional tax burdens. For example, if rich

Table 10.7

Local tax rates under conventional fixed-unit equalizing[a] at different levels of school expenditure per student[b]

District (1)	Income level (2)	Expenditure per student (3)	State aid (4)	Local tax (5)	Local tax rate (mills) (6)
A	$ 60,000	$1,200	$ 200	$1,000	16.7
B	25,000	1,000	375	625	25.0
C	20,000	1,000	500	500	25.0
D	15,000	1,000	625	375	25.0
E	10,000	1,200	750	450	45.0
Total	130,000	5,400	2,450	2,950	22.7

[a] Table 10.6.
[b] Individual figures and column totals have been rounded.

districts have relatively few children per household, they will pay taxes at lower rates than the poorer districts. Lastly, the Strayer-Haig scheme is moved toward progressiveness in burden if the state tax is progressive and toward regressiveness if the state tax is regressive.

Let us now examine arithmetic illustrations of the working of the percentage equalizing grant. This particular grant arrangement is basic to such of its variants as "district power equalizing" and "guaranteed valuations"; these we will consider in the next chapter.

The operation of the state aid grant was described in equation (10.2). Here we will restate it as:

$$A_1 = \left[1 - \left(0.5 \times \frac{\text{assessed valuation per student in the district}}{\text{assessed valuation per student in the state}} \right) \right]$$
$$\times \text{ expenditures in the district} \tag{10.3}$$

Suppose statewide assessed valuation per student is \$20,000.[33] Let assessed valuation per student in school district 1 (Table 10.8), a relatively wealthy district, be \$30,000. In school district 2, a poor district, let the corresponding figure be \$10,000. Suppose further that both districts wish to spend \$1,000 per student in their public school programs. Let enrollment in district 1 be 5,000 and in district 2, 10,000. Obviously, total expenditure in district 1 is intended to be \$5,000,000 (5,000 students times \$1,000 per student), and total expenditure in district 2 is to be \$10,000,000. Let us compute state aid and local tax rates. For district 1,

$$A_1 = \left[1 - \left(0.5 \times \frac{30,000}{20,000} \right) \right] \times \$5,000,000$$
$$= (1 - 0.75) \times \$5,000,000$$
$$= 0.25 \times \$5,000,000 = \$1,250,000$$

local expenditure in district 1 = total expenditure − state aid
$$= \$5,000,000 - \$1,250,000$$
$$= \$3,750,000$$

$$\text{tax rate in district 1} = \frac{\text{local expenditure}}{\text{tax base}} = \frac{\$3,750,000}{\$150,000,000}$$
$$= \$2.50 \text{ per } \$100 \text{ of assessed valuation}$$

[33] This figure is chosen to simplify computation. The figure is not computed from Table 10.8, which figures in this discussion. The reader may assume that the three districts in Table 10.8 are in a state in which there are many other districts; overall, statewide wealth comes out at \$20,000 per student.

Table 10.8
Comparing example districts under percentage
equalizing grant (in dollars)

	District 1 (5,000 students)	District 2 (10,000 students)	District 3 (5,000 students)
Assessed valuation per student	$ 30,000	$ 10,000	$ 60,000
Expenditure per student	1,000	1,000	1,000
Total assessed valuation	150,000,000	100,000,000	300,000,000
Total expenditures	5,000,000	10,000,000	5,000,000
Total state aid	1,250,000	7,500,000	−2,500,000
Local tax rate (per $100 of assessed valuation)	2.50	2.50	2.50

And for district 2,

$$A_2 = \left[1 - \left(0.5 \times \frac{10,000}{20,000} \right) \right] \times \$10,000,000$$
$$= (1 - 0.25) \times \$10,000,000$$
$$= 0.75 \times \$10,000,000 = \$7,500,000$$

local expenditure in district 2 = total expenditure − state aid
$$= \$10,000,000 - \$7,500,000$$
$$= \$2,500,000$$

tax rate in district 2 $= \dfrac{\text{local expenditure}}{\text{tax base}} = \dfrac{\$2,500,000}{\$100,000,000}$
$$= \$2.50 \text{ per } \$100 \text{ of assessed valuation}$$

The local tax rates in districts 1 and 2 are the same—$2.50 per $100 of assessed valuation, even though district 2 has only one-third the wealth per student of district 1 and even though district 2, the poor district, is twice as large as district 1. Under a fully operational percentage equalizing grant the rule holds: Any set of districts that chooses the same expenditure level per student will obtain that expenditure at equal local tax rates, regardless of the wealth of the districts.

This kind of relationship between the state and local authorities under which, in effect, the price of educational services stands in a precise one-to-one status with expenditures has been hailed as an achievement in equity. Surely such a system would be preferable to one under which poor districts must submit to high tax rates to finance meager programs, while rich districts provide themselves with lavish school programs at low tax rates. However, it is extremely difficult to put a percentage equalizing grant into full operation. There are two major reasons: First, differences in assessed valuation per student vary more widely than shown in the example, where district 1 has three times the wealth per student of district 2. It is not uncommon for differences to run as high as 10 to 1. So suppose we add to the example a district 3 (Table 10.8) having 5,000 students, an expenditure of $1,000 per student, and an assessed valuation per student of $60,000. The formula for district 3 would read:

$$A_3 = \left[1 - \left(0.5 \times \frac{60,000}{20,000}\right)\right] \times \$5,000,000$$
$$= (1 - 1.5) \times \$5,000,000$$
$$= -0.5 \times \$5,000,000 = -\$2,500,000$$

local expenditure in district 3 = total expenditure − state aid
= $5,000,000 − (−$2,500,000)
= $7,500,000

tax rate in district 3 $= \dfrac{\$7,500,000}{\$3,000,000,000}$

= $2.50 per $100 of assessed valuation

The formula produces a negative aid ratio of −0.5. Thus district 3 must be expected to pay for its school program in full *and* make a contribution of $2,500,000 from its own local taxes to the other districts of the state. State governments are not generally inclined to demand such self-sacrifice of rich areas.[34] Instead they frequently provide a *minimum school aid grant* to districts, even the very richest.

---

[34] If the coefficient of 0.5 in the state aid formula (Table 10.8) were reduced to 0.1, then the negative grant implied in the original would disappear:

$$A_3 = \left[1 - \left(0.1 \times \frac{60,000}{20,000}\right)\right] \times \$5,000,000$$

$$= (1 - 0.3) \times \$5,000,000$$

$$= 0.7 \times \$5,000,000 = \$3,500,000$$

District 3 now receives state aid for schools in the amount of $3,500,000, instead of (theoretically) being charged $2,500,000. However, as the coefficient is reduced from 0.5 toward 0.1, the state share of total educational spending rises: The state share is given by (1 − 0.5) = 0.5, or (1 − 0.1) = 0.9, or, in general, by (1 − x). This example,

Second, for the percentage equalizing grant to be fully operational in the sense of matching up tax rates and expenditures, one of two conditions must hold: Either the state places a ceiling on educational expenditures per student that applies to all districts, or the state shares in educational expenditures with districts at whatever level of spending the local districts choose.[35]

Some people would prefer to preserve the kind of local freedom to spend that now exists. That is, under percentage equalizing the state would share in locally chosen expenditure levels without limit. Some state officials see this as giving local districts a blank check. It is a troublesome problem, moreover, because aid ratios can rise to 90 percent and above; poor local authorities can buy expensive educational programs with 10 cents per dollar or less of local money. Only in Wisconsin and Utah—and only under the constraint of rigid audit procedures—has there been serious experimentation with major open-ended grant programs.

The course commonly chosen by states that have used the percentage equalizing grant is to provide for state sharing of locally determined expenditures *up to a point and not beyond*, while allowing districts to exceed the state-sharing maximum if they wish. This compromise makes the percentage equalizing grant into a foundation program plan for all practical purposes, especially when most districts actually do spend beyond the point at which the state stops its contribution.

Using our simple examples of the three districts, let us see the effect on local tax rates of the combination of a minimum grant of $300 per student and a ceiling on state sharing of $1,000 per student (Table 10.9). Assume all figures as before, *except* that a minimum grant of $300 per student is provided and all three districts now decide to spend $1,200 per student (the state ceiling for sharing, as noted, is assumed to be $1,000). For district 1, then

$$A_1 = \left[1 - \left(0.5 \times \frac{30,000}{20,000} \right) \right] \times \$5,000,000$$
$$= 0.25 \times \$5,000,000 = \$1,250,000$$

---

where $x = 0.1$, implies 90 percent state support—in effect, full state assumption of costs. Thus, the only way the percentage equalizing grant can accommodate extreme ranges in local assessed valuations per student is by establishing state assumption of educational costs.

[35] John E. Coons, William H. Clune III, and Stephen D. Sugarman, *Private Wealth and Public Education* (Cambridge, Mass.: Harvard, 1970).

Table 10.9

Comparing example districts under percentage equalizing grant, with minimum grant and state aid ceiling (in dollars)

	District 1 (5,000 students)	District 2 (10,000 students)	District 3 (5,000 students)
Assessed valuation per student	$ 30,000	$ 10,000	$ 60,000
Expenditure per student	1,200	1,200	1,200
Ceiling on state sharing	1,000	1,000	1,000
Minimum state grant per student	300	300	300
Total assessed valuation	150,000,000	100,000,000	300,000,000
Total expenditures	6,000,000	12,000,000	6,000,000
Total state aid	1,500,000	7,500,000	1,500,000
Local tax rate (per $100 of assessed valuation)	3.00	4.50	1.50

This computation reflects that only $1,000 per student is recognized for state sharing; but the computed amount of aid, $1,250,000, falls short of the district's minimum aid of $300 per student (5,000 students × $300 = $1,500,000). So A_1 = $1,500,000, *not* $1,250,000 as the formula suggests.

$$\text{local expenditure in district 1} = \$6,000,000 - \$1,500,000$$
$$= \$4,500,000$$

This computation reflects that the district is now spending $1,200 per student ($1,200 × 5,000 students = $6,000,000).

$$\text{tax rate in district 1} = \frac{\$4,500,000}{\$150,000,000}$$
$$= \$3.00 \text{ per } \$100 \text{ of assessed valuation}$$

For district 2,

$$A_2 = \left[1 - \left(0.5 \times \frac{10,000}{20,000}\right)\right] \times \$10,000,000$$

$$= 0.75 \times \$10,000,000 = \$7,500,000$$

Aid remains the same as in the previous example.

local expenditure in district 2 = $12,000,000 − $7,500,000
= $4,500,000

$$\text{tax rate in district 2} = \frac{\$4,500,000}{\$100,000,000}$$
= $4.50 per $100 of assessed valuation

To provide the same quality program, district 2 must now sustain a tax rate 50 percent higher than in district 1.

For district 3,

$$A_3 = \left[1 - \left(0.50 \times \frac{60,000}{20,000}\right)\right] \times \$5,000,000$$

$$= -0.5 \times \$5,000,000 = -\$2,500,000$$

However, the minimum grant comes into play, and district 3 receives a sum determined as 5,000 students times $300. So $A_3 = \$1,500,000$, *not* −$2,500,000 as the formula suggests.

local expenditure in district 3 = $6,000,000 − $1,500,000
= $4,500,000

$$\text{tax rate in district 3} = \frac{\$4,500,000}{\$300,000,000}$$
= $1.50 per $100 of assessed valuation

Note that the three districts (Table 10.9) that have equal expenditures per students now have unequal tax rates, and the richer the district, the lower the rate. That is precisely what has gone wrong with the state equalizing plans in use today, which provide a minimum grant per student. States have also put ceilings on the expenditures per student that the state will recognize for reimbursement or sharing. As districts move above the ceiling, clearly these extra, or marginal, expenditures are going to fall more heavily on a low-wealth district than on a high-wealth district.

Suppose, finally, that district 3 chose to spend $2,000 per student. Its budget would rise to $10,000,000. Its state aid would hold constant at $1,500,000, and its tax rate would be $8,500,000/ $300,000,000 = $2.83 per $100 of assessed valuation. Rich district 3 thus would spend $800 more per student than the poor district 2, but its tax rate would be $1.67 per $100 lower. This demonstrates the inverse relationship between expenditures and tax rates that is characteristic of most state aid systems in the United States. And that is the situation the courts have been complaining about.[36]

Summary

General-purpose grants in education are the means used to link together state and local revenue sources to supply funds to run the schools. Much effort has been expended to try to devise grant arrangements that can overcome the large disparities in local wealth of school districts in most states. The foundation program plan is one such grant scheme. When established in its original form, it assures that all school districts can provide an adequate school program for each of their students at a local tax rate no higher than that required of the richest district. That is, no greater effort is required of poor districts than rich to put forward a standard school program. An alternative plan is percentage equalizing, under which the state shares in whatever level of expenditures the local district chooses, but at a higher rate in poor districts than in rich. The intent is to effectively equalize local wealth per student. Unfortunately, few states have managed in practice to come close to either of these ideal plans. Tax and expenditure disparities have become sufficiently large that state courts have begun to demand reform of educational finance, which is the topic of the next chapter.

[36] In the percentage equalizing examples, we do not show the burden of state taxes added to local because the examples are sufficiently complicated as they stand. The reader might wish to add the state tax as an exercise.

Selected Bibliography

Blinder, Alan S., et al. *The Economics of Public Finance.* Washington, D.C.: Brookings, 1974.

Break, George F. *Intergovernmental Fiscal Relations in the United States.* Washington, D.C.: Brookings, 1967.

Cohn, Elchanan. *Economics of State Aid to Education.* Lexington, Mass.: Lexington Books, 1974

Johns, Roe L., et al. *Economic Factors Affecting the Financing of Education.* Gainesville, Fla.: National Educational Finance Project, 1970.

National Center for Educational Statistics. *The Condition of Education, 1976.* Washington, D.C.: U.S. Government Printing Office, 1976.

Tron, Esther O. *Public School Finance Programs, 1975–76.* Washington, D.C.: U.S. Government Printing Office, 1976.

Chapter Eleven

The Reform of Finance of Education

From the early 1960s onward, a number of economists, sociologists, and educational administrators have been arguing that arrangements under which we pay for schooling of the young are in serious disarray. What has come to be called the *educational finance reform movement* received an immense push forward on August 30, 1971, when the California Supreme Court indicated that the system of paying for schools in the state probably stood in violation of constitutional guarantees of equal protection of citizens. State legislatures across the country have been busy since that decision to see if systems of finance in their own states had problems similar to those pointed out by the California Supreme Court and, if so, to revise them.

Our tasks in this chapter are several. First, we shall note briefly some of the seminal works that launched the reform movement. Second, we shall examine the role of the courts in reshaping school finance, and we shall take account of the kinds of revisions in finance systems that have been proposed to achieve equity. Third, we shall recognize the difficulties of implementing new financial arrangements, and we shall consider what the state governments have been able to accomplish so far. Fourth, we shall suggest what remains to be done.

Antecedents of the Reform Movement

The assumption that children of different income classes receive more or less equal school services was strongly attacked by Patricia Sexton in her 1961 volume *Education and Income.*[1] The book was a thorough study of the workings of schools in a large eastern city, identified simply as Big City, and covered "all relevant and available facts about the 285,000 students, 10,000 teachers and almost 300 schools in Big City." Schools were grouped by income levels of parents. The performance of schools was judged primarily on the basis of achievement, as measured by the Iowa Achievement Test. Sexton noted that by the fourth grade, the children in the highest strata of school (in terms of parental income) were, on the average, two years ahead of the children in the lowest strata. Since basic skills, such as reading, are essential for later progress of children in school (formal education is substantially cumulative), such early learning differences are almost certain to put the low-income children under a lifetime learning disability.

Sexton then pointed out that home and neighborhood conditions offered obvious advantages to high income children over low. It might then be assumed that (a) given the fact that, for whatever reasons, low-income children tended quickly to fall behind in school, and (b) that environmental conditions were, in any case, inimical to a low-income child's progress, the school attended by low-income children might be *at least equal* in staff and facilities to those attended by rich children.[2] The conditions Sexton observed violated even the rudimentary rule of fairness. Low-income schools had far more substitute teachers than did high-income schools, and at the time the study was made, a substitute teacher was not required to hold a teaching certificate.[3] Average class size was large in low-income schools.[4] Buildings used by low-income students had fewer science labs, auditoriums, and facilities for instrumental music and speech than did those used by high-income children; the schools used by low-income children were also more likely to be rated as fire hazards than the (generally newer) facilities used by the richer children.[5] All

[1] Patricia Cayo Sexton, *Education and Income: Inequalities of Opportunity in Our Public Schools* (New York: Viking, 1961). The material in this paragraph is based on pp. 20 (including the quotation) and 27 of this book.
[2] However, Sexton did not confine herself to recommendations for equalizing resources. She also dealt with problems in the use of I.Q. tests, the curriculum generally, the teaching of reading, field trips, extracurricular acitivities, classroom discipline, and many other topics. See especially Ibid., chap. 7.
[3] Ibid., pp. 116–122.
[4] Ibid., pp. 113–114.
[5] Ibid., pp. 130–134.

in all, Sexton's book was an impressive indictment of social policy toward children.

Also in 1961 James Bryant Conant published his provocative study *Slums and Suburbs*.[6] Whereas Sexton drew attention to disparities among schools of a single large city district, Conant's interest was focused on inequalities that existed between the schools of central city slums and the schools of favored suburban districts. Conant made the following observations about resource distributions:

> The contrast in the money spent per pupil in wealthy suburban schools and in slum schools of the large cities challenges the concept of equality of opportunity in American public education. More money is needed in slum schools.. . . Social dynamite is building up in our large cities in the form of unemployed out-of-school youth. . . . More teachers and perhaps more pay for teachers are necessary for schools in the slums than in either the high income districts of the large cities or the wealthy suburbs.[7]

Because of the high standing held by Conant in American educational circles, his observations could not easily be brushed aside.

Four years after Sexton and Conant published their books, this writer published a volume, *The Cheerful Prospect*, that sought to show that the disparities to which Sexton and Conant had drawn attention were systematically derived.[8] That is, the disparities flowed from the use of a particular system of finance in which the amount of resources made available to any given student was set predominantly by the size of the tax base of the school district in which the student attended school. Given that there are many thousands of school districts in the United States, some large but most small, it would not be surprising if the amount of taxable property per student in different districts varied widely. The argument was stated as follows:

> [T]here is good reason to be concerned about the continued existence of thousands of . . . small school districts, namely, that many of them represent islands of privilege; they are districts whose boundaries have been drawn to produce high

---

[6] James Bryant Conant, *Slums and Suburbs* (New York: McGraw-Hill, 1961).

[7] Ibid., p. 146. Like Sexton, Conant did not content himself just with making recommendations about resource allocations. He paid attention as well to guidance programs, revision of curriculum in both city and suburban schools, integration of school staffs, decentralization of administration, etc. These various observations are summed up in Chapter 6.

[8] Charles S. Benson, *The Cheerful Prospect* (Boston: Houghton Mifflin, 1965).

property values for each resident pupil. The local share of the education bill is paid primarily from taxation of real property located in the district. Hence, the power of some districts to include estates or large industrial holdings within their boundaries but to exclude high-density residential areas allows these districts to provide expensive educational programs at extremely low tax rates. The other result, of course, is that poorer districts (in terms of local real property base) must levy taxes at high rates in order to finance even a minimum program. The gerrymandering of the real property tax base excludes a substantial portion of local wealth from the support of schools. Where . . . small districts exist, the state governments, moreover, have been unable to compensate effectively for the variations in property tax base per pupil by the use of such devices as grants-in-aid.

[Attention was drawn to the disparities in property tax base per student in California and the argument continued.] All the way across the country, in Maine, there was [in the early 1960s] a range in local valuation per pupil from $1,727 to $620,000.[9]

What were seen as the results of wealth disparities among local school districts? Wealth disparities came to be reflected in educational resource differences of the following kinds:

1. Salaries paid to teachers are notably higher in high-wealth, high-expenditure districts than in low-wealth, low-expenditure ones.
2. Size of classes tend to be larger in low-wealth, low-expenditure districts than in economically favored districts.
3. School facilities, including playing fields, are generally more attractive in high-wealth, high-expenditure places than in poor ones.[10]
4. High-wealth, high-expenditure districts provide a more generous amount of auxiliary services, for example, school libraries, than do low-wealth, low-expenditure districts.

These differing conditions can be expected to influence teacher recruitment.

[9] Ibid., pp. 44–45.
[10] Ibid., p. 23. At the time of writing that earlier volume, this author, citing evidence, was able to say, "In our affluent society many children attend school in dank, foul-smelling, rat-infested squalor."

A teacher who is looking for a job will see that some districts pay much lower salaries than others do. Further, he will note that these are the same districts in which he stands a relatively high chance of getting stuck with an oversize class meeting in an old, run down school building where, in any case, he will have relatively few auxiliary materials and services to make use of. Altruism aside, it is clear to which district he will send his application.[11]

This author then commented that those districts offering their resident students a superior quality of school program often did so while levying school tax at a low rate, citing the example of Beverly Hills (see above, Chapter 6).[12] At this point, we may well wonder whether primary emphasis is placed on inequities handed out to children or to inequities imposed on taxpayers—mainly adults. Conceivably the two problems could be solved—or appear to be solved—separately. A state could simply mandate that all districts offer programs costing x dollars per student. And if x dollars was a higher figure than the foundation program or its equivalent (see Chapter 10), then equity in providing basic school programs would be improved but tax rate disparities would be increased. Alternatively, the state could adjure districts to keep their school expenditure levels where they were and take action to raise local tax rates in high-expenditure districts and lower them in low-expenditure ones. This would presumably enhance taxpayers' equity but would not help children who were receiving low-grade educational inputs.

To this writer, first interest has always been attached to reducing inequities among different groups of children. The only reason for having drawn attention to the school tax rate situation was to indicate that low-school expenditures *do not* exist because taxpayers in low-expenditure districts fail, or are unwilling to accept, rates of taxation that are reasonably high. Indeed, if low-wealth

[11] Ibid., pp. 24–25. This problem might appear to have been alleviated by the teacher surplus of the mid-1970s. However, even though low-wealth districts may now receive large numbers of applications from unemployed teachers, so still do high-wealth districts. Common logic suggests that the high-wealth districts will succeed in skimming off the superior applicants (at least with respect to the ways that high-wealth districts define superiority of teacher).

[12] Nothing in this analysis explains directly the intracity disparities in provision to which Patricia Sexton drew attention. However, because state governments established and maintained a local district structure of the kind we have described, then clearly the responsible educational authority (the state government), by its own action, condoned gross inequities in the provision of services to children. Thus, the states set no contrary example to the cities.

districts attempted to match per-student expenditure in high-wealth districts, they would likely have to levy school taxes at rates that were practically confiscatory. In this author's opinion, *school tax reform* is the handmaiden of reducing inequitable treatment among groups of children, not the other way around. It should be added, finally, that the present topic is concerned with reform of finance of the basic school program, which serves the typical child in the typical school in the typical district. Such reform is not a substitute for improvement in the distribution of categorical aid (monies to serve needs of children who in one way or another are not typical), but neither is an increase in categorical funding a substitute for removing inequities in the basic program. Otherwise, the basic inequities can cancel out the intended effects of the categorical aids.

In 1967 Arthur Wise, then of the University of Chicago, published a volume, *Rich Schools, Poor Schools*, in which he made the suggestion, the first suggestion, that higher courts might find state practices in financing schools unconstitutional.[13] He posed the following questions:

> School-finance legislation, in effect, classified school districts (and the students in them) on the basis of their wealth. As a result of the way in which these laws operate, wealthy districts enjoy the benefits of high expenditures for public education whereas poor districts must make do with low-school expenditures. . . . [T]he classification which results from a state's school-finance legislation must bear a reasonable relation to the state's purpose in education. The question is then: If the amount of money spent on the education of a student is determined primarily by the wealth of the area in which he lives, does this constitute a reasonable classification? In other words, is the wealth of the local geographical area the relevant criterion for determining how much is spent on the education of students?[14]

Wise then proposes that if the courts were willing simply to employ a *negative standard* of equality of educational opportunity—in the absence of a *positive standard*—they might conclude otherwise:

[13] Arthur E. Wise, *Rich Schools, Poor Schools: The Promise of Equal Educational Opportunity* (Chicago: University of Chicago Press, 1967).
[14] Ibid., p. 121.

Equality of opportunity exists when a child's educational opportunity does not depend upon either his parents' economic circumstances or his location within the state . . . [T]his definition has the virtue of being precise . . . [A]s a negative definition . . . it is useful for demonstrating that equality of educational opportunity does not exist. All that need be shown is that two children of the same abilities who happen to live in different parts of a state are receiving different assistance in developing those abilities. The definition does not, however, specify the conditions for equality.

Nevertheless, the Supreme Court might employ this limited definition to declare present school finance statutes unconstitutional. It closely resembles the reasoning employed by the Court in recent voting cases. The Court held that a citizen's vote could not be made to depend upon where he happened to live or upon his economic circumstances, thereby basing the decision on an essentially negative definition of equality in voting rights. The definition does not specify the conditions of equality; it merely states the conditions of inequality. The Court thus begged the question of standards. There is no reason to think that the Court would not do likewise about equality of educational opportunity. The Court might well again employ a limited, negative definition, leaving the issue of standards for equality to the lower courts and the states.[15]

The final antecedent work, *Private Wealth and Public Education*—John E. Coons, William H. Clune III, and Stephen D. Sugarman, three lawyers, not educators or economists—led directly to court action.[16] The first part of the book is devoted to an analysis of state and local systems of financing education, showing that so-called equalizing plans leave low-wealth districts in the unenviable position of choosing between an educational program of relative inadequacy and a school tax rate of confiscatory proportions.[17] The last third of the book broke new ground and provided the legal analysis necessary for courts to attack school finance schemes on *equal protection*

[15] Ibid., pp. 146–147.
[16] John E. Coons, William H. Clune III, and Stephen D. Sugarman, *Private Wealth and Public Education* (Cambridge, Mass.: Harvard, 1970).
[17] In actuality, low-wealth districts will do some of both—find educational programs that fall short of generally accepted standards of quality and submit to school tax rates that are above state average.

grounds. The authors suggest one major guiding principle in equity, which they called Proposition 1: "the quality of public education may not be a function of wealth other than the total wealth of the state."[18] This is, of course, the simple negative statement of equality of educational opportunity proposed earlier by Arthur Wise. But the lawyers extend their arguments to show that educational finance is entitled to a place "within the inner circle of equal protection. . . . The best hope for Proposition 1 lies in the demonstrated willingness of the Supreme Court to carve out from among the populous herd of equal protection issues seeking its attention an inner circle of cases to be given special scrutiny on substantive grounds."[19] Among the arguments developed were the following:

1. Education is a "fundamental interest" of the people, thus deserving "strict scrutiny" of the means by which it is distributed. The assertion of fundamental interest was defended on such grounds as the role of education in maintaining free-enterprise democracy, its compulsory character, the universality of its relevance, that education is a "continuing process," and that education is uniquely a service through which the state seeks to shape the human personality.[20]

2. Wealth of school district, i.e., the amount of locally taxable property per student is an inappropriate variable, is a "suspect classification," when used to guide the distribution of educational resources to different groups of children.

3. No special state interest is served by using district wealth to regulate the distribution of educational resources.

4. There are available practical alternatives that satisfy legitimate state goals without perpetuating existing forms of discrimination.[21]

The particular alternative that the lawyers recommended is a state and local financial arrangement called *district power equalizing,* essentially a free-form version of a percentage equalizing grant. The intent is to equalize taxable capacity among all school districts of a given state; we shall examine the details of the plan shortly.

---

[18] Ibid., pp. 303–304. The lawyers chose not to apply the standard to interstate variations in expenditure, partly because education is a function of government reserved by the federal constitution to the states.

[19] Ibid., p. 339.

[20] Ibid., pp. 415–418.

[21] Ibid., p. 396.

Enter the Courts

On August 23, 1968, a suit was filed by school children and their taxpaying parents of a number of Los Angeles school districts. The case, *Serrano v. Priest*, listed the state treasurer, the state superintendent of public instruction, and several other state and local officials as defendants. Plaintiffs claimed that there were disparities in educational provision among the districts of California; that these disparities arose primarily as a result of differences in taxable wealth per student; and that educational opportunities in low-wealth districts were substantially inferior to those available to children attending schools in high-wealth districts.

Early on, the case did not fare well. The complaint was dismissed by the California Superior Court and such action was affirmed by the California Court of Appeals. However, on August 30, 1971, the California Supreme Court reversed the decision of the lower court in dismissing the complaint and sent the case back to trial court for further proceedings. The case might not at this point have attracted national attention had not the California Supreme Court delivered a rather extensive discussion of the case, offering statements to the effect that if the evidence was of the character claimed by plaintiffs, the California educational finance system would appear to stand in violation of both federal and state constitutional guarantees of equal protection.

The Court first recognized that expenditure disparities existed among California school districts:

> [I]n Los Angeles County, where plaintiff children attend school, the Baldwin Park Unified School District expended only $577.49 to educate each of its pupils in 1968–69; during the same year the Pasadena Unified School District spent $840.19 on every student; and the Beverly Hills Unified School District paid out $1,231.72 per child. . . . [T]he source of these disparities is unmistakable: in Baldwin Park, the assessed valuation per child totaled only $3,706; in Pasadena, assessed valuation was $13,706; while in Beverly Hills, the corresponding figure was $50,885—a ratio of 1 to 4 to 13. . . . Thus, the state grants are inadequate to offset the inequalities inherent in a financing system based on widely varying local tax bases.[22]

[22] Serrano v. Priest, printed as Appendix A in Joel S. Berke, *Answers to Inequity* (Berkeley, Calif.: McCutchan, 1974), p. 182.

Following essentially the legal arguments developed by Arthur Wise and John Coons, the Court then declared that wealth was a suspect classification to regulate the distribution of educational resources among school districts:

> The commercial and industrial property which augments a district's tax base is distributed unevenly throughout the state. To allot more educational dollars to the children of one district than to those of another merely because of the fortuitous presence of such property is to make the quality of a child's education dependent upon the location of private commercial and industrial establishments. Surely, this is to rely on the most irrelevant of factors as the basis of educational financing.[23]

The second main point developed by the California Supreme Court was to declare education a fundamental interest, and it repeated almost verbatim the arguments in the Coons, Clune, and Sugarman volume.

Third, the Court declared it could find no compelling state interest served by the particular form of California's school finance arrangement.

> We find that such financing system as presently constituted is not necessary to the attainment of any compelling state interest. Since it does not withstand the requisite "strict scrutiny"; it denies to the plaintiffs and others similarly situated the equal protection of the laws. If the allegations of the complaint are sustained, the financial system must fall and the statutes comprising it must be found unconstitutional."[24]

Had the Court stopped its argument at this point, it would probably have been clear that remedy should focus on the rights of children to suitable educational opportunities, irrespective of the size of local tax base in their school districts. Actually, the Court recognized a second course of action:

> Additionally, the parents allege that they are citizens and residents of Los Angeles County; that they are owners of real property assessed by the county . . . and that as a direct

[23] Ibid., p. 185.
[24] Ibid., pp. 192–193.

result of the financing system they are required to pay taxes at a higher rate than taxpayers in many other districts in order to secure for their children the same or lesser educational opportunities.[25]

In recognizing the second cause of action, instead of saying simply that children were being harmed because local taxpayers could not meet their needs even when they submitted to property levies at onerously high rates, the California Supreme Court introduced an ambiguity. Is the *Serrano* case primarily a case about equity to groups of children or is it a case about equity to taxpayers?

Conceivably, if tax rates bore a close relationship to school expenditures per student—and this could happen if the tax bases of districts by means yet to be discussed were made more or less equal—so that high-expenditure districts had high school tax rates and conversely for low-expenditure districts, a standard of equity sufficient to satisfy the California Supreme Court would be deemed to prevail. But from the point of view of the school child, and assuming that education is a matter of fundamental interest in the private as well as the social sense, does it matter whether his educational program is relatively deficient, whether, that is, he suffers educational insult, on account of a low level of district taxable wealth or on account of whether the district taxpayers who vote on this program are stingy? This matter has been left hanging by the *Serrano* case and others like it that have followed.[26]

The *Serrano* case subsequently went to trial in the Superior Court of Los Angeles; and on April 10, 1974, after a five-month trial, that Court declared the California system of educational finance unconstitutional, being in violation of state constitutional guarantees of equal protection. Between the time of the California Supreme Court's statement on the *Serrano* case and the Superior Court's finding, the legislature had passed changes in the financing system, raising the value of the foundation program by a large amount and placing expenditure limits (per student) on high-spending districts. However, these changes failed to satisfy the Superior Court. It pointed out that California still provided $125 per-student aid regardless of wealth of district (the minimum grant discussed in Chapter 10); that residents of districts could vote to override the state-imposed expenditure limits; and that, in spite of the reform of educational finance in

---

[25] Ibid., p. 194.

[26] This is not to imply that tax-base equalizing is worthless as an act of social policy. It reduces pressure on suburban communities to exclude low-income families with school-age children from their populations, for one thing.

the state, variations in expenditure per student and in local tax rate remained unconscionably wide.[27]

While the *Serrano* case was proceeding through the courts, a similar case, *Demetrio P. Rodriguez* v. *San Antonio Independent School District*, was filed in Texas and heard before a three-judge court. The court rendered an opinion in December 1971, holding the Texas educational finance system unconstitutional under the equal protection clause of the Fourteenth Amendment of the U.S. Constitution. The State of Texas appealed the case to the U.S. Supreme Court; and on March 21, 1973, that Court reversed the decision of the Texas District Court, thereby stopping a uniform, nationwide attack on inequities in the distribution of school resources. In effect, the Supreme Court declared that the Texas system of finance and all related systems in other states did not violate the equal protection guaranties of the federal constitution. State courts were still free, of course, to declare systems unconstitutional on the basis of their own state constitutions.

Why did the U.S. Supreme Court so decide?

1.   The Court held that plaintiffs had at best proven a *relative* disadvantage in the schooling of some children, not absolute deprivation. The Court then stated that the equal protection clause does not require "absolute equality or precisely equal advantages."[28] That is, as long as all children had available to them some minimum standard of schooling, the Court was satisfied that rough justice was being done.

2.   The five-vote majority of the Court stated that plaintiffs had not clearly identified a "suspect" or disadvantaged class of persons.[29] Essentially, this argument stated that since some families of low income lived in districts rich in locally taxable wealth, the proposed remedy of tax-base equalizing could work to the disadvantage of low-income families.

3.   The Court held that educational policy was a matter to be determined by the states, not the federal government, and that the Supreme Court lacked expertise to make judgments on state educational policies.[30]

Though the U.S. Supreme Court decision halted a national movement toward reform of educational finance, activities in the

---

[27] Lawyers' Committee on Civil Rights Under the Law, *Update on Statewide School Finance Cases* (Washington, D.C., 1976), pp. 2–3.

[28] Berke, *Answers to Inequity*, p. 213.

[29] Ibid., pp. 214–215.

[30] Ibid., pp. 215–219.

states continued. As of 1976, major cases were before the courts in Alaska, California (final appeal of the *Serrano* case), Connecticut, Florida, Georgia, Kansas, Maine, Missouri, New Jersey, New York, Ohio, Oregon, and West Virginia.

The New Jersey case[31] is especially interesting because the New Jersey Supreme Court established a second version of constitutional violation, one not based on equal protection. The Court held that the state's educational finance system was illegal because it failed to provide the constitutionally mandated system of education throughout the state that is "thorough and efficient."

In Michigan and Kansas substantial reforms were put in place partly in response to statewide finance cases.[32] In Colorado, Illinois, Utah, and Wisconsin major reforms were instituted as a kind of general response to the *Serrano* issue. Finally, in December 1976, the California Supreme Court gave its own final ruling.[33] It restated its earlier legal arguments on education as being a fundamental interest and upheld the judgment of the trial court that wealth-related disparities in both school expenditures (per student) and local school tax rates must be eradicated by 1981.

We should not conclude, however, that *proposals* for reform were discovered by the courts. We noted earlier Morrison's plea (in Chapter 10) for statewide financing of school services. In 1965, the author recommended to the California legislature a reform package that included a statewide property tax, statewide teacher salary schedules, and state assumption of teaching costs.[34] If the proposals had been accepted, the *Serrano* case could not have been mounted. The contribution of the courts was to push reform proposals from the discussion stage toward implementation. In that process, the nature of reform proposals became more or less standardized.

Reform Proposals of the Post-*Serrano* Period

Two main types of reform proposals dominated the scene in the wake of the 1971 analysis of the *Serrano* case by the California Supreme

---

[31] Robinson v. Cahill, 62 N.J. 473, 303 A. 2d 273, 1973.

[32] W. Norton Grubb, "The First Round of Legislative Reforms in the Post-*Serrano* World," *Law and Contemporary Problems*, 38, no. 3 (Winter-Spring 1974): 472–492.

[33] Serrano v. Priest, 135 *California Reporter* 345, 1977.

[34] Charles S. Benson et al., *State and Local Fiscal Relationships in Public Education in California* (Sacramento, Calif.: State Senate Fact-Finding Committee on Revenue and Taxation, 1965).

Court. One was *full-state funding* and the other was *district power equalizing*. We will consider them in turn.

Full-State Funding

Under full-state funding the state government becomes the sole source of educational resources, whether for school operation or capital outlay.[35] But complexities arise in designing a process of transition from present schemes of state and local finance to a state-only system; in determining the grants to particular districts, and in shifting administrative responsibilities among state, regional, and local authorities.

Transition   In almost all states, expenditures per student vary among districts. This is what the *Serrano* case is all about. At what level, then, of expenditure per student is the state to provide basic support. Assume, as is not unrealistic, that the range in expenditure per student is from $600 to $4,000, with the median level being $1,600. If the state enforces an expenditure per student at the median level, half the districts of the state must make absolute cuts in expenditure. Such districts would be forced to drop programs—in art and music, athletics, bilingual education, summer activities, and so on—and morale would no doubt be seriously affected.

On the other hand, the state can hardly afford to keep everybody happy by raising expenditures in all districts up to the level of the highest, $4,000. Not only would this call for an immediate doubling or tripling of the total public school budget in the state but it would also be economically wasteful.[36] How, then, under the device of full-state funding, can the inherited wealth-related disparities in expenditure be removed?

The standard approach to the problem consists of two stages of action. First, the state acts immediately to establish a minimum level of basic expenditure per student at some point above existing

---

[35] Full-state funding proposals were recommended strongly in the immediate post-*Serrano* period by *The Fleischmann Report on the Quality, Cost, and Financing of Elementary and Secondary Education in New York State* (New York: Viking, 1973), I, chap. 2 and III, app. 14A; and by the Advisory Commission on Intergovernmental Relations, *Financing Schools and Property Tax Relief—A State Responsibility* (Washington, D.C., 1973), chap. 9. The current state finance programs in Florida and New Mexico are full-state funding plans.

[36] Forcing expenditures up sharply in the short run can convert those expenditures into quasi-rents as teachers, say, receive a large increase in pay but are not quickly enabled to work any differently from the way they were working before the pay increase.

average expenditures—this is the *leveling up* procedure. Second, the state takes action to see that higher expenditure districts will eventually be overtaken by a rising floor of the state's own program and hence incorporated into that state level of basic expenditure.

For example, following almost immediately upon the 1971 *Serrano* finding, the Fleischmann Commission in New York issued its recommendations that New York State take over full responsibility for financing educational services of districts within its borders. The commission recommended more specifically that the state level up basic operating expenditures to a sum of $1,143 per student, which represented the 65th percentile of spending per student in the base year (1970-71).[37] Thus, districts were to be leveled up to a point somewhat above median expenditures. Second, the commission recommended that districts spending at a higher level than the 65th percentile be frozen—kept at their existing level of spending—until the statewide base level of expenditure caught up to their level, at which point they would start moving ahead with the main body of the state's districts.

Though the Fleischmann Commission eschewed absolute cuts in expenditures in any district, their recommendation did imply cuts in the real value of services in high-spending districts. Accepting the fact that the economy is inflationary, to hold a group of districts at a constant dollar sum of expenditures means that the real value of school outlays per student in the high-spending districts must fall. Assuming that the state will try to protect the real value of expenditures in the large number of districts operating at the state's base expenditure amount (initially, say, the 65th percentile figure of the Fleischmann Commission recommendations) and assuming that organized teachers will encourage the legislature and the governor to so act, the length of the transition period—the time required to even out wealth disparities in basic school expenditures and get all districts operating at the statewide basic expenditure level—becomes a function of the rate of inflation. The higher the rate of inflation, the more quickly the gap will be closed. Ironically, one of the few positive contributions inflation can make to our social life is to quicken the achievement of equity in education.[38]

---

[37] *The Fleischmann Report*, III, 408.

[38] Of course, an absolute freeze on expenditures in high-spending districts is not essential, just that those districts be sufficiently constrained that the other districts can catch up within a reasonable period. But, anything other than an absolute freeze means a longer transition period. These points are further discussed in Charles S. Benson, "Equity in School Financing: Full-State Funding" (Bloomington, Ind.: Phi Delta Kappan Educational Foundation, Fastback No. 56, 1974).

Full-state funding clearly implies a shift from local taxation toward state taxation for education. But it does not follow that the use of property taxation to pay for school programs fades away. Educational reform proposals ordinarily incorporate a recommendation that the state levy a school property tax at a uniform rate (in the case of the Fleischmann recommendations, the rate was $2.04 per $100 of assessed valuation), with the statewide school property tax rate being set at a level sufficient to raise approximately that amount of revenue that the districts previously had obtained from property taxes for schools. This step makes the transition to a statewide system easier than if the state had to replace school property taxation by raising income tax rates, sales tax rates, and so on: Massive tax shifts of that kind produce many unintended windfall gains and losses.[39]

Determination of Grants to Particular Districts   The basic intent of full-state funding is to make distribution of educational resources more economically rational. Wealth-related disparities are clearly irrational, as the California Supreme Court stated. As a judicial body, the Court did not see fit to go beyond that negative position. But what is rational? Edging toward the positive, the Fleischmann Commission stated: "The state shall determine a defensible basis of distributing money to school districts. Equal sums of money shall be made available for each student, *unless a valid educational reason can be found for spending some different amount.*"[40]

What are valid educational reasons for spending different amounts? First, clearly, the learning needs of students. For their education, some young people require more resources than others. The Fleischmann Commission recommended two massive programs of categorical aid: one for the educationally disadvantaged, with a weight in the distribution formula of 1.5 (as compared with 1.0 for the typical child but with the state's contribution standing in addition to federal compensatory grants), and the second for handicapped children, with a weight of approximately 2.0. Similar extra distributions could well be provided for students in vocational programs, for the artistically gifted student, for the scientifically inclined student, and so on.

---

[39] Of course, taxpayers in certain districts may receive a shock, nevertheless. Where low-income households live in high property wealth districts and where such districts have previously enjoyed low school tax rates, the movement to a statewide school property tax may cause such low-income households to face quite large increases in property tax. This situation leads to the use of "circuit breakers" in almost all major school finance reform proposals (see below, this chapter).

[40] *The Fleischmann Report*, I, 62.

Nothing in the idea of full-state funding implies that equal dollars be spent on each student. To adopt full-state funding means that wealth-related disparities must first be removed, and this implies making basic educational expenditures equal in the first instance. From then on, resource allocation would be directed in accordance with the learning requirements of children. As we have seen in the discussion of educational production functions, information is not yet available to precisely identify educational resource needs of different types of students. The most we can look for is rough justice, which is surely better than those state-mandated injustices that the present system of educational finance contains.

Are there reasons to think that state assumption of financing education would produce a distribution of funds that better recognizes the learning requirements of different students than would a system that allowed local authorities to continue to determine the size of their budgets? Here are some possible reasons. If the state becomes the responsible agent for raising and distributing the entire amount of funds for elementary and secondary education, then the state is ultimately responsible for the levels of student achievement produced in the schools—and responsible as well for disparities in achievement from one school to the next. Local districts can always pass the blame for deficiencies in school programs to the higher level of government, claiming that the state did not provide the local district with enough money, that state regulations prevented the local district from spending the money as well as it knew how to, and so on. Since education is the constitutional responsibility of state governments, full-state funding should give reality to the idea that "the buck stops here."

Not only does legal responsibility rest with the states but so also does the financial consequence of educational failure. The largest share of welfare distributions are drawn from state tax sources, not federal or local. The state, thus, has a direct financial interest in seeing that the incidence of educational failure is reduced. Would full-state funding help the state government to pursue that interest? In the first place, full-state funding implies that the locus of collective bargaining on major economic issues shifts from the local school board to the state legislature and executive. The state could seek to negotiate agreements with teachers so that experienced and well-trained teachers would be available to take posts in "difficult" schools. If local authorities sought strong controls on teacher assignment, the unions might threaten some form of local withdrawal of services, such as a strike. But statewide strikes are much harder to mount than local, and the potential of state power is consequently stronger. In the second place, continuity of educational policy is more likely to be maintained at the state level than the local, partly because the civil service bureaucracy at the state level is larger and more professionally staffed than are local school administrations and partly because state legislatures are less subject to massive turnover than are local school boards. Hence, because of greater continuity of policy, the state government should have more interest than local government in developing long-term accountability systems and the appropriate information feedback systems. Information so obtained could be used by the state to adjust resource distributions more closely in accordance with the learning requirements of students.

Another ground for establishing differences in expenditure per student from one district or school to the next is variation in input, or resource, prices. This factor, and differences in learning requirements of students, are the two chief educational criteria that fit the Fleischmann Commission specification on full-state funding: no differences in expenditure except those that can be justified on *educational grounds*. Indeed, unless the second criterion is adequately recognized, attempts to adjust expenditures to student learning requirements can be rendered null and void. Suppose it is intended to provide an extra amount of teaching service in a certain low-income district and suppose further that a sum is issued to the district to hire additional staff under the stipulation that newly hired teachers be of demonstrated competence. If the district has a reputation as a difficult place to work and if no extra pay (above, say, a statewide scale) is offered, the district may fail to receive applications from teachers of demonstrated competence. Not only can we imagine that some districts have to pay more than others to engage teachers of a given level of ability, it is also certainly true that some districts must pay higher prices than others for school sites, for building maintenance and repair, and for money (though the higher interest rates commonly charged to low-wealth districts would no longer be a problem if state governments took over finance of school construction). In summary, then, an early task of a state government in establishing a full-state funding scheme is to arrange a distribution of money to school districts that takes account of differences among districts in learning requirements of students and of differences in prices that must be paid by districts for school resources. Both adjustments are required to recognize the "needs of children." And, as Stefan Michelson has said, commenting favorably on the concept of full-state funding,

> Justice in the allocation of school resources to children is most likely to be achieved if the distribution question is separated from questions pertaining to revenue, thus eliminating the

potential for decisions based on the desires of adult tax-payers. Accordingly, the needs of children themselves will probably be more determinative when finance decisions are made by a unit of government that is less responsive to direct parental pressure than is the school district.[41]

Distribution of Responsibilities Among Governmental Levels　The third aspect of full-state funding that must be dealt with in any serious policy context is how public responsibility toward education shall be divided. One common misconception should be cleared away. Full-state funding does not imply that local districts are abolished or lose all their powers. The full-state funding proposals that were recommended by the Advisory Commission on Inter-governmental Relations, by the Fleischmann Commission, and that received legislative consideration in Minnesota and Michigan left local school districts in place.[42]

Local districts would no longer be responsible under full-state funding for balancing the local school budget by levying a local tax nor would they be responsible for establishing a salary schedule for teachers (though local authorities would continue to exercise power to hire, and fire, and promote teachers).[43] But it is just these issues of local school tax and teachers' salary schedule that take up so much time of local educational administrations—often to so little point—and serve effectively to distract local administrations from dealing with real educational questions—with, for example, who should be taught what, at what ages, by whom, and under what conditions, in order to reach what kinds of intended outcomes. Free-ing local educational authorities from the tasks of revenue raising and of negotiating with teachers on major economic issues (though pre-sumably boards would be enabled to negotiate on details of working

[41] Stefan Michelson, "What Is a 'Just' System for Financing Schools? An Evaluation of Alternative Reforms," *Law and Contemporary Problems*, 38, no. 3 (Winter-Spring, 1974): 457.

[42] Advisory Commission on Intergovernmental Relations, *Financing Schools and Property Tax Relief.*

[43] The point about full-stage funding shifting the locus of bargaining to the state level can be put in a straightforward way. At the local level, there would be nothing to bargain about except how much money to shift around in the fixed local budget, how much to shift from other items of expenditures to teachers' salaries. Naturally, teachers' unions would want to direct their bargaining energies toward the sources of funds—the state legislature. But statewide collective bargaining does not necessarily imply absolutely uniform salary schedules across the state. City salaries might be set at different levels from suburban, for example; and at the first, almost certainly there would be regional salary schedules to reflect past differences in salary standards.

conditions) could yield them more time to deal with the requirements of participatory democracy.

Moreover, there is nothing inconsistent between moving to full-state funding and increasing the powers of parental advisory groups to exercise control over expenditure policies and curricular matters at the site of the school. Full-state funding proposals, that is, can be joined with proposals to increase local control at the school site, the point where influence would seem to make the most difference to parents.

At the state level, as we have indicated, powers would be expanded to supply the total of school revenue; to arrange for a period of transition from local finance to full-state funding; and to establish a set of distributions to school districts, reflecting, as well as information allows, the need to spend money on children in different types of school districts. Finally, to improve efficiency in delivering educational services, it would surely be wise to strengthen the capacity of regional educational authorities to supply high-cost and highly specialized instructional programs, along the line we discussed in Chapter 8.

District Power Equalizing

The second major response to the *Serrano* issue is a form of state and local finance called *district power equalizing* (hereinafter called DPE). Basically DPE represents tax-base equalizing. Suppose every school district in the state relied solely on property tax to meet local costs of education and suppose further that every school district contained taxable property worth $10,000 per student. Any two districts that spent an average of $1,000 per student would have a local school tax rate of 10 percent, or $10 per $100 of assessed valuation.[44] Any two districts that spent an average of $1,200 per student would have a tax rate of 12 percent, or $12 per $100 of assessed valuation, And, in general, any two districts that laid out the same sum of dollars per student would tax themselves locally at an equal rate. Differences in local taxable wealth would not affect local tax rates; only the expenditure level chosen by the district would. To put it another way, differences in local wealth would not constrain any district from producing as many dollars per student for education as any other district, nor would any district, by having large sums of taxable property, be able

[44] That is not to say that the $10,000 represents full value; most assessments are pegged at some fraction of full value, say, 25 percent.

to finance expensive educational programs at low tax rates.[45] This, of course, is a fictional situation, because in no state is assessed valuation per student precisely equal among all the school districts. However, DPE is an arrangement between the state and its localities to produce a one-to-one positive relationship between expenditures per student and school tax rates, exactly in accord with the situation that would prevail *if tax bases (per student) were equal all over the state.* This is also the result of the strict application of the percentage equalizing formula, equation (10.3), we discussed in Chapter 10. DPE is simply a set of free-form versions of percentage equalizing grants.

For example, states might establish a schedule between local property tax rates and allowable expenditures (per student) on the basic K–12 program as shown in columns (1) and (2) in Table 11.1. Under the Schedule A, the state decrees a minimum school tax rate of $4.00 per $100 of assessed valuation, with which is associated a minimum school expenditure of $800 per student, as regards to the basic education program (sums received by the district as categorical aids would be in addition to the amounts allowed in the DPE distribution). From the minimum point on, increases in local tax rates call forth additional basic expenditures per student. Under Schedule A, all districts having $5.75 as a school tax rate would be allowed basic expenditure of $1,150 per student—no more, no less.

In Schedule A, increments in school expenditures are uniform (each is equal to $50) throughout the range of tax rates, which, in turn, rise in increments of $0.25. More generally, DPE schedules are drawn up with a *kink,* as illustrated in Schedule B in Table 11.1. At lower tax rates, increases in expenditure are fairly wide, while at higher tax rates they become narrower. This is illustrated diagramatically in Figure 11.1.

The kink in Schedule B occurs at a tax rate of $6.00 and an expenditure level of $1,400. In effect, the state is giving the following message to its school districts: "We, the state authorities, believe that

---

[45] DPE does nothing directly or in the short run to equalize household incomes among school districts. Hence, to say that districts of equal taxable property—or districts as existing once a full-fledged DPE system is in place—have equal capacity to pay for schools is patently false. The districts in which household income is higher or, more to the point, in which the number of low-income households is small, are in a much better position to put up school tax rates at high levels than are those in which the majority of households are poor. DPE seeks to remove the influence of size of property tax base on school spending, but only that, at least in its more common versions. Later in this chapter we shall note that it is possible to design DPE plans that are "progressive" with respect to household income, that is, that attempt to correct for both taxable wealth and household income disparities.

Table 11.1
Illustration of district power equalizing of basic school finance

| Local tax rate (per $100 of assessed valuation) (1) | Expenditures per student | |
	Schedule A (2)	Schedule B (3)
$4.00 (minimum)	$ 800	$ 800
4.25	850	875
4.50	900	950
4.75	950	1,025
5.00	1,000	1,100
5.25	1,050	1,175
5.50	1,100	1,250
5.75	1,150	1,325
6.00	1,200	1,400
6.25	1,250	1,425
6.50	1,300	1,450
6.75	1,350	1,475
7.00	1,400	1,500
7.25	1,450	1,525
7.50	1,500	1,550
7.75	1,550	1,575
8.00	1,600	1,600

$1,400 is an appropriate sum to provide a good education to the typical child in the typical school district and we encourage you to spend that much by leading you up at $75 increments in spending per student for each $0.25 on your school tax rate. On the other hand, we do not want you to overspend, because outlays in excess of $1,400 are either not justified in terms of educational output or, if justified, create too much educational inequality in an era of reform. Especially if you are a low-wealth district do we hope you do not overspend, because the costs to the state budget of subsidizing your program are large. So we decree that expenditures above the $1,400 level rise only by $25 per student, not by the previous $75 increment, for each $0.25 addition to your tax rate." The kink, then, is established in DPE schedules to curb local propensities to spend money on schooling.

DPE schedules ordinarily embody the concept of *recapture:* High-wealth districts are more or less forced into the position of

Figure 11.1
Alternative forms of simple DPE

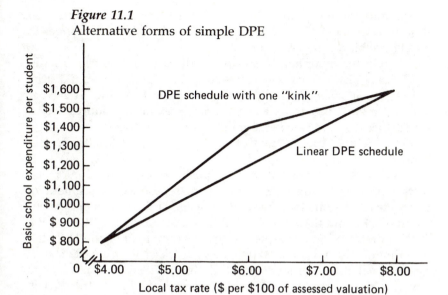

raising more dollars for schools from their local tax bases than they are allowed to spend. Consider again Schedule A of Table 11.1. Imagine that there is in the state school district X with $40,000 assessed valuation per student. Assume the district chooses to spend $1,200 per student in its basic program. Reading across Table 11.1 to the left, we see that this district, along with all others that decide to pay out $1,200 a student, must levy a local school tax of $6.00 per $100 of assessed valuation. But a $6.00 tax rate in district X yields, not $1,200 a student, but $2,400. The extra $1,200 raised by district X is thus turned over to the state's general education fund and recirculated to poorer districts.[46] Under Schedule A, all districts having assessed valuations in excess of $20,000 per student will be subject to recapture. When values of residential properties are rising rapidly, as in the later 1970s, and when assessors do their job of keeping assessments up to date, more and more districts will find themselves

---

[46] To see why recapture is an essential part of DPE, recall the analysis at the end of Chapter 10, in which we saw that the only way for a state that uses a matching grant scheme to avoid requiring rich districts to tax themselves in excess of their actual expenditures is for the state to take over practically all of the financing of schools—to move, in effect, to a full-state funding system. But this avoids recapture only in the procedural sense, because any imaginable version of full-state funding takes more money out of rich school districts (by means of state taxes) than it puts back (by means of state grants).

354   *The Reform of Finance of Education*

falling into the recapture category. This suggests that a state may wish to revise its DPE schedule periodically to recognize changes in locally taxable values (per student).

On the other hand, low-wealth districts are net beneficiaries of DPE. Let district Y have a tax base of $10,000 per student. If district Y, in terms of Schedule A in Table 11.1, chooses to expend $1,200 per student in basic program, it levies a $6.00 tax rate, produces $600 a student locally, and receives a grant of $600 a student from the state. Under Schedule A all districts of valuation less than $20,000 are net beneficiaries.

To see better the alternative positions of rich and poor districts, consider Figure 11.2. This figure reproduces a segment of Schedule A. Assume that the state is engaged in a gradual implementation of DPE and that, initially, DPE extends up to but not beyond a $6.00 tax rate and $1,200 expenditure level (point I of Figure 11.2). Let us examine the position of two new districts: W with $22,500 of assessed valuation per student and Z with $17,500. Let each seek to advance its tax rate to $7.00. In the absence of DPE, district W will move to an expenditure level of $1,575 (as shown by the dotted line I–II), and Z will go to $1,225 (as shown by the dotted line I–III). For the same absolute increase in local tax rate, W's expenditure rises by $375 per student (from $1,200 to $1,575) and Z's by only $25. Now, let the state extend the upper limit of the DPE schedule by a $1.00 increment in tax rate to a $7.00 tax rate, with a $1,400 expenditure per student limit. If districts W and Z choose to hold their tax rates constant at $7.00, each will now have an expenditure of $1,400; W will contribute an additional $175 to the state's educational fund (shown by distance II–IV), and Z will receive an additional grant of $175 from the state (the distance III–IV). Clearly, district W would prefer to operate on its own tax-base line—the dotted line I–II—because it has a steeper slope (more school dollars generated by any given increase in school tax rate) than the state-imposed DPE schedule. District Z should prefer the DPE schedule to its own tax-base line (I–III) because its slope is less steep than the state's DPE schedule. We shall make use of Figure 11.2 later in discussing pressures on local governments to shift functional responsibility from one local unit of government to another in response to measures of school finance reform.

DPE schedules typically establish a minimum school expenditure level and a minimum local school tax rate. There are at least two reasons for so doing: First, in some districts, whatever their degree of wealth, there may be such a degree of disinterest in education by the adult members of the community that school expenditures would be set at such a level as to represent a serious disadvantage to resident

Figure 11.2
Districts' own-tax line compared with DPE

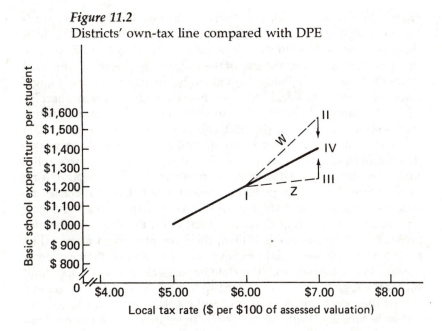

children, unless the district is required by the state to provide adequately (Table 11.1 incorporates such a minimum). The second reason has to do particularly with high wealth districts. As we have seen, these districts are required to raise more money for schools than they are allowed to spend on their own local schools. It might well be to the financial advantage of such communities to push school tax rates down practically to zero and provide themselves with private schooling. But some residents might prefer public schools; and some residents might be poor and be unable to afford the required tuition fees. The statutory minimums in DPE plans protect the interests of minority members of rich school districts.

What about upper limits on expenditures? Practice varies, and we shall note the possibilities. But we must first point out that when DPE is imposed, the interest of state government in the level of maximum expenditures shifts markedly. Under the foundation program plan, it is a matter of relative indifference to state government if certain districts vote to spend large amounts of money on their schools because these sums come mainly or exclusively out of local district taxation. That is, once a district decides to raise its expenditure level beyond the amount of the foundation program, it is expected to find the extra money from its own resources, not from state grants. When a state adopts DPE, the state makes a pledge, in principle, to share school costs with local districts at whatever level of local spending those districts choose to maintain. The state's educational budget, then, becomes subject to choices made by voters in hundreds of local districts. Not only does the size of the state budget become somewhat unpredictable, but the budget is vulnerable to major increase if large, low-wealth districts decide to raise their expenditure levels sharply.

Figure 11.3 shows alternative forms by which state governments seek to control maximum levels of expenditure. Alternative *A* is one in which the state places no upper limit on expenditures nor on its own obligation to share in meeting those outlays; it simply relies upon the kink in the DPE schedule to restrain districts from raising expenditures to very high levels. Alternative *B* likewise carries no absolute limit on local district expenditures, but after a point the state foregoes further sharing of costs—point *O* on the diagram. Beyond point *O*, districts are on their own; the amount of extra money they raise for any given tax rate increase is a function of their property wealth. With alternative *C*, the state imposes an absolute upper limit on local expenditures per student (point *p*). As districts in general extend their expenditures toward point *p*, *C* takes on characteristics of full-state funding. With alternative *D*, the state places no upper limit on expenditures; but after point *q*, no further local contribution is required. Ordinarily, *D* carries with it the right of the state to approve in detail all budgets of school districts that are spending at levels in excess of *q*.[47]

How does the government of a given state go about designing a DPE plan? Essentially, there are four variables to be worked upon: minimum expenditure level; minimum local tax rate; slope(s) of the DPE schedule; and provisions, if any, for maximum expenditure levels. In fitting a DPE plan into the fiscal condition of a state, money can be saved by setting the minimum expenditure level low and the minimum local tax rate high. The slope of the schedule should be flat rather than steep if the objective is to obtain reform on the cheap. But a flat schedule, other things equal, will increase the number of districts in the recapture category, at the same time that the amount of recapture demanded of high-wealth districts becomes very large (and their opposition to the plan presumably increases). States can also save money by controlling the upper limits of expenditures toward which they will contribute. A state that had a favorable budget situation and that wanted to adopt a generous DPE plan would take opposite action in setting the parameters of its new finance program.

[47] Wisconsin operated a DPE scheme using alternative *D* in the early 1960s. See Charles S. Benson, "State Aid Patterns," in *Public School Finance: Economics and Politics*, ed. Jesse Burkhead (Syracuse, N.Y.: Syracuse University Press, 1964), p. 225.

Figure 11.3
Alternative forms of control on DPE expenditures

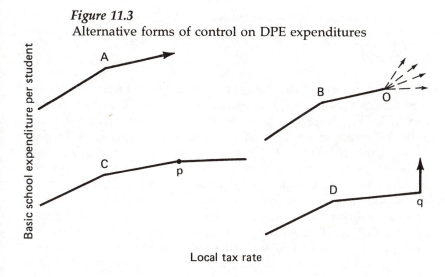

Once a general estimate of the parameters is in mind, precise design of a DPE plan is greatly aided by computerized simulations of school districts' responses to the financial arrangements. If a given simulation indicates that the plan is not likely to cost the state government as much as the state government wishes to spend, then the four parameters, or some of them at least, can be adjusted to raise the state share of the educational budget or to stimulate higher levels of expenditure with state share staying constant, or both. In making simulations of school finance plans, assumptions must be made about the behavior of different types of districts. For example, one assumption might be that high-wealth, high-expenditure districts would reduce their expenditure levels over a three-year period of time to a point halfway between their existing outlays and state average expenditure. Low-wealth districts that levy school taxes at high rates might be assumed to reduce their tax rates (if they didn't under DPE, their school expenditures would rise very sharply) to some point, say, two-thirds above the state average school tax rate. There is no set procedure for making such assumptions; hence, it is best to prepare alternative simulations based on alternative assumptions to help establish boundaries around the likely budgetary impact of a given DPE proposal on state government.[48]

[48] Examples of simulations of DPE and full-state funding are given in Charles S. Benson et al., *Final Report to the Senate Select Committee on School District Finance* (Sacramento: State Senate, California Legislature, 1972), I, chap. 4.

Alternative Forms of District Power Equalizing

We shall discuss three alternative forms of the district power equalizing concept.

Guaranteed Valuation   Long popular in England, guaranteed valuation guarantees a revenue yield for low-wealth districts as if each district had a certain standard amount of valuation per student, with the standard amount set at or near state average valuation. High-wealth districts are left to use their tax base as they see fit, and high-wealth districts do not receive grants for their basic programs. At first glance, this might appear to be discrimination *against* high-wealth districts, but actually the reverse is the case. All districts having wealth above the guaranteed base are in a privileged position, because they can finance any given level of expenditure at a lower tax rate than any district subject to the guaranteed valuation. Another way to put it is this: Guaranteed valuation does not embody recapture.

Those points are illustrated in Figure 11.4. Assume that the state guarantees an assessed valuation per student of $20,000. Measuring tax base per student along the horizontal axis, we see that the local tax rate required to finance a program costing $1,400 per student is constant at $7.00 per $100 of tax base for all districts having valuations less than or equal to $20,000. At higher valuations, the tax rate required to pay for the same valued program falls steadily. At greater educational expenditure levels, the required tax rates are larger, but the same pattern of relationship is preserved: uniform tax rates for a given level of expenditure in all districts poorer than or equal to the guarantee level, lower tax rates in higher wealth districts.

Guaranteed valuation plans are appropriate in cases when the politics of the situation make it impossible to recapture excess revenues from high-wealth districts. These plans do succeed in putting a strong floor under the financial capacity of poorer districts, but it is doubtful if they would meet the *Serrano* criticism of removing the influence of district wealth on educational expenditures.[49]

Progressive DPE   At the other extreme of the policy spectrum is *progressive DPE*, which recognizes not one but two ability characteristics of local school districts: assessed valuation per student

---

[49] For a thorough discussion of alternative reform mechanisms, see Stephen M. Barro, "Alternative Post-*Serrano* Systems and Their Expenditure Implications," in *School Finance in Transition: The Courts and Education Reform*, ed. John Pincus (Cambridge, Mass.: Ballinger, 1974), pp. 25–80.

Figure 11.4
Guaranteed valuation plan

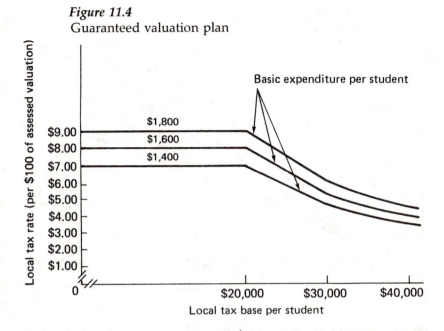

and household income. Districts in which household income is average for the state are dealt with in the ordinary way—see Schedule I, Figure 11.5. Districts in which household income is on the average low are assigned a more generous DPE schedule, like Schedule II, Figure 11.5; districts in which household income is high are given a more restrictive schedule, III in Figure 11.5 Under this tripartite arrangement (actually, the relationship between DPE schedule and household income could be continuous), the tax rate required to support a $1,400 program is $6.00 in districts of average income, $5.50 in districts of low household income, and $8.00 in high-income districts. The intent of progressive DPE is to remove the effects of both taxable wealth differences and household income differences on educational expenditure, by mandating that a given tax rate brings more educational dollars in low districts than high.[50] Progressive DPE can serve to increase sharply the amount of recapture required under financial reform.

Split-Roll DPE As we have seen, the local property tax base is made up of residential and nonresidential properties, the latter being mainly industrial and commercial holdings. Given this, an

[50] Benson et al., *Final Report to the Senate Select Committee*, pp. 83–85.

Figure 11.5
Progressive DPE

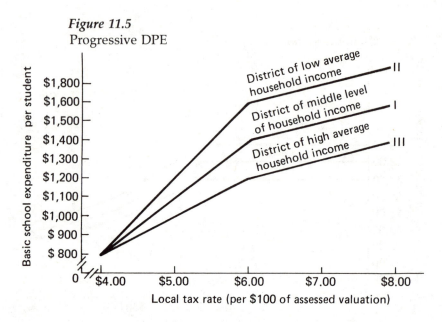

undesirable consequence of progressive DPE is to award preferential tax treatment to concentrations of industrial and commercial properties that may exist in school districts of low-household income. This kind of selective tax shift could not easily be justified. One solution is to place commercial and industrial property strictly under statewide taxation, or at least statewide taxation for schools—to split the tax roll, that is, dealing separately with residential properties and with commercial-industrial. Presumably, all industrial and commercial property would be taxed at the same rate, regardless of the school district in which it is located (that rate could be set as the statewide weighted average of locally determined school rates on residential properties).

Split-roll DPE can be justified even when the DPE system is not explicitly progressive. Wherever there are concentrations of profit-making taxable properties, we can expect, inter alia, that school tax rates are low. This indicates, of course, that commercial-industrial properties have the benefit of a tax haven. This problem becomes serious under school finance reform, which almost certainly means that tax rates will rise in districts with heavy concentrations of non-residential properties if the quality of school programs is to be preserved. But the owners of the property will be motivated to campaign against those very increases. If successful, they will preserve for themselves the financial advantage of tax avoidance but at the price of causing harm to school children. If the tax rate increases required under reform are blocked, the necessary consequence is a sharp fall in school expenditures per student.

Problems in the Path of School Finance Reform

Though many states have made substantial progress in school finance reform since the mid-1960s, hardly any one of them has established a thoroughly fair system. It is thus appropriate to consider some of the difficulties that reform entails.

Mismatch Between District Wealth and Household Income

The *Serrano* judicial argument deals with the inequities that flow from the uneven distribution of taxable values, one school district to the next. We could take a highly formalistic attitude toward reform and say that reform exists when a state establishes full-state funding or a DPE plan, period. But, if reform is viewed in its historical meaning, it applies to an improvement in the plight of poor people. The issue becomes dramatic in school reform because, in industrial states, large numbers of poor people reside in property-rich districts.[51] We might claim that these poor people have been gaining unfair advantage of our educational system by managing to locate themselves in high-wealth districts, but poverty in America is a sufficiently terrible experience that if the end result of *Serrano*-produced reform is to lay additional tax burdens on large numbers of low-income households and to reduce educational expenditures in the schools their children attend, then that reform effort is perverse.

In its larger aspects, this problem arises chiefly because there are large numbers of low-income households who live in central cities. (In Chapter 6 we noted that, excepting rural areas, low-income families are more or less forced to inhabit central cities because of the absence of cheap housing in the suburbs.) Large cities have significant amounts of industrial and commercial properties, and this increases their apparent wealth as school districts. Further, in computing assessed valuation per student, the procedure in most states is

[51] In New York State, a majority of low-income children attend schools in high-wealth districts, mainly because low-income families are concentrated in New York City. That city, its financial difficulties aside, is, in terms of the distribution of state aid for schools, a rich district. See *The Fleischmann Report,* I, 83–86.

to divide the total value of taxable properties by the number of students in average daily attendance (ADA). This works to the disadvantage of city residents because ADA in cities is reduced by three factors: high proportion of students attending private schools, high rates of truancy, and unusually large numbers of high school dropouts. To some extent these conditions reduce cost pressure in public schools and to some extent they do not. But in combination they serve to inflate the apparent wealth of central city school districts. As high-wealth districts, then, the cities are targets for action under *Serrano* type reform, just as are high-wealth suburbs, though the latter are more likely to be populated by middle- to high-income households. We defer further discussion of the big city problem per se until the next chapter.

There is, nevertheless, a particular fiscal device to ease the plight of low-income households who find themselves in high-wealth districts during a period of educational reform—the *circuit breaker*. The idea is that the state government "breaks the circuit" when property tax levies on a certain set of households become excessive. As of 1975, 27 states used such a form of property tax relief though, in many cases, relief is confined to property owners (not renters) and to elderly property owners at that.[52]

Such restriction to a special segment of the population is inequitable; and if educational reform is to proceed smoothly, the circuit breaker should apply to all households. The basic arrangement might be as follows: Let the state reimburse residential property owners for taxes paid on their chief place of residence with a smoothly declining ratio inverse to household income; that is, let the state reimburse, say, 96 percent of residential property taxes paid by households with income under $3,000; 88 percent of property taxes paid by households having income between $3,001 and $4,500, and so on, down to zero reimbursement for households having income over $12,000. It is necessary to put an upper limit on the size of the residential property tax bill eligible for reimbursement (this might be set at the level of the median property tax bill in the state). The reason for having the limit is to forestall some rich households, for example, those who obtain income from tax-exempt bonds and who report little income to the state, from gaining reimbursement for property taxes on large, expensive homes.[53]

For renters, circuit breaker relief must be designed on the basis of rules of thumb, since, as we have already seen in Chapter 9,

---

[52] See Education Commission of the States, *Compact*, Spring, 1976, p. 21.
[53] A thorough-going proposal for a circuit breaker is shown in Benson et al., *Final Report to the Senate Select Committee*, pp. 14–20.

there is no clear evidence about who pays what proportion of property tax on rented properties, about how much, that is, is paid by the owner and how much by the tenant. One proposal is to assume that, on the average, gross rent is about 25 percent of income and that property taxes represent about 20 percent of gross rent. Thus, one might allow low-income renters to file a claim for property tax reimbursement equal to 5 percent of adjusted gross income (as the term is defined for federal income tax purposes).[54] Whatever the precise details, the interest in adopting or extending the use of circuit breakers is to see that sudden increases in property tax rates in some school districts do no serious damage to the disposable income of low-income households.

Withdrawal of High-Income Households from the Public School System

A second problem to be faced when putting school finance reform proposals in place is: Those proposals may loosen the allegiance of upper income families to the public school system. If the state takes action to control the level of school expenditures in suburban districts, rich families may decide that they must turn to private schools to protect the quality of education their children enjoy. If the state adopts tax proposals that draw far more money out of high-income suburbs than the state allows those suburbs to spend, the rich families may be inclined to move to a low-tax jurisdiction and send their children to a privately managed institution.

This would be an unfortunate consequence because this would lead us to a two-class school system, something that has been avoided. Admittedly, some public schools are more highly regarded than others, but for the present argument this is beside the point. What is important is that when public high school graduates from low-income families apply for college admission, they are subject to no systematic bias because they attended a public school; after all, the same type of institution is used in full measure by high-income families, even though they have the means to choose private institutions. This suggests that reform should be accompanied by serious attempts by state and local governments to improve the quality of public education. (Certain suggestions about this point were given in Chapter 8.)

[54] The criteria for an optimum circuit breaker have been analyzed in W. Norton Grubb and E. Gareth Hoachlander, "Optimal Circuit Breaker Schedules and Their Application in California" (Childhood and Government Project, University of California at Berkeley, 1975).

Capitalization Effects

We observed earlier (in Chapter 6) that differences in service levels and local tax rates tend to be capitalized into property values. If reform means that certain school districts suddenly face large changes in tax rates, then property values can be expected to move up (if the district enjoys a tax cut) or to move down (if the district has a tax increase) and in sharp measure. Losing districts could mount a tax-payer revolt against the reform measures, possibly to the lasting damage of the public educational system.

There is also a matter of equity at stake. Take the case of a school district that offers superior school programs, that contains large amounts of taxable residential property per student, and that has low tax rates. Under reform it is probable that the state would force school tax rates to rise. Since the residents get good schools and pay low tax rates, on its face, this is unfair. But it is likely that many of the residents bought their way in by paying higher prices for their houses and lots than they would have paid for equivalent property in a district that did not have particularly good schools. A current tax rate is not a terribly good measure of what access to good schools has cost these families. To penalize such households by forcing down the value of their homes might itself be regarded as unfair.[55] This argument suggests, not that reform be set aside, but that it move at a judicious pace, the better to avoid large-scale capitalization effects.

Budgetary Shifts

In discussing DPE we noted its effects on districts of different wealth. Examining Figure 11.2 again, we see that a high-wealth district has to put up more dollars for schools than it can keep, while a low-wealth district gains considerably more on the DPE line than it could get if it was on its own tax-base line. Ordinarily, school finance reform proceeds independently of reform in other units of local government. Imagine, now, that school districts and certain small cities are coterminous. Let city A be rich and city B be poor in taxable wealth. After DPE reform, city A is on line I–IV in Figure 11.2 for financing schools, but it remains on its own tax-base line, I–II, for financing other municipal services.[56] It is clearly to the advantage of city A to move

---

[55] For further discussion of this problem, see Robert D. Reischauer and Robert W. Hartman, *Reforming School Finance* (Washington, D.C.: Brookings 1973), pp. 51–53.

[56] The same argument would apply if a state adopted a full-state funding scheme, except that the target of policy would be the state legislature. Rich districts would

functions out of the school budget and into the municipal accounts. Take libraries, for example. If city *A* is thinking of improving school libraries by, say, $40,000, and if the transaction is handled by the schools, the required increase in taxes might be in the order of $70,000: $40,000 for school libraries and $30,000 paid to the state in recaptured funds. But if school libraries are transferred to the municipal library system, then the city can forego providing the state with the recapture funds—the city can finance the library improvement, not on the DPE line, but on its own tax-base line. The reader can reasonably demonstrate that just the opposite pressures apply in district *B*; that is, it moves items out of the municipal budget and into the school budget.

Such budgetary shifts may not be consequential in terms of quality of services provided, but that they may possibly occur suggests that simply to judge the effect of school reform by comparing pre- and post-reform school budgets in different types of districts may well overstate the magnitude of those effects. What we have described is simply an example of entrepreneurial activity that public authorities engage in. A district that is hard pressed financially by school reform might also begin to charge fees for certain of its services (transport, music lessons, and so on), and it might also become more assiduous in seeking grants from public agencies (like the National Institute of Education) and from private foundations.

Illustrative Changes in State and Local Relationships in Education

School finance plans in the various states have complexities in structure and peculiarities of definition that defy simple description; they are almost constantly in a state of revision. What must serve our purpose in this section is an indication of the kinds of changes that have been taking place in the wake of court-inspired reform. We will look at such changes in six states—Michigan, Maine, Illinois, Florida, California, and New Mexico.

In 1973–74 Michigan established a guaranteed valuation plan. As of 1975–76, the state guarantees $42.40 per student per mill of local tax for the first 20 mills and $38.25 for the next 7 mills, a total state

---

petition against increases in statewide school expenditure levels and poor districts would petition for them. Under full-state funding, the collectivity of rich districts has an incentive to finance school-related needs out of the municipal budget, and so on.

guarantee of $1,115.75 per student at the maximum local tax rate of 27 mills. In 1977–78, the guarantee is $47.00 for the first 20 mills and $42.40 for the next 10 mills, etc. But there is as yet no recapture in the Michigan system: Districts having more assessed valuation per student than $47,000 in 1977–78 are allowed to retain the revenues that are in excess of state guarantees for their own uses.[57]

A second important feature of the Michigan school finance plan is recognition of *municipal overburden.* When a school district is in a city that has high local tax rates to support its noneducational services, the assessed valuation of the school district is reduced—not in actuality and not as employed in raising local revenues, but as used in computation of grants from the state for its schools. Reducing the computational value of assessed valuation directs more state school money to districts where noneducational local property taxes are unusually high.[58]

In Maine, the 1975 School Finance Act established a uniform property tax for schools intended to raise annually 50 percent of school expenditures in the state. Recognizable expenditures (statewide average at elementary and secondary levels) are determined in relation to previous levels of expenditure, adjusted for inflation. In terms of basic state grants, low-spending districts receive extra financial assistance, and high-spending ones are squeezed downward to state average. Additional to the basic state programs is a power equalizing local add-on, such that districts can levy local tax up to two-and-one-half mills in excess of the statewide property tax. However, while the state guarantees $50 per mill per student—which benefits low-wealth districts—the maximum that can be raised by this local supplement is $125 per student.[59]

Thus, the Maine system is in the direction of full-state funding: state distribution of sums for basic expenditures; a statewide property tax; and a closely bounded DPE add-on. There is also a set of

---

[57] The most comprehensive source of information about state aid arrangements, and one used extensively in this section, is Esther O. Tron, *Public School Finance Programs, 1975–76* (Washington, D.C.: U.S. Government Printing Office, 1976). See also W. Norton Grubb, *New Programs of State Aid,* National Legislative Conference, 1974; and John Callahan and William H. Wilken, eds., *School Finance Reform: A Legislator's Handbook,* National Conference of State Legislatures, 1976.

[58] In the next chapter, there is further discussion of the special needs of central cities and of the concept of municipal overburden.

[59] As of 1976, the Maine educational finance system was under attack in the courts on the grounds that the recapture of money implied in the statewide uniform school tax was unconstitutional, but no decision had been handed down. See Lawyers' Committee for Civil Rights, pp. 5–6. Utah and Wisconsin are two other states in which recapture of funds from high wealth school districts is provided for. See Grubb, *New Programs of State Aid,* pp. 42–49.

categorical aids for special education, vocational education, student transport, and school facilities.

Illinois has kept the foundation program plan of school finance. But in 1973 a DPE plan was set alongside it. Districts choose one or the other arrangement; generally low-wealth districts have chosen DPE. Unit districts (K–12 districts) are guaranteed a valuation of $42,000 per student (in 1975–76), up to a tax rate of $3.00 per $100. In high-taxing districts that elect DPE (districts with rates historically at levels above $3.00), the state applies a *roll back* provision requiring them to work back down to the upper limit recognized for state subsidy. Because the foundation program plan is still in place and because (as we have seen) recapture is not part of that form of finance, recapture is not an essential feature of the Illinois plan. But the count of students used in Illinois is weighted in the districts by the ratio of compensatory education children to attendance; thus, districts having a high percentage of poverty children receive extra state aid, not just in categorical grants but in the computation of basic state distribution itself. This is a strong equity feature of school financing in Illinois.

In Florida, the 1973 Education Finance Act included a number of interesting features. On the one hand, the Florida plan could be described as full-state funding, in that there is a statewide property tax for schools and relatively little local leeway to spend in excess of state distributions. The distributions are themselves remarkable for the detailed weightings, some 25 in number, to take account of different learning characteristics of students and their programmatic costs. The distributions are also unusual in that they attempt to regulate the flow of funds in terms of the prices districts in different parts of the state have to pay for educational resources; that is, the distribution formula incorporates a cost-of-education index, based mainly on differences in teachers' salaries.

On the other hand, the Florida plan emphasizes decision making in the local school. Principals and teachers, in consultation with parents, are expected to establish educational objectives for their schools and to monitor progress toward meeting those objectives. Categorical aids, essentially the student weightings mentioned above, are tracked directly into the schools in accordance with a given school's number of affected children. Thus, while educational reform in Florida was intended to increase the power of the state in financing schools (centralization), it was also intended to distribute greater powers from school districts to the school site (decentralization).

California continues to rely on the foundation program plan as its basic means of financing education. However, major changes have been made in recent years. In 1972 the legislature raised the amounts of the foundation program, effectively doubling them and increasing substantially the proportion of school costs borne by the state. Also, provision was made to adjust the amounts of the foundation program year by year in accordance with an inflation index. An expenditure limit was established, which regulated total basic expenditure in any district in accordance with numbers of students in attendance and with expenditures per student in the previous year. These revenue limits apply to both state and local spending and can be avoided only if the local citizens vote in favor of an expenditure override. Moreover, high-spending districts are "squeezed" to the foundation program, in that their revenue limits are adjusted downward by a special index in the form of a ratio of the foundation program to their previous year's expenditure per student. (A district that has had high expenditures and that is losing enrollment is placed in a double budgetary bind.)

In 1977 California added DPE for all equalization districts that spend in excess of the foundation program. In such high-spending districts, low-wealth sites will draw more dollars than their local tax base would give them, and high-wealth districts will be subject to substantial recapture especially for voted overrides.

In New Mexico, 87 percent of nonfederal school revenue is provided by the state (as of 1975–76). A statewide property tax is levied at a uniform rate on assessed valuation in the districts. Special learning requirements of students are recognized by a weighting scheme, and districts employing teachers with high levels of training and experience are compensated for the extra amount of salaries this implies. Though it is somewhat in the tradition of New Mexico, that state can be described as a full-state funding operation, and it has in recent years strengthened its commitment to that idea.

Preliminary Economic Assessment of Educational Reform

Most studies of the effects of school finance reform so far conducted deal with changes in expenditures (per student), revenues, and school tax rates among the different school districts of a given state, pre- and post-reform. These studies may conveniently be grouped in three types: theoretical, descriptive, and econometric.

One theoretical analysis, by R. Hartman and R. Reischauer, predicts the responses of contrasting high- and low-expenditure districts to alternative forms of district power equalizing (different in terms of the slopes of the expenditure tax rate schedule and level of

minimum state guarantee) on the basis of price and income elasticities.[60] The general conclusion is that the steeper the slope of the
expenditure tax-rate schedule and the lower the minimum expenditure guarantee, the greater will become disparities in expenditure
between formerly high-expenditure and formerly low-expenditure
districts. This same general theoretical analysis is frequently used in
simulations of interdistrict responses to state-specific DPE plans.[61] In
an early analysis, S. M. Barro advanced the theoretical discussion by
considering interdistrict differences in the composition of local tax
base as well as differences in household income.[62] One interesting
conclusion of Barro's study is that where residential property values
are high because of locational factors, distribution of state aid on
equalizing principles can have a perverse effect on school expenditures per student.

The major descriptive studies conducted to date have been
undertaken by A. Hickrod and his associates at Illinois State University.[63] The basic techniques are, first, to calculate pre- and post-
reform coefficients of revenue inequality—on such variables as assessed valuation per student and household income per student—
and, second, to compute linear regressions of state and local revenues
per ADA on local tax rate. Hickrod concluded: "Movement was made
[in the Illinois reform plan] toward the goal of fiscal neutrality, variation in revenues per pupil and tax rates were reduced, reward for
effort was increased, and movement was made toward the goal of
equal expenditures for equal effort. Furthermore, Illinois became one
of the leading states in the nation to at least begin to meet the
expensive educational needs of students in its urban areas."[64] But
Hickrod warns that his results are for an extremely short-run period
of response to reform and that once districts of high-income households sense a relative decline in quality of school services, they are
likely to take greater advantage of the reward-for-effort provisions in

[60] R. W. Hartman and R. D. Reischauer, "The Effect of Reform in School Finance on
the Level and Distribution of Tax Burdens," in *School Finance in Transition: The Courts and
Education Reforms*, ed. John Pincus (Cambridge, Mass.: Ballinger, 1974).

[61] Benson et al., *Final Report to the Senate Select Committee*.

[62] S. M. Barro, *Theoretical Models of School District Expenditure Determination and the
Impact of Grants-in-Aid*, R-867-FF (Santa Monica, Calif.: RAND Corporation, 1972).

[63] G. A. Hickrod et al., "The 1973 Reform of the Illinois General Purpose Educational
Grant-in-Aid: A Description and an Evaluation," in *Selected Papers in School Finance*,
Office of Education, U.S. Department of Health, Education, and Welfare (Washing-
ton, D.C.: U.S. Government Printing Office, 1974); and G. A. Hickrod et al, *Measurable
Objectives for School Finance Reform: A Further Evaluation of the Illinois School Finance
Reform of 1973* (Normal: Illinois State University, 1975).

[64] Hickrod, *Measurable Objectives*, p. 77.

the new plan than are districts of low-income households. Thus, previously existing inequalities will be restored.[65]

The main line of econometric inquiry is presented in the work of M. S. Feldstein.[66] Defining *price* of educational services to a school district as the amount the local district must put up for an additional dollar's purchase of school resources, Feldstein establishes that wealth neutrality (zero influence of variation in tax base of districts on expenditures) exists when the price in a given district is regulated by the ratio of wealth elasticity of expenditure to price elasticity. By examining the results of a highly constrained DPE system in Massachusetts, Feldstein concluded that the value of price elasticity of expenditure is far greater than wealth elasticity. Hence, DPE formulas, if they are to achieve wealth neutrality, must be written to produce less dollars of expenditures per student for a given rise in local tax rate in low-wealth districts than in high-wealth ones. The argument is more compelling when considering school district-municipal district expenditure transfers (when these are possible) than it is in predicting voter behavior between rich and poor districts. In this connection, it might be noted that the theoretical works mentioned earlier use local school tax rate, not local sharing ratio, as the relevant price of educational services.

R. P. Inman has conducted an econometric analysis of the response of school districts to reform, incorporating as response variables the propensity of households to move from one school district to another and to substitute private for public schooling of their children.[67] Other econometric investigations have been conducted by D. Stern and W. N. Grubb and S. Michelson.[68]

A second main group of studies is concerned with changes in budget allocations within units of local government. These studies, like the previous group, fall into three categories: simple descriptive, econometric, and analytical surveys.

R. Mize conducted a multiple case study of the response of California school districts to major increases and decreases in reve-

[65] Ibid., pp. 36–37.

[66] M. S. Feldstein, "Wealth Neutrality and Local Choice in Public Education," *American Economic Review*, 65, no. 1 (March 1975): 75–89.

[67] R. P. Inman, "Optimal Fiscal Reform of Metropolitan Schools: Some Simulation Results with a General Equilibrium Model" (Department of Economics, Harvard University, 1975).

[68] D. Stern, "The Effects of Alternative Formulas for Distributing State Aid for Schools in Massachusetts," *Review of Economics and Statistics*, 55, no. 1 (February 1973): 91–97, and W. Norton Grubb and S. Michelson, *State and Schools* (Lexington, Mass.: Lexington Books, 1974).

nue.[69] Limitations of data prevented her from reaching firm conclusions, but she was inclined to predict that low-spending districts faced with an inflow of funds would distribute the increase to produce a set of budget allocations conforming to the typical pattern of budget allocations in the state. Depending on the previous patterns of expenditure, this might not result in directing the funds toward instructional services. M. W. Kirst examined budget allocations of school districts in Los Angeles County before and after implementation of the school finance reform package of 1972–73 (Senate Bill 90).[70] He found that contrary to the assertions of Daniel Moynihan,[71] teachers salaries in districts receiving large increases in revenue increased less rapidly than did teachers' salaries in the state as a whole. Most of the new money was used by the low-wealth districts to employ additional instructional personnel and to establish new programs. S. Horvath conducted a case study in Northern California to see whether changes in school revenue in a large school district resulted in discriminatory treatment of low-income or handicapped youth.[72] His findings were that no such discrimination existed, but it is obviously hard to generalize from a single case.

Econometric analysis of school district budget allocations has been conducted by S. M. Barro and S. J. Carroll using data from 195 large districts in Michigan.[73] The main technique was multivariate regressions. In the cross-sectional part of the study, dependent variables were per-student expenditures for teachers, class size, teacher experience and education, average teacher salaries, and so on. Independent variables were size of district budget, price variables, and socioeconomic characteristics of districts. In a second stage of analysis, attention was directed to the ways in which discretionary funds were spent, for example, funds not previously committed to teachers already employed, to fixed charges, and so on. One major finding was that per-pupil expenditures for teachers increase less rapidly than the budget overall; and expenditures on specialists, supplies, and equipment increase more rapidly. J. G. Chambers, in a

[69] R. Mize, "Winner and Losers," in Benson et al., *Final Report to the Senate Select Committee,* app. III-C.

[70] W. M. Kirst, "What Happens at the Local Level After School Finance Reform" (School of Education, Stanford University, 1976).

[71] Daniel P. Moynihan, "Equalizing Education: In Whose Benefit?" *Public Interest,* no. 29, Fall 1972, pp. 69–89.

[72] S. Horvath, "Spending Patterns Within a School District: A Case Study" Graduate School of Public Policy, University of California at Berkeley, 1975).

[73] S. M. Barro and S. J. Carroll, *Budget Allocations by School Districts: An Analysis of Spending for Teachers and Other Resources,* R-1797-NIE (Santa Monica, Calif., RAND Corporation, 1975).

highly sophisticated study of resource allocations in public school districts, reached a similar conclusion: "[A] one percent increase in school expenditure will, on the average, lead to between a 0.20 to 0.26 percent increase in the demand for teachers." [74]

A somewhat different topic of econometric investigation has been pursued by J. C. Weicher. He sought to explore the fungibility of grants to overlapping or coterminous units of government. His general conclusion is that when governments are coterminous, it is a matter of indifference which one receives an increase in a state or federal grant: "expenditure increase for any will be the same per dollar of aid, whether the aid is earmarked for that service, for another service performed by the same government or for some function performed by some other government serving the same population." [75]

Analytical surveys of response of government to revenue change is best illustrated by the work of F. T. Juster, a major venture in survey research to investigate the results of general revenue sharing (GRS). On the one hand, the study was directed to the impact of GRS on expenditures and taxes: "In essence, we asked respondents how their budget situation would have been different if the Revenue Sharing program had not existed."[76] On the other, the study sought to discover how decision-making processes and government structure had changed, if they had, under revenue sharing. The questions in the first instance were broadly phrased, but the respondents were helped in making their replies by hundreds of detailed specific inquiries. Since no one can know with certainty what the situation would have been in the absence of revenue sharing, this method seems well suited to getting as close as possible to the truth. Indeed, the Juster study appears to be as close as one can come to a model for investigating intradistrict effects of school finance reform.

In summary, it seems clear that the educational reform movement has had some success in producing changes in some states. Further, though insufficient time has passed fully to allow complete assessment of the effects of these changes, preliminary assessment indicates a direction toward equity in the distribution of

---

[74] J. G. Chambers, "A Model of Resource Allocation in Public School Districts: A Theoretical and Empirical Analysis" (School of Education, University of Rochester, 1975), p. 18.

[75] J. C. Weicher, "Aid, Expenditures, and Local Government Structure," *National Tax Journal*, 25, no. 4 (December 1972): p. 582.

[76] F. T. Juster, ed., *The Economic and Political Impact of General Revenue Sharing, A Report to the National Science Foundation* (Washington, D.C.: U.S. Government Printing Office, 1976), p. 3.

school resources and possibly toward the use of resources in new and creative ways.

Summary

Long-standing disparities among school districts in expenditure per student and in tax rates have come, since the 1960s, to be viewed as violations of constitutional rights and mandates. The main corrective actions fall into two categories: assumption of educational costs by state government and tax-base equalizing. These reforms do not necessarily advance the interests of low-income households; accordingly, reform legislation often includes features of categorical grants for low-income youth and income-specific property tax relief. Notwithstanding the complexity of the issues, improvements in equity under the school finance reform movement can be claimed in a number of states.

Selected Bibliography

Alexander, Arthur. *Inequality in California School Finance: Dimensions, Sources, and Remedies.* Santa Monica, Calif.: RAND Corporation, 1975.

Benson, Charles S., et al. *Planning for Educational Reform: Financial and Social Alternatives.* New York: Harper & Row, 1975.

Berke, Joel. *Answers to Inequity: Analysis of the New School Finance.* Berkeley, Calif.: McCutchan, 1974.

Coons, John E., William H. Clune, and Stephen D. Sugarman. *Private Wealth and Public Education.* Cambridge, Mass.: Harvard, 1971.

The Fleischmann Report on the Quality, Cost, and Financing of Elementary and Secondary Education in New York State. 3 vols. New York: Viking, 1973.

Garms, Walter, James Futhrie, and Lawrence Pierce. *School Finance: The Economics and Politics of Public Schools.* Englewood Cliffs, N.J.: Prentice-Hall, 1977.

Pincus, John, ed. *School Finance in Transition: The Courts and Education Reform.* Cambridge, Mass.: Ballinger, 1974.

Thomas, J. Alan. *The Productive School.* New York: John Wiley, 1971.

Chapter Twelve

Federal Aid and the Future of Education in Central Cities

Historically, the federal government has played a strategic albeit minor role in elementary and secondary education. Indeed, the traditional federal contribution can be easily summarized: The central government puts its money into school operations when either one of two conditions exist—a significant number of local districts are required to meet extra costs of provision, such costs being incurred for reasons beyond the control of the local districts, but without such provision the national interest would suffer; and by virtue of some federal action the revenue position of certain local districts has been damaged. An example of a response to the first condition is federally funded compensatory education programs (Title I of the Elementary and Secondary Education Act of 1965). An example of the second is *impact aid*—federal grants intended to protect the fiscal position of local school authorities from the possible adverse consequence of their having tax-exempt federal properties within their borders (Public Laws 864 and 815).

The educational policy of the federal government is different from that of most other central governments. In many countries the central government seeks to exercise a degree of control over input prices—teachers' salaries and school construction costs, for example. Other governments—the French being the most commonly cited—seek to set the content of the curriculum. Governments overseas often provide financial support to private as well as to public schools.

With rare exceptions, our federal government has chosen to play the more limited role just described.[1]

Our task in this chapter is two-fold. First, we shall examine certain major pieces of federal legislation to see how they are working. These include grant programs for vocational education, compensatory education, and the schooling of handicapped children. We shall also consider impact aid. Second, having first taken account of the financial plight of central city school systems, we shall examine the question of whether support of educational services in those cities is a reasonable cause for federal action. In this exercise we shall see that the federal role in education is afflicted with its own peculiar contradictions.

Federal Legislation in Education

We begin our discussion of federal legislation with acts concerning vocational education.

The Vocational Education Acts

Federal grants for vocational education began with the Smith-Hughes Act of 1917. The intent was to stimulate state and local activity in what was regarded as a neglected area of education: High school programs were seen as strongly oriented toward preparation for college; students whose plans did not include college were offered little instruction in preparation for useful employment. Also, labor shortages contributed to the passing of the act. Six million dollars was authorized to support salaries of teachers of agriculture, home economics, trades and industry, and distributive occupations.

Vocational legislation has been expanded and modified many times, most notably in the George-Barden Act of 1946, the Vocational Education Act of 1963, and the Education Amendments of 1976. But certain principles of administration have been adhered to throughout.

---

[1] Possibly *the* major exception is the National Defense Education Act of 1958, which was passed in response to the Soviet Union's early lead in space exploration. The act's primary focus was raising the effectiveness of instruction in science, mathematics, and foreign languages. It also was intended to influence prices of educational resources, for example, prospective teachers who took out loans under the act could obtain partial forgiveness of those loans if and when they actually took up classroom teaching. Obviously, the intended effect was to increase the supply of newly prepared teachers over what it would otherwise have been.

Distribution of Grants   The sums authorized ($1,030 million in fiscal 1976) and appropriated by Congress are treated in closed-end fashion: The available sums are allocated among the states on the basis of a weighted population formula (see Chapter 10). The main weights presently used represent state shares of population in various age groups, with special emphasis on the ages of 15 to 19. The Smith-Hughes and George-Barden Acts were predominantly weighted toward rural populations, but urban areas have become better represented from the time of the Vocational Education Act of 1963. The 1976 Education Amendments retain a secondary weighting to take account of interstate differences in per capita income, though this adjustment has never been strong enough to shift any large amount of funds from rich states to poor.[2] Except for a possible deduction related to a matching requirement, the amount of money to which a given state is entitled is determined by a set of demographic data; actions of the state in improving the performance of its vocational programs thus do not enter into the federal-state allocation process.

Allocations within states are regulated by a state plan, by a set of rules and guidelines developed in each state, which specifies the procedures under which local authorities may apply to the state for funds and the criteria for project approval. The federal government sets the general nature of these criteria by requiring, for example, that the state governments will give priority to school districts located in economically depressed areas and in areas with high rates of unemployment. Second, preference is to be shown to districts that "propose programs which are new to the area to be served and which are designed to meet new and emerging manpower needs and job opportunities in the area and, where relevant, in the State and Nation. . . ."[3] States are proscribed from making across-the-board allocations on the basis of enrollment or as related to some fixed percentage of local expenditure.

Control of Funds   How to assure that federal monies are additive to state and local expenditures, not merely substituting for what state and local authorities would have spent anyway, is a vexing problem. It has been so since the earliest legislation. There is a general

---

[2] Bruce F. Davis and Philip D. Patterson, Jr., *Vocational Education and Intergovernmental Fiscal Relations in the Postwar Period* (Washington, D.C.: Georgetown University, 1966, p. 93).
[3] U.S., Congress, House, *Education Amendments of 1976*, Report no. 94-1701 (Washington, D.C.: U.S. Government Printing Office, 1976), p. 105.

matching provision type, that state and local authorities must spend one dollar on vocational programs for each federal dollar they receive; but this provision has become virtually meaningless. In 1973 the average state and local expenditure per dollar of federal funds was $5.29; in Massachusetts, New York, and Oregon over $10.00 in state and local money was spent for each federal dollar obtained.[4] When federal appropriations are increased, then, states can legally claim their allotted shares of increase while holding their total vocational budgets constant.

Naturally, then, we would expect the federal government to seek out alternative mechanisms of control. We have already noted that the intrastate distribution of funds is regulated by a state plan. Incidentally, the federal government also requires state governments to pledge that "federal funds made available under this Act will be used to supplement, and to the extent practicable, increase the amount of state and local funds that would in the absence of such federal funds be made available for the uses specified in the Act, and in no case supplant such state and local funds."[5] Yet, since there is no way to estimate what would be the actions of state and local authorities in the absence of any increment of federal funding, the data needed to enforce such a stipulation are simply not and never will be available. A second traditional measure to obtain compliance with federal intent is the requirement that state and local agencies establish advisory committees to establish and administrate vocational programs. Committee membership represents people who have close knowledge of labor power requirements in different sectors of the economy and of training possibilities.

The Education Amendments of 1976 added new features to the control process. Categorical matching (though in less strict degree than the basic one-to-one matching of the whole vocational budget) is now required in certain national priority programs, such as vocational programs for disadvantaged persons, for persons with limited English-speaking ability, and for recent high school leavers who are unemployed. A second feature recognizes that the state plans under which vocational programs have been administered have lacked flexibility and have failed to establish operational objectives—for the most part. Under the 1976 Education Amendments, states are now required to develop five-year plans that "set out explicitly the goals the state will seek to achieve by the end of the five-year period . . . in

---

[4] U.S., Congress, Senate, *Education Amendments of 1976*, Report no. 94-882 (Washington, D.C.: U.S. Government Printing Office, 1976), p. 47.
[5] Vocational Education Act, 1973.

meeting the need for particular job skills." [6] These goals are to be derived from an exhaustive analysis of skill requirements and of training capacity already in place. Moreover, the five-year plans are to be divided into annual program plans, each of which shows how the five-year targets are to be advanced upon in the given fiscal year. This planning procedure is modeled after that used in education ministries and planning commissions in the developing countries. If it does not assure that each and every federal dollar is additive to state and local funds, at least it should bring about a more efficient use of the total vocational education budget.

Title I of the Elementary and Secondary Education Act of 1965 (Compensatory Education)

To understand the nature of Title I, it is appropriate to review briefly the history of the search for an expanded federal role in education. In 1946 Senator Robert Taft, then a leading figure in the Republican party, threw his substantial prestige behind a bill (Senate 181, 79th Congress) to provide federal money for teachers' salaries. This bill would have offered sizeable grants to poor states; the rich would have received none. On August 1, 1946, Senator Taft stated on the Senate floor:

> I have felt very strongly that education is a state and local responsibility. . . . However, the difficulty which has developed . . . is that in many states, although they are devoting as much or more than the average amount, on the basis of their wealth and the current income spent on education of the entire Nation, nevertheless they are unable to provide an adequate basic minimum education for their children, due to the great difference in income as between the states. . . . So I feel that the Federal government does have a responsibility to see that every child in the United States has at least a minimum education in order that each child may have the opportunity which lies at the very base of the whole system of our Republic. [Aid to all states, however, would be inimical to the stated goal:] [I]t would mean that we would be paying to states which already provide a good basic education for their children money which is needed by states which are not able to provide such education at the present time. [7]

[6] U.S., Congress, House, Report no. 94–1701, p. 108.
[7] U.S., Congress, Senate, *Congressional Record*, 1946, 92, pt. 8: 10620.

Such a bill was passed by the Senate on April 1, 1948. One of the changes from its original form was provision of a minimum grant to each state, regardless of need or ability. This same bill was passed again by the Senate on May 5, 1949, but neither in 1948 or 1949 was the companion bill reported out of the House. From mid-1949 until 1960, the attention of Congress was directed mainly toward such matters as aid for federally impacted areas and categorical assistance for defense purposes.

But in 1960, the interest of certain important groups turned once again to general aid for equalization. The Committee for Economic Development (CED) issued a statement on national policy in which it took a strong stand against general federal aid for education and an equally strong stand in favor of general-purpose aid for the poor states. In particular, the committee stated:

> The majority of the Committee agree that further extension of the scope of Federal government activities in the field of elementary and secondary education is undesirable. We find that in most of the country additional Federal school support is unnecessary. Hence, we oppose Federal grants to support schools throughout the country. However, we also find that some parts of the nation cannot, with any probable allocation of their own resources, support their schools at a level that meets the nation's requirements. Although we are reluctant to see further expansion of the Federal role in education, we conclude that to secure adequate schools throughout the country it is necessary for the Federal government to supplement school finance in the states where incomes are the lowest.[8]

As demonstration of its position, the Committee advanced a proposal for federal general-purpose school aid. It was a rather weak form of the foundation program plan idea. The minimum expenditure level (per student) in public elementary and secondary schools was set at 80 percent of the national average expenditure. The state and local contribution rate toward that minimum level of expenditure was set equal to the national average of state and local expenditures, relative to personal income in the several states. The federal government was then to make up the difference between the minimum level

---

[8] Committee for Economic Development, *Paying for Better Public Schools* (New York, 1960), p. 34.

of expenditure in a state and the amount that would be raised if the state (and its localities) levied taxes equal to national average.[9] Like Taft's legislation, this proposal would have distributed money to the poorer states and given none to the rich. It was estimated to cost $489 million in 1960–1971. But the proposal was never written into legislation.

What passed the Senate in 1960 was a bill identified as *Senate 8*. It provided authorization for $20 per child, aged 5–17, as general-purpose federal aid. The appropriation would have been distributed to the states under the standard type of federal equalizing formula. For each state, an *allotment ratio* was to be multiplied by the number of children aged 5–17. A state's share of the appropriation was determined by the ratio of its product (the number of children times allotment ratio) to the total of all the products. The allotment ratio was:

$$1 - 0.5 \times \frac{\text{income per child of school age in state}}{\text{income per child of school age in U.S.}} \qquad (12.1)$$

There was a stated upper limit of 0.75 in the allotment ratio (which penalized the poorest states) and a lower limit of 0.25 (which helped the richest ones). This formula is of the type we described in discussing the weighted population grant. Clearly, it would distribute funds in direct proportion to the number of school-age children in a state (as a measure of expenditure requirement) and in inverse proportion to the income of residents (as a measure of the grantee's fiscal capacity). But how thoroughly?

The cost of Senate 8 in 1960 was estimated at $917 million, roughly twice the cost of the CED proposal. Yet, because Senate 8 distributed money to every state, it was much weaker as an equalizing device. Consider this comparison: Distributing $917 million in federal funds, Senate 8 would have reduced the tax burden in Mississippi to provide a federal school program at 80 percent of national average (the CED plan) from 5.90 percent of state income to 5.13. The CED plan, at a distribution of only $489 million, would have brought

---

[9] The formula would work this way: First, calculate a figure equal to 80 percent of national average school expenditures per student— call it $1,200. Second, divide the total of state and local expenditures by the total of personal incomes of the states. This gives us a weighted average of state and local school effort, relative to income levels— call it 4 percent. Third, compute the yield of 4 percent of personal income in each of the states. Fourth, disregarding all states in which the hypothetical state and local tax yield (4 percent of state personal income) was in excess of the educational expenditure requirement (80 percent level of expenditures times number of students), the government would provide grants to all those in deficit, and by the amount of the deficit.

it down to 3.20 percent. While distributing nearly a billion dollars under an equalizing formula, Senate 8 would have left interstate differences in tax rate at a range of over two to one, poor states compared with rich. Senate 8 did not pass the House.

There was, of course, opposition to federal support of the schools in the early 1960s. Some church groups demanded that money for parochial schools be a part of the program; other church leaders thought that money should not be made available to nonpublic institutions. Some southern spokesmen thought that federal school aid would be used to speed up the process of desegregation and were opposed to it on that ground. Not all conservatives agreed with the 1946 position of Senator Taft that school aid could be a tolerable exception to their general opposition to expansion of the federal budget.

Yet, there also was substantial sentiment toward enlarging the federal role in education, and the amount of money Congress had in mind was $1 billion. The objective was equalizing opportunity. To obtain any noticeable amount of equalization for $1 billion in a situation in which a majority of children live in relatively rich states called for one of two things: If the state was to serve as the unit toward which distribution of federal funds were to be distributed, then the rich states would have to be excluded from the grant; or some new formula in which the state was not the receiving unit would have to be developed. The first alternative had been considered not politically acceptable from 1946 when Senator Taft's original bill had been defeated. The second alternative languished because no one had advanced a workable formula.

Had a bill like Senate 8 been passed, the Congress could well have seen that the money was distributed in more or less indifferent measure to all the states. Until recently state aid formulas did not have a strong equalization bias themselves, so the federal aid, as a supplement to state aid, would probably have been passed to all the school districts within the states in indifferent measure. To vote $1 billion to obtain a token rise in educational expenditure was not enticing enough to carry a school bill over the opposition of the church groups, the southern segregationists, and the financial conservatives. Since the early 1960s, the political scene has changed somewhat: Opposition to federal grants to schools is centered more on grounds that other programs, such as health insurance, housing, and environmental protection, are more cost-effective in promoting the national welfare. But a general lesson can be drawn from that earlier experience: As long as the federal government is a junior partner in financing the educational enterprise, the politics of the situation demand that federal money be directed to some *special purpose.*

In the spring of 1965 the Elementary and Secondary Education Act was passed. For the year ending June 30, 1966, the Congress appropriated $1,392 million to implement the (then) five titles of the act. Of the amount, $1,175 was for Title I, the program for the education of disadvantaged students. What had served to break the barriers to a (relatively speaking) large-scale federal addition to support of school services? In part, the formula of distribution. As passed by the 89th Congress, the act provided that funds under Title I should be distributed through the states to the local district on the basis of the count of children in the district living in families with an annual income less than $2,000 and the count of children living in families that received more than $2,000 under the program for aid to dependent children. The sum of these figures was multiplied by one-half the average current expenditures per student in the state in the second preceding year. This product thus became the basic entitlement of a local school district.

The distribution formula did two things. First, it channeled money to the poorer states. In 1965–66, the 20 poorest states had 28.5 percent of national daily attendance and received 38.9 percent of total Title I disbursements. Second, the formula, together with guidelines and regulations on the uses to which Title I funds could be put, assured that distributions within the wealthy states would improve the schooling (for the most part) of poor children, not rich. In sum, the formula emphasized equalizing opportunities (the necessary element of special purpose), while allowing all states, regardless of wealth, to participate to some degree (the necessary element of political sharing). This was the compromise the Congress had been searching for.

The monies under Title I represent categorical aid in the sense that the districts were to spend the funds only for the educationally disadvantaged. The program, that is, was intended to be categorical by client, as distinct from being categorical by program (for example, vocational versus academic) or type of purchase (for example, educational television). Local districts had a great deal of latitude in designing Title I projects, though they were early furnished with a shopping list of suggested, or illustrative, types: in-service training of teachers, full-day summer schools, work-experience programs, and so on.

The Title I distribution formula was substantially modified by the Elementary and Secondary Education Amendments of 1974. One change had to do with the poverty criteria under which children eligible for assistance are counted. A problem that needed to be recognized was the following:

> Under the . . . Title I formula there is (prior to the 1974 Amendments) a flat income criterion so that only those poor children from families with incomes under $2,000 a year are considered poor. Thus, if a family has an income of $1,999 and one child, that child is counted under Title I. However, if a larger family has an income of $2,001 and has six children, those children are not counted under the Title I formula even though that family is by far the more poverty stricken.[10]

The 1974 Amendments struck out the flat income criterion and substituted a measure of poverty known as the *Orshansky poverty index*. This index takes into account the number of children in the family, the sex of the head of household, and the farm or nonfarm status of the family. Its dollar basis is a minimum food budget for different types of families, and it assumes that poverty exists when the family income is less than three times the dollar cost of the minimum food budget. The index is adjusted from one time to the next to reflect changes in consumers' prices.

A second problem had to do with interstate variations in expenditure level. As we have seen, Title I allotments originally were determined by multiplying the count of poverty children by a dollar sum equal to 50 percent of the state average expenditure per student. As we noted earlier, expenditures per student vary widely among the states; furthermore, those variations are positively associated with per capita income in the states. Poverty children in high-expenditure states (states that are rich in household income) were entitled to many more dollars of compensatory aid than poverty children in low-expenditure states.[11]

The procedure was changed in 1974 to the following: The count of poverty children is multiplied by 40 percent of state average

---

[10] U.S., Congress, House, *Elementary and Secondary Education Amendments of 1974*, Report no. 93–805 (Washington, D.C.: U.S. Government Printing Office, 1974), pp. 12–13.

[11] This problem showed up in the earliest days of Title I. In 1965–66, Westchester County, New York, the sixth richest county in the country, received $2.8 million in Title I allocations, while Breathitt County, Kentucky, one of the nation's poorest, got $340,000. U.S., Congress, House, *Congressional Record*, 1967, p. H5587. An important reason for this kind of discrepancy was the use of state average expenditure in calculating Title I awards.

expenditure, except when the state average expenditure is less than 80 percent of national average, in which case 80 percent of national average is used as the relevant expenditure level, and except when state average expenditure is greater than 120 percent of national average, in which case the 120 percent figure is employed.[12] This reduces the effect of interstate variations in expenditures on the amount of the state-by-state entitlements.

Just as in vocational grants, there is a problem in seeing that federal funds are additive to what the states and localities might be spending on compensatory education. And there is a further problem to see that the grants reach poverty children, that is, to see that they are *targeted* to children of educational disadvantage. We shall examine both of these concerns together.

Throughout the history of Title I, the matter of targeting has been handled by requiring that Title I payments be treated as excess cost of programs and projects designed to meet the special educational needs of educationally deprived children who live in school attendance areas having high concentrations of low-income families. It also permitted, at the discretion of the local district, money to be spent in schools outside such an attendance area, provided the proportion of poverty children in the given school is roughly the same as the proportion of poverty children in the low-income attendance area. Further, districts are enjoined to obtain a sufficient concentration of resources in each Title I school that reasonable progress in meeting the needs of the educationally disadvantaged can be expected.

These provisions reflect a concern that Title I funds, if spent in absence of such legislative control, might be diluted into a form of general aid, thus becoming a token add-on to the budgets of all schools. They also reflect a belief that small additions to budgets of schools are unlikely to produce measurable change in the environment of any child. Finally, they reflect a belief that concentrations of poverty children in a single school represent an accentuation of the force of educational disadvantage over and beyond what it would be if the children were dispersed throughout the educational system.

The school, then, is the unit of measurement for the final distribution of Title I money. The funds flow to schools that enroll students from low-income neighborhoods *and* that are located in

---

[12] It should not be inferred that the dollar size of the Title I program has become smaller because the count of poverty children is applied to 40 percent instead of 50 percent of state average expenditure. It has, instead, grown larger, mainly because the poverty criteria (Orshansky index) have been made more realistic.

low-income neighborhoods. Additionally, schools outside low-income areas may be designated as target schools if they enroll an unusually high proportion of poverty children. Title I administrators in the early 1970s became concerned that while Title I money in Title I schools might be additive to what had been previously spent in those schools, it still might not serve to raise expenditure levels in the schools up to or much beyond average district expenditures. This could happen if the district deliberately (or unintentionally) discriminated against schools attended by low-income youth (the problem to which Patricia Sexton drew attention, see Chapter 11). From this concern developed the *comparability guidelines,* for example, the requirement that Title I schools show an expenditure level from state and local funds at least equal to districtwide average.[13]

What are the difficulties with the Title I approach to improving the schooling environment of the educationally disadvantaged? We will discuss some of them.

Targeting   Title I assumes the existence of residential segregation by income class. If this begins to break down in a given city or region, the allocation process fails to work as it is supposed to. Suppose, for example, there are socially mixed areas in a city and that middle- and upper-income families enroll their children in private schools. The poor children are educationally segregated, but they may not be entitled to help.[14] A similar problem has to do with interdistrict differences in proportion of poverty families. To take a hypothetical example, suppose that the proportion of poverty families in district *A* is 20 percent and in district *B,* 30 percent. Imagine that a student lives in an attendance area where the proportion of poverty families is 25 percent. If that student were living in district *A,* he or she might attend a school that received Title I funds; if the student lived in *B,* he or she might not, regardless of whether his or her family was a poverty family.

Title I administration also assumes that schools are segregated by social class. If poverty children attend predominantly middle-class schools, they probably will not receive Title I assistance, even though their degree of disadvantage from home and neighborhood may be just as great as low-income children who attend segregated schools. Although exceptions can be obtained, the general

---

[13] There are certain loopholes in the guidelines, one of which is the provision that seniority payments to teachers may be excluded from the expenditure comparisons.
[14] As we have seen, the district may provide Title I allocations to such a school, but it is not required to do so.

direction of Title I administration is in contradiction to the general direction of school integration.

Once Title I monies are placed in a given school, poverty criteria vanish and degree of educational deprivation (lack of achievement) takes over as the allocating mechanism. Accordingly, some rich children may receive Title I money if they attend a Title I school and have low achievement. This is, of course, a minor problem because the amount of social mixing in the schools is not terribly great. Furthermore, to use a poverty criterion within the social setting of a school would be cruel and humiliating.

However, a difficulty remains. Take a poverty child in a Title I school who does moderately well. He or she does not receive, in theory, Title I assistance. Yet, that student may be potentially a very high achiever and may, because of deprivation, need help to reach his or her attainable level of performance, just as the low achiever needs help to climb out of educational failure. Title I is not well targeted to release the energies of potentially high achieving, low-income students.

Additivity As long as state governments were not themselves spending any money on compensatory education, the comparability guidelines might have been sufficient to guarantee that federal money bought additional services. Indeed, where ghetto schools had been discriminated against, the guidelines might produce expenditure increases in excess of the Title I distributions. But in 1975–76, 14 states operated compensatory programs from their own resources, totalling $240 million.[15] In this situation, the comparability guidelines fail to preserve additivity. Suppose a group of influential legislators in the state capitol were about to pass—and the governor to sign—a bill to increase state and local spending on compensatory education. Suppose that the legislators and the governor learned that the federal government was about to enact legislation that would increase the size of Title I allotments. It is easy to imagine that the state authorities would shelve or reduce the size of their own compensatory legislation and use the money for some other worthy purpose. This is a type of supplanting action that Title I legislation, as presently constituted, simply cannot control. Indeed, the existence of the guidelines may positively discourage states from attempting to serve poverty students who attend school in nontarget schools, since the fiscal effects of such programs in the first instance (the effects of

[15] Esther O. Tron, *Public School Finance Programs, 1975–76* (Washington, D.C.: U.S. Government Printing Office, 1976), pp. 16–17.

raising state and local expenditures in nontarget schools over the level of that in target schools) would be to render some of their districts ineligible for Title I assistance.

Education for All Handicapped Children Act

The Education for All Handicapped Children Act, also known as P.L. 94–142, represents a new vintage of federal educational legislation. Coming into effect in the school year 1977–78, the act establishes high levels of fund authorization for programs for handicapped children: $387 million in the first year rising to over $3 billion in 1981–82. It provides that authorization will be scaled upward in relation to the national average rate of change in per-student expenditure in all public elementary and secondary education.

There are two important innovative features of the act. In the first place, the act requires each state, as a condition of becoming eligible for federal money, to provide appropriate public education to all of its handicapped children. The U.S. Office of Education has the power under the act to define service standards for schooling of children suffering from different types of handicaps; moreover, the Office of Education can specify these standards in terms of real resource inputs. Whether federal dollars are matched precisely thus becomes an irrelevant question. Instead of dollar-for-dollar matching requirements or comparability guidelines, and so on, there is an embryonic contractual arrangement between the federal and state levels of government to ensure delivery of specified services. If in some states there is already nearly ample provision for handicapped children, such that in order to provide them appropriate public education little additional expenditure is required, presumably the federal grant would allow a diversion of some state and local funds that are presently used for the handicapped to other educational services. The main emphasis in the act is on service accountability, not dollar accountability. The former is the stronger concept, and the passage of P.L. 94–142 raises the question of whether service accountability can be applied some day to schooling of the educationally disadvantaged.

A second innovative feature is derived from the joint operation of two provisions of the act. First, it is stated that federal money, when received by a local school district, is to be used to defray part of the excess cost of programs for the handicapped. Second, the education of the handicapped is to be offered in the "least restrictive environment," that is, in the regular elementary or secondary classroom, whenever possible. The provisions together imply an intent to track federal money through to the individual student, rather than, as in Title I, only as far as the schoolhouse door. If such a procedure is workable for the handicapped, it may also be workable for the educationally disadvantaged.

The Impact Laws

There are two *impact laws*, P.L. 874 and P.L. 815, designed to protect school districts from the loss of local revenue that might occur when tax-exempt federal installations are located in the area. P.L. 874 provides grants for current operating expenses of school districts. The grants are paid directly to school districts and are the closest the federal government has come to general aid: School districts that receive the funds are free, practically speaking, to make such uses of the money as they are allowed to do with their locally raised revenues. In 1974–75 a sum equal to $636 million was appropriated by Congress for P.L. 874 grants. P.L. 815 is a grant arrangement of smaller size ($16 million being reserved by Congress for P.L. 815 distribution in 1974–75) and provides money for school construction.[16]

    The idea behind the two programs is that the federal government as a property owner has the responsibility of the normal citizen in the community to participate in the financial support of local government services. However, since most federal properties enjoy exemption from local taxation, it would seem equitable for the federal government to pay the local government a sum equivalent to what they would have received if the properties had been taxable. This sum could be paid to all the overlapping governments that could claim rights to tax the property if it were not a federal installation.

    The main provisions of P.L. 874 (and P.L. 815 is basically similar) are otherwise. The procedure is the following. First, a local contribution rate, which is intended to measure the locally financed costs of operating the schools, is computed. At the option of the district, this may be calculated as current expenses per student in comparable districts in the state, less state aid, or as 50 percent of state average current expenses per student, or as 50 percent of national average current expenses per student. Second, students in local public schools whose parents live on federal property or work on federal

---

[16] U.S., Commissioner of Education, "Administration of Public Laws 81-874 and 81-815" in *Annual Report of the U.S. Commissioner of Education, Fiscal Year 1975* (Washington, D.C.: U.S. Government Printing Office, 1976), app. A, pp. 234, 324.

property or both live and work on federal property are counted. Students whose parents live or work on federal property are counted as one-half, while students whose parents both live and work on federal property (as in the armed services) are counted as one. Third, the sum of these weighted federally connected students is multiplied by the dollar amount of the local contribution rate; the product is the amount of grant to which the district is entitled. The distinction between categories of students is intended to recognize that when federally connected parents live or work on private property they make, or there is made in their behalf, a certain payment toward the operation of the schools. This payment comes from the private sector. When parents live and work on federal property, no such property tax payment from private sources is likely to be forthcoming, and the grant thus is larger for their children.

To see a difficulty in the operation of these grants, consider this example: Suppose there are two contiguous school districts, *A* and *B*, of equal size and in all aspects (number of students, assessed valuation per student, and so on) the same. Let the tax base of each be comprised of residential properties and taxpaying farmland that is gradually being converted to housing. Let a federal work installation be placed on some of the farmland of *A* and let workers new to the area be employed in that installation. Suppose all the new workers choose to live in new tract houses in *B*, and let these homes be of assessed value equal to the average value already prevailing in *B*. Now, what changes have occurred in the fiscal situation of local government in the area? School district *A* has lost part of its tax base without compensatory change in school expenditure requirements. Further, all the local governments that were taxing the farmland in *A* have lost a tax base; that is, the local governments that provide fire, police, recreation and library services, inter alia, have suffered a decline in revenue base. On the other hand, school district *B* has lost no tax base and has suffered no decline in assessed valuation per student. Yet, all the P.L. 874 money generated by the federal installation will flow to school district *B*, not *A*. The impact acts favor places where school expenditures are incurred, not places where the loss in revenue base takes place; further, these acts favor school expenditures over other types of local government outlays. Such anomalies have led state governments in various ways to incorporate P.L. 874 grants into their own equalization schemes.

Having reviewed four major federal programs in education, we turn to the second topic of this chapter, the condition of education in the central cities.

Table 12.1
Enrollment in nonpublic elementary and secondary
schools, 1970-71

State and city	Percentage in nonpublic schools	State and city	Percentage in nonpublic schools
Massachusetts	14.5%	Illinois	15.9%
Boston	23.9	Chicago	24.5
New York	17.7	Michigan	10.9
New York City	24.1	Detroit	20.0
Pennsylvania	17.6	Ohio	11.7
Philadelphia	31.7	Cleveland	32.2

Source: National Center for Educational Statistics, U.S. Department of Health, Education, and Welfare, *Statistics of Non-public Elementary and Secondary Schools, 1970-71* (Washington, D.C.: U.S. Government Printing Office, 1973), pp. 28–29, and *Non-public Schools in Large Cities, 1970-71* (Washington, D.C.: U.S. Government Printing Office, 1974), p. 5.

Schools in Central Cities

In earlier times, schools in large cities were held in high regard. Parents who lived in the suburbs often took special pains to remove their children from their neighborhood schools and enroll them in the schools of the central city. The century's earliest educational reformer, Ellwood P. Cubberley, had as his mission to uplift suburban and rural schools to the standard of city institutions.[17] Some rural schools still display low standards of performance, but otherwise the situation has changed dramatically: Suburban schools are generally more highly regarded than are those of central cities.[18]

To examine some evidence on this point, we may start with attendance patterns. The figures in Table 12.1 indicate, for selected states and central cities, the proportion of children enrolled in nonpublic elementary and secondary schools in 1970–71. Thus, in some of the largest, heavily industrialized cities, there is a propensity by

[17] Ellwood P. Cubberley, *School Funds and Their Apportionment* (New York: Teachers College, Columbia University, 1906).
[18] That is not to say that all central cities face the same degree of difficulty in managing their schools. The problems of Minneapolis' schools are much less severe than Detroit's. Nor should we imagine that schools within any given city are all alike. See Annie Stein, "Strategies for Failure," *Harvard Educational Review*, 41, no. 2 (May 1971): 159–160.

Table 12.2
Proportion of city school enrollment compared with
proportion graduating, 1974–75

City	Percentage of statewide public school enrollment	Percentage of high school graduates
Boston	7.1	5.5
New York City	31.9	23.9
Philadelphia	11.8	7.6
Chicago	23.2	14.9
Detroit	12.0	8.7
Cleveland	5.6	4.6

Source: National Center for Educational Statistics, *Statistics of Public Elementary and Secondary Day Schools, Fall 1975* (Washington, D.C.: U.S. Government Printing Office, 1976), pp. 29–31.

parents to use private schools in excess of that of parents in the state as a whole.

With respect to retention of students through completion of high school, the figures in Table 12.2 are illustrative. The first column shows city enrollment in public schools in 1974–75 as a percent of statewide public school enrollment. The second column shows proportion of graduates of regular day secondary schools as a proportion of statewide high school graduates in 1974–75. Consistently, the cities graduate fewer students than their enrollment would indicate they should.[19]

With respect to achievement of students, we may note that in the National Assessment of Educational Progress, the 13-year-olds in large cities were below national median performance in science, writing, reading, literature, music, social studies, and mathematics. (Though the scores of city children are not as far below national median performance as are the scores of children in extreme rural areas, they are consistently and notably lower than the scores of

[19] The obvious explanation for the discrepancy is student wastage, but it is also likely that some students at the completion of elementary school change to suburban schools or enter private schools in the city and eventually graduate. These shifts in enrollment, however, reflect lack of parental regard for city public schools. Finally, the discrepancy could be explained by a recent disproportionate increase in enrollment in the lower grades of the city public schools. But in the case of the particular cities listed above, this has not happened.

Table 12.3
New York State pupil evaluation program:
percentage of pupils tested scoring below statewide
reference point[a]

	New York State		New York City	
	1970–71	1975–76	1970–71	1975–76
3rd grade				
Math	21	16	39	32
Reading	27	19	46	38
6th grade				
Math	32	33	54	53
Reading	30	30	50	49

[a] The statewide reference point represents a New York State normed score of "minimum competency" in the given subject in the given grade. Students scoring below that point are regarded as in need of special attention.
Source: David Seeley and Adele Spier, "Productivity in New York City's Schools: Fiscal Reality and Educational Quality," *City Almanac*, 2, no. 3 (October 1976): 3. Reprinted with permission.

children in the urban fringe of metropolitan places, that is, the suburbs.)[20]

In the case of the largest public school system, New York City, the figures in Table 12.3 reveal a distressingly dramatic situation. Approximately *one-half* of the 6th graders in New York City public schools in the mid-1970s are identified as potential educational failures, absent special and effective means of intervention.[21]

Yet, in the mid-1970s the fiscal condition of New York City, compounded by the financial difficulties of New York State, renders it unlikely that strong and effective intervention can be provided:

> Public schools [in New York City] where alternative educational modes, such as open classrooms and team teaching, have been nurtured have suffered staff turnovers as high as

[20] National Center for Educational Statistics, *Digest of Education Statistics, 1975* (Washington, D.C.: U.S. Government Printing Office, 1976), p. 189.
[21] A similar condition is indicated for Detroit in Betsy Levin et al., *The High Cost of Education in Cities* (Washington, D.C.: Urban Institute, 1973), p. 66. Earlier, in Chapter 6, we alluded to deficiencies in student achievement in San Francisco.

> 50 percent and these programs have died while they were still young because the young teachers committed to them have been laid off.[22]

In the three years, 1973–1976, the average age of New York City teachers rose from 28 to 41.

> Class size, in general, has increased markedly from teacher-pupil ratios of 1 to 20 three years ago to 1 to 25 today and it is not at all unusual to have classes of 40 students or more . . . Interscholastic sports, after-school recreational programs, adult education, evening trade high schools and summer school programs have been cut to the point where administrators, teachers and students alike doubt their viability.[23]

Ironically, when budget cuts require the dismissal of teachers, as was true in New York City, the cost of teachers' services per teacher go up because, under seniority rules, it is the younger, lower paid teachers who must be dismissed first. When financial difficulties occur in a time of stable or rising enrollments—New York City's enrollment in the mid-1970s was approximately stable—there are then likely to be twin pressures to increase class size: Because some teachers had to be fired in the first place and because the reduced budget must be accommodated to a higher price for teachers' services, additional dismissals, and so on, are likely.[24] Though New York City may be an extreme example of a big city in trouble with its schools, New York's problems are only marginally removed from those of Boston, Newark, Philadelphia, Chicago, Cleveland, Detroit, and Washington, D.C., among others.

What is at risk is the survival of certain basic historical principles of American education—that schools are open to all regardless of birth and background and that families of quite different socioeconomic status all make use of one public school system. (The

[22] Fred Ferretti, "Financial Crisis Crippling New York's Public Schools," *New York Times*, December 12, 1976, p. 1.

[23] Ibid. In Toledo, the public schools were shut down in early December 1976 for lack of funds, and school officials predicted that in the 1978 fiscal year, the schools might have to close as early as October.

[24] On November 13, 1976, Albert Shanker, president of the United Federation of Teachers, which represents the teachers of New York City, took the unprecedented step of declaring that collective bargaining in the city should be suspended: "When there's nothing to be bargained for, it's a form of torture to send people in to bargain." *New York Times*, November 13, 1976, p. 1.

second principle does not require that every child attend public schools, just that significantly large representations of all classes in a given geographic area participate.) There is emerging, in large metropolitan areas, a three-class educational system. In the city live many rich families, and these mainly use private schools and academies. That is one class. In the suburbs live mainly middle-class families, and these use their local public schools. These schools are protected from low-income families of the central city by the practice of geographic entitlement. That is the second class. In the central cities live very many poor families who have no choice but to use the central city public schools. That is the third class. Although it could never be claimed there was a thoroughly integrated public school system, looked at school by school, until recently there was at least a system in which the different classes all made significant use of the public schools *within any given large local authority*. This is what appears to be breaking down in metropolitan areas. And as it breaks down, the openness of American education, through the schools to the higher educational institutions, seems bound to suffer.

Fiscal Aspects of the Big City School Problem

School officials in large city districts often cite shortage of funds as the reason why they find it difficult to compete with suburban districts and with private schools for students (excepting those students who have no place else to go). Their argument is in two parts: extra cost and inadequate sources of revenue.

Costs It is contended that the costs of providing school plants in central cities are extraordinarily high because land costs in cities can be extreme. This affects the ability of school systems to reduce overcrowding, where it still exists, and to replace outmoded facilities that stand in undesirable neighborhoods. A related point is this: School construction in central cities is constrained by the high cost of land to be multistory; multistory schools are reported to be 20 to 30 percent more expensive per student place than are the conventional one- to two-story suburban buildings.[25]

Second, on operation and maintenance it has been stated that "the large city requires greater expenditures per pupil for operation and maintenance of the school plant. City standards require licensed

[25] Norman Drachler, "The Large-City School System: It Costs More to Do the Same," in *Equity for Cities in School Finance Reform* (Washington, D.C.: Potomac Institute, 1973), pp. 22–25.

Table 12.4
Families below poverty level in income, 1969

City	Citywide percentage	Statewide percentage
Boston	11.7%	6.2%
New York	11.5	8.5
Philadelphia	11.2	7.9
Chicago	10.6	7.7
Detroit	11.3	7.3
Cleveland	13.4	7.6

Source: John J. Callahan et al., *Urban Schools and School Finance Reform: Promise and Reality* (Washington, D.C.: National Urban Coalition, 1973), p. 28. Reprinted with permission.

engineers for operation of heating plants . . . Vandalism, which accompanies bigness . . . adds to higher operation and maintenance costs."[26]

Third, because many city districts reached maximum enrollments some years before suburban districts, they tend to have teaching staffs of greater seniority. Since a prime determinant of teachers' pay is seniority, this serves to increase teaching costs.

Fourth, large cities have disproportionate numbers of children who require services appropriate to the mildly handicapped; the cities also accept obligations to run a greater variety of vocational programs than does the typical suburban district. The extra costs of these programs are not always fully met by categorical aid from state and federal governments.

Fifth, the cities have disproportionate numbers of families of low income (see Table 12.4). If the cities were to pay heed to requirement to improve the out-of-school environment of young people in the ways we noted in Chapter 8 (physical security in after-school hours, protection from excessive household work requirements, places of refuge for quiet study and recreation, and so on) and if the cities were to take serious steps to assure adequate nutritional status of pregnant women and infants—in other words, to mitigate the effects of a poverty environment on school performance—then they would be assuming fiscal obligations for such services far beyond the needs of the typical suburban community.[27]

[26] Ibid.
[27] Kenneth J. Arrow, "A Utilitarian Approach to the Concept of Equality in Public Expenditures," *Quarterly Journal of Economics*, 85, no. 3 (August 1971): 409–415.

Table 12.5
Taxable property per public school student, 1972

City and state	Amount citywide	Amount statewide
Boston, Mass.	$20,794	$26,666
New York, N.Y.	53,960	37,767
Philadelphia, Pa.	22,860	19,804
Chicago, Ill.	52,490	38,491
Detroit, Mich.	40,063	40,147
Cleveland, Ohio	60,260	47,126

Source: John J. Callahan et al., *Urban Schools and School Finance Reform: Promise and Reality* (Washington, D.C.: National Urban Coalition, 1973), p. 26. Reprinted with permission.

Revenue Base In most large cities, taxable property per student stands at a higher level than the average relationship for the state. Four of the cities in Table 12.5 could be classified as property rich—New York, Philadelphia, Chicago, and Cleveland—and would receive less in equalizing school aid than the average-wealth district—and much less than low-wealth districts. This apparent wealth of the cities arises from a certain concentration of commercial and industrial properties within their boundaries and from the high value of residential properties of their remaining rich households. It might thus appear that the cities are fully able to meet their special needs from their own taxable resources. The response of the cities to such an assertion is generally in two parts.

First, it can be pointed out that other high-wealth districts—Great Neck and Scarsdale in New York, Grosse Pointe in Michigan, Shaker Heights in Ohio—are able to devote their locally taxable resources to the education of children without having to meet the special expenditure requirements of four cities we just listed. In other words, a properly functioning state aid formula should discriminate among districts in terms of locally taxable wealth *and* in terms of expenditure requirements. Most formulas now in use deal only with the former variable and treat all equally wealthy districts alike with respect to size of grants, regardless of whether those districts differ in their need to spend money.

Second, the cities are inclined to make much of the concept of municipal overburden. The idea is that cities have unusually strong requirements to finance such services as police, fire, sanitation, health and hospitals, and, in the case of New York City, public welfare. These expenditures push total city tax rates—school and municipal tax rates together—to levels above total tax rates of suburban communities, thus making it difficult if not impossible for city school districts to increase their own school tax rates. Thus, so it is said, the low school tax rates some cities enjoy are not a sign of affluence but a sign of municipal poverty relative to their social needs.[28]

As we noted in Chapter 11, only Michigan has so far recognized municipal overburden in its state aid formula. (When total tax rates are unusually high, a computational deduction is made in assessed valuation per student in determining state school aid.) Actually, the municipal overburden argument is seriously flawed. First, no one can yet estimate what share of municipal costs can be attributed to the excessively high wage and salary levels of municipal employees. Some public-sector unions are notoriously aggressive, and it is simply not clear whether city administrations bargain carefully with these unions or whether they are inclined to make settlements that are simply too generous.[29]

Second, some part of municipal costs may be incurred to cater to tastes of city residents for expensive services. Possibly suburban dwellers would like to have similar services but feel the need to restrain their appetites. If this is so, it might be unwise to demand that suburban families subsidize the extravagances of the city. Third, uncritical acceptance of the municipal overburden argument, leading to massive increases in general support of city government, and a general lowering of the city tax rate, could have as one of its effects the subsidization of rich municipal property owners, some of whom might be regarded as absentee exploiters of the urban predicament.

Federal and State Responsibility for Cities' Decline

Although the problems of certain large cities may be caused by (in part) mismanagement of municipal officers, it is also true that state governments, and more especially the federal government, have contributed to the cities' decline. The removal of the middle-class from the cities has been aided by federal and state outlays to create freeway networks, thus allowing suburban dwellers to hold jobs in cities but

[28] For an outstanding analysis of municipal overburden, see Harvey E. Brazer et al., *Fiscal Needs and Resources: A Report to the New York State Commission on the Quality, Cost and Financing of Secondary Education* (New York, 1971).

[29] Bernard Jump, Jr., "Compensating City Government Employees: Pension Benefit Objectives, Cost Measurement, and Financing," *National Tax Journal*, 29, no. 3 (September 1976): 240–256. See also Harry H. Wellington and Ralph K. Winter, Jr., *The Unions and the Cities* (Washington, D.C.: Brookings, 1971); and Jack Stieber, *Public Employee Unionism* (Washington, D.C.: Brookings, 1973).

to live outside. Likewise, federal subsidy and guarantee of home mortgages helped many hundreds of thousands of families to purchase their single-family, detached homes in the suburbs. Local property taxes are deductible under federal personal income tax returns and under some state tax returns; interest on home mortgages is commonly deductible under both.

As Robert Reischauer has stated:

> Many have argued that certain federal policies in the transportation, housing, and tax areas have significantly abetted the middle-class exodus from the nation's largest cities, leaving them with disproportionately poor populations.[30] [As for the specific effects of tax policy:] Currently the federal tax code permits persons to include in their itemized deductions most taxes paid to state and local governments. In fiscal year 1976, it is estimated that federal revenues will be reduced by $16.1 billion by these provisions—$5.3 billion alone coming from the deductability of property taxes on owner-occupied housing. For many governments, this provision is not unlike an open-ended general purpose federal matching grant . . . When a community raises its taxes, a fraction of each dollar of increase is picked up by the federal government in the form of a reduced federal tax liability for local taxpayers . . . it is likely that wealthy suburban communities receive a disproportionate share of the total. This is because the size of the benefits depends upon whether a taxpayer itemizes his deductions, the amount of local taxes paid, and the taxpayers' marginal tax rate. While the taxes levied on central city residents may be higher than those elsewhere, the low level of home ownership in many cities means that a smaller fraction of the population is likely to itemize deductions and then avail itself to the benefits. Taxpayers with lower incomes face lower marginal tax rates; this characteristic of the tax expenditure also works to the city's disadvantage.[31]

Once a sufficient proportion of the middle-class leave a city, the remainder feels it must turn to private schools for the education of its children. But here the constitutional position against public support

[30] Robert D. Reischauer, "The Federal Government's Role in Relieving Cities of the Fiscal Burdens of Concentrations of Low-Income Persons," *National Tax Journal*, 29, no. 3 (September 1976): 307.
[31] Ibid., pp. 307–308.

of private elementary and secondary education results in their being faced with intolerably high tuition charges. Hence, this remainder is "pushed out."

The policies of the federal government to combat inflation have hit the cities in particularly distressing ways. Part of the policy is to curb demand and moderate union aggressiveness by tolerating high levels of unemployment. Those who are most susceptible to a contracyclical unemployment policy are concentrated in the inner cities. Thus, costs of poverty are accentuated, city budgets rise in response, and employers threaten to move their firms out of the city because of high taxes, and so on. Mothers are induced to leave their children to take any kind of paying job to supplement (or to provide) the family income, but young children who might benefit from a mother's care are thereby neglected. Their progress in school may consequently be diminished.

A second part of the federal government's policy on inflation is to use tight credit to control demand. Cities must make frequent use of the municipal bond market. Their interest costs rise on two counts: high rates due to tight credit in general and falling credit ratings due to their precarious fiscal position.[32]

The States' Limited Role in Aiding Cities

For two reasons at least, it seems unlikely that the state governments can be of any great assistance to the large cities. In the first place, the political structure of many state legislatures renders any show of favoritism toward large cities anathema. In the second, the resolution of *Serrano* type issues is likely to absorb the energies and the finances of state legislators in the social service field for the next decade. Attacking fiscal disparities is important work, and low-wealth suburban districts need the assistance that the *Serrano* case has opened up to them. But that general approach does little, as we have seen, for large cities.

There is, however, one long-term action within the power of the states to take. Because its effects are relatively mild in the short run, it may be within the realm of political possibility. That step is to establish a scheme of incremental metropolitan tax base equalization.

[32] Between 1964 and 1975, average net interest costs for A-rated public borrowers—and few big cities have a better credit rating, while some have worse—rose from 3.17 percent to 6.57 percent. This more-than-doubling of the interest rates cost the big cities many millions annually. See National Center for Educational Statistics, *Bond Sales for Public School Purposes, 1974–75* (Washington, D.C.: U.S. Government Printing Office, 1976), p. 4.

The example is to be found in the Minneapolis metropolitan area. In a seven-county area, including the City of Minneapolis, 40 percent of the increase in tax yield attributed to increase in assessed valuation is pooled and redistributed over the seven-county area under an equalizing formula. This is a share-the-growth plan, and its effects are to protect the central city against loss of a proportionate share of taxpaying properties to the suburbs. Businesses and households alike are free to locate themselves outside the city limits, but they are nevertheless required to make a contribution to the financial needs of the central city.

Federal Responsibility Toward Public Education in Large Cities

We began this chapter by noting that in the field of education the federal government seeks a special purpose to intervene in the affairs of state and local authorities. On the argument that basic principles are at stake in the survival of city educational systems serving a cross-section of families, the federal government can properly focus its attention on the needs of those cities. Indeed, as of the mid-1970s, it is surely correct to say that big-city schools represent the number one educational problem in the country.

Before proceeding further, however, we must recognize that big cities require more than an enlightened federal educational policy. Programs to provide jobs and housing should take first priority and improvements in health and nutrition, second.

As for educational policy itself, the federal government, in dealing with the large cities, must search for programs that recognize the great diversity among the cities; it must also seek programs that contain a nexus between improvement in performance and cash—the former being a requirement to receive the latter.

It is suggested here that the four different forms of aid discussed in the first part of this chapter can be adapted to establish a federal presence in big-city education.

The Planning Model In federal support of vocational education, five-year and annual plans are developed by states to specify targets and short-term objectives for improvement and expansion of occupational training. A similar approach could be taken toward improving central city school systems. The state could prepare plans for such development, ideally including arrangements for making inner city schools more attractive to the middle classes. Plans approved by state and federal agencies could be funded under a weighted population grant from the federal government.

The Title I Model   Title I grants are categorical by client. The program could be expanded in size, and the entire central city school population might be designated as clients. It might be wise to make categorical restrictions by program as well, specifying that the money should be spent on costs of year-round education, expenses of keeping schools open on weekends as study and play refuges, adult supervision in places where children congregate, and so on.

The Contractual Model   As we saw in considering the Education for the Handicapped Children Act, it is now possible to see a contractual arrangement developing between the central government and the states and localities with regard to the provision of educational services. A similar contractual arrangement could be developed between the federal government and the states with regard to establishing professional schools in central city areas (see Chapter 8 for a discussion of such schools).

The Impact Aid Model   Federal policies have served to weaken the fiscal base of several of central cities. To recognize this condition the federal government could offer matching dollars toward the establishment of share-the-growth schemes of the Minneapolis type. These schemes, as we noted, protect the central city from movement of taxable assets beyond its own borders into the suburbs. But some federal stimulus appears necessary to encourage their wider use. Whatever sum was generated by growth in taxable value for redistribution across the whole metropolitan area could be supplemented by a given ratio of federal support. Admittedly, this could be a broader program of federal assistance than one confined to educational services, since it is hard to improve education in central cities when the general environment is deteriorating. Hence, we need a kind of *Serrano* approach—a partial tax-base equalization, toward local public services generally in the large cities.

Summary

Federal aid for elementary and secondary schools is directed toward certain narrowly defined purposes: improving vocational education, helping low-income youth overcome educational disadvantage, assuring properly organized school programs for the handicapped, and compensating school districts for tax exemption of federally owned properties. Considerable problems attend the administration of these federal programs, of which the chief ones are: assuring that federal monies are additive to state and local spending and assuring that federal funds are spent on those certain programs that the central government seeks to subsidize.

Deterioration of educational activities in major central cities has reached distressing proportions. The difficulties may be beyond the capacity of state governments; hence, it is suggested that improving education in central cities is the next appropriate and logical objective for the federal government to undertake as it seeks strategic intervention in education.

Selected Bibliography

Crecine, John P. *Financing the Metropolis.* Beverly Hills, Calif.: Sage, 1970.

Ferman, Louis A., Joyce L. Kornbluh, and Alan Haber, eds. *Poverty in America.* Ann Arbor, Mich.: University of Michigan Press, 1969.

Institute for Educational Leadership. *Federalism at the Crossroads: Improving Policy-Making.* Washington, D.C.. George Washington University, 1976.

Riles, Wilson C. *The Urban Education Task Force Report.* New York: Praeger, 1974.

Sacks, Seymour. *City Schools, Suburban Schools: A History of Fiscal Conflict.* Syracuse, N.Y.: Syracuse University Press, 1972.

Epilogue

The various chapters of this book have dealt with major aspects of educational policy. We have examined the values that undergird that policy and the types of evidence that are used to shape its details. We have noted recent directions of change in the approach to the schooling of young people, at least as far as this approach can be described in terms of resource allocation.

At the close of this volume, it seems appropriate to speculate about what the future holds for educational policy. In the view of this writer, the most urgent matter is discussed in the last chapter, where we considered deterioration in central city schools, the apparent inability of state governments to come to grips with that problem, and the search for a federal solution. If there is desperation among the youth of the country, it exists in concentrated form in the central cities. Earlier, assertions that central city financial difficulties were the consequence of weak bargaining by local public administration may have had some basis in fact. To say now, however, that city administrations had wasted money in the past is not to conclude that taking money away will help what is turning into a very depressing situation. Furthermore, central city salary scales are increasingly being placed under the control of state government. Today, the taxpayer can be reasonably confident that money put into central city budgets buys improvement in services.

A second important prospect is that the contribution schooling can make to life outside the work place will receive greater
recognition. It has become clear that not everyone is going to have the
jobs they would like or for which they have been trained. But work
need not set finite limits to human existence. Indeed, nonwork activities can be as intensive, rewarding, and challenging as those activities
undertaken for pay, if the schools help prepare people to find accomplishment and satisfaction outside of what they do in the labor market.

The third likely direction of change is toward giving students
a greater degree of choice in their educational programs. To allow
students to develop interest and capabilities that will serve them well
in their private lives calls for more specialization in school activities.
There are means available to give choices to students without sacrific-
ing whatever degree of social integration has been achieved. An
example is the use of vouchers for educational activities outside the
standard curriculum.

Fourth, changes will occur in the system of financing schools.
In general, these changes will advance equity in the distribution of
educational services and in tax burden as well. We must beware,
however, of simple solutions. When high-wealth districts are con-
stricted in spending under implementation of school finance reform,
it becomes necessary to ask which types of children live in such
districts and whether cutbacks in programs redistribute income from
rich to poor or, as can easily happen, from poor to rich.

Lastly, this writer would like to think it probable that the
career of teaching will become more interesting and intellectually
rewarding. Teachers have played an insufficient part in the development of the substance of their professional lives. That they should
come to do so is the best hope for raising the quality of education in
the United States.

Name Index

Aaron, H., 129–130, 285n, 291
Agelasto, Michael A., II 150–151n
Alexander, Arthur, 373
Alonso, William, 152n
Archibald, Brenda M., 220n
Arrow, Kenneth J., 396n
Averch, Harvey, 192, 196–197, 198n, 217, 247

Barro, Stephen M., 358n, 369, 371
Baumol, William J., 133, 280n
Becker, G. S., 87–88, 103, 133
Benson, Charles S., 24n, 72n, 149n, 153n, 179, 189n, 196, 220n, 266n, 300n, 333–335, 343n, 345n, 356n, 357n, 359n, 362n, 369n, 373
Benveniste, Guy, 153n
Berg, Ivar, 94–95
Berke, Joel S., 339n, 342n, 373
Blechman, Barry M., 21, 263
Blinder, Alan S., 329
Boat, John C. G., 153n
Bowen, Howard R., 303n
Bowles, Samuel, 73n, 101–103

Brazer, Harvey E., 398n
Break, George F., 291, 329
Buchanan, James M., 144, 150n, 179
Burkhead, Jesse, 133, 196, 200, 217

Callahan, John, 366n, 396–397
Carlyle, Thomas, 5n
Carnegie Corporation, 227n
Carnoy, Martin, 179
Carroll, S. J., 371
Chambers, Jay, 171–174, 176, 371–372
Chase, Samuel B., 204n, 259
Chiang, A., 59n
Clune, William H., III, 325n, 337–338, 340, 373
Cobb, C., 58–61
Cohn, Elchanan, 75, 194–195, 217, 329
Coleman, James S., 189n, 192n, 196, 217
Coleman Report, 138n, 192, 196, 212, 247
Conant, James Bryant, 21, 237–238, 333

Subject Index